AMSTERDAM URBAN DEVELOPMENT 1975–2025

Maurits de Hoog

AMSTERDAM URBAN DEVELOPMENT 1975—2025

nai010 publishers

CONTENTS

FOREWORD

In this year of Amsterdam's 750th anniversary, we inevitably see our city through a historical lens. Cities are the built expression of social, economic, cultural, and political histories. But more than most, Amsterdam's shape is not the accidental outcome of shifting forces – it is the result of deliberate choices and targeted interventions. From the canal belt to Cornelis van Eesteren's General Expansion Plan, Amsterdam has long been a global model of urban planning. Amsterdam as a carefully constructed city.

This anniversary offers a perfect moment to reflect on our city's recent past. How has Amsterdam evolved over the past fifty years, since its last major jubilee, into the city we know today?

What lessons can we draw from the demolition of parts of 19th-century neighborhoods, from the forced relocation of residents to new suburbs and growth centers? From the once-unshakable faith in urban highways and high-rise housing blocks? And from the blind spot for existing neighborhoods and their inherent qualities?

How do we, quite literally, rebuild the city? Fifty years on, it is impossible not to feel both astonishment and quiet admiration for the city's remarkable transformation – from decline to renewal, from stagnation to vitality. Despite all the undeniable downsides – an overheated housing market, mass tourism, just to name a few – the city is in an incomparably better state than it was half a century ago.

The results invite critical reflection, as explored in countless publications and debates. But a thorough account of how this massive urban transformation actually unfolded has been missing – until now. This book tells that story: a chronicle of the major spatial changes Amsterdam has undergone in the past fifty years. It is also the story of a profession that has had to confront, absorb, and respond to well-founded criticism.

And, of course, no retrospective would be complete without a glimpse ahead. This book sets the stage for Amsterdam's next milestone – its 800th anniversary – and invites us to imagine the city's future, together.

Femke Halsema
Mayor Amsterdam

INTRODUCTION

In 2025, Amsterdam celebrates its 750th anniversary. Who could have imagined, fifty years ago, how well the city would be doing today? The city now has 935,000 residents, and in the last five years alone, 75,000 new jobs have been created. Amsterdam's residents rate their city an average of 7.5 for livability, and in 2024, it was once again named the most attractive city to live in the country.[1]

This was quite different in 1975. Over 40,000 Amsterdam residents left that year, exchanging their old, often noisy, and small homes for houses outside the city, in growing towns such as Purmerend, Lelystad, and Hoorn. While the city's population was 872,428 in 1959, it had dropped to 756,650 by early 1975. The city was in decline.

1975 was a memorable year for the capital, marked by the Nieuwmarkt riots, the arrival of tens of thousands of Surinamese immigrants, political crises involving councilors Riethof, Lammers, and Van Duijn, and also by groundbreaking new events such as Sail Amsterdam, the marathon, and the Festival of Fools, all part of the 'Amsterdam 700' celebrations.

The tall ships docked along the quays of the IJ (Amsterdam's central lake) attracted hundreds of thousands of visitors. Sail Amsterdam showcased the proud history of the harbor. At the same time, the event symbolized the end of the old industrial and port economy. While the post-World War II reconstruction and the expansion of the welfare state had driven strong growth in the urban economy, decolonization and the rise of aviation had already significantly diminished the port's role in the 1950s and 1960s. Consolidation and mergers in the shipping industry in the 1970s resulted in one large shipping company, Nedlloyd, based in Rotterdam, and eventually led to the closure of the large shipyards in North Amsterdam and the machine factories of Stork and Werkspoor.

The city's recovery was slow. By the end of 1984, the lowest point was reached, with the city's population down to 675,570. From that year on, the population steadily increased. Fueled by the waves of globalization, individualization, and informatization in the 1990s and 2000s, the service sector became the primary engine for population and job growth. The financial and business services, healthcare, education, culture, tourism, and more recently the rapid rise of the tech industry, all contributed to tens of thousands of new jobs. Along with the service economy and mass tourism, Schiphol Airport grew rapidly.

In the fifty years between 1975 and 2025, unimaginable transformations have taken place in the city: nearly 200,000 new homes were built, four metro lines and a ring road were opened, parks were created and expanded, and hundreds of offices, hotels, and businesses were established, not to mention all the renovations, small and large renovations, street and square reconfigurations, and the renewal of miles of cables and pipelines – in short, a massive reconstruction.

The growth of the city is, of course, not an isolated phenomenon; the region has also undergone significant development. In 1975, the first homes were built in Almere, which now boasts a population of 230,000. The Amsterdam Metropolitan Area (MRA) grew from 1.8 million inhabitants in 1975 to over 2.6 million by early 2025.[2]

With the city's 750th anniversary in 2025 in mind, it is interesting to reflect on and reconstruct the remarkable development of the city over the past fifty years, examining how this development took shape. What was the spatial policy, which strategies were used, and how was the planning executed? How did ideas evolve, and how were shifts in the economy and broader society addressed?

The city's success also has its downsides. The city center is extremely crowded, partly due to approximately 22 million overnight visitors per year and a sharp rise in the number of cyclists. In recent years, the influx of internationals has also led to explosively rising house prices and a completely blocked housing market. Traffic congestion on the roads surrounding the city has made a post-pandemic comeback, as has the noise pollution from the flight paths around Schiphol Airport.

Equally intriguing is the need to look ahead. Are the shocks from the COVID-19 pandemic, the wars in Ukraine and the Middle East, and the crises in the energy and housing markets mere setbacks, or are they signals of structural changes to come? What might the major developments of the coming decades be? And how might the city look by 2075?

In *Urban Development Amsterdam 1975–2025*, the focus is on the spatial development of the city. Political developments are extensively covered in other publications, including the books by Geert Mak, James Kennedy, Herman de Liagre Böhl, and Fred Feddes, as well as more recently by Tim Verlaan, Marcel van Engelen, and Bas Kok.[3] The central focus of this overview is the documentation and analysis of the actual creation of the city, from housing and amenities to the construction of infrastructure and green spaces. In addition to the text, maps and photos tell the story. This could build on the annual project documentation *Gebouwd in Amsterdam (Built in Amsterdam)*, the editions of *Plan Amsterdam*, and a whole series of other municipal publications: *50 Years AUP*, *Nooit Af* (*Never Finished*), *Stadsplan Amsterdam 1928–2003* (*City Plan Amsterdam 1928–2003*), the *Major Projects* book, and more recently, the *Public Space Amsterdam 2019* and *Amsterdam Urban Design, Work in Progress 2020*.[4]

Looking at the period as a whole, the development of the city can be understood in terms of five movements. The concept of 'movement' was introduced in the *Structural Vision Amsterdam 2040: Economically Strong and Sustainable* in 2011, and was used to describe the spatial dynamics in the city, such as 'the roll-out of the city center' and 'the rediscovery of the waterfront'. Municipal policy had to relate to these movements and give shape to them. For this historical overview, the concept provides an interesting starting point.[5] The development of the city is not a linear process but is characterized by various processes that coexist, complement each other, and sometimes even obstruct each other.

A movement, in this context, is understood as a societal process in which many spatial decisions made by individuals, organizations, and municipal policy and design come together over an extended period. Sometimes the municipality initiated a movement or actively encouraged a development; in other cases, municipal policy followed, whether willingly or reluctantly, the decisions or preferences of other parties. The character of these movements also evolved over time.

This publication distinguishes five movements. Movement 1, 'renewal of the existing city', describes the development of the city as it was in 1975. It covers urban renewal in the old city, but also the renewal of post-war neighborhoods and the Bijlmer. Movement 2, 'low-rise on the city's edge', began early and is exemplified by areas like Gein, Nieuw Sloten, and De Aker. Other examples, such as De Bongerd, Elzenhagen-Noord, and the DIY housing projects since 2012, are also part of this movement: all aimed at reducing the exodus of young families moving to the new towns or to nearby cities like Haarlem and Zaanstad. The transformation of the area outside the dikes around the IJ is addressed in movement 3, 'water city'. Movement 4, 'southward', describes the relocation of many metropolitan work functions and services from the city center to the stations and areas on the outskirts of the city, as well as towards Schiphol, and everything that followed. Finally, the large-scale redevelopment of the city center itself, with a focus on the establishment of new cultural facilities, hotels, and the reduction of car traffic in public spaces, is discussed under movement 5, 'supercluster city center'.

The book opens with 'Chronicle of a Turbulent Celebration Year', a description of what took place in and around the celebratory year of 1975 in the city. The motto of *Amsterdam 700* was 'wonen, werken, spelen' (living, working, playing), with a nod to Provo. In the lead-up to 1975, many questioned the modernist dogma of separating functions – spatially distancing living, working, recreation, and traffic. 'Playing' aligns much more with the city's new role, focused on interaction, cultural exchange, and innovation. But one could also view the urban development since 1975 as a game – a postmodern game: sometimes with lofty ambitions and serious issues, but mostly centered around the joy of collectively creating a pleasant city.

In Part 1, the strong societal dynamics of the past fifty years are described, and a periodization is presented: 'reversing the decline', 'recovery', 'rapid growth', and 'shocks'. This sets the context for Part 2, where the major movements are discussed: 'renewal of the existing city', 'low-rise on the city's edge', 'water city', 'southward', and 'supercluster city center'. In Part 3, the developments are summarized and placed in the professional debate and regional development. Finally, there is cautious speculation about the city's development towards 2075.

The idea for this book has existed for a long time, but in 2024 and the spring of 2025, it was realized, together with Tim Ruijs, Laura Smits, Arjan Verhoef, and Isis de Vries. Thanks for the intensive and cheerful collaboration! Many of the photos in the book were specially taken by Rindert van den Toren. They are new interpretations of situations previously captured by Jusopo Muhamad Arsath Ro'is (1919–1993). In the Image Bank of the City Archive, nearly 18,000 of his photos are included – early shots from the early 1950s, but mostly from the period when he documented the changes in the city for the municipal services, from 1958 until his death in 1993. They are not 'interesting' photos, but often 'incidental' ones, as Hans Aarsman aptly noted.[6]

The actual making of a book is a craft in itself. Marja Jager and Marcel Witvoet of nai010 publishers offered valuable advice on the structure and form of the book and guided the production process. Editor Els Brinkman ensured consistency and accuracy in names and toponyms, and pressed for a number of essential clarifications. Designer Maud van Rossum beautifully solved the complex puzzle of text, maps, photos, tables, fold-out pages, timeline, and notes. The colour palette throughout the book subtly reflects the richness and diversity of the period described.The publication was supported in part by funding from the Municipality of Amsterdam.

Thanks also for all the special material and the encouragements, observations, and corrections: Ruwan Aluvihare, Niek Bosch, Ed Degenkamp, Ireen Dubel, Matty Gaikhorst, Paul Gravemaker, Kevin Krieger, Sabine Lebesque, Nick van Luit, Anne Meijer, Erik Pasveer, Erjen Prins, Ton Schaap, Annika Smits, Simon Sprietsma, Wil Val, and Thijs de Wit. A concept version of the manuscript was meticulously reviewed by Han Goes, Frits Palmboom, Duco Stadig, Koos van Zanen, and Wil Zonneveld. Should the publication still contain errors or ambiguities, the author is responsible.

The text only includes a few references to employees of the Municipality of Amsterdam. Urban development is teamwork, and between 1975 and 2025, hundreds of professionals from all kind of disciplines were involved in shaping the city.

During my time working for the Municipality of Amsterdam, I also had the opportunity to reflect on policy and projects.[7] This helped to foster internal debate and dialogue with all those strong-minded Amsterdammers who passionately engage with their city. I hope this publication also contributes to the ongoing conversation—about the city's development over the past fifty years, and about its future. It's important to note that the questions and suggestions in the epilogue, which looks ahead, are entirely the responsibility of the author. I'm curious to see what kind of city Amsterdam will become in the next fifty years!

1975 AMSTERDAM 700

CHRONICLE OF A TURBULENT CELEBRATION YEAR

Under the motto '700 Years of Living, Working, and Playing', Amsterdam celebrated its 700th anniversary throughout 1975 with 260 large and small events.[1] The city opened its doors – quite literally: over the course of the year, the municipal government hosted 36,614 guests at 131 official receptions, 14,354 people were invited on 121 canal cruises, and 3,711 guests attended 47 formal dinners!

A fascinating overview of the festivities can be found in the *Stedelijk Jaarverslag 1975* (Municipal Annual Report 1975)[2]. To commemorate the anniversary year, a special, richly illustrated edition was published. In addition to covering the celebrations, it also documented the more turbulent events of the year, such as the riots that broke out when squatted buildings in the Nieuwmarktbuurt were cleared and the hostage situation at the Indonesian consulate. The report also marked Suriname's independence on November 25.

A recurring theme in the annual report is the sharp political and administrative controversies – not between the city government and the opposition on the council, but within the city government itself, as well as on the streets and in countless meeting rooms. Change was in the air. Ultimately, 1975 marked the end of a long period of political consensus about the city's direction and the beginning of something new. Modernist ideals and the belief in progress gave way to a more diverse and dynamic political and cultural climate.

The 1973 city council proposal for the *Amsterdam 700* theme (see page 11) referenced the ongoing debates at the time about housing and the economy but also emphasized the importance of culture and quality of life. While not without controversy, the anniversary events appear to have contributed to a new sense of self-awareness. In the decades that followed, this helped lay the foundation for Amsterdam's evolution into a highly desirable place to live and a popular destination.

Quote from City Council Proposal for Amsterdam 700
October 1973.[3]

'(...) we believe it would be advisable to frame all activities surrounding the 700th anniversary within a specific theme. This theme should reflect the diversity of life in a large and dynamic city like Amsterdam. It should convey that it is not the municipal government, but rather the community itself that is celebrating its 700-year existence. Moreover, it should highlight certain aspects of life for Amsterdam's residents – both now and in the future – that deserve special attention.

The first and foremost focus should be on living in Amsterdam. As the city stands on the brink of an urban renewal process that will profoundly impact both its residents and its structure, housing must take center stage in the anniversary's theme. Another key point of reflection should be Amsterdam's economic role. The city's rise and prosperity have always been closely tied to specific economic activities. The ongoing debate revolves around how best to adapt to changing circumstances. The outcome of this discussion will be crucial in shaping the future of Amsterdam's economy.

A final emphasis must be placed on culture in the broadest sense of the word. Not only must Amsterdam continue to function as a hub for creative and performing arts, but it must also ensure there are ample opportunities for leisure, sports, and recreation – both for Amsterdammers and visitors alike.

The diversity of life in Amsterdam, the aspects that deserve particular attention, and the integration of this commemoration into everyday life – all of this is expressed in the theme: Amsterdam: 700 Years of Living, Working, and Playing.'

Quote from article by Jan van Oostrom, Chairman of Bureau Amsterdam 700, in: *Amsterdam werkt*
(Amsterdam Works), No. 10, October 1973.[4]

'The city government has expressed the hope that, through this celebration, Amsterdam will gain something of lasting value from the events of 1975. I think that's an excellent idea. We should make an effort to fulfill that wish. (...) This could take the form of a permanent exhibition, a sports hall, a neighborhood facility – but it could just as easily be a cultural event, a new sense of momentum, or something more abstract and therefore harder to define.'

➔ Posters Amsterdam 700 (on the right, the poster designed by Gielijn Escher on behalf of Bureau Amsterdam 700)

CHRONICLE OF AMSTERDAM 1975

as featured in the *Municipal Annual Report 1975*

January

Concert by the Amsterdam Philharmonic Orchestra in the Westerkerk, with speeches by Professor Frits de Jong Edz. and Professor I.A. Diepenhorst; anniversary New Year's overture by Sieto and Marijke Hoving at the Stadsschouwburg; opening of the Jewish Historical Museum in *De Waag* on Nieuwmarkt and the Historical Medical-Pharmaceutical Museum.

February

Opening of the symposium *Tussentijds Bestek 1975* (*Interim Review 1975*) by Queen Juliana; operetta *The Bartered Bride* at Carré; publication of *700 Centenboek* by Jos Houweling (commissioned by the *Gemeentegiro* municipal bank, 55,000 copies) and *De Jarige Stad* (*The Birthday City*) by Han G. Hoekstra and Veronica van Vliet (for preschools); opening of the exhibition *The Amsterdam Stock Exchange 1475–1975*; release of the *Amsterdam 700 Years* postage stamp.

March

Award ceremony for the National Violin Competition at the Van Gogh Museum; *Plant Your Own Tree* campaign; donation of 17,000 flower bulbs by Keukenhof; opening of the Marriott Hotel at Leidse Bosje and the Sonesta Hotel at Hekelveld; distribution of 1,700 CJP youth culture festival passports as part of the *Amsterdam laat naar je kijken* (*Amsterdam Shows Itself to You*) project; eviction of squatted buildings on Rechtboomssloot in Nieuwmarktbuurt, leading to demonstrations.

1

2

4

1 Amsterdam 700 tram GVB: 'Keetje Stippel', design by Marte Röling
2 Taxi with Amsterdam 700 logo
3 June 1975, Holland Festival on water
4 Tableau of the troupe Festival of Fools in front of Shaffytheater
5 Poster for Festival of Fools 1975, design by Gielijn Escher
6 Cover Han G. Hoekstra: *De jarige stad*. Gouden Boekje, De Bezige Bij
7 Cover Jos Houweling: *700 centenboek*, Gemeentegiro Amsterdam
8 June 24, 1975, Opening Mokum 700, RAI

3

April

Opening of the western section of the A10 ring road; eviction of buildings on Lastageweg, sparking demonstrations; unveiling of the *Women of Ravensbrück* monument at Museumplein; gift of 15,000 tulips to New York on its 350th anniversary; planting of 700 Austrian spruces in Rembrandtpark; inauguration of city-wide decorative lighting; gifts from 700 Amsterdam children for the birthday of Queen Juliana and Prince Pieter van Vollenhoven.

May

Opening of the *Florijn 75* exhibition at Amstelpark; International Diamond Congress; laying of the first stone for a miniature Amsterdam at the *Mokum 700* exhibition in the RAI convention center; introduction of the *event hotline*; exhibition of children's drawings at the Bijenkorf department store; launch of the ten-day *Book and City* literary and film festival at Museumplein and the Stedelijk Museum; children's *diorama exhibition* at the Tropenmuseum; *Amsterdam 700* marathon; public transport rally; release of the LP *Ik zing van Amsterdam* (*I Sing of Amsterdam*), featuring *D'r is een Amsterdammer doodgegaan* (*An Amsterdammer Has Died*), sung by Johnny Kraaykamp.

June

Opening of a sculpture exhibition at Amstelpark featuring 160 works and a sculpture route at Museumplein; opening of *Art as a Matter of Government* exhibition at the Royal Palace; new location of the Bijbels (Bible) Museum on Herengracht; launch of the *Amsterdam 700* card game; extension of the *100 Posters, 100 Years of Amsterdam (1875–1975)* exhibition at Icon Gallery, Frederiksplein; test rides on the new metro *Oostlijn* (East Line); exhibition *Open Tube* by GVB (public transport operator) at the new Weesperplein metro station; ballet and musical fleet performance as part of the Holland Festival; The Werkteater performs in a tent at Museumplein; photography exhibition *Images of Amsterdam* at the Van Gogh Museum; *Mokum-700* event at the RAI; performances by the Concertgebouw Orchestra; Open Amsterdam Klaverjassen Championship (card game tournament); Chinese fireworks display.

5

6

7

8

July

Opening of the *Amsterdammers Draw Their City* exhibition at Arti et Amicitiae, featuring 180 drawings commissioned by the Municipal Archives since 1934; opening of the photo exhibition *A City for Everyone* in the restored Dritt Sjoel and Obbene Sjoel synagogues on Nieuwe Amstelstraat by Jerusalem mayor Teddy Kollek and Amsterdam mayor Ivo Samkalden; NIPO survey finds that 88% of Dutch people are aware of *Amsterdam 700*; opening of the antiques market at Nieuwmarkt.

August

Amsterdam 700 soccer tournament, final match: Ajax vs. Molenbeek (2-5); *Sport in Motion* exhibition at Amstelpark; opening of the *Halte 75 – 100 Years of Trams, 75 Years of GVB* exhibition at the Van Gogh Museum; four-day *Sail Amsterdam 700* maritime event featuring 18 tall ships, a million visitors, a mock sea battle, harbor carnival, 300 admiralty-style sailing boats, a harbor exhibition, rowing races, and fireworks; Sweelinck organ competition at the Oude Kerk; celebration of 300 years of the Portuguese-Israelite Synagogue; publication of the photobook *The Old Jewish Quarter of Amsterdam Now* by Mozes Heiman Gans; opening of *De Pintohuis* on Sint Antoniesbreestraat by Princess Beatrix.

September

Closing of *Amsterdam 700* outdoor activities in Vondelpark; opening of a new youth hostel at Zandpad; inauguration of the Electric Museum Tram Line to Amsterdamse Bos; tram parade; music festival featuring wind and brass orchestras at the former Koopmansbeurs stock exchange; *Pieremegoggel '75* competition (for whimsical boat designs); carillon contest; *The Night Watch* painting at the Rijksmuseum attacked with a knife; publication of the *Amsterdam Charter Book Up to 1400*; exhibition *The History of Amsterdam-Noord* at the Tolhuis; *Flowers for Amsterdam* floral parade; International *City in Motion* Congress at the Tropenmuseum; opening of Sporthallen Zuid; opening of the *Amsterdam Played for Fun* exhibition at the Theater Museum; *A Future for Our Past* heritage exhibition at the Rijksmuseum as part of the 1975 Monuments Year; reopening of the restored Rembrandt House and Ronde Lutherse Kerk.

1

2

1 Admiral sailing on the IJ, Sail Amsterdam 700, August 1975
2 Festive lighting on Geldersekade
3 Opening of the Amsterdam Historical Museum, October 27, 1975
4 Magic box shop, information stand Amsterdam 700 at Museumplein, December 1975

October

Performances by amateur choirs at Jaap Edenhal; opening of the *Spinoza* exhibition at Arti et Amicitiae; premiere of the musical *The Angel of Amsterdam* at Carré; October 27: anniversary celebrations with fruit and flower gifts for hospitals and nursing homes, a public holiday for municipal employees, extended café hours, flags, *beschuit met muisjes* (traditional Dutch treat) for families of newborns, sports festival, opening of the Amsterdam Museum on Kalverstraat by Queen Juliana, and a grand fireworks display over the IJ; opening of *The Kopenhagen Family* exhibition at Ronde Lutherse Kerk; opening of the Netherlands Film Museum at the Vondelpark Pavilion; national street vendor competition at Dam Square; launch of *Eva-nement and A'dam-benemend* feminist event by the Federative Women's Council at the Van Gogh Museum; *Jumping Amsterdam 700* equestrian event.

November

Urban planning simulation game *Amsterdam as a Playground for Spatial Decisions* at VU University; opening of the *Europort* exhibition at the RAI by the Swedish Minister of Labor; reopening of the restored English Reformed Church at Begijnhof in the presence of the Queen Mother of England; symposium on *Prosperity for Amsterdam?*, a brochure by Jan Lambooy; Saint Nicholas plants one of twelve elm trees at Dam Square as part of the *Groene Hart van Amsterdam* (*Green Heart of Amsterdam*) initiative; *Jacob Olie and Amsterdam* photography exhibition at the City Archives; symposium on 75 years of the Municipal Port Authority; events marking Suriname's independence; opening of *700 Years of News in Amsterdam* exhibition at the University Library.

December

Hostage crisis at the Indonesian consulate; publication of *I Need to Look for a Smaller Home Because My Family Is Growing*, by Egbert Ottens, commemorating 60 years of the Municipal Housing Department; resignation of Alderman Han Lammers (PvdA); vote of no confidence against Alderman Roel van Duijn (PPR); 150 years of municipal gas supply; *Amsterdam 700* concert by the Vienna Philharmonic at the Concertgebouw; Eurovision broadcast of the Christmas matinee by the Concertgebouw Orchestra; *Crea-Festival* featuring 150 performances by 1,500 artists for 10,000 Amsterdammers; *Amsterdam in Fragments* film festival at Ronde Lutherse Kerk; opening of Slotervaart Hospital; *Amsterdam 700* retrospective on national TV on New Year's Eve.

3

4

A New Formula

What a Celebration! Looking at the range of festivities and events, the first category consists of well-known or 'established' types of events, such as symposia, exhibitions, drawing competitions, tree planting, music competitions, klaverjas, chess and bridge tournaments, and the flower parade. The 'Mokum 700' event in the RAI could also be included here: a six-day 'fair' featuring various festivities set against a cardboard canal backdrop. Additionally, more than 150 sports and play facilities were renewed or newly constructed throughout the city.[5] On the actual anniversary of the city on October 27, primary schools had the day off, carillons rang, and a grand fireworks display lit up Museumplein in the evening.

Truly innovative were events where the city itself became the stage, such as the marathon and Sail, both of which would later become annual or quinquennial traditions. These new types of events attracted large audiences, not only from Amsterdam but also from the region and the rest of the Netherlands. Less widely known is that both the Festival of Fools and Kwaku were first organized in 1975. The 'tent-happening' in the summer of 1975 on Museumplein was a precursor to the Uitmarkt and De Parade; from the 'musical fleet' during the Holland Festival in June 1975, it is only a small step to the Prinsengracht Concerts and the Canal Parade.

A second innovation was the significant investment in new cultural, sports, conference, and tourism facilities. Some of these may have been planned earlier and independently of Amsterdam 700, such as the renovation of the Rembrandt House and the Ronde Lutherse Kerk. This likely also applies to the opening of the Sporthallen Zuid, the Bijbels Museum on the Herengracht, and the Nederlands Filmmuseum in the Vondelpark Pavilion. Direct investments as part of Amsterdam 700 included the renovation of the former Burgerweeshuis on Kalverstraat into the Amsterdam Historical Museum, the opening of the Jewish Historical Museum in the Waag, and city illumination projects, which involved lighting up bridges and significant buildings. Additionally, 1975 saw the opening of the Marriott Hotel and the Sonesta Hotel, both featuring over 600 rooms and conference facilities for 750 and 550 participants, respectively. In the celebratory year, 60 international congresses were held in the city.[6]

A third element of innovation was the use of various media: in addition to booklets, flags, ties, posters, and trams featuring the Amsterdam 700 logo, a magazine was published, and a telephone information service was launched. Additionally, surveys were conducted regularly. Radio and television broadcasts brought the events into people's homes.

Amsterdam 700 thus laid the foundation for city promotion and urban tourism as it would take shape in the 1980s and 1990s. It is no surprise that KLM was one of the main sponsors of the festival, but the city itself bore the bulk of the costs. The expenses incurred by Bureau Amsterdam 700 amounted to 3.5 million guilders, including half a million for publicity and nearly 100,000 as a contribution to Sail Amsterdam. Municipal services contributed an additional 3.7 million guilders, with the largest expenditures allocated to city illumination (0.8 million), subsidies for cultural activities (0.8 million), and the construction of sports and play facilities in neighborhoods (1.3 million).[7]

1 Cartoon Opland, *Parool*, April 1975
2 Poster European Monuments Year 1975
3 Call for demonstration March 11, 1972, joint Amsterdam action groups

1

2

3

Provocations, Farewells, and New Beginnings

Just before the city's official anniversary at the end of October 1975, the European Heritage Year M'75 was concluded at a well-attended international congress in the RAI with the Amsterdam Declaration.[8] This charter called for a renewed appreciation of the qualities of historic European city centers: an end to slum clearance, a halt to large-scale office developments and traffic breakthroughs, and a commitment to preservation – not only of monuments but also of characteristic historical ensembles, with attention to social and community aspects.[9]

The congress took place at a crucial moment. In March of that year, a fierce battle had erupted in the Nieuwmarkt neighborhood during the eviction of squatted buildings slated for demolition to make way for the construction of the East Line metro. This confrontation was the climax of a broad urban debate (hearings, pamphlets, letters to newspapers, council petitions, exhibitions, sit-ins, [bicycle] demonstrations) that had unfolded since the mid-1960s. Key moments in this debate included the Ban de Bank protests against the expansion of the ABN Bank on Vijzelstraat (1966), the City Hall competition (1967–1968), the construction plans for De Nederlandsche Bank (1968), the proposed traffic breakthroughs in the Nieuwmarkt neighborhood and Haarlemmerhouttuinen (1970), the university development plans for Valkenburg (1971), and finally, the metro construction.[10]

Two camps stood opposed: modernists and preservationists. The modernists included PvdA politicians influenced by Joop den Uyl and Han Lammers, as well as a new generation of municipal architects and urban planners, such as Siegfried Nassuth, Ton de Gier, and Willem Duyff.[11] Riding the wave of economic prosperity, these designers developed a new model for urban development in the early 1960s. The pre-war vision of Amsterdam as a tram and bicycle city was expanded into a metro and car city, with new extensions to Amstelveen, Zaanstad, and Weesperkarspel (later the Bijlmermeer). This metropolitan area was envisioned as the core of a larger region, incorporating state-designed new towns. In this vision, Amsterdam's inner city would naturally evolve into the region's central hub for offices, culture, specialized retail, and an expanding university. Each new urban expansion was planned to have its own secondary center.[12]

The protectors were led by sculptor and publicist Geurt Brinkgreve, who had been working since the 1950s to prevent large-scale demolition in Amsterdam's inner city.[13] He was the founder of the Vereniging Vrienden van de Amsterdamse Binnenstad (VVAB).

However, the counter-movement was much broader and was also fueled by the new youth culture, which took shape in the 1960s around music venues such as Provadya, Fantasio, the Melkweg, and Paradiso, as well as magazines like *Hitweek* and *Aloha*.[14]

The most political and activist branch of this movement was Provo, founded in 1965 by Roel van

Duijn, Rob Stolk, and others. Provo called for various playful protests, such as those staged during the wedding of Beatrix and Claus in early 1966. They also developed a series of 'environmentally friendly alternatives' that satirized the new Amsterdam urban model. Well-known examples include the white bicycle plan, the white housing plan, and the white chimney plan.[15] In June 1966, Provo secured a seat on the city council. Though the movement was officially disbanded in 1967, the seat in the council remained occupied by successive Provo members, who surprised the municipal government with cheerful initiatives. Luud Schimmelpenninck, for instance, launched the idea of the Witkar, a small electric vehicle that members of the Witkar association could rent from charging stations for short trips within the city center.

In 1970, the Kabouter Party, which emerged from Provo, won five council seats, though it too was short-lived. However, the protectors succeeded in having the De Pinto House on Sint Antoniesbreestraat designated as a national monument after a long struggle in 1968. As a result, the planned traffic road through the Nieuwmarkt neighborhood was definitively abandoned.

A few years later, a serious experiment with the Witkar project began. In 1974, Irene Vorrink, Minister of Health and Environmental Hygiene in the progressive Den Uyl cabinet, opened the first charging station on the Amstelveld.[16]

These events seemed to foreshadow a bold experiment following the municipal elections of May 1974: the formation of a left-wing program coalition with aldermen from the PvdA, CPN, PSP, and the newly established Progressive Party of Radicals (PPR). In the 1972 national elections, the PPR won seven seats in the House of Representatives and provided ministers for the Den Uyl cabinet. The Amsterdam branch of the PPR then put forward former Provo member Roel van Duijn as an alderman. This resulted in a municipal executive with outspoken opponents: Han Lammers (PvdA) and Harry Verhey (CPN) versus Roel van Duijn (PPR) and Huib Riethof (PSP). This led to unlikely debates within the executive board and the city council, running parallel to preparations for the celebration year. Modernists and preservationists now stood in direct opposition within the municipal government as well.[17]

To build or not to build a metro? After much debate, it was decided at the end of 1974 to proceed with metro construction but to reconstruct the Nieuwmarkt neighborhood according to its original street pattern after demolition. Architect Theo Bosch, partner of Aldo van Eyck, was commissioned to develop the urban plan. Nevertheless, tensions in the Nieuwmarkt neighborhood escalated.[18]

In February 1975, a bomb attack on one of the metro stations under construction was thwarted. In a statement from the municipal executive, accusations were directed at the activists, though these later proved to be unfounded. Van Duijn refused to sign the statement, while Huib Riethof did. As a

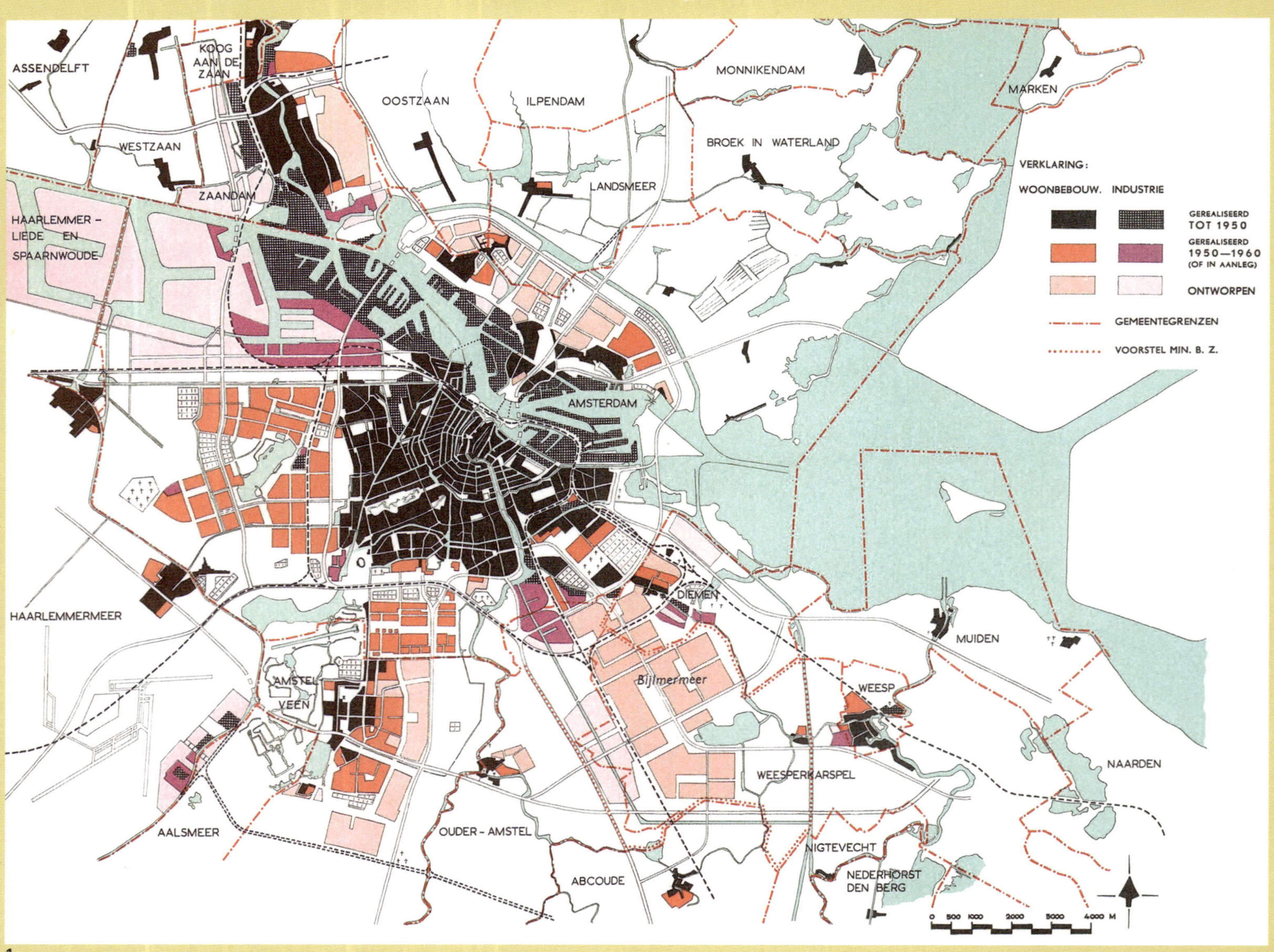

1

1 Structural diagram of the Amsterdam Agglomeration 1962: transformation of the city center for offices-culture-retail-university-government, new urban expansion in lobes/fingers with their own retail centers
2 Witkar station Amstelveld 1975, design by Luud Schimmelpenninck

2

result, Riethof was forced by his party to resign as alderman. The situation further deteriorated. A council's decision in mid-March to construct only the East Line and abandon plans for other metro lines failed to prevent major riots during evictions the following week. The mounting conflicts ultimately led to the resignations of Han Lammers in December 1975, followed by Roel van Duijn a week later. At the beginning of 1976, a more traditional multi-party coalition was formed.

Only after the 1978 elections did policy shift. Under a new generation of PvdA leaders – Jan Schaefer, Walter Etty, and Michael van der Vlis – the focus turned to large-scale renewal of the existing city and new urban expansions to counter suburban migration and retain young families. The 'compact city' became the new policy concept.

The City's Appearance 1975–2025

The transformations of Amsterdam's inner city in the 1960s and 1970s took on a different character than those in Utrecht and The Hague. In Utrecht, large-scale demolition made way for the colossal Hoog Catharijne shopping and office complex. In The Hague's Spuikwartier, an entire series of large office buildings for ministries was constructed alongside the new city hall. While much was demolished in Amsterdam as well, the original plans for large-scale developments were, fortunately, never fully realized or were carried out in significantly altered forms.

The drastic breakthrough at the Haarlemmer Houttuinen, intended to connect a major traffic route to the widened Prins Hendrikkade, was ultimately narrowed, with the urban fabric largely restored. The most severely affected area was the already battered eastern inner city, suffering from the demolition of Vlooienburg to make way for the Stopera, the Weesperstraat-Valkenburgerstraat corridor leading to the IJ Tunnel with its vehicle and pedestrian underpasses at Mr. Visserplein, and the complete redevelopment of Kattenburg and Wittenburg.

The planned IJ Tunnel route turned out quite differently in the 1980s than originally envisioned. The Nieuwe Leeuwarderweg and Gooiseweg were never extended toward Leeuwarden and Het Gooi, leading to a painfully slow process of downgrading, repair, and redesign. As early as 1983, the unsafe pedestrian tunnels beneath Mr. Visserplein were sealed off. The Maupoleum on Jodenbreestraat made way for the Theatre School in the early 1990s, the Mr. Visserplein vehicle tunnel was closed in 1996, and Valkenburgerstraat was transformed into a narrow urban street. Visitors to the temporary underground play center Tun-Fun, located in the abandoned tunnel trench, could see that the foundation for the new Film Academy had been built straight through the tunnel structure. In 2010, the large roundabout at Mr. Visserplein was replaced by simpler, yet still confusing, intersections. From 2012 onward, Wibautstraat underwent a full redesign from façade to façade. Other elements still await further modifications. Instead of an outright closure, narrowing Weesperstraat to two single lanes seems to be the logical next step.

These gradual changes exemplify the long-term process of reversing decline and restoring the city in the decades after 1975. Following the debates and heated clashes between modernists and preservationists in the 1960s and 1970s, urban renewal gained momentum in the early 1980s. From 1985

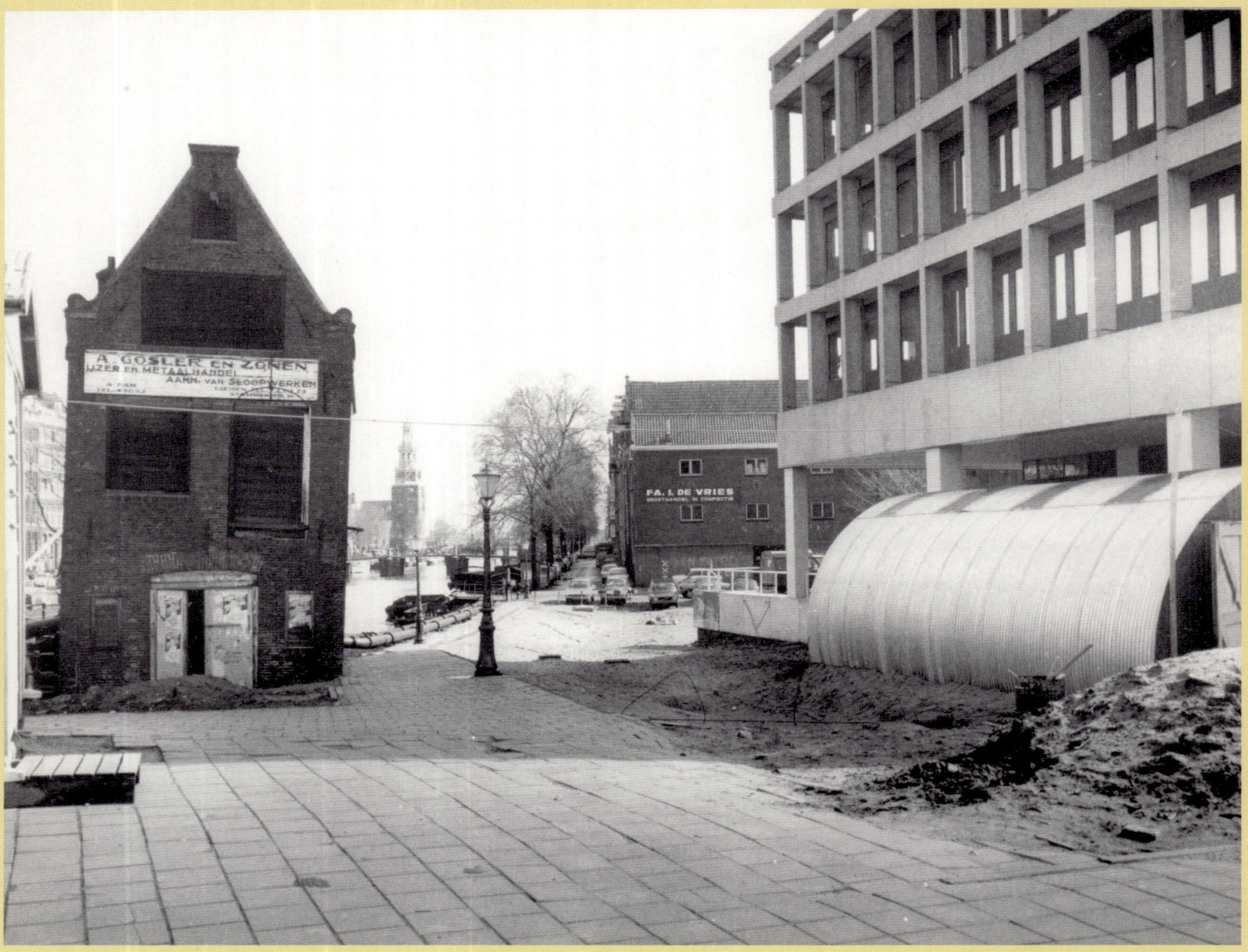
A. GOSLER EN ZONEN
IJZER EN METAALHANDEL
AANN. VAN SLOOPWERKEN
FA. I. DE VRIES
GROOTHANDEL IN CONFECTIE

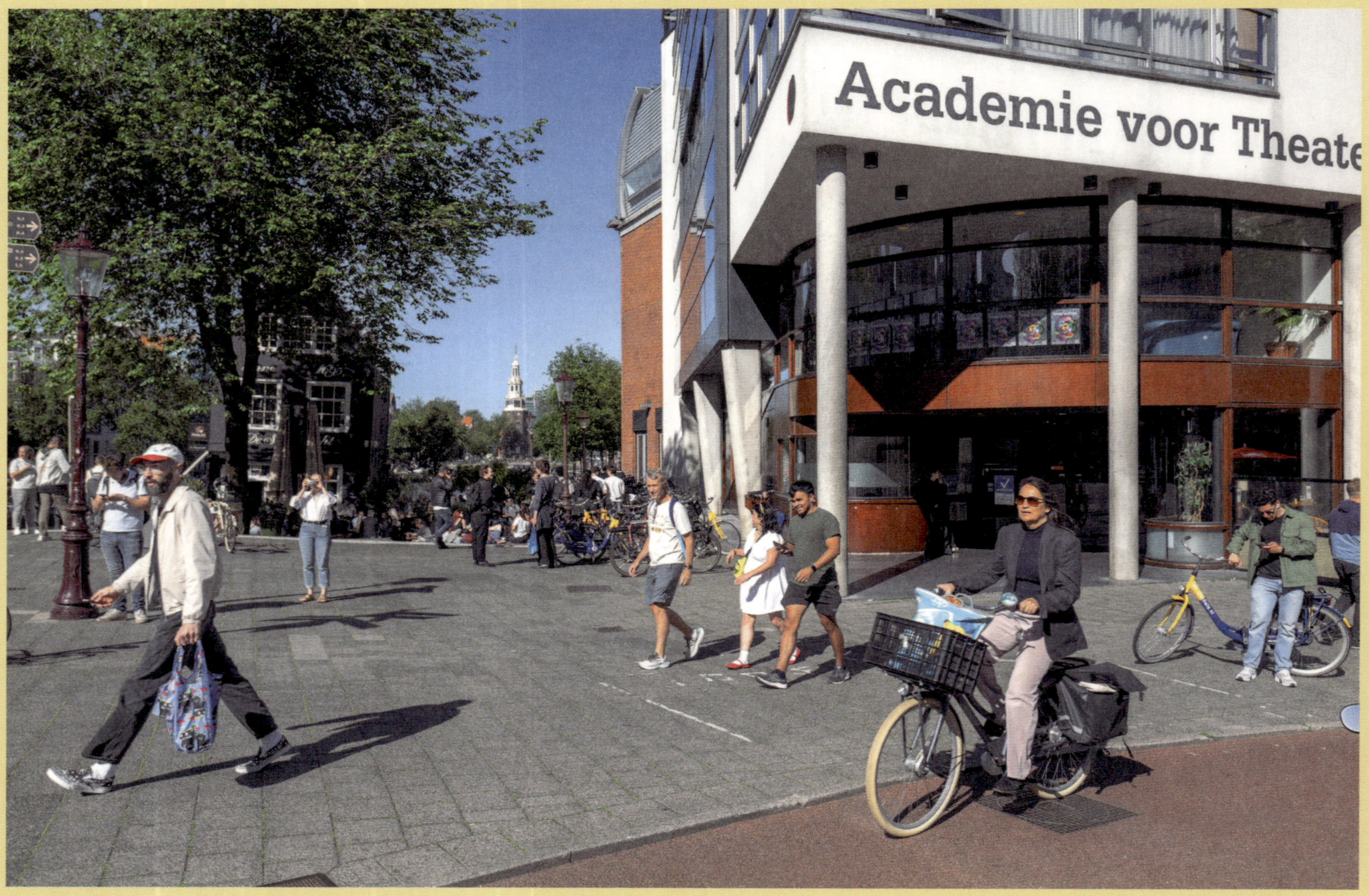
Academie voor Theate

← Jodenbreestraat seen towards Oude Schans and Montelbaanstoren, 1975–2025

onward, the city's population began to grow again, largely due to new expansion areas with many low-rise homes, such as Nieuw Sloten, De Aker, and Oostzanerwerf.

The transformation of the harbor islands in the Eastern Port Area set the stage for an enormous growth spurt, driven by three developments that were not yet fully foreseeable in 1975: the port and industrial areas on both sides of the IJ transformed into a mixed-use urban district, the Zuidas and ArenAPoort developed into new city centers, and the inner city became an international cultural and tourist hotspot.

Thus, the city's appearance changed entirely after 1975. How did this transformation take shape?

The philosophy underpinning these five major urban developments is often referred to as 'post-modernism'. City leaders, policymakers, and designers drew inspiration from successful examples in Amsterdam's own history, opting for a mixed-use and a high degree of differentiation. New construction in Amsterdam would no longer consist of 10,000 identical homes in a rigid grid, as seen in the Bijlmermeer, but would instead feature distinct neighborhoods with a diverse range of housing types and block designs to accommodate different urban communities. A key priority was the creation of a pleasant, accessible, and sustainable public space – one with trees, brick-paved streets, natura stone curbs, benches, good lighting, and, most importantly, minimal car traffic!

Quote from a conference speech by Jan Mastenbroek, Head of the Public Information Department, Municipality of Amsterdam, member of Bureau Amsterdam 700, November 1975.[19]

'The significance [of Amsterdam 700 – MH] can be formulated as follows: Amsterdam has once again become acutely aware of itself. Very large segments of the population have taken action for the city. Various aspects of the city have been newly emphasized. The past has been reflected upon in a highly engaging manner. The possibilities for the future have become clearer. A sense has emerged that Amsterdam can foster great solidarity and togetherness.

Amsterdam is a city with problems, but these no longer obscure its potential; instead, they can be seen as challenges. Amsterdam will survive! Amsterdam is more than worth the effort.

The value of this celebration is, of course, determined by emotion. After all, it is wonderful to be an Amsterdammer. Gains can indeed be measured in emotions and not just in money. We all feel that, through this year, Amsterdam has grown mentally stronger. It can face the future again. This, I would say, is the meaning of this celebration.'

PART 1
SOCIETAL DYNAMICS

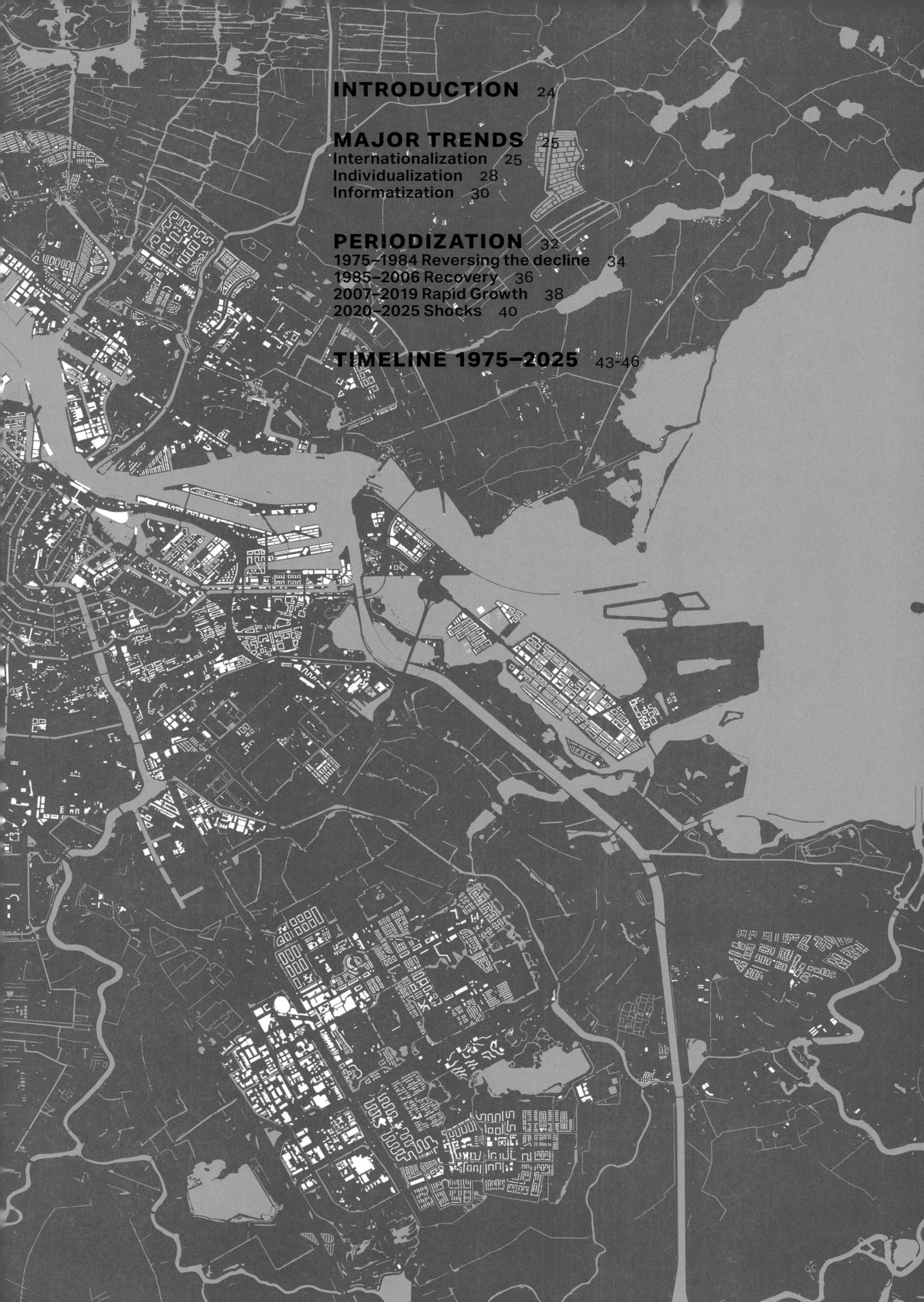

INTRODUCTION

In the development of Amsterdam between 1975 and 2025, several long-term trends emerge, closely linked to major societal shifts and changes in the city's position within the Netherlands, the EU, and the world. Reviewing reports from the Scientific Council for Government Policy (WRR) and the Netherlands Institute for Social Research (SCP), three key trends stand out: internationalization, individualization, and informatization.[1] These trends have deep historical roots, but over the past fifty years, technological breakthroughs and economic policies focused on liberalization and privatization have fundamentally transformed society.

The first section examines how these societal dynamics have shaped life in the city and influenced its development. This is followed by a periodization of Amsterdam's urban evolution. The city's development follows a classic pattern, divided into four phases. The period from 1975 to 1984 marks a phase of *Reversing the Decline*, characterized by efforts to halt further deterioration and stabilize the city, largely driven by local government initiatives. The second phase, from 1985 to 2006, is a period of *Recovery*, during which market forces and private enterprises play an increasingly dominant role. From 2007 to 2019, the city experiences a phase of *Rapid Growth*, fueled by waves of internationalization. However, from 2020 onward, the COVID-19 pandemic and wars in Ukraine and the Middle East trigger a phase of *Shocks*.

For this periodization, shifts in the city's population growth serve as key reference points – decline, modest growth, strong growth, and extremes. These demographic patterns closely align with broader phases in Amsterdam's socioeconomic development. A brief characterization of these four periods, along with a map illustrating construction activity in the city, provides an initial insight into the interrelationship between social and spatial developments.

Finally, this chapter presents a fold-out timeline covering the years 1975–2025.

How have the major societal trends of internationalization, individualization, and informatization over the past fifty years influenced life in and the development of the city? Below, several key aspects are highlighted.

Internationalization

Since 1975, Amsterdam has transformed into a highly diverse, international city. The 1975 Yearbook of the Amsterdam Bureau of Statistics focused primarily on migration patterns between Amsterdam, surrounding municipalities, and the rest of the Netherlands. However, the 1976 Yearbook, which reported on 1975 data, included for the first time a table categorizing residents by nationality. Out of Amsterdam's 750,000 residents at the time, 40,200 were classified as having an 'alien nationality'.

By 2025, an estimated 560,000 residents will have foreign roots – accounting for 60% of the population. This marks a profound shift from the situation in 1975 and also sets Amsterdam apart from the Netherlands as a whole.

Decolonization

The most significant event in 1975 regarding the Netherlands' relationship with its overseas territories was the independence of Suriname on November 25. In Paramaribo, Oranjeplein was renamed Onafhankelijkheidsplein (Independence Square), where the Surinamese flag was raised for the first time. This marked the end of more than three centuries of colonial rule. In Amsterdam, the Surinamese flag was also displayed above the entrance of City Hall, an initiative by the Welsuria foundation, and a large celebration took place at Bijlmerplein.

Many studies view 1975 as the final chapter of the global decolonization process that followed World War II.[2] That same year, Angola and Mozambique also gained independence, and the Vietnam War came to an end. While most countries in North, Central, and South America had already achieved independence in the 18th and 19th centuries, by the mid-1970s, nearly all nations in Africa and Asia had done the same. However, this did not necessarily mean that post-colonial relations became fully equal. As a result, many Surinamese sought opportunities outside their homeland. Between 1970 and 1980, 150,000 Surinamese settled in the Netherlands – 40,000 of them in 1975 alone. Many found housing in the newly built apartment complexes in the Bijlmermeer. Some eventually returned to Suriname, but the majority remained.

By early 2025, Amsterdam had 62,000 residents of Surinamese descent. Together with 13,000 Antilleans and 23,000 Indonesians, the city now has nearly 100,000 residents with roots in the former colonies, making up 10% of the population.

European integration

Global power dynamics also underwent a profound shift around the time of World War II. Former colonial powers such as France and the United Kingdom not only relinquished their colonies but also lost their dominant positions on the world stage to the United States and the Soviet Union. This led to the emergence of what became known as the First, Second, and Third Worlds. By the 1960s, an 'Iron Curtain' ran through Europe, dividing Western and Eastern Europe.

Economic cooperation among the Benelux countries – Belgium, the Netherlands, and Luxembourg – and former wartime adversaries such as West Germany, France, and Italy took shape during the postwar reconstruction period. This led to the creation of new alliances, including the European Coal and Steel Community (ECSC) in 1952 and the European Economic Community (EEC) in 1958. In 1973, Denmark, the United Kingdom, and Ireland also joined the EEC.

Southern Europe experienced democratic transitions during this period as well. Portugal held democratic elections in 1975 following the Carnation Revolution of 1974, and Greece transitioned to democracy after the fall of its military junta. In Spain, democracy was restored after the death of dictator Francisco Franco. In the following years, these countries also joined the EEC. The 1970s were thus a hopeful period for democratization and international cooperation.

That hope turned into euphoria with the fall of the Berlin Wall in 1989. After the Schengen Agreement in 1995 and the official introduction of the euro in 2002, the European Union expanded to include seven Eastern European countries. By early 2025, the EU consists of 27 member states with a total population of approximately 450 million.

The principle of 'free movement of people and goods' has made Amsterdam increasingly a European city. In 1975, nearly 19,000 Amsterdammers held a European nationality. By early 2025, that number has grown to 162,000 – 17% of the city's population – including both students and expats. After Brexit, the number of EU bachelor's and master's students in Amsterdam increased rapidly, as studying in the UK now required a visa and became significantly more expensive.[3]

Labor migration and refugees

Alongside decolonization and European integration, the global process of globalization also brought significant changes. A key driver of globalization is the redistribution of production processes between low-wage and high-wage countries. For example, clothing can be manufactured much more cheaply in low-wage countries than in the Netherlands or Western Europe. Meanwhile, employment in cities like Amsterdam has increasingly concentrated in sectors such as media and technology. This shift has led to a dramatic increase in global trade and, over time, has radically transformed Amsterdam's economy.

A transitional phase in the 1960s and 1970s saw an influx of workers willing to take on jobs in the Netherlands for relatively low wages. Initially, these workers came mainly from Southern Europe, but before long, laborers were also recruited from

Population Amsterdam by nationality 1975 and origin 2025
(Source O&S Amsterdam)

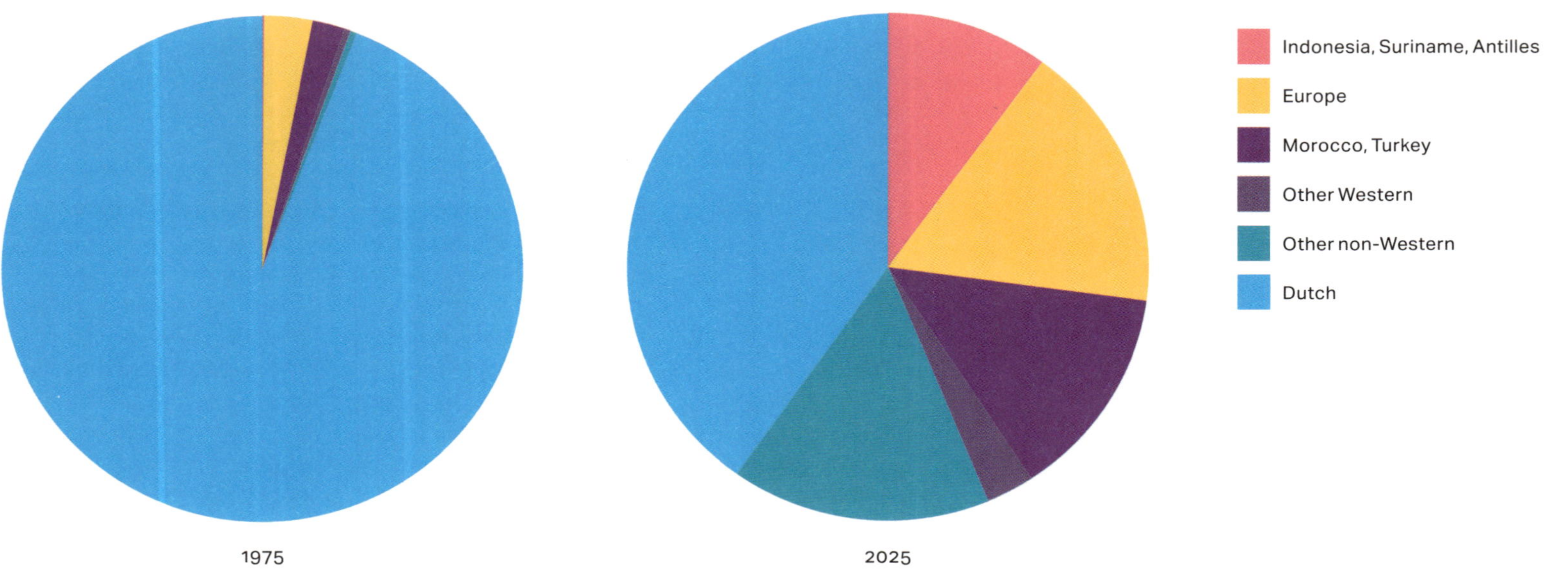

Morocco and Turkey. By the end of 1975, Amsterdam was home to around 14,000 residents – predominantly men – from these two countries. They were originally considered 'guest workers' who were expected to return to their home countries after a few years. However, in 1974, the Den Uyl government introduced the Family Reunification Act, allowing workers to bring their spouses and children to the Netherlands. Instead of being housed in barracks, such as the Atatürk residential complex near the NDSM shipyard, these families gained the right to proper housing. Today, approximately 126,000 Amsterdammers have Moroccan or Turkish roots, making up 13.5% of the city's population.

Eventually, much of Amsterdam's industrial production relocated to other countries, often outside of Europe. This process first affected the city's textile industry and later its wood, paper, metal, and shipbuilding industries. Mergers and acquisitions ultimately led to a wave of business closures around 1980. Other regions in the Netherlands faced similar industrial declines, particularly in mining and textiles, resulting in widespread unemployment.

Throughout the 1980s and 1990s, Amsterdam's economy became increasingly service-oriented. While traditional sectors such as healthcare, culture, education, and government remained important, the strongest growth occurred in business services, finance, and tourism. In recent years, the so-called tech industry has emerged as the fastest-growing sector, attracting a highly educated workforce, not only from neighboring countries but also from outside Europe – particularly from India. In 1975, only around 3,000 Amsterdammers were from 'other Western countries'. By early 2025, that number had risen to approximately 26,000, or 3% of the city's population.

Amsterdam has become a global city, and as such, it has also become a destination for many immigrants from non-Western countries, including both refugees and economic migrants. In 1975, the number of Amsterdammers with a non-Western migration background (excluding Moroccans and Turks) was 2,782. By early 2025, that number had grown to 150,000 – nearly 16% of the population. The largest groups come from Ghana, the former Soviet Union, China, and Egypt, while smaller groups include refugees and asylum seekers from Eritrea, Afghanistan, Syria, and Ukraine.

Decolonization, European integration, and globalization have profoundly shaped the city's development and daily life. At the end of 1975, 5% of Amsterdam's residents had a migration background. Fifty years later, that number has risen to 60%.

Business activity

The process of internationalization manifests not only in the composition of Amsterdam's population but also in its evolving economic landscape. In her influential 1991 publication *The Global City*, Saskia Sassen described the new role that cities such as New York, London, and Tokyo play in an increasingly integrated global economy.[4] These cities function as key nodes through which capital, goods, and information flow worldwide. Stock exchanges and headquarters of multinational financial institutions – surrounded by consulting firms – form the backbone of this global network.

Amsterdam participates at a secondary level in this network, though its banking sector has played a less dominant role since the financial crisis of 2007–2008. The banking sector underwent early consolidation through mergers and clustering. In 1964, NHM and Twentsche Bank merged to form ABN, while in the same year, Amsterdamsche Bank and Rotterdamsche Bank merged to create AMRO Bank. These two entities later merged in 1992 to form ABN AMRO, expanding their operations across the US, UK, Belgium, Brazil, and Italy. A similar trajectory led to the creation of ING. In 1979, the Gemeentegiro Amsterdam was acquired by the newly formed Postbank, which itself had emerged from the 1977 merger of the Postgiro and Rijkspostspaarbank. Postbank was privatized in 1986 and merged in 1989 with the Nederlandse Middenstandsbank. The 1991 merger with Nationale Nederlanden led to the formation of ING. By 2007, ING had grown into one of the world's twenty largest financial institutions, operating in over fifty countries with 140,000 employees and total assets of €1.313 trillion.

Both ABN AMRO and ING established their headquarters near Amsterdam Zuid Station and the World Trade Center (WTC), which opened in 1985, in what became known as the Zuidas district – just a stone's throw from Schiphol Airport. Numerous law firms and consulting firms also established offices in this area, including both Dutch and international companies such as NautaDutilh, Accenture, PwC, EY, and Deloitte. Major Dutch corporations also relocated their headquarters to Zuidas, such as AkzoNobel (2007) and Arcadis (2010), both of which moved from Arnhem. Initially, Philips located its headquarters near Amstel Station but is set to relocate to Zuidas in 2025.

Many Dutch companies have since engaged in mergers or joint ventures with foreign firms or have been acquired, becoming part of larger European or global corporations. Examples include Euronext, Ahold, ICL, and Cargill. Conversely, several foreign companies have chosen Amsterdam as the location for their headquarters, such as Calvin Klein and Tommy Hilfiger in the fashion industry. Around Schiphol Airport, numerous Japanese companies have established their European distribution centers, including Canon, Sony, Hitachi, and Mitsubishi.

Since the financial crisis of 2007–2008, Amsterdam's position as a financial center has shifted. In 2007, ABN AMRO was acquired by the Belgian bank Fortis, but in 2008, the Dutch government was forced to take over Fortis's shares. ING also received government support, and Nationale Nederlanden was spun off in 2014. From that point onward, Dutch banks have operated on a more modest scale. ING has since concentrated its operations in Amsterdam-Zuidoost, while ABN AMRO is following suit, maintaining only a significantly downsized headquarters on the Zuidas.

Privatization and autonomization

The formation of ING was part of a broader trend of privatization and the corporatization of state-owned enterprises. In response to deindustrialization and economic stagnation, the Dutch government under Prime Minister Lubbers, following recommendations from the Wagner Commission in 1981 and 1982, adopted a radically new economic policy. This policy prioritized a more market-driven approach with a reduced role for the government. It was implemented through deregulation, lower taxes, the introduction of market mechanisms in traditionally public sectors such as healthcare, and the corporatization and privatization of state-owned enterprises.[5] Nationally, companies like PTT and NS were split and partially sold, while the Postgiro and Rijkspostspaarbank were privatized entirely. The expectation was that these newly independent companies would provide services more efficiently and cost-effectively in a competitive market.

This transformation was also evident in Amsterdam. In 1975, the city had a large number of municipal enterprises, including the Abattoir, the Burgerweeshuis, the aforementioned Girokantoor, the Department of Public Works with its road workers and divisions for parks and sewage, the GEB (Municipal Energy Company), the Stadsdrukkerij (City Printing Office), the GWL (Municipal Water Company), the WSBZ (Municipal Laundry, Cleaning, Bathhouse, and Swimming Facilities), the Social Services Department, the Municipal Police, the Municipal Housing Company, and the staff of the municipal Binnengasthuis and Weesperplein hospitals. The largest municipal service was the GVB (Municipal Transport Company), employing 3,426 people. In total, Amsterdam employed 28,128 municipal workers in 1975.[6] By the end of 2024, this number had been reduced to approximately 18,000.

Several municipal enterprises were privatized or merged into provincial, national, or even international companies and organizations.[7] This also applied to KTA (Kabeltelevisie Amsterdam), which was established in 1976 in collaboration with Amsterdam's housing corporations and was sold in 1995 to A2000 for 700 million guilders. The GVB, after much debate, remained a municipal enterprise. The Port of Amsterdam was corporatized but remains 100% city-owned, and Schiphol's shares have not been publicly traded.

GEB and Municipal Housing Corporation

The spatial implications of these developments make it worthwhile exploring the transformation of two major municipal enterprises in more detail: the GEB (Municipal Energy Company) and the Gemeentelijk Woningbedrijf (Municipal Housing Company).

Until 1985, the City of Amsterdam owned both the distribution network and power plants of the GEB, located in Noord and at the Hemweg. In 1985, the GEB was corporatized, leading to the establishment of UNA. This company was privatized in 1998 and sold for a significant sum to the American company Reliant Energy. Meanwhile, provincial energy companies had already begun merging, resulting in the formation of Nuon in 1994. In 2003, Nuon acquired UNA. Following the separation of the distribution network in 2008, Alliander was formed, while Nuon focused solely on energy production. In 2009, the Swedish state-owned company Vattenfall took over Nuon.

Vattenfall's Dutch headquarters is now located near Bijlmer ArenA Station at Hoekenrodeplein. As of 2025, the company supplies energy to approximately two million customers in the Netherlands. Coal-fired power plants, including the one at Hemweg, have been shut down, and gas plants are undergoing a transition. In late 2024, Vattenfall decided against converting the Diemen plants to biomass fuel, opting instead for an e-boiler system.

The Gemeentelijk Woningbedrijf was established in 1915 to develop and manage affordable worker housing while also facilitating urban renewal and slum clearance. Many of its early housing projects were built in the garden villages of Amsterdam Noord. After World War II, housing corporations took the lead in construction, but from 1975 onward, the municipal housing company was increasingly utilized by the city for complex new developments and the renovation of acquired buildings. This included the transformation of former squatted buildings, such as the Groote Keijser and the Handelsblad complex. By the end of 1991, the Woningbedrijf managed nearly 40,000 homes in the city.

In 1994, the company was privatized following the so-called 'bruteringsoperatie' (Brutering Operation, a financial restructuring measure) under

State Secretary Heerma, leading to the creation of housing association Ymere. Government subsidies for social housing were abolished, requiring new developments to be financed through rental income and property sales. Liberalization also allowed housing corporations to sell existing social housing units and develop market-rate homes. Many corporations merged and established real estate development divisions. Ymere expanded by merging with corporations in Almere, Purmerend, Haarlemmermeer, Alkmaar, Heerhugowaard, and Weesp, becoming a major regional housing provider. As of 2023, Ymere managed 72,165 homes, including 65,075 social rental units and 7,090 market-rate rentals. Other corporations like Stadgenoot and De Alliantie followed similar paths, abandoning their original association structures and becoming foundations.

The liberalization of the housing market also opened the door for private developers and investors. In 1996, Amsterdam's housing stock consisted of 55% publicly owned social housing, 34% private rental units, and 11% owner-occupied homes. By the end of 2023, the distribution had shifted dramatically: 36% of housing was social rental owned by corporations, 11% was private-sector social rental, 24% was other private rental, and 29% was owner-occupied – marking a significant transformation![8]

During the real estate crisis, liberalization was partially reversed, and housing corporations were subjected to a 'landlord levy.' They were no longer allowed to develop properties for sale, leading many to divest their development branches and sell key land holdings. In 2023, this annual levy was abolished, but high costs continue to make new social housing development challenging. As a result, many housing corporations still prioritize the sale of existing rental properties.

Homes Amsterdam by sector 1996–2023
(Source O&S Amsterdam)

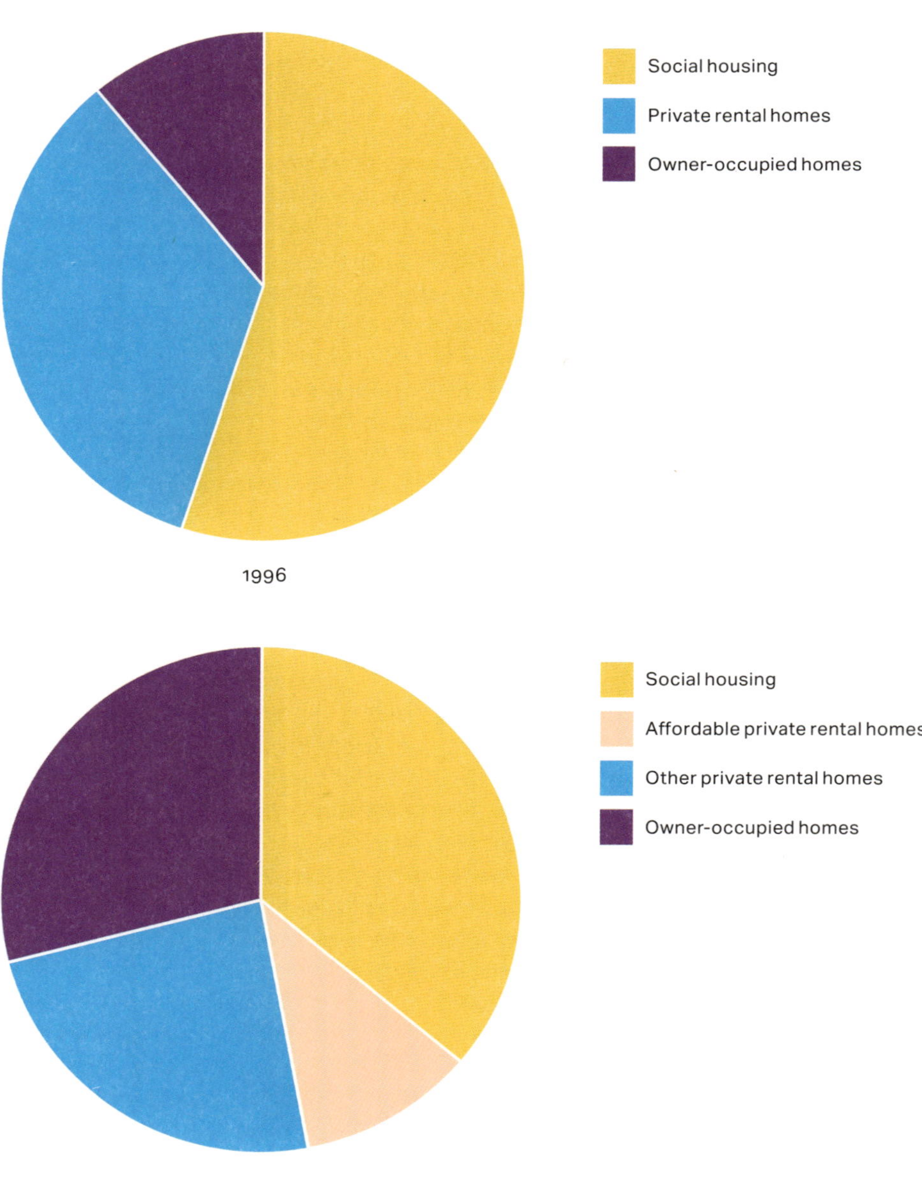

Education and research

Scientific research and debate are inherently internationally oriented. True collaboration received a significant boost through EU funding for research programs, such as Horizon 2020, and student exchanges through the Erasmus program. Following the Schengen Agreement and more recently after Brexit, the number of Amsterdam students from European countries has increased significantly. Both the University of Amsterdam (UvA) and Vrije Universiteit (VU) offer part of their bachelor's programs, but in fact, their entire master's and PhD programs are taught in English. In the academic year 2023–2024, UvA and VU had 35% and 20% international students, respectively. In the current academic year, the number of first-year bachelor students at both UvA and VU has decreased, but the number of foreign master's students at UvA has once again risen.[9]

Culture, sports, and tourism

Between 1975 and 2025, Amsterdam has become a highly sought-after destination for foreign tourists. The number of hotel beds in the city increased from 20,000 in 1975 to 92,000 in 2023; the number of overnight stays rose from 2.8 million to 22.1 million. The integration within the EU, the expanded network of Schiphol, and relatively low ticket prices have played a role in this, but so has the city's offerings. The entire cultural infrastructure of the city has been renewed and significantly expanded, including an impressive array of events, from now-established and popular events like 'King's Day' and the Canal Parade to the Amsterdam Dance Event. With just a few clicks, one can book tickets, travel, and accommodation.

In 1985, Amsterdam bid to host the 1992 Summer Olympics. While the Games were ultimately awarded to Barcelona, the city did retain the Nieuw Sloten area (the proposed Olympic Village), the Arena, and a modernized Olympic Stadium. The Gay Games held in Amsterdam in 1998 were a cheerful and successful alternative to the 'official' event.

Individualization

A similarly profound change is seen in the way Amsterdammers shape their daily lives. The ideal nuclear family from the post-war period – a working man, a housewife, and two or more children – has been replaced by a broad range of living and household forms. Currently, about 280,000 Amsterdammers are single. That is 30% of the population, but 54% of the number of households. What happened?

Emancipation

1975 was declared by the United Nations as the International Year of the Woman, and in Mexico City, the first International Women's Conference was held that year. The Charter from 1948 included gender equality between men and women as a prominent part, but in practice, little of that had been realized. The situation was actually the opposite: economic independence and the right to self-determination for women were hardly in place in many countries, including in the Netherlands. Organizations such as Dolle Mina, Man-Woman-Society, and Wij Vrouwen Eisen started advocating against this from the late 1960s. In 1973, the Amsterdam Women's House opened.

During the celebratory year of 1975, the Van Gogh Museum hosted the event Eva-nement and A'dam-benemend, organized by the Amsterdam Women's Council, founded in 1974. The Tropenmuseum organized a broad thematic exhibition called Vrouw ben je (You are a Woman), which was later also displayed in Utrecht during the Emancipade that year. At the end of October, the festive musical De Engel van Amsterdam (The Angel of Amsterdam) played at Carré. With lyrics by Lennart Nijgh and music by Joop Stokkermans, Jasperina de Jong sang *Vrouwen, vrouwen, vrouwen, voorwaarts in de strijd. We moeten het juk van die kerels 'ns kwijt* ('Women, women, women, forward in the fight. It's time to cast off the men's yoke tonight'). More significant were the actions for equal pay in the spring of 1975 and the occupation of the Bloemenhoven Clinic in the following year.

In the aforementioned Yearbooks of the Amsterdam Statistics Bureau from the 1970s, no distinction was made between men and women in terms of the workforce. However, the size of the labor force in 1975 (305,000 people, 53% of the population aged 15 to 75) suggests that a limited number of women were in paid employment. In 2020, the labor force participation rate was 68% on average, with 65% for women. That seems like a significant step, but of the working women, (only) 48% currently work 35 hours a week or more; for men, it is 73%.[10]

Singles

Notably, the number of single people in Amsterdam in 1975 was already relatively high: 173,400, 23% of the population, and nearly 47% of the number of households! The city had traditionally offered unique forms of housing, such as courtyards in the old city and housing complexes for single people or specifically for single women, such as Otter-Knoll at Eikenplein, Het Nieuwe Huis and Huize Lydia at Roelof Hartplein, the Oranjehof at Geuzenkade, the Louise Wenthuis at Wibautstraat, and the Westereindflat in Slotermeer.[11] Specially built for students were the Weesperstraatflat, the Zilverberg, and Casa 400. The city also had 63 'retirement homes' with 7,068 'beds' in 1975.

Altogether, however, this amounted to little more than 10,000 households. The majority of single people lived in 'ordinary' homes, mostly in the older parts of the city, such as in the Jordaan and Oud-West. In these two neighborhoods, the majority of one- and two-room apartments were concentrated. For example, in the northern part of the Jordaan, the share of such apartments in the housing stock in 1975 was 72%, and in the Jacob van Lennepbuurt, it was even 78%. Single people made up two-thirds of the number of households there. The average household size was therefore extremely low: 1.90 and 1.85, especially compared to family neighborhoods like the Concertgebouwbuurt (2.96), Geuzenveld (3.20), Tuindorp Buiksloot (3.01), or rural areas (average 4.01).

It is interesting to look more closely at the population trends in the early 1970s. The total city population decreased from 831,463 to 751,054 by the end of 1975.[12] Mainly families with children left, mostly to municipalities in the region; a classic pattern of suburbanization. In total, from 1971 to 1975, the net migration between the city and other municipalities in North Holland and Flevoland was 70,855 people. Amstelveen, Zaanstad, and the new generation of new towns (Hoorn, Purmerend, Haarlemmermeer, and Lelystad) each accounted for about 6,000 people. In 1975 alone, nearly 9,500 families (comprising 27,000 people) left the city. Of course, families also settled, but the net result was -5,100.

At the same time, more single people moved into the city than left: 8,600 in 1975, mostly young adults. The share of 20-29-year-olds in the city's population increased rapidly. Amsterdam became a city for youngsters. This was especially evident in neighborhoods with many small homes. The share of young adults in the aforementioned northern part of the Jordaan and in the Van Lennepbuurt increased from 16%, respectively 18% in 1965, to 24% and 27% in 1970, and 29% and 34% in 1975.

Young Adults City

The growth in the number of young adults in the city is undoubtedly linked to the strong growth in the number of students during this period. At VU and UvA, just over 10,000 students were enrolled in 1960. By 1970, this number had risen to 25,000, and by 1975, it had reached 31,000. Additionally, 18,000 students were enrolled in some form of higher vocational education that year. Only a portion of these students lived in the city and managed their own households, but this was, of course, an important development for the character and atmosphere of the city. Many chose to stay in the city after their studies.[13]

The character of the city as a youth hub has only strengthened in recent decades. In 2023, nearly 75,000 students were enrolled at VU and UvA; nearly 47,000 more at the Hogeschool van Amsterdam. The gender ratio has also changed significantly. In the VU Yearbook of 1960, the term 'lady students' was still used. There were 483 of them at the time, 17% of the total. Nowadays, women make up the majority in higher and scientific education. This also applies to the city as a whole, especially in terms of young adults and the elderly. There are nearly 15,000 more women than men in the city's 18-30 age group. Of the households, only 15% are two-parent families with children.

Gay Capital

The large number of one- and two-person households in the city is partly explained by the relatively high number of gays and lesbians living in the city. Exact numbers are not known, but with the waves of youth culture in the 1960s, homosexuality began to play a more significant role in city life, including in public life.[14] In 1977, the first demonstration was held, concluding with a speech by Annemarie Grewel at Leidseplein. In the years that followed, the infrastructure of the gay community developed spectacularly, with dozens of cafés, bars, and nightclubs, including the RoXY and the iT. In 1987, the Homomonument was erected at the Westermarkt. Leading up to the 1998 Gay Games, the first Canal Parade took place in 1996 with 45 boats and 20,000 spectators. In 2001, Mayor Job Cohen officiated the first same-sex marriage in the world. Amsterdam had become the Gay Capital, at least of Europe.

But this also included the AIDS outbreak starting in 1982. Thousands of Amsterdam residents died from the disease. Research programs and campaigns from the GGD (Public Health Service) and UvA played a key role in combating and preventing the disease.

Under the LGBTQI+ flag, gay culture has expanded in recent years. At the same time, the number of nightlife venues has decreased, and acceptance seems less taken for granted.

Informatization

A very different but equally important long-term trend in recent decades is the informatization of society, also known as digitization. The new information technology has made communication and information exchange much easier.

Amsterdam is an important hub in the associated new networks. An important step in 1975 was the founding of Nikhef, the National Institute for Subatomic Physics and High Energy Physics, a collaboration between the Foundation for Fundamental Research on Matter (FOM), the Institute for Nuclear Physics Research (IKO), the University of Amsterdam, and the Catholic University of Nijmegen. The new institute was established alongside the Mathematical Centre and the Institute for Atomic and Molecular Physics (AMOLF) at the particle accelerator of the IKO in a building complex opened in 1978 on Kruislaan in the Watergraafsmeer. Nikhef still exists today as the National Institute for Subatomic Physics. The Mathematical Centre became the Centrum Wiskunde & Informatica (CWI). Like AMOLF, these institutes have become part of the Netherlands Organization for Scientific Research (NWO).

Over time, a whole cluster of research institutes has emerged in the Watergraafsmeer area, supported from 1980 by SARA, the Foundation for Academic Computing Amsterdam, and connected to the world by bundles of cables. In 1988, the first 'open' internet connection was made from Europe to the United States. AMS-IX, founded in 1994, grew into one of the largest internet hubs in the world in the years that followed.[15] After the move of the UvA's Faculty of Science to the area in 2010, the cluster was named Amsterdam Science Park. By now, the university sports center, University College, several housing projects, and a whole series of data centers have been established at the Science Park. Close to the internet hub, these data towers are the most expensive and sought-after places for data storage in the Netherlands.

Digitalization

But 1975 is of course primarily the year of the founding of Microsoft, followed by Apple in 1976. These companies are now among the largest in the world, measured by their market value, but also by

Housing stock and new construction Amsterdam 1975–2025
(Source O&S Amsterdam)

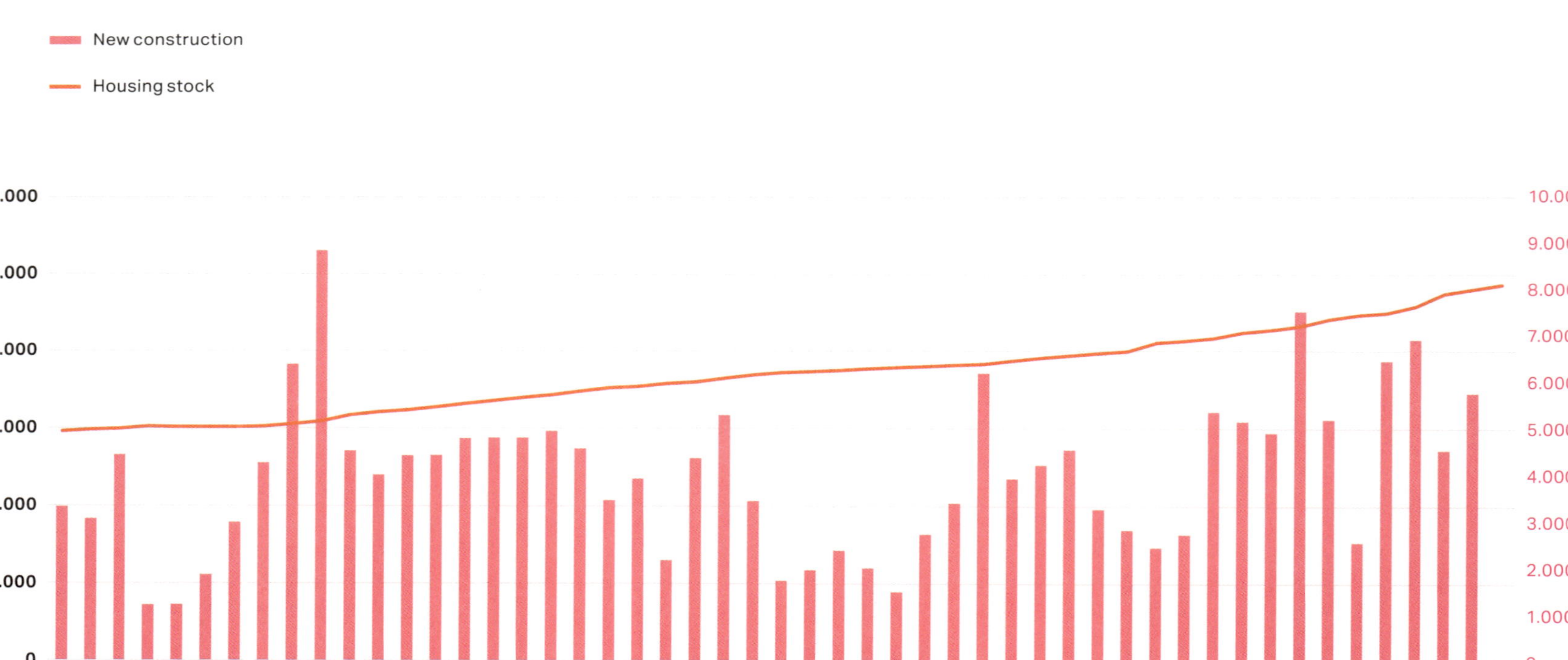

their influence. While IBM had already developed large computer systems for business applications in the 1960s, Microsoft and Apple subsequently expanded these technologies for personal use in PCs, laptops, and mobile phones. In 1975, Amsterdam had 282,000 telephone connections for 750,000 residents and 31,000 business establishments. In 2022, the Netherlands had 20.64 million mobile phone connections, a coverage rate of 120%.

The Amsterdam economy traditionally had a mixed character, with industrial production alongside large sectors like trade, banking, government, healthcare, and education. As of 2025, nearly all employment is in the service sector. Deindustrialization and the simultaneous expansion of the knowledge-intensive service sector have been accompanied by a different form of employment organization: large industrial companies like ADM, NDSM, and Werkspoor with thousands of employees made way for countless self-employed individuals (zzp'ers) and temporary contract workers in the service sector, who operate in flexible networks and often from their homes. This explains the enormous increase in the number of business establishments in Amsterdam: 31,000 in 1975 and 206,190 in 2024.[16]

Concentration and location preferences

At the same time, however, there is also a noticeable trend of concentration in the service sector. Mergers and efficiency, as well as encounters and proximity, play a role in this. This is particularly true for the financial sector. Conglomerates such as ABN AMRO and ING opted for a high degree of clustering of their activities in the city. On the ING campus in Zuidoost, 2,800 people work. Similar movements can also be seen in education and healthcare. The number of hospitals in Amsterdam has been significantly reduced. Since 1975, the Binnen- and Wilhelmina Gasthuis, the Emma Children's Hospital, the Andreas, Slotervaart, and Prinsengracht Hospitals, as well as a whole series of smaller clinics, have closed. Amsterdam UMC had 19,500 employees at the two locations, AMC and VUMC, in 2024.

What stands out is the difference in location preference for service-oriented businesses. While most large companies in the financial and legal sectors moved out of the city center, the city center itself became a popular place for specialized banks, small law firms, and various new companies in the creative and tech sectors. This applied to both startups and scaling businesses, as well as well-established brands like TomTom and Booking. The payment service Adyen took over the vacant department stores of Hudson's Bay on Rokin in 2020, with 1,000 employees.

New logistics

The closure of department stores such as Hudson's Bay, but also V&D and Marks & Spencer, is the tip of what can easily be described as an earthquake in retail. While supermarkets have been replacing small-scale food shops since the 1980s, online orders and home deliveries in the last ten years have led to a radical change in the cityscape. The excess sales floor space in neighborhood and district centers has been filled with new services like phone shops and nail studios. The parades of delivery vans from DHL, UPS, PostNL, Picnic, and HelloFresh, as well as bicycle couriers from Deliveroo, Flink, and Domino's, are also completely new phenomena. Enormous distribution centers are part of this. The Centrale Markthal on the grounds of the Food Center Amsterdam on Jan van Galenstraat closed its doors in 2006, while colossal new halls were built on the outskirts of the city, such as the fully automated sorting and distribution centers of Albert Heijn and PostNL, or the brand-new, stacked logistics city hub for last-mile delivery services at the North Sea Canal.[17] *Digitization takes over.*

Cables and electrification

The digital revolution was accompanied by the deployment of kilometers of new underground cables, in various colors and sizes, from different, heavily competing 'providers' who sometimes literally built on the cable networks of telephones and television. The city of Amsterdam operated its own cable television network starting in 1976, together with, among others, housing corporations: KTA (Cable Television Network Amsterdam). Anyone who wanted could get a free connection. It was rolled out by the city in two years. After its sale in 1995 to A2000 and through various intermediaries, this network formed the basis for the current Ziggo network.

The distribution and especially the storage of all the new information consumes a lot of electricity, especially in data centers. Added to trends like electric cooking and driving, serious problems with electricity supply have arisen in and around the city in recent years. 'Congestion' on the grid is intensified by the irregular (return) supply of electricity from non-fossil sources like solar and wind. The congestion prompted the municipalities of Amsterdam and Haarlemmermeer to implement a stricter data center policy since 2020: no, unless...

Meanwhile, the internet hub AMS-IX achieved an 80% reduction in the electricity required by one of the new data centers. In terms of energy consumption and (temporary) energy storage, there is still a lot to be gained in the city.

The development of the city between 1975 and 2025 was not a straightforward, continuous process. A periodization can give more definition to the differences. The turning points in population development have been used as the basis for distinguishing periods. Below is the justification for the periodization; the figures are derived from the yearbooks of Research and Statistics (O&S) of the city of Amsterdam and its predecessors. On the following pages, maps of construction activities in the city during the four periods are included with an explanation.

1975–1984 Reversing the decline

In the first ten years, the population continued to decline, reaching 676,000 inhabitants by 1984. This was also the period of significant changes in the traditionally strong industrial sector. Breweries and printing companies left the city; shipping companies merged, and countless wood, metal, and shipbuilding industries closed their doors, leading to high unemployment.[18] In municipal politics, the focus shifted to reversing further decline, primarily through the initiation of urban renewal.

When zooming in on population development, it becomes clear that the decline was mainly caused by 'domestic emigration'. From 1968 onwards, between 35,000 and 45,000 Amsterdammers left the city each year; often families moving to new towns such as Hoorn, Purmerend, Lelystad, and from 1976, Almere. The population decline was somewhat mitigated by relatively stable flows of new arrivals from other parts of the country (around 20,000 per year) and from abroad (10,000-12,000 per year). 1975 was an exceptional year, with 18,422 new arrivals due to the independence of Suriname. From the early 1980s, the number of people leaving the city decreased, eventually reaching 25,000 per year. In 1984, for the first time since 1972, there was a birth surplus.

1985–2006 Recovery

In the period from 1985 to 2006, the population grew again, reaching 743,000 inhabitants. The city's economy also recovered. Influenced by European integration and national economic policies aimed at liberalization and privatization, the financial sector and aviation experienced rapid growth. Technological breakthroughs, such as the large-scale application of containers and the introduction of the internet, brought significant changes to transport, logistics, and the service sector. This development led to what Spanish-French sociologist Manuel Castells called 'the rise of the network society'.[19] Amsterdam transformed into a post-industrial service city and prepared itself for a role as a global city around the newly formed conglomerates of ABN AMRO and ING, the Euronext stock exchange, and the internet hub AMS-IX.[20]

Students and young adults increasingly stayed in the city for longer periods, eventually forming families there. The number of elderly residents declined, as many middle-aged residents who had lived in Amsterdam during the 1970s and 1980s moved to the new towns. While births and deaths were nearly in balance in 1985, the number of births

Population development and total population Amsterdam (+ Weesp in 2022)
(Source O&S Amsterdam)

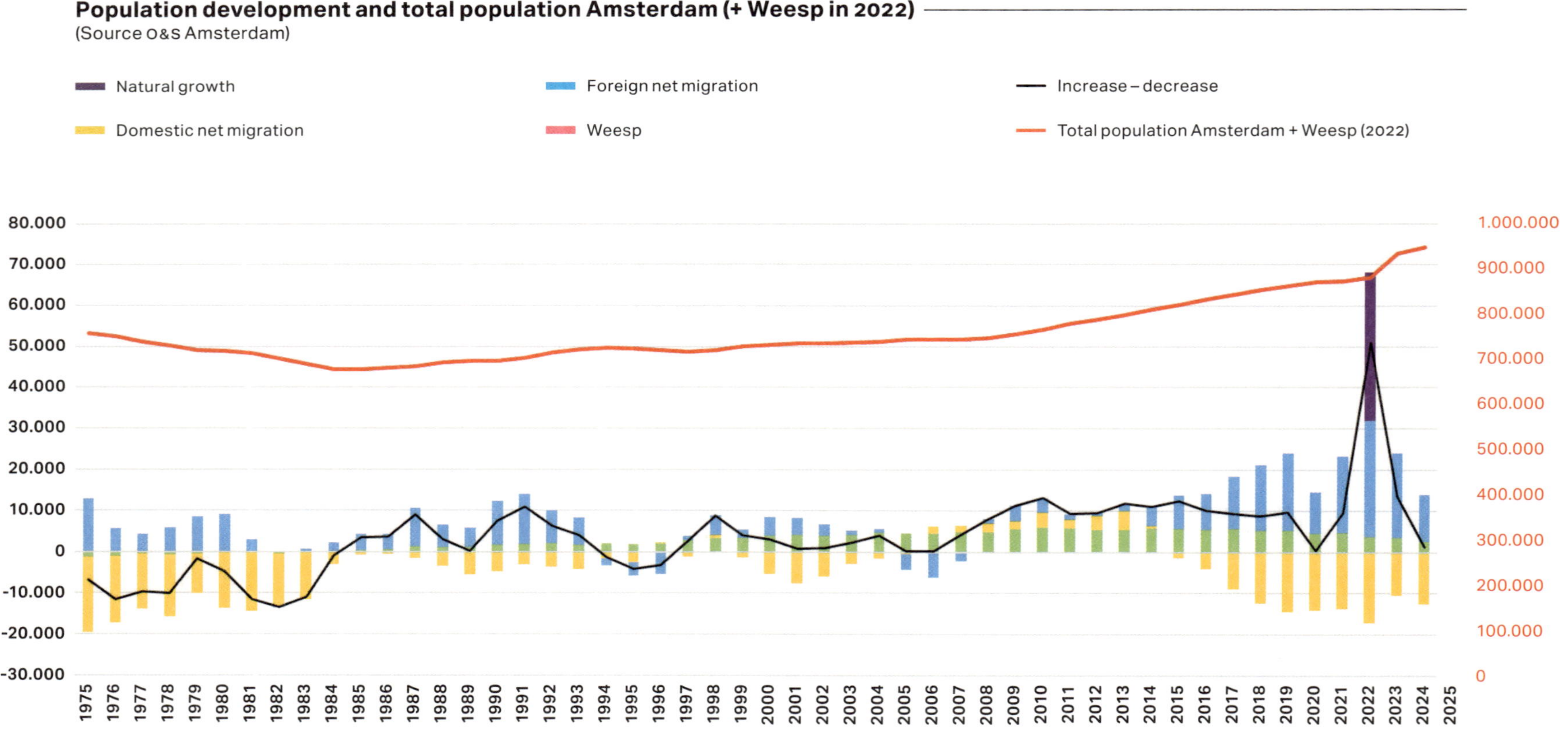

steadily increased from 7,800 to 10,200 per year between 1985 and 2006. At the same time, the number of deaths decreased from 7,500 to 5,750, leading to a greater share of natural population growth. Over the entire period, natural growth was relatively high, averaging 3,000 per year.

Migration played a less significant role in the population growth. The net migration was on average 475 per year. However, migration patterns were different from the previous period. Domestic migration (settlement and departure) remained relatively stable around 25,000 and 28,000 per year, respectively, throughout the period. Many of those leaving the city were young families with children. Rob van Engelsdorp Gastelaars and David Hamers referred to this phenomenon as 'the escalator'.[21] Young adults meet in the city, form a family, and after a few years, move outside the city, either to the suburbs or elsewhere in the country. The 'stayers' form a stable group of 'new city dwellers'.

Foreign migration fluctuated significantly. On average, 16,000 people settled in Amsterdam, while 13,000 left the city each year.

2007–2019 Rapid Growth

Starting in 2007, a new phase began, influenced by a population growth spurt and strong internationalization. The city's growth (and prosperity) stands in stark contrast to what was happening elsewhere in the Netherlands. The 2007–2011 credit crisis led to a sharp decline in exports and a global recession. However, against the tide, the city proved to be a great place to start a career. While housing production slowed down, the city grew by an average of 10,000 people annually, reaching 872,000 by the end of 2019. Initially, the growth was mostly from the Netherlands, but from 2016 onward, there was an increasing influx of migrants from abroad – particularly from the UK, India, the US, and Spain. The economy also grew, but in a different way from the 'global city' scenario. Now, the creative and tech sectors, along with 'other business services' and tourism, experienced strong growth. Rather than becoming a hard global city, Amsterdam increasingly evolved into a city of innovation and cultural interaction. Housing prices skyrocketed.

Unlike in the previous period, migration played an important role in this growth spurt. While the natural population increase continued to rise, with a peak of 11,000 births and a natural increase of 6,000 in 2010, the migration balance also increased, reaching an average of 4,500 people per year. Perhaps even more remarkable was the significant rise in the scale of migration movements. In the previous period, the number of arrivals and departures was relatively stable, with about 6% of the population changing each year. From 2007 onward, this increased rapidly. In 2019, no less than 81,000 people moved to the city (9.4% of the total population). In the same year, 76,600 people left the city (8.9%); a huge dynamism.

Within this strong migration movement, there was also a notable difference between domestic and foreign migration. The number of domestic settlers remained relatively stable, around 34,000 throughout the period. However, the number of domestic departures increased significantly over this period, from 30,000 in 2007 to an unprecedented 50,000 in 2019, a higher number than during the exodus in the 1970s. While the number of foreign departures remained relatively stable at around 26,000 per year, the number of settlers increased dramatically, from nearly 20,000 in 2007 to more than 46,000 in 2019.

Amsterdam has become a characteristic example of what architectural historian Michelle Provoost refers to as 'a city of coming and going'.[22]

2020–2025 Shocks

The COVID-19 pandemic in the spring of 2020, Brexit, and the wars in Ukraine and the Middle East marked a harsh end to the optimism, leading to unprecedented migration movements. The Amsterdam economy was relatively hard-hit in 2020, with a contraction of 6.4% in its Gross Regional Product (BRP). While the economy recovered, the rising energy prices and strong inflation significantly increased the cost of living. The congestion on the electricity grid made new connections difficult, and expanding capacity would take time. Furthermore, the prospects for further integration of the global economy and Europe became uncertain.

Nevertheless, the number of jobs continued to rise, from 690,000 at the end of 2019 to 746,000 by the end of 2023. The number of overnight stays in the city in 2023 matched the record set in 2019, at 22.1 million.

Domestic migration continued to increase, with nearly 56,000 people leaving the city in 2024. Foreign migration, however, fluctuated significantly. In 2022, nearly 52,000 people from abroad settled in Amsterdam; by 2024, that number dropped to 36,000. By early 2024, there were 5,500 Ukrainian refugees living in the city. A notable trend during this period was the decline in the number of births.

1975–1984

The decline of the city was reversed starting in 1975 through significant investments with substantial public funding, not only in the completion of expansion neighborhoods in the Banne and the Bijlmer but also, and especially, in the renewal of the existing city. A key moment in the celebratory year of 1975 was the opening of the Amsterdam Historical Museum, marking confidence in a new direction. Initially, housing production declined, but in 1984, a record number of new homes were completed: almost 9,000.

The large urban renewal operation in the city center and 19th-century neighborhoods was made possible by tight coordination from City Hall (the newly established Coordination Department for Urban Renewal) and the creation of 'outposts' of the Bureau of Administrative Contacts. These administrative project groups, operating autonomously from municipal services, made planning and decision-making efficient. The government contributed with generous financial support (Interim Saldo Scheme, ISR). For the success of the operation, it was equally important that almost all new homes were built in the social rental sector, by housing associations or the Municipal Housing Company. Additionally, the city purchased around 30,000 private rental homes, which were resold to housing associations and received either major or minor refurbishments.

In addition to renewal, efforts were also made to strengthen the residential function through the development of 'supplementary housing locations', often on land previously designated for business activities, such as the Venserpolder, the former ADM shipyard site (now IJplein), and the fairgrounds at Marcanti. The reservation for the 'extended' Lelylaan in Osdorp was also developed.

At the same time, large infrastructure projects planned as early as the 1960s were carried out: the East Line Metro, as well as the construction of the western and southern sections of the A10 ring road and the Ringspoorbaan with the new Zuid and RAI stations. A series of new urban facilities were also created: the hospital complexes of the Academic Medical Center (AMC) and Slotervaart, the Sports Hall South, and the expansion of De Mirandabad. Under the festive banner of the Floriade, Gaasperpark was opened in 1982.

In 1982, the Preliminary Design Structure Plan 'The City at the Center' was published. This further developed and broadened the new 'compact city policy' and outlined the direction for the city's development in the coming decades.

➔ Map Built in Amsterdam 1975–1984

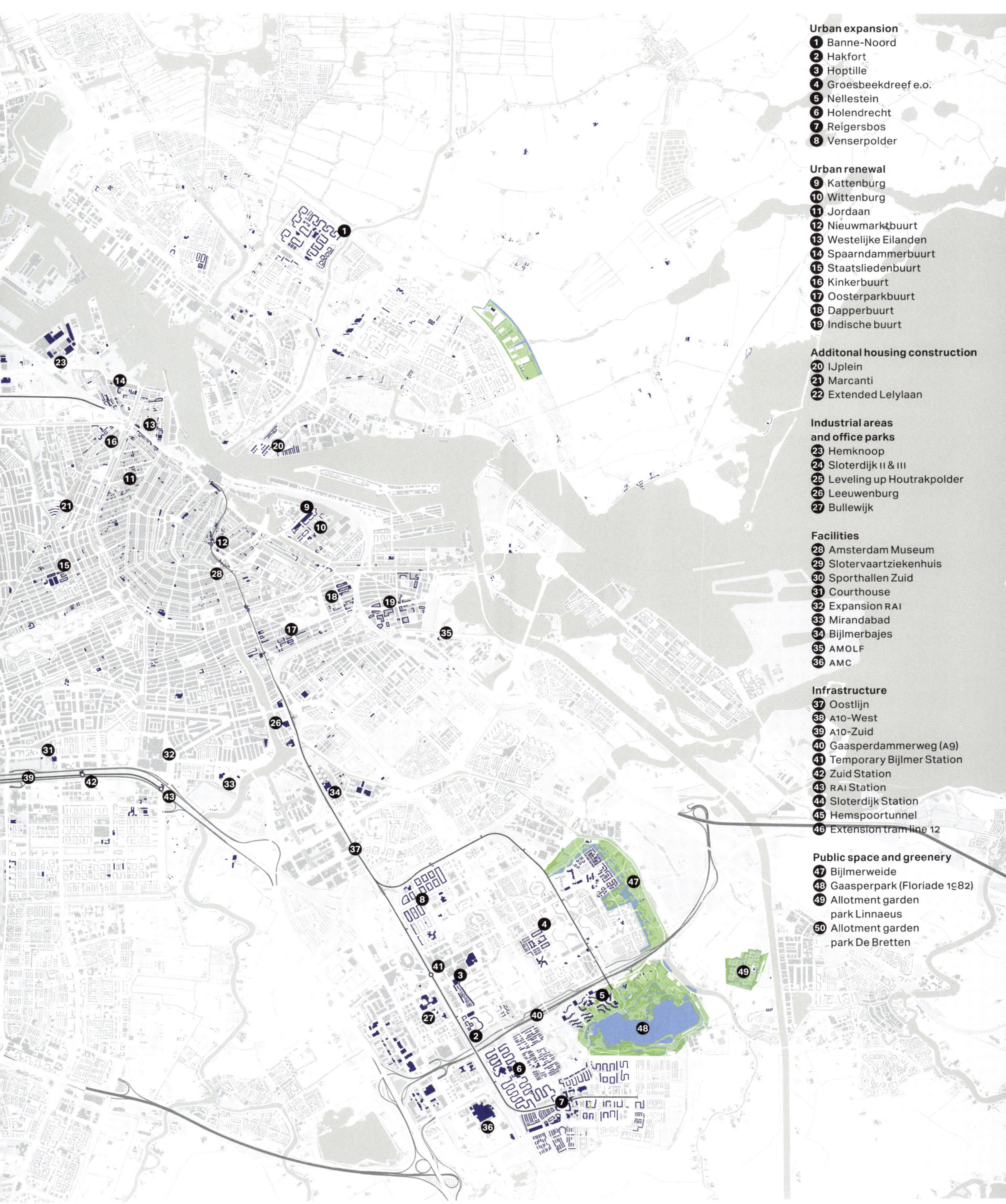
Urban expansion
1 Banne-Noord
2 Hakfort
3 Hoptille
4 Groesbeekdreef e.o.
5 Nellestein
6 Holendrecht
7 Reigersbos
8 Venserpolder
Urban renewal
9 Kattenburg
10 Wittenburg
11 Jordaan
12 Nieuwmarktbuurt
13 Westelijke Eilanden
14 Spaarndammerbuurt
15 Staatsliedenbuurt
16 Kinkerbuurt
17 Oosterparkbuurt
18 Dapperbuurt
19 Indische buurt
Additonal housing construction
20 IJplein
21 Marcanti
22 Extended Lelylaan
Industrial areas and office parks
23 Hemknoop
24 Sloterdijk II & III
25 Leveling up Houtrakpolder
26 Leeuwenburg
27 Bullewijk
Facilities
28 Amsterdam Museum
29 Slotervaartziekenhuis
30 Sporthallen Zuid
31 Courthouse
32 Expansion RAI
33 Mirandabad
34 Bijlmerbajes
35 AMOLF
36 AMC
Infrastructure
37 Oostlijn
38 A10-West
39 A10-Zuid
40 Gaasperdammerweg (A9)
41 Temporary Bijlmer Station
42 Zuid Station
43 RAI Station
44 Sloterdijk Station
45 Hemspoortunnel
46 Extension tram line 12
Public space and greenery
47 Bijlmerweide
48 Gaasperpark (Floriade 1982)
49 Allotment garden park Linnaeus
50 Allotment garden park De Bretten

1985–2006

Urban renewal initially focuses on completing the large projects in the city center and the 19th-century neighborhoods. In the late 1980s, the renewal also begins in what becomes known as the 'belt '20–'40,' the neighborhoods built during the interwar period under the Berlage Plan. With the exception of the Indische Buurt, renovation takes precedence here. The rapidly deteriorating living conditions in the Bijlmermeer lead to the drastic decision in 1993 to demolish a large number of high-rise flats in the G-district.

The compact city policy, outlined in the 1986 Structure Plan 'The City at the Center,' first manifests itself in the creation of several new expansion areas with compact low-rise housing. In addition to rental homes in the social sector, private homes are also built here – initially as subsidized, so-called premium-A and premium-B homes, later also in the free sector. The largest new low-rise neighborhoods are Gein, Oostzanerwerf, Nieuw Sloten, and De Aker.

A second aspect of the new policy is the transformation of the Eastern Port Area. After transforming the sites of the Veemarkt and the Abattoir on Cruquiuseiland, the KNSM, Java, and Borneo Islands, Sporenburg, and finally the Eastern Handelskade follow, with the Music Building and Passenger Terminal Amsterdam at the tip.

Altogether, a large number of homes were built in the city between 1985–1999: 63,918, averaging 4,260 homes per year.

A third element is the development of new employment hubs in the periphery of the city around the new stations on the western and southern branches: Sloterdijk, Zuid, and Bijlmer. The opening of the WTC in 1985 marks the city's new international orientation.

The bursting of the internet bubble in the spring of 2000 leads to a decrease in economic growth. This results in rising mortgage rates and a much lower housing production rate in the period 2000–2006: 15,718 homes, averaging 2,245 homes per year.

Under this gloomier economic backdrop, the renewal of the Western Garden Cities begins, with the first experiments in Geuzenveld, Bos en Lommer, and Osdorp. The development of IJburg on a series of newly reclaimed islands in the IJmeer is vigorously undertaken, but housing construction starts slowly. The first homes are completed in 2002.

→ Map Built in Amsterdam 1985–2006

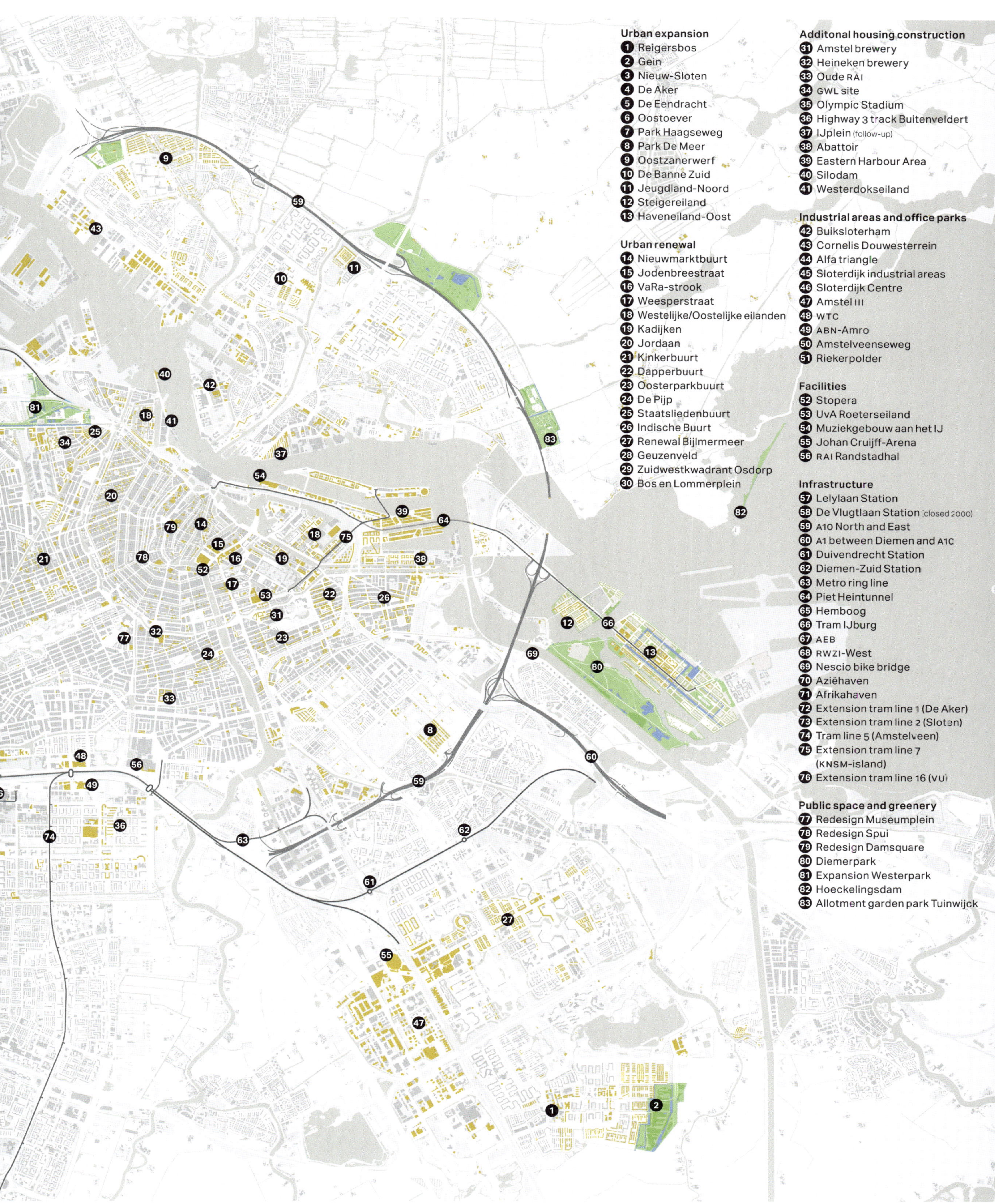
Urban expansion
1 Reigersbos
2 Gein
3 Nieuw-Sloten
4 De Aker
5 De Eendracht
6 Oostoever
7 Park Haagseweg
8 Park De Meer
9 Oostzanerwerf
10 De Banne Zuid
11 Jeugdland-Noord
12 Steigereiland
13 Haveneiland-Oost
Urban renewal
14 Nieuwmarktbuurt
15 Jodenbreestraat
16 VaRa-strook
17 Weesperstraat
18 Westelijke/Oostelijke eilanden
19 Kadijken
20 Jordaan
21 Kinkerbuurt
22 Dapperbuurt
23 Oosterparkbuurt
24 De Pijp
25 Staatsliedenbuurt
26 Indische Buurt
27 Renewal Bijlmermeer
28 Geuzenveld
29 Zuidwestkwadrant Osdorp
30 Bos en Lommerplein
Additonal housing construction
31 Amstel brewery
32 Heineken brewery
33 Oude RAI
34 GWL site
35 Olympic Stadium
36 Highway 3 track Buitenveldert
37 IJplein (follow-up)
38 Abattoir
39 Eastern Harbour Area
40 Silodam
41 Westerdokseiland
Industrial areas and office parks
42 Buiksloterham
43 Cornelis Douwesterrein
44 Alfa triangle
45 Sloterdijk industrial areas
46 Sloterdijk Centre
47 Amstel III
48 WTC
49 ABN-Amro
50 Amstelveenseweg
51 Riekerpolder
Facilities
52 Stopera
53 UvA Roeterseiland
54 Muziekgebouw aan het IJ
55 Johan Cruijff-Arena
56 RAI Randstadhal
Infrastructure
57 Lelylaan Station
58 De Vlugtlaan Station (closed 2000)
59 A10 North and East
60 A1 between Diemen and A1C
61 Duivendrecht Station
62 Diemen-Zuid Station
63 Metro ring line
64 Piet Heintunnel
65 Hemboog
66 Tram IJburg
67 AEB
68 RWZI-West
69 Nescio bike bridge
70 Aziëhaven
71 Afrikahaven
72 Extension tram line 1 (De Aker)
73 Extension tram line 2 (Sloten)
74 Tram line 5 (Amstelveen)
75 Extension tram line 7 (KNSM-island)
76 Extension tram line 16 (VU)
Public space and greenery
77 Redesign Museumplein
78 Redesign Spui
79 Redesign Damsquare
80 Diemerpark
81 Expansion Westerpark
82 Hoeckelingsdam
83 Allotment garden park Tuinwijck

2007–2019

The development of the city center into an attractive interaction space is marked in 2007 by the opening of the new headquarters of the Openbare Bibliotheek Amsterdam (OBA) on Oosterdokseiland. Around the Central Station (CS), two new, compact urban neighborhoods are being developed: Westerdokseiland and Overhoeks. After the reopening of the renovated Stedelijk Museum and the Eye Filmmuseum in 2012, 2013 becomes a true 'jubilee year' for the city with the reopening of the renovated Rijksmuseum, celebrations surrounding the inauguration of King Willem-Alexander, the 400th anniversary of the canal ring, and the first Amsterdam Light Festival. The number of hotel overnight stays in the jubilee year reaches 11 million, growing to 17.5 million in 2019.[23]

Many projects that laid the foundation during the recovery period come to fruition in these years, although the construction pace is initially not very high: IJburg, the Zuidas, and the renewal of the Bijlmer, Nieuw-West, Banne Zuid, and the Waterlandplein neighborhood. New low-rise neighborhoods are developed in De Bongerd and Elzenhagen-Noord. Hospitals, universities, and colleges begin an extensive process of mergers and clustering, such as at the Science Park and the Amstel Campus at the tip of Wibautstraat. The Andreas Hospital is replaced by residential buildings.

Due to stagnating housing construction, the strong population growth is initially absorbed within the existing housing stock – in basements and attics, and by sharing a single home with multiple 'friends'. The city functions like a sponge. When the crisis is over in 2014, a significant leap in construction production is made. The Zuidas, in particular, undergoes a spectacular development. During the 'seven fat years' from 2014–2019, more than 30,000 new homes are under construction, including in Houthavens, Noord, Oostpoort, Amstelkwartier, and on Zeeburgereiland.

In the western part of the city, the A5 opens in 2013 alongside the Second Coen tunnel. After significant delays in construction, the Noord/Zuidlijn starts operation in 2018. Around the Noord Station, the expansion of the Buikslotermeerplein shopping center into a full-fledged urban area begins.

By the end of 2019, the city's population reaches 873,000 again, just as it was in 1959, but on a much larger surface area.

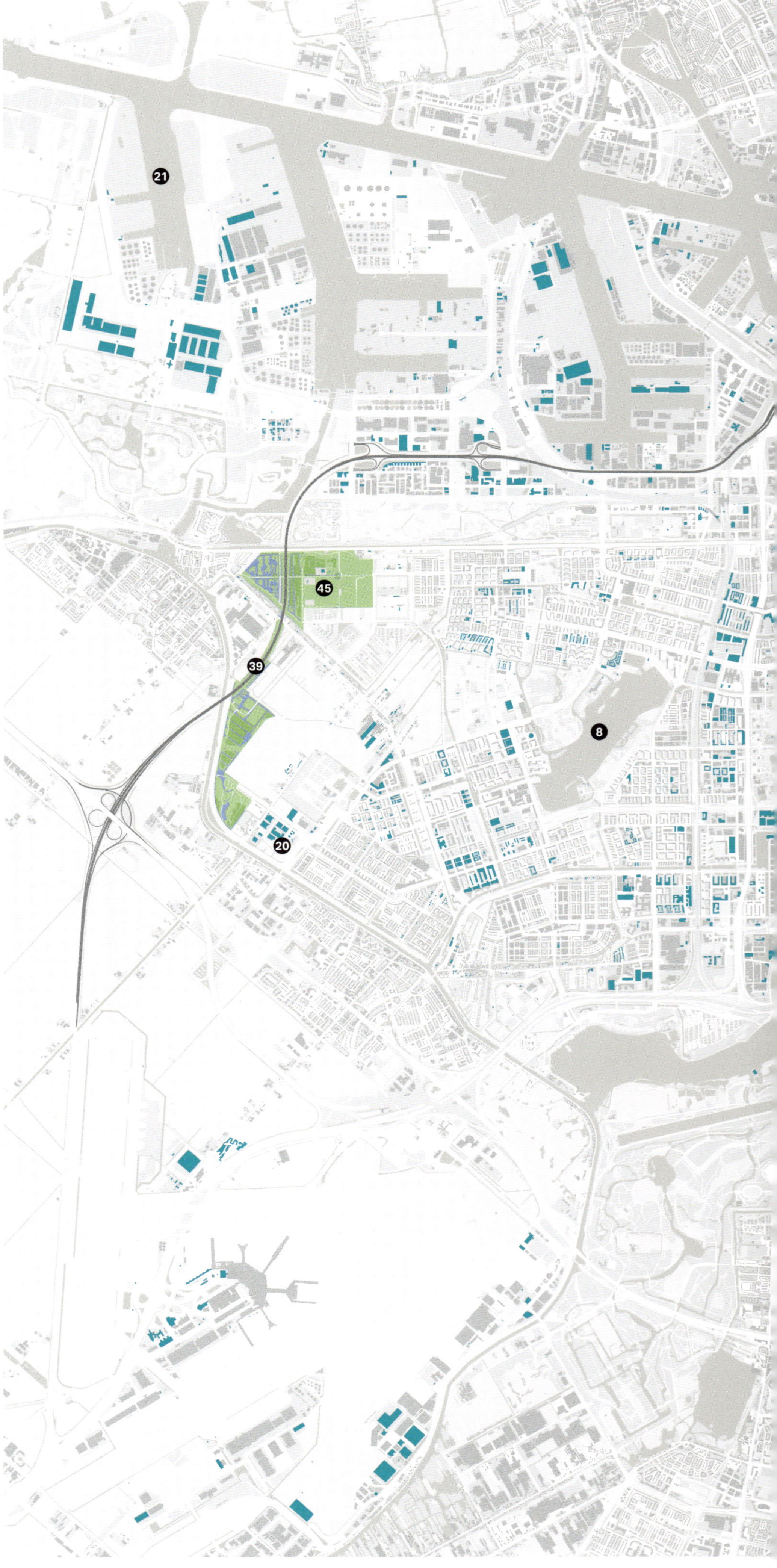

→ Map Built in Amsterdam 2007–2019

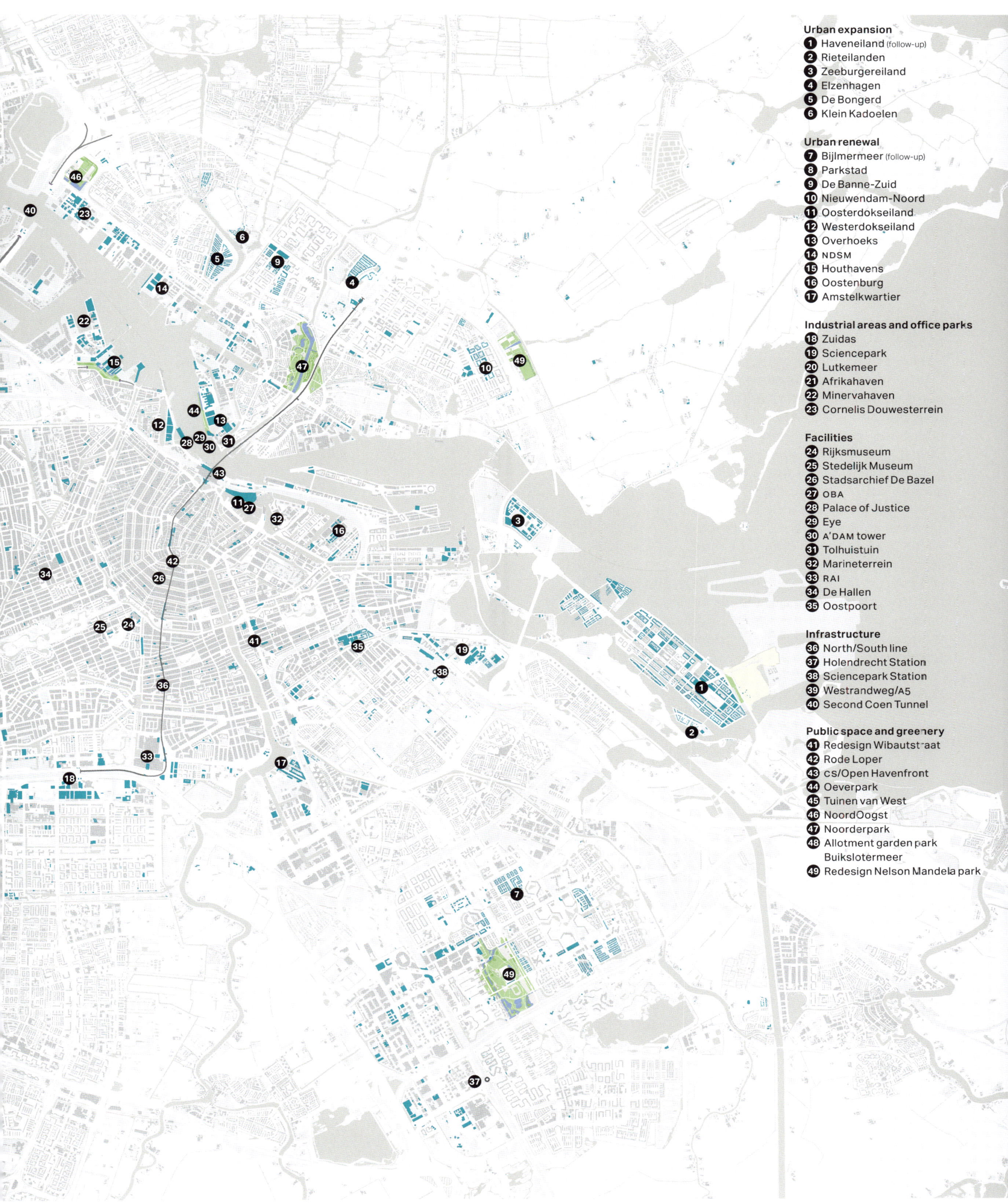
Urban expansion
1 Haveneiland (follow-up)
2 Rieteilanden
3 Zeeburgereiland
4 Elzenhagen
5 De Bongerd
6 Klein Kadoelen
Urban renewal
7 Bijlmermeer (follow-up)
8 Parkstad
9 De Banne-Zuid
10 Nieuwendam-Noord
11 Oosterdokseiland
12 Westerdokseiland
13 Overhoeks
14 NDSM
15 Houthavens
16 Oostenburg
17 Amstelkwartier
Industrial areas and office parks
18 Zuidas
19 Sciencepark
20 Lutkemeer
21 Afrikahaven
22 Minervahaven
23 Cornelis Douwesterrein
Facilities
24 Rijksmuseum
25 Stedelijk Museum
26 Stadsarchief De Bazel
27 OBA
28 Palace of Justice
29 Eye
30 A'DAM tower
31 Tolhuistuin
32 Marineterrein
33 RAI
34 De Hallen
35 Oostpoort
Infrastructure
36 North/South line
37 Holendrecht Station
38 Sciencepark Station
39 Westrandweg/A5
40 Second Coen Tunnel
Public space and greenery
41 Redesign Wibautstraat
42 Rode Loper
43 CS/Open Havenfront
44 Oeverpark
45 Tuinen van West
46 NoordOogst
47 Noorderpark
48 Allotment garden park Buikslotermeer
49 Redesign Nelson Mandela park

2020–2025

While the city holds its breath, work continues on the completion of a large number of iconic projects, such as the new courthouse on Parnassusweg. In 2021, the new complex is put into use. With the opening of the Jakoba Mulderhuis at Rhijnspoorplein in 2022, the clustering of faculties at the Hogeschool van Amsterdam is completed. The same is true, for now, for the renovation of Central Station and its surroundings. The new bicycle parking facilities beneath the Open Havenfront (in front of Station Island) and under the quay along the IJ give the city a pleasant entrance.

The Jewish Cultural Quarter around the synagogues at Mr. Visserplein has been expanded with the Holocaust Names Monument (2021) on Weesperstraat and the Holocaust Museum (2024) in the old Hervormde Kweekschool on Plantage Middenlaan. At the same time, the memorial site Hollandsche Schouwburg has been renovated.

After the downturn in 2020, high new construction numbers are again achieved in the following years, with a record 8,400 new homes under construction in 2022, including the first towers in the new Sluisbuurt on Zeeburgereiland, residential construction in Buiksloterham, Oostenburg, Cruquius, the Bajeskwartier, and further in Bullewijk. The renewal of the centers at Buikslotermeerplein and Osdorpplein is also accelerating. The Houthavens, Centrumeiland, and Overhoeks are nearing completion.

However, a high interest rate and high prices for materials and energy make the market uncertain once again. In 2024, fewer than 5,000 homes are under construction, 800 of which involve the transformation of existing buildings. Housing prices in the free rental and purchase sectors are rising sharply, and waiting times are increasing.

In March 2022, Weesp merges with Amsterdam, adding nearly 21,000 new residents. On January 1, 2025, Amsterdam's population reaches 935,000.

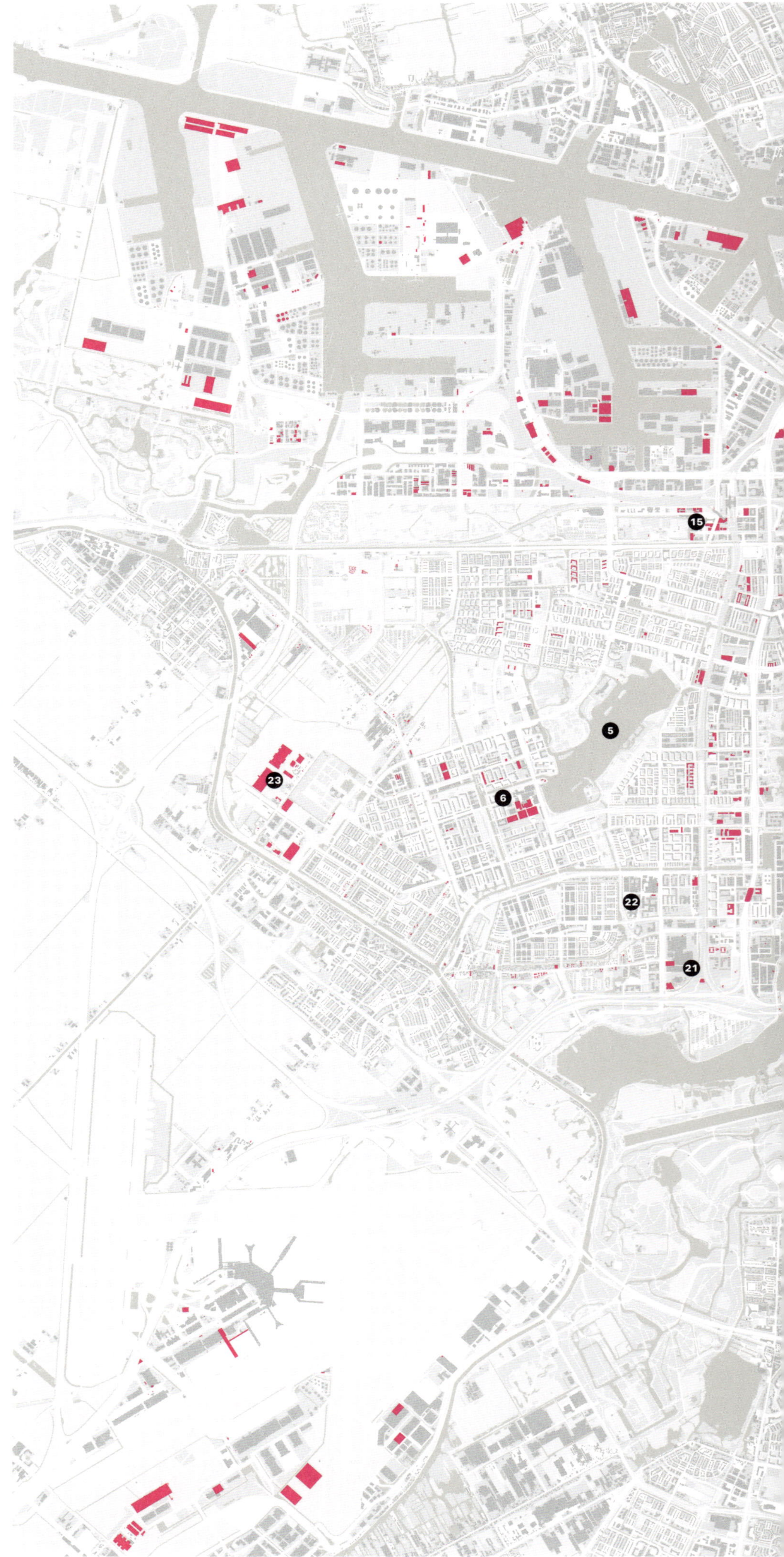

→ Map Built in Amsterdam 2020–2025

→ **Next page:** Entrance North/South line Rokin Station

INTRODUCTION

In the *Structuurvisie Amsterdam 2040* (*Structural Vision Amsterdam 2040*), *Economisch sterk en duurzaam* (*Economically Strong and Sustainable*), published in 2011, the term 'movements' is used to describe spatial developments in the city. Sometimes, these refer to autonomous trends that are difficult to influence, such as the migration of many internationally oriented companies to the station areas in the southern part of the city. In most cases, however, these movements result from an interplay of societal trends, municipal policy, and urban design. A prime example is the transformation of the waterside city around the IJ.

Looking at the entire period from 1975 to 2025, five major movements emerge in the spatial development of Amsterdam: 1. Renewal of the existing city 2. Low-rise housing at the city's edge 3. Waterside city 4. Southward expansion 5. Supercluster city center

Renewal of the Existing City

The first movement traces back to the groundbreaking municipal elections of 1978. The newly elected city government broke away from plans for a radical modernization of the existing city and instead opted for rapid yet cautious renewal. In the early years, the focus was still on demolition and new construction, but over time, the emphasis shifted toward renovation and sustainability. Many businesses, shops, schools, barracks, gas factories, and – more recently – offices left the city. The vacated sites were repurposed for supplementary housing and, in many cases, new public amenities. In essence, this movement represents a process of *de-mixing and intensification.*

As a result, the old city as it existed in 1975 has increasingly transformed into a residential city – where many Amsterdammers now work from home. The renewal process continues to this day. Scaffolding and construction fences have become a permanent part of the urban landscape. Large-scale redevelopment is now concentrated in parts of Slotermeer and in several neighborhoods built in the late 1970s, including Banne Noord and Holendrecht.

Low-rise housing at the City's Edge

The Structural Plan 'De stad centraal' (The City Central) of 1986 introduced a second movement. This was more of a strategic intervention aimed at reversing a societal trend. By creating an attractive supply of low-rise housing on the city's outskirts, the aim was to slow the outflow of families with young children to designated new towns. After an initial experiment in Gein, the approach was expanded in the 1990s with large developments in Sloten and De Aker. Many more followed, including smaller-scale initiatives such as self-build projects on found land starting around 2010.[1]

Space for larger residential developments was created by buying out agricultural businesses and relocating sports parks and allotment gardens. The city's sports infrastructure is now used far more intensively than in 1975. The Main Green Structure of the city, established in the Structuurvisie Amsterdam 2040 (Structural Vision Amsterdam 2040) in 2011, provides protection for sports parks and allotment gardens. The most recent relocations in Noord made way for the development of the Elzenhagen-Noord neighborhood.

Water City

Already during the development of the previously mentioned Structural Plan of 1986, a third movement began to take shape. The old port economy was changing at a rapid pace. Islands such as Kattenburg, Wittenburg, and Kadijken had already undergone a transformation. On the vacated site of the ADM shipyard in Noord, the IJplein was developed. By relocating still-active businesses and urban infrastructure to the Western Port Area, space was also freed up in the Eastern Port Area for housing development – starting with the site of the former Abattoir. This was followed by the Nieuwe Entrepot, the KNSM, Java, and Borneo islands, as well as Sporenburg.

In the decades that followed, the water city along the IJ evolved into a vast and vibrant part of Amsterdam, featuring large new islands such as IJburg and newly developed mixed-use neighborhoods around Central Station and along the Northern IJ waterfront. Unlike the low-rise neighborhoods on the city's outskirts, this new water city has a much more urban character – something that also applies to IJburg.

Southward

The Structural Plan of 1986 also set a definitive course for addressing the immense demand for development opportunities driven by the rapidly growing service economy. Further expansion within the city center was ruled out. Earlier plans, such as Structural Plan Part C: Working in Amsterdam (1978), had already designated space near Amstel Station and around the newly established NS stations Sloterdijk, Lelylaan, Zuid, RAI, and Bijlmer on the city's periphery. In addition to their connection to the rail network, these new business districts were also accessible via the newly constructed A10 ring road. Throughout the 1980s, these areas experienced rapid development, marked by large-scale projects such as Atlas, the Fokker headquarters near Bijlmer Station, and the WTC at Zuid Station.

In 1996, ABN AMRO's decision to establish its headquarters near Zuid Station prompted a shift in policy. The focus turned to large-scale office development around Zuid, emphasizing direct connectivity via road and rail to Schiphol and the other major cities of the Randstad. This emerging Zuidas was envisioned as a Central Business District – one that might not rival Docklands in London or La Défense in Paris, but could still compete with financial hubs in cities like Milan and Frankfurt. A new North/South metro line was planned to link this business district with both the city center and Schiphol.

The city's rapid growth from 2007 onward led to a significant policy shift in the Structural Vision Amsterdam 2040 (2011). The new guiding principle for all major developments became a high-density mix of residential and commercial functions – not only in the Zuidas, Amstelkwartier, and ArenAPoort, but also deeper into Zuidoost, where office buildings in Bullewijk are rapidly being replaced by residential towers.

City Center

The movement southward created space for the remarkable makeover of the city center in the past few decades, the fifth movement. The relocation of major financial institutions, law firms, and accounting offices in the 1990s made many buildings in prominent locations in the city center available for new purposes. The clustering of faculties from the University of Amsterdam, the Amsterdam University of Applied Sciences, and the Amsterdam School of the Arts, as well as the relocation of facilities like the city hall and the OBA (Public Library), strengthened this process. Most of the vacated buildings were taken over by hotel chains and sometimes by other urban functions for which they were not originally intended, such as the Beurs van Berlage and De Bazel.

It is noteworthy that many companies from the creative and tech sectors, as well as international institutions, prefer to establish themselves in the city center. This applies to many small companies but also large ones like Booking, Adyen, and Tommy Hilfiger, as well as organizations such as Amnesty and the Goethe-Institut.

The redesign of public spaces has been a key driver of this development. Many squares have been reconfigured for pedestrians and a pleasant stay: Museumplein, Nieuwmarkt, Spui, Dam, Damrak, Rokin, Rembrandtplein, and Leidseplein, Oosterdok, and in the 2020s, the Open Havenfront and the IJ side of Central Station. Bicycle parking has gone underground.

Around Central Station (CS), the city center expanded towards the IJ. The relocation of the Public Library to Oosterdokseiland and the Dutch Film Museum to Overhoeks contributed significantly to this. The renovation of Central Station, along with the newly designed quay along the water, has turned the IJ into one of the city's most important public spaces.

In the following paragraphs, these major movements will be explored in more detail. Four aspects are central. First, the movement is described in broad terms, including a look back at the period before 1975. Some movements have a long buildup or form an explicit response to what occurred earlier. Then, the approach in terms of policy, strategy, and design is addressed. Next, the development of housing, block, and layout forms are examined. Finally, for each movement, five representative public investments is documented.

RENEWAL OF THE EXISTING CITY — 'YOU CAN'T LIVE IN NONSENSE'

→ Echtenstein Amsterdam Southeast, 1975–2025

The old residential neighborhoods in the city presented a depressing sight in the early 1970s. According to the initiative note 'Open gaten' (Open Gaps) from 1972, there were more than 700 gaps in façade walls and around a hundred sections, partly demolished.[2] The Jaarboek 1975 (Yearbook 1975) from the Bureau of Statistics shows that the situation only worsened between 1970 and 1974.[3] While new construction occurred only sporadically, almost 400 homes were declared uninhabitable and 514 were demolished. Moreover, more than 3,000 homes were 'taken out of use', meaning they were evacuated and boarded up, but in many cases, they were later reoccupied: 'gekraakt' (squatted).

From 1978, the renewal of the existing city became a top priority: 'bouwen voor de buurt' (build for the neighborhood). By 1993, nearly 36,500 new homes had been constructed within the old city inside the Ring, and 70,000 homes in the social housing sector had been renovated, both through minor and major repairs and high-level renovations. 20,000 private rental homes were improved with subsidies.[4]

In the following years, more than half of the honeycomb flats in the Bijlmer were demolished and replaced with new construction, mostly in the form of low-rise buildings, totaling around 7,000 homes. The renewal of other post-war neighborhoods started in the 1980s with relatively small infill projects, but from 2000 onwards, it was approached in an integrated manner. The city of 1975 is looking great today!

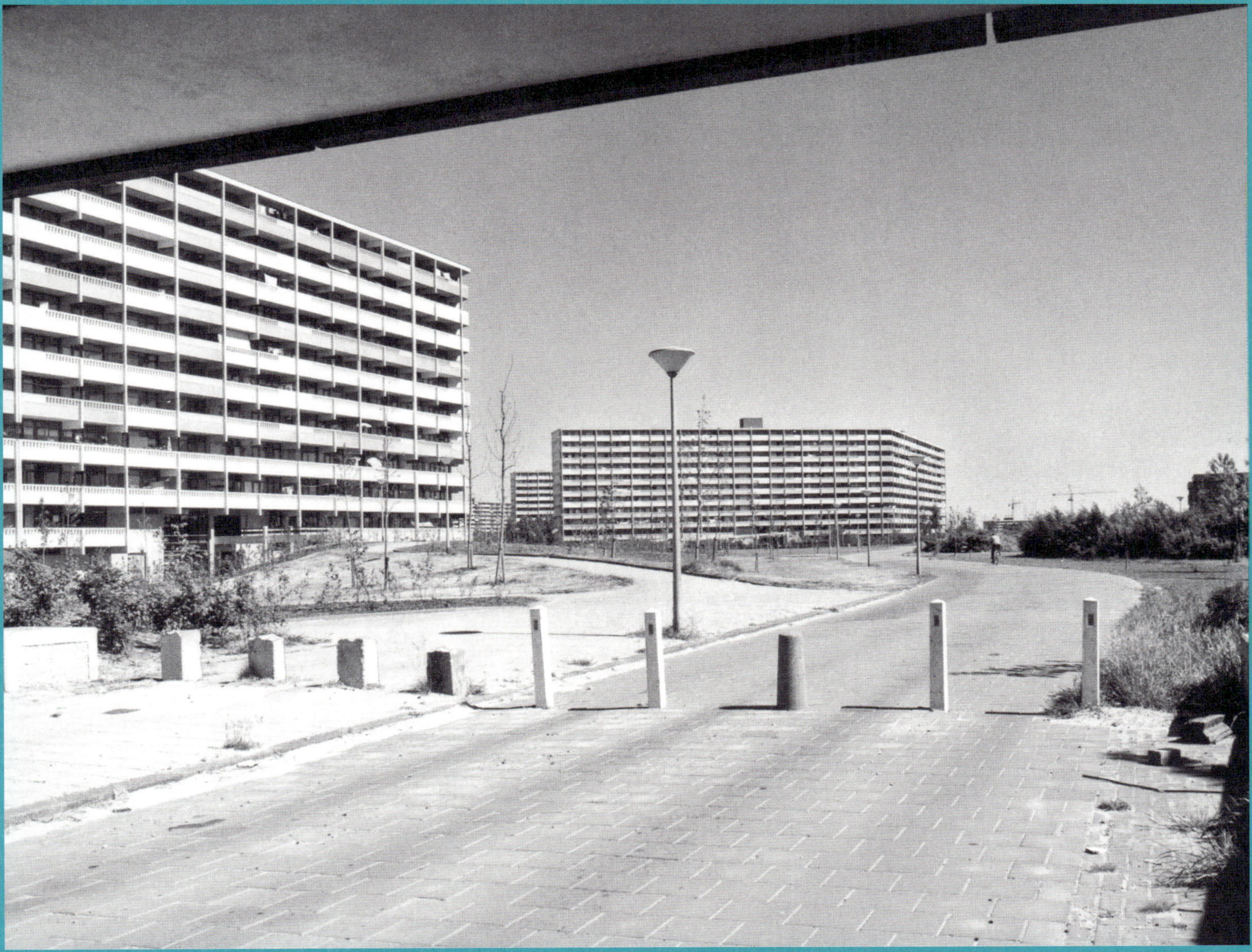

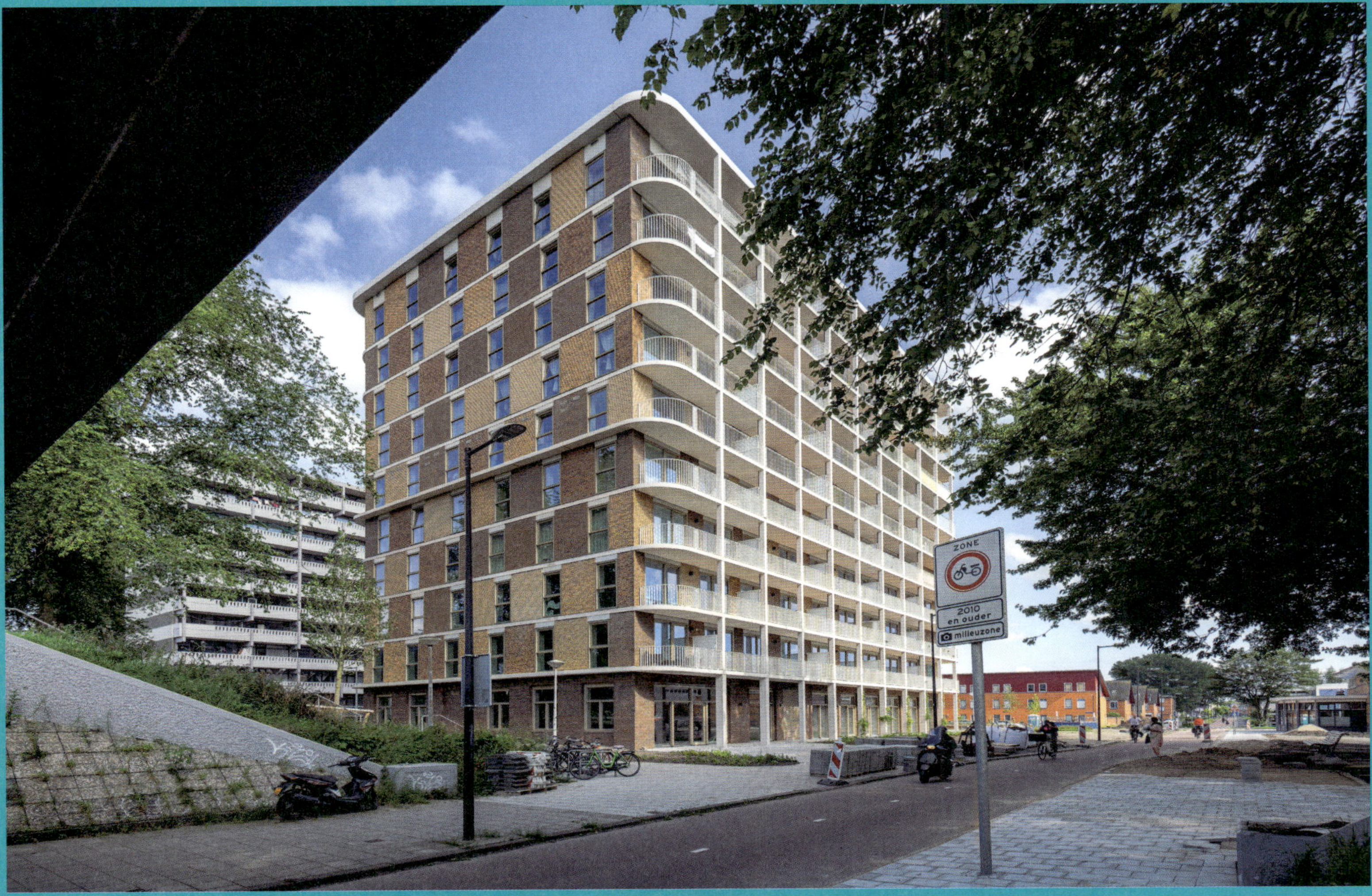
ZONE
2010
en ouder
milieuzone

The city of 1975 was much smaller than it is today. The pre-war city and Nieuw-West formed a more or less continuous urban area. The 'border' of this city was defined by the dikes along the IJ, the Kruislaan in the Watergraafsmeer, the Zuidelijke Wandelweg, Prinses Irenestraat, and IJsbaanpad in the south, the edges of Osdorp and Geuzenveld in Nieuw-West, and the Haarlemmerweg. Buitenveldert was still relatively close, 'behind the sports fields,' but the high-rise Bijlmer, Old North, and the part of North between the IJ dikes and the projected A10 were far away.

All these areas have undergone more or less significant renewal over the past decades. Many homes have been renovated, refurbished, or replaced by new ones; the 'movement' is primarily a process of de-mixing and intensification. The historical city center remained very mixed, but in the Jordaan, the islands, the 19th-century belt, and neighborhoods from the interwar period, many shops and business spaces on the ground floor have been converted into housing. Daily amenities are concentrated in the main streets. These broader, lively 'city streets' sharply contrast with the quieter residential streets. It is important to note that many businesses, barracks, gas factories, schools, churches, and, more recently, offices left and made way for housing. The city that existed in 1975 has increasingly become a connected residential city.

The 'additional housing' initially focused on building on sites in post-war neighborhoods reserved for road construction but deemed 'overcomplete' by the newly elected municipal government in 1978. In Buitenveldert, the already constructed embankment for national road 3 to Rotterdam was dug up and developed. The same occurred in Nieuw-West with embankments meant to extend the Lelylaan and create the Geerban. In North, the extension of the Nieuwe Purmerweg and the construction of the Zuiderzeeweg, which was part of the highway to Lelystad via the projected Markerwaard, were abandoned. In the following years, a whole series of parking areas were entirely or partially developed: at the shopping centers on Osdorpplein and Buikslotermeerplein, around the RAI, and at Stadionplein.

More significant was the dynamism in the old city itself. Many of the industrial companies founded in the 19th century modernized and relocated their production in the 1970s to locations in Sloterdijk or outside the city, such as the merged breweries Heineken and Amstel, or the factories of CSM, Klene, and Maschmeijer. But the entire 19th-century basic infrastructure of the city also underwent major changes. After the discovery of the Groningen gas field, the three municipal gas factories in the West, South, and East closed at the end of the 1960s. The opening of new pumping stations in Heemstede and at Gaasp near Driemond (1976) made it possible to close the Municipal Waterworks pumping station on the Haarlemmerweg. The City Wharf on Van Reigersbergenstraat and the Bodecentrum site on Pontanusstraat (with sheds for transport and order services) moved to Sloterdijk. The District Court and the House of Detention relocated from their old site at Kleine-Gartmanplantsoen to Parnassusweg and the Penitentiary Institution Amsterdam Overamstel (the 'Bijlmerbajes'). The municipal hospitals (Binnengasthuis and Wilhelmina Gasthuis) moved in 1980 with the Emma Children's Hospital to the massive new AMC complex in Zuidoost. Should churches also be considered part of the city's basic infrastructure? The Koepelkerk at Leidsebosje, the Willibrordus, Augustinus, Bonifatius, Rita, Majella, and Vincentius churches were all closed down and, in many cases, demolished. The municipal bathhouses also closed after most of the old homes had been fitted with showers during renovation. However, most of them were designated as monuments and repurposed.

A special part of the 19th-century basic infrastructure was the defense complexes along Sarphatistraat. Traditionally, the Marine Establishment, originating from the Admiralty, was located in the city, but by the end of the 19th century, as part of the construction of the Stelling van Amsterdam (Defense Line of Amsterdam), various barracks and supporting services were housed in and around the city, including a clothing warehouse, a hospital, grain silos, and a drinking water extraction site. The capital had to be able to withstand a war for a long time. Throughout the 1970s and 1980s, almost all of these special functions left the city, with only the Navy remaining.

Across the city, many sites became available for repurposing. In most cases, housing was chosen, often in combination with neighborhood amenities, as was eventually realized on the old RAI site. There, in the early 1980s, in addition to 250 homes, Sporthal De Pijp, a children's farm, and a nursing home for the elderly were also built. Similar developments took place on the Amstel Brewery site, the WG site, and the GWL site.

Some sites were polluted. With a special national subsidy scheme, the soil was remediated. Especially the land under the gas factories was heavily contaminated. At the Westergasfabriek, a limited remediation was chosen. A large part of the factory buildings could therefore remain, but the site is not suitable for residential development. The desire to build homes on the sites of the Ooster- and Zuidergasfabriek required radical remediation. Almost all buildings were demolished. Only the Sportfondsenbad and the Ketelhuis in Oostpoort, and the Watertower and a few residential buildings in the Amstelkwartier, still remind us of the gas factories.

Three renewal zones stand out: the Singelgracht zone, the area along the Kostverlorenvaart, and the Ring zone in the West, around the A10 and the Ring Line. In the increasingly connected residential city, these areas still represent special forms of mixing today. These are explained in more detail below.

Singelgracht Zone

After the decision to construct the Nieuwe Hollandse Waterlinie (New Dutch Water Line) in 1815, the seventeenth-century fortifications of the city lost their function. In the following decades, the walls were dismantled, and most of the gates and bastions were gradually removed. The Singelgracht was straightened in many places, and the strip of land between the canal and the street inside the 'rampart' was developed. To this day, it remains a very differentiated area. Various urban functions that had no place in the old city or benefited from good accessibility, such as the vegetable market, police posts, a fire station, the first gas factory, the Schouwburg theater, the District Court, the House of Detention, and a whole series of barracks along Sarphatistraat, were pragmatically established.[5] The most monumental part was around the Amstel Hotel (1867) and the Palace of Industry (1864) near the already existing Weesperpoort Station, built in 1843. The Leidseplein also developed into a large urban square in the early 20th century with the department store building for Hirsch & Cie, the American Hotel, and the City Theater; all of these were taller buildings with distinctive architecture. Along Leidsebosje, the robust brick buildings of the youth organization AMVJ and Hotel Atlanta followed.

After the Palace of Industry burned down in 1929, plans were made to build a new town hall on that site, but this quickly became a protracted issue. Ultimately, in 1968, De Nederlandsche Bank was built

↑ Sketch movement – Renewal of the existing city combined with (in yellow) 'additional' housing on available sites

here, designed by Marius Duintjer. The design sparked many critical reactions, especially when it was revealed that the District Court and the House of Detention would move, and the hotel operator from Zandvoort, Nico Bouwes, presented his plans for the location at Kleine-Gartman-plantsoen in early 1975. The activist group *Bouw'es wat anders* (Build Something Else) convinced the city council and the mayor and aldermen of alternative plans in which Paradiso and the District Court building could remain. In 1979, a temporary theater opened in the old District Court building, which later became part of the art and debate center De Balie. The prison building was integrated into the new development around the new Max Euwe-plein, but it is hardly recognizable as such. Over the square, a bike connection to the Vondelpark was created.

Safer cycling traffic also played a role in the redesign of the 'inner ring' during that same period. After the construction of the

1 Aerial view of new development plan for a hotel complex at Leidseplein commissioned by Nico Bouwes
2 Rijksacademie of Fine Arts, transformation of the Cavalry Barracks, design by Koen van Velzen, 1992
3 Windmill De Otter 2005
4 Allebéplein Nieuw-West, 1975–2025

Torontobrug over the Amstel in 1969, the outer avenue along the canal, formed by Nassaukade, Stadhouderskade, and Mauritskade, began functioning as a ring road for car traffic; the inner ring of Marnixstraat, Weteringschans, and Sarphatistraat was redesigned for trams and cyclists. This has now become one of the busiest cycling routes in the city.

The five barracks along Sarphatistraat were repurposed in the 1980s and 1990s. These are all quite imposing, severe buildings. Since they are monuments, not much could be done to the façades along the Sarphatistraat side. Only when you enter through the gates into the inner areas do you see the transformation. In addition to housing, you can find, for example, the Rijksakademie van Beeldende Kunsten (State Academy of Fine Arts) in the building complex of the Cavalry Barracks, renovated by Koen van Velsen, and offices, including those of housing corporation Stadgenoot, renovated by American architect Steven Holl. The Singelgracht zone has thus remained a fairly mixed area.

Kostverloren Canal

Outside the Singelgracht, many 'nuisance' businesses had already settled from the 18th century on; in the 19th century, they were followed by various industrial companies, especially along the Amstel and Kostverlorenvaart (Kostverloren Canal), the connecting routes to the hinterland by water.

There is a striking difference. On the Weesperzijde strip along the Amstel, the companies were located on the inner plots behind the new housing along the Weesperzijde. Only Utermöhlen had an office on the Amstel. The companies around the northern part of the Kostverlorenvaart were all located directly on the water. This characteristic has been maintained in the transformation. Behind the Weesperzijde, there are still a few surprising relicts, including from the Luycksfabriek in a quiet residential courtyard, and notable new buildings, such as an office first orange and then apple green, renovated by MVRDV.

The Kostverlorenvaart, though primarily a residential area due to gradual transformation, has strong spatial differentiation. This makes it a distinctive part of the 19th-century city. In a few cases, the waterfront has been made public in housing projects, and you can walk along it (Awic site/Meander, Jacob Catskade, Van Reigersbergenstraat, Marcanti Island), while others in the northern part are located directly on the water. Between the new developments stands the restored sawmill De Otter, the 'oldest sawmill in the world' from 1631.

Further south along the Kostverlorenvaart – and its extension, the Schinkel – there is also a beautiful collection of urban phenomena from very different periods: the Slatuinen, the Landje van Ome Kick on the site of the former iron foundry Zimmer, the village-like Bellamybuurt, the Westermoskee, the Sieraad, the Aalsmeerder Veerhuis, the converted Bankgirocentrale and the 'Lightfactory,' and at the very end of Sloterkade, where Jaagpad begins, the cemetery Huis te Vraag. Across from this is the tram depot Havenstraat. It's a shame that you cannot cycle through there to the Schinkeleilanden and the Amsterdamse Bos.

All in all, about 2,500 homes have been built along the Kostverlorenvaart on former industrial sites.

Ring Zone

In the 'Ringzone', the transitional area between the pre- and post-war city in Nieuw-West around the A10 and Ringspoorbaan, many more homes have been added. In this very well-connected area, with the Lelylaan train station and the metro sta-

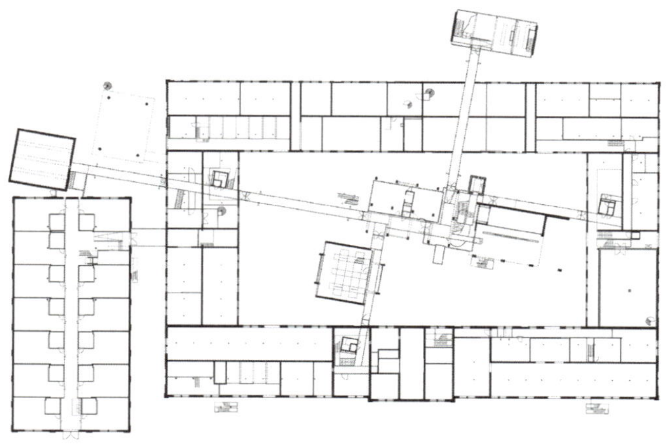

2

3

4

tions of the Ring Line, the number of homes increased by almost 12,000 between 2000 and 2021 – a density increase of 72%.[6] In the Kolenkitbuurt, the number of homes more than doubled, from 2,634 to 6,027.

The intensification in the Ringzone is a successful response to the peculiar deviation that Amsterdam's urban designers made in the implementation of the General Expansion Plan (AUP) in the 1950s and 1960s. In the 1935 AUP, the main outlines for the western city expansion were set: a series of green garden cities outside the Ringspoorbaan around the newly dug Sloterplas. To create a good transition from the old city to the new expansions, residential areas with urban densities were designed within the Ringspoorbaan, interspersed with parks and sports fields.

In the implementation, from the early 1950s to the late 1970s, two fundamental plan changes were made that had disastrous consequences. First, with the aim of accommodating growing car traffic, the framework of roads and green spaces was radically altered. The planned Multatuliweg and Einsteinweg were not executed as wide avenues but as a highway on an embankment, the A10 West. In its wake, the Roëllstraat, Lelylaan, and Sneevlietweg were also elevated. The consequence, however, was that incoherent and unsafe situations arose in many places, full of barriers.

A second change was the substitution of part of the residential construction in the Ringzone for new large-scale urban facilities. Instead of continuous residential neighborhoods, four hospitals, the Confection Center, and a whole range of schools, offices, and businesses were built, including the GAK and a GVB bus garage. The Kolenkit, Overtoomse Veld, and Westlandgracht became flawed urban neighborhoods. They were also cut through or bordered by heavy infrastructure, which made them less optimally integrated into their surroundings.

However, the strong dynamics in the area from the early 1990s offered opportunities to improve urban quality. For example, the Amsterdam Pirates baseball and softball club moved to Sportpark Ookmeer, the Turnace gymnastics school to Sportpark Sloten, and Sportpark Jan van Galen became largely available for housing. The Laan van Spartaan was built here with 1,600 homes at high density. After the merger of the Andreas Hospital and Sint Lucas Hospital, 500 homes could be built at the Andreas site. A whole series of housing projects have also been realized on and around the Koningin Wilhelminaplein. The 'bridge buildings' on the Bos en Lommerweg literally bridge both sides of the A10 West. Various housing projects, such as Rhapsody, de Leeuw van Vlaanderen, de Tribune, and the redevelopment of the GAK building, have come up with inventive solutions for dealing with the noise pollution from the ring road. Thus, the Ringzone was urbanized after all.

Despite the conversion of offices and facilities into housing, many businesses are still located in the Ringzone. In Slotervaart alone, these provide employment for almost 25,000 people.[7] Therefore, the Ringzone has become a super-diverse urban area, both in terms of population mixing and function. A new mixed urban area has emerged between the pre-war city 'inside the ring' and the Western Garden Cities 'outside the ring.' There are now more 'eyes' on the streets, and a bike ride in the evening or at night no longer takes you through an eerie area between 'the city' and Nieuw-West.

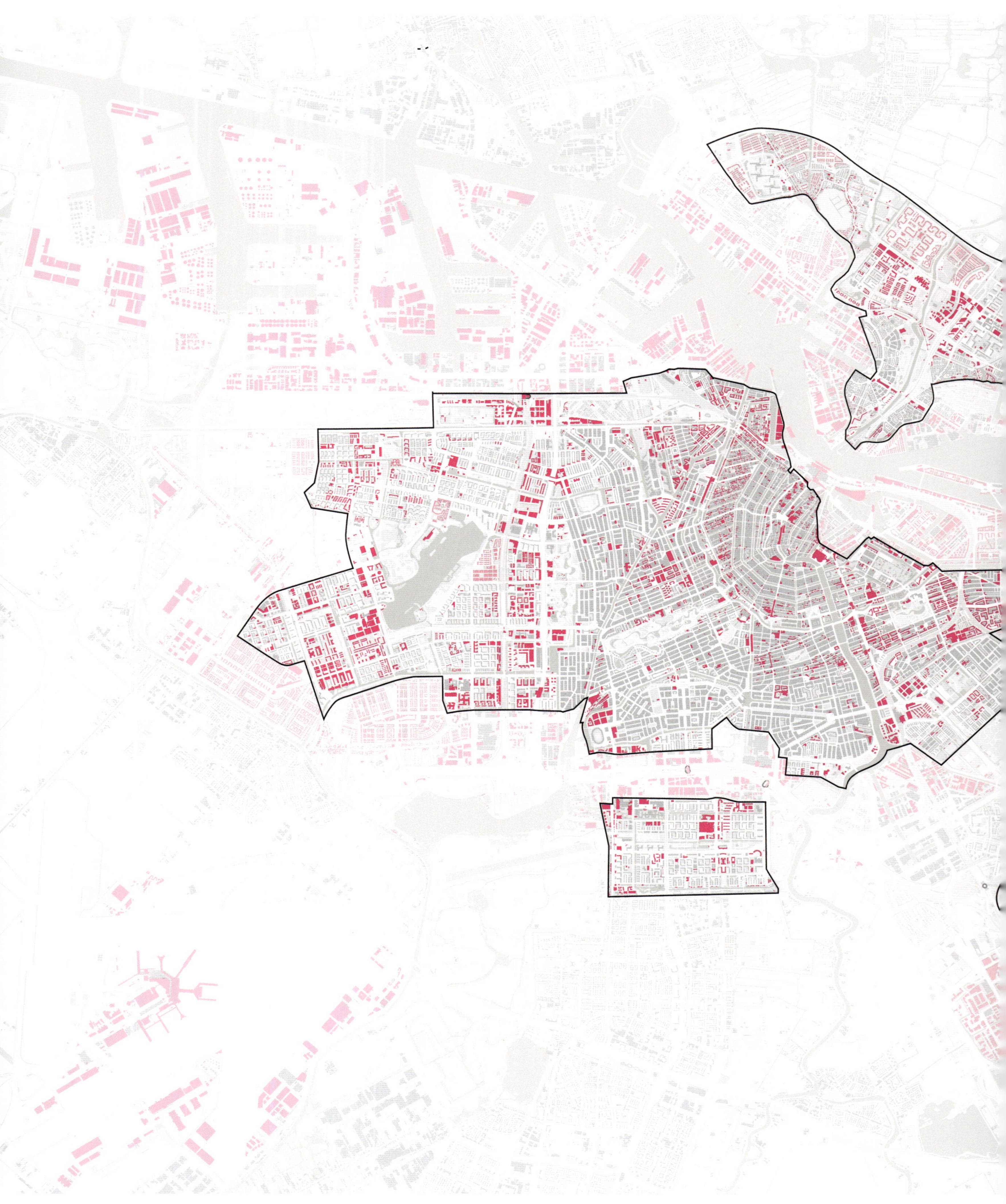

It took an extremely long time for the renewal of the existing city to gain momentum. The stagnation was primarily related to the focus on expanding the city during the post-war period. This was when the post-war housing shortage had to be addressed. There was little to no experience, tools, or financial resources to tackle the renewal process.[8]

Most of the literature on this period in the city's history emphasizes the differences of opinion between and within political parties, between the municipal apparatus and residents' organizations, and across generations. For example, Herman de Liagre Böhl chose 'The Struggle for Urban Renewal' as the subtitle for his monumental study on this period, *Amsterdam op de Helling* (Amsterdam on the Slope).[9] Looking back now, the 1970s appear as a typical transition period. Through trial and error, and accompanied by confrontations in city hall and on the streets, a new approach had to be developed. Years later, and in a less intense form, this process repeated itself when determining the approach for the renewal of Bijlmermeer and the garden cities in Nieuw-West and Noord.

From Slum Clearance to Preservation and Restoration

It is therefore interesting to delve deeper into the controversy within the municipal apparatus during the 1970s, leading up to the large-scale renewal operation, between the urban planners of Public Works (PW) and the housing builders of the Municipal Housing Department. PW was a service with a long tradition, dating back to the 'city carpenters' and 'city surveyors' in the seventeenth century! Besides urban expansion, PW also traditionally played an important role in the city's infrastructure, designing and managing all streets, quays, bridges, and trees in the city. The Municipal Housing Department was established in 1915 and flourished in the 1920s and 1930s under the socialist aldermen Wibaut and De Miranda.

When it came to the development of the existing city, PW's focus from the end of the 19th century was on traffic. The widening of Damstraat (1868), the breakthrough of Raadhuisstraat (1895), and the widening of Vijzelstraat (1917–1935) are well known, but around 1900, a whole list of interventions was already being dis-

← Map Built in the renewal of the city, 1975–2025

cussed in the municipal council that were considered necessary by the department to make the city center accessible for the rapidly growing traffic.[10] For the Housing Department, however, improving living conditions, i.e., slum clearance, was the central issue.[11]

A major joint success was the clearance of the 'squalid neighborhoods' around Ridderstraat and Jonkerstraat in the Lastage near Nieuwmarkt and on the islands of Uilenburg and Valkenburg in the 1920s and 1930s. The residents were offered alternative housing in new developments in the Transvaalbuurt in the East and in the garden villages in the North. Acquisition, expropriation, demolition, and new construction were made possible by hard-fought financial contributions from the national government.

During these clearances, entire streets were removed, and city blocks were expanded in depth. On the newly formed large inner courtyards in the Lastage, for example, the still-existing playground De Waag was created. Nieuwe Uilenburgerstraat became 15 meters wide. Much of the construction on Valkenburg was also replaced in the 1930s, but the Valkenburgerstraat received an even broader profile – 25 meters – suitable for through traffic and a tram line. The widening aligned with a planned breakthrough towards Jodenbreestraat and Waterlooplein. This allowed for the creation of an 'inner ring', according to the General Regeneration Plan from 1930.[12]

In post-war plans, this approach was extended and strongly amplified. In 1953, PW presented three interconnected post-war reconstruction plans for the severely affected eastern city center, focusing on the neighborhoods around Nieuwmarkt, Jodenbreestraat, and Weesperstraat. The Jewish population of these neighborhoods had been deported; many houses were looted, and some were demolished.

The publication of the reconstruction plans marked the beginning of a long series of studies and equally numerous debates in which the traffic problems in the eastern city center took center stage, in combination with the construction of the city hall at Waterlooplein. This debate continues to this day, and it seems likely that a few major steps still need to be taken.

It is notable that the way in which the urban fabric was approached in the reconstruction plans received little attention in the discussions. In all three sub-plans, it was proposed to merge and expand city blocks, clear courtyards, and widen road profiles – essentially, the same approach that had been used in the 1920s for Ridderstraat and Jonkerstraat. The post-war plan for Weesperstraat was gradually but mostly realized over the 1960s, 1970s, and

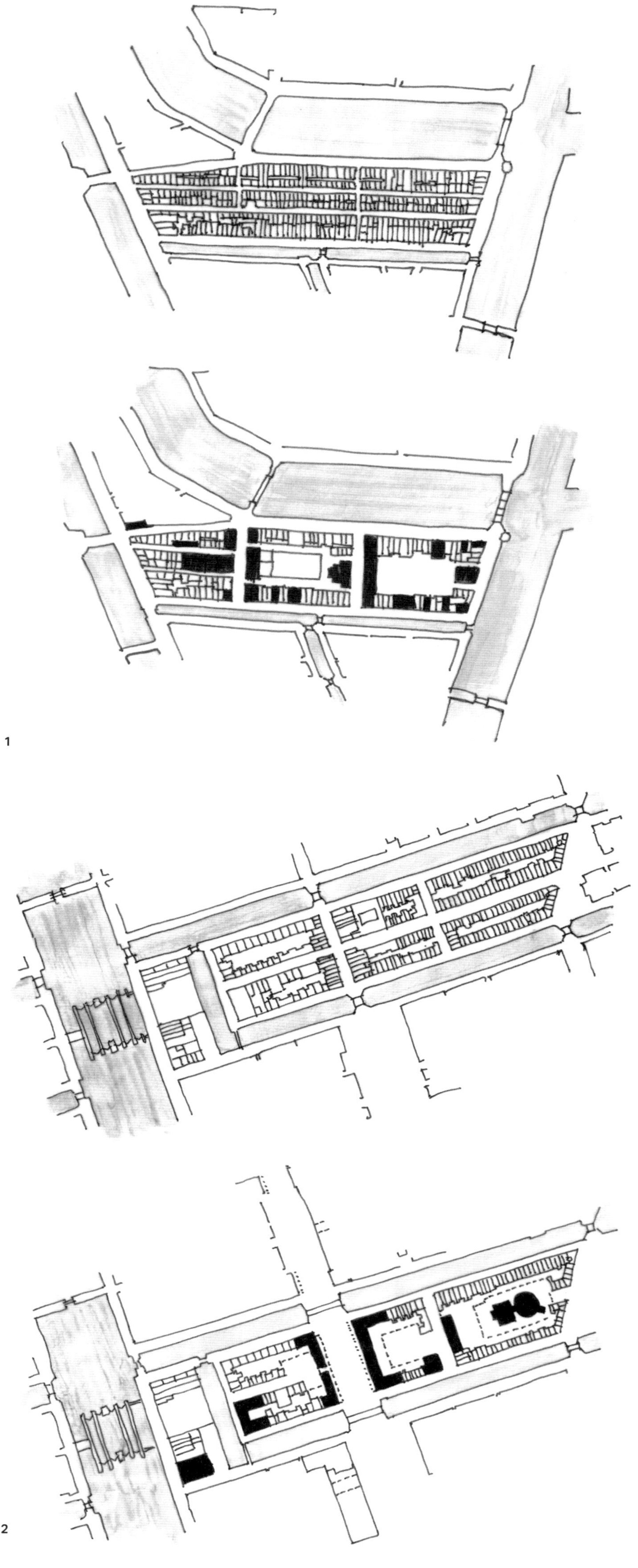

1

2

1980s, including an intervention in the urban fabric. Between Nieuwe Prinsengracht and Nieuwe Achtergracht, Lepelstraat disappeared, along with nearly all of its buildings. Only in the section near Carré do two rows of houses still stand. On the side of Roetersstraat, a new courtyard area saw the construction of the Dr. E. Boekmanschool. Behind the pink office building on Weesperstraat, where the C&A headquarters was once located, there is now a gloomy parking lot in the place of the demolished buildings on Lepelkruisstraat.

In all of PW's plans for the renewal of the Jordaan and the 19th-century neighborhoods in the 1970s, the theme of modernizing the urban fabric returned: the city blocks were considered too cramped, and the streets too narrow, meaning that many homes did not get enough light and air, and the living environment was deemed unsuitable for families with growing children. The existing city did not meet 'modern requirements'.

Changing the street plan could be justified when most existing buildings were in a very poor condition, but that was almost never the case. The rents for new homes were also much higher. In all the neighborhoods of the old city, there was discussion with residents' organizations about the planned comprehensive demolition and changes to the urban fabric. The Housing Department, Alderman Schaefer, and ultimately the municipal council opted for a different approach at the end of the 1970s: 'take a photo from above', making the existing street plan the starting point for renewal. Good quality buildings could remain, while bad ones would be replaced.

Dapperbuurt

Scattered throughout the city, you can still find remnants of the old approach in many early urban renewal areas, such as in the blocks around Borgerstraat in the Kinkerbuurt and in the northeastern corner of the Staatsliedenbuurt. In the Spaarndammerbuurt, Krommeniestraat disappeared, and a school was built on the large new inner courtyard.

The Roomtuintjes project in the Dapperbuurt is another example of such a relict. It was part of a renewal plan for the entire neighborhood designed by Willem Duyff from Public Works (PW). The plan was abandoned, and ultimately, a neighborhood-initiated plan was implemented. Architect Hans Borkent was one of the designers.[13] This shift is characteristic of what happened in many other neighborhoods in the 19th-century belt.

Duyff's plan went even further than just merging blocks. It unmistakably referenced the large-scale renewal programs carried out in many English cities at the end of the 1960s under the Wilson government (slum clearance). Single-family homes on long streets in many 19th-century neighborhoods were replaced by stacked maisonettes in a meandering courtyard layout, accessed by raised pedestrian decks with parking underneath. You can find some beautiful examples of this in the Camden neighborhood in London, but most of these projects are now in poor condition due to deferred maintenance. It's fortunate that this idea was not implemented on a large scale in Amsterdam.

In Duyff's plan, the streets also disappeared. Dappermarkt would have been concentrated at the central Dapperplein. The first part of the plan, the Roomtuintjes on the old Bodecentrum site in the northeastern corner of the neighborhood, was a simplified version of the plan: no maisonettes, but gallery flats, no pedestrian decks with parking underneath, but barren parking lots. This certainly did not help with enthusiasm for the plan, if there was any to begin with.

According to the neighborhood's proposal, far fewer homes were eventually demolished. Where demolition did occur, it was done in phases, allowing residents to move from their old homes to new ones. This became an important principle in all later urban renewal plans.

In terms of housing type, the porch apartment layout was revived: four floors, storage rooms and an apartment for elderly residents on ground-floor, with two apartments per floor above, and sometimes even small units on the fifth floor.[14] Shifts in the building lines and balconies added life to the streetscape. The only parking garage built in the early years of urban renewal is located on Sparrenweg in the Oosterparkbuurt. All other cars park on the streets.

By the 1980s, the emphasis increasingly shifted towards 'preservation and restoration'. Homes that had been purchased for demolition turned out to still be livable after a small maintenance overhaul. A large portion of these buildings still stands today, renovated and in good condition. If demolition did occur, it was often done in the 1990s through small projects of a few plots. Material usage and detailing were also more in line with the qualities of existing buildings: dark brick, flat façades.

1 Diagram of urban fabric of Jonker- and Ridderstraat area before and after implementation of the 1929 Reconstruction Plan with merging of building blocks
2 Diagram of urban fabric of Lepelstraat area before and after implementation of the 1953 Reconstruction Plan for Weesperstraat with merging of building blocks
3 Plan-Duyff 1972 and neighbourhood plan 1974

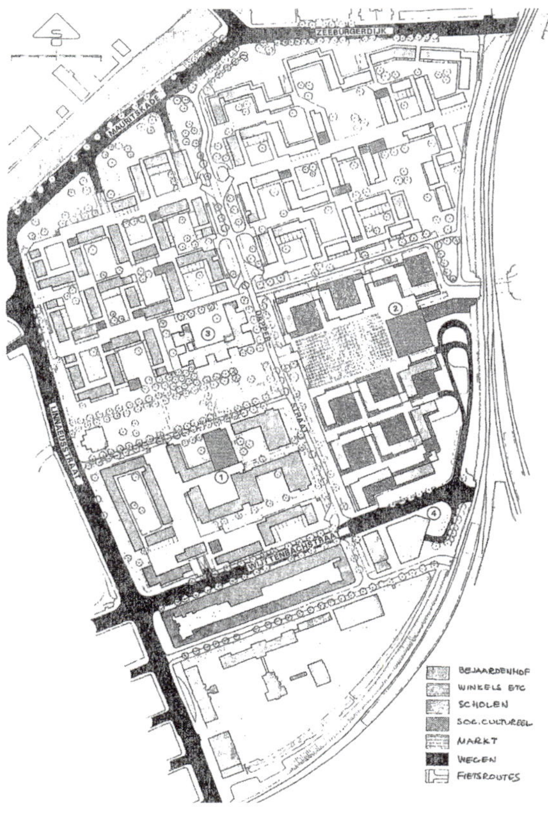

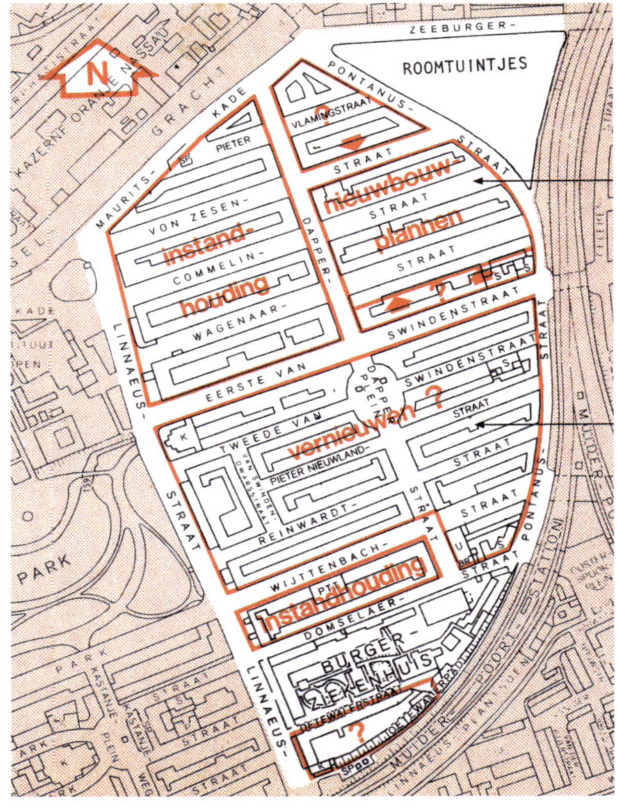

3

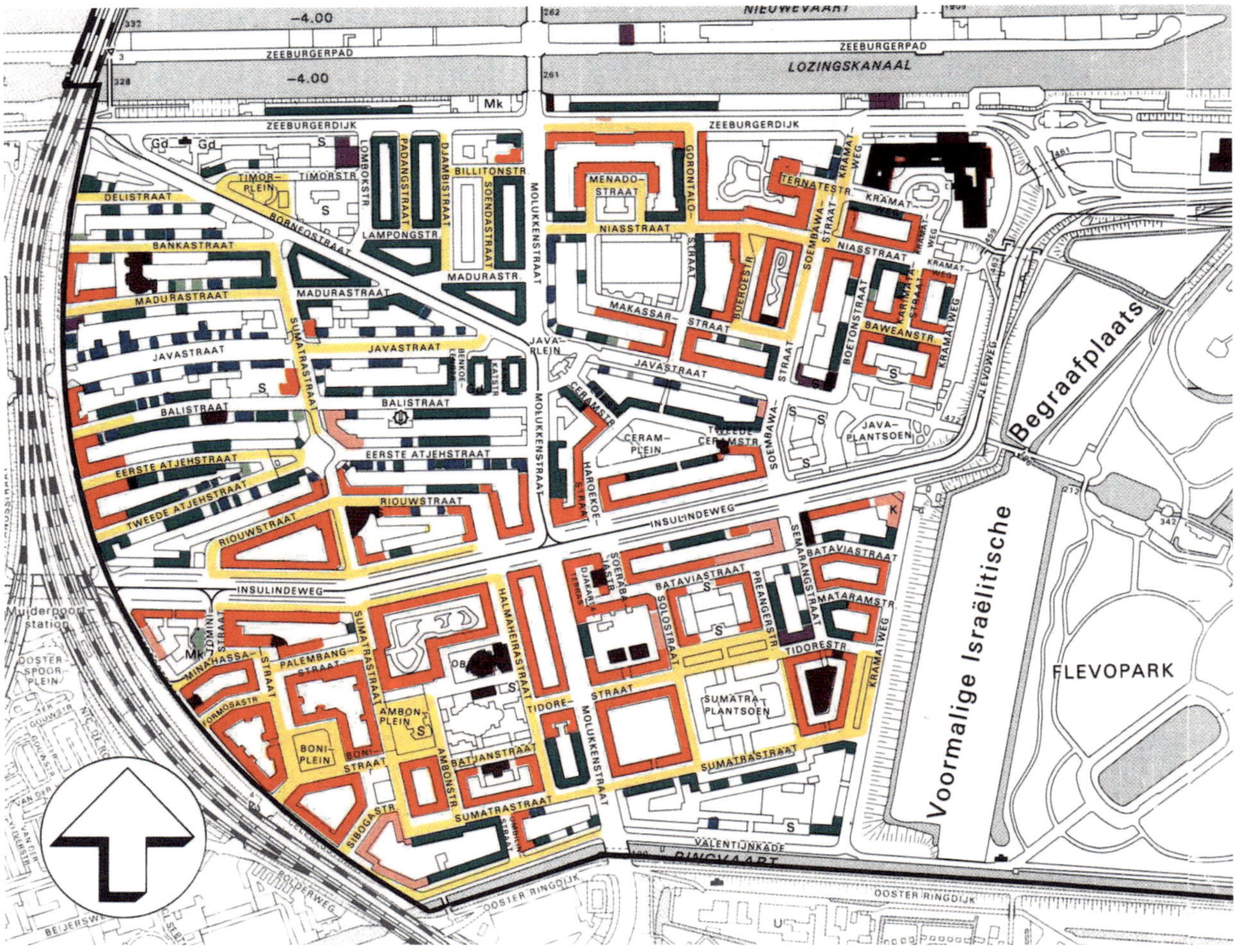

1 Renewal of the Indische Buurt: red/pink demolition-new construction, green/blue renovation

2 Van Beuningenplein Staatsliedenbuurt, 1975–2025

1

In the 1920s–1940s belt, most of the buildings were thoroughly renovated, including the monumental complexes of the Amsterdam School in Spaarndammerbuurt, De Pijp, and around Mercatorplein. Only in the Indische Buurt and Transvaalbuurt a significant number of structurally poor buildings was replaced. The foundations of entire blocks were faulty. In particular, in the Indische Buurt, much was demolished – almost 80% of the buildings constructed during the crisis years of the 1930s.

Schaefer's choice to 'take a photo from above' meant that the street pattern in the 19th-century city was preserved, including the pleasant distinction between busy streets and quiet inner courtyards within the closed building blocks. However, the consequence of this choice was that public outdoor space remained limited, making its use very intensive. There were few opportunities for street play. Scattered throughout the old city are numerous small squares, playgrounds, and schoolyards that were redesigned. Successful examples include Van Beuningenplein in the Staatsliedenbuurt, Kastanjeplein in Oost, and Balboa- and Columbusplein in De Baarsjes. In the relatively spacious Indische Buurt, new schools were built on some of the redesigned squares, including those designed by Herman Hertzberger. These are free-standing buildings with three stories, cheerful, open façades, stairs, and terraces. In many other neighborhoods, such solutions were not possible. Many streets in the 19th-century city are filled with cars and bicycles.

Bijlmermeer

By the late 1980s, it was concluded that the renewal of the old city was almost complete.[15] Attention shifted towards the post-war neighborhoods but soon focused on the renewal of the Bijlmermeer. Some of the 'honeycomb flats' were already facing vacancies and management issues early on; especially Gliphoeve was notorious. By 1984, the problems had become so severe that twelve housing associations decided to place their properties in the Bijlmer under one corporation: Nieuw-Amsterdam. Imagine this: ten to fifteen years after construction, the 'city of the future' turned out to be completely unsustainable. With a subsidy of 100 million guilders, management measures were implemented to combat the deterioration. Vacancy rates decreased somewhat, but the problems did not disappear. The elements that proved particularly difficult to manage in daily functioning were the parking buildings and the internal streets. The parking buildings had multiple floors and were publicly accessible. The long internal streets on the first floor of the flats connected the parking buildings with the elevators. Collective facilities along these internal streets struggled to come to fruition.

On October 4, 1992, an El Al airplane crashed into the Groeneveen and Kleinkruitberg flats. The disaster claimed at least 43 lives. Partly because of this, the debate on the future of the Bijlmer accelerated: What would the future of the Bijlmer look like?

In a 1985 study, Rem Koolhaas had already advocated for a radicalization of the Bijlmer concept. Instead of a 'photo from above' like in the 19th-century belt, he proposed a redesign. The idea was to keep the honeycomb flats but demolish the parking buildings and redesign the ground level. On the sites of the parking buildings, a series of residential towers could be built around the central, elevated Bijlmerdreef.

However, in 1993, a different approach was chosen: lowering the Bijlmerdreef and experimenting with demolition and new construction in the G-district. The Bijlmerdreef was given a profile similar to that of Apollolaan in Berlage's South district, with four rows of trees and residential blocks ranging from four to eight floors, with their entrances along the new avenue. Where the honeycomb flats stood, low-rise neighborhoods were created according to an urban plan by Donald Lambert, who was appointed as the external city planner.

The pilot project was positively evaluated. In the end, nearly 7,000 homes were demolished – more than half of the honeycomb flats. They were replaced by new construction, mostly in the form of low-rise houses in well-structured street layouts.[16] Most of the avenues were lowered, including the Karspeldreef in the southern part,

2

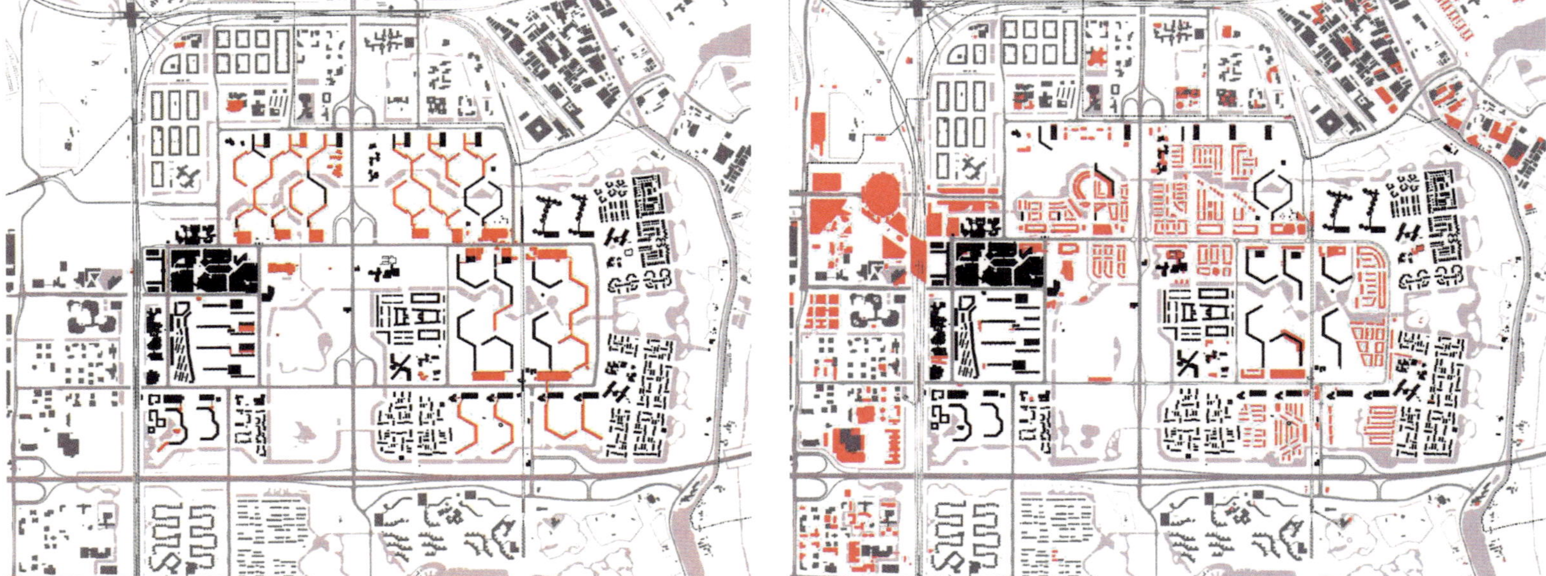
1

although here, the classic Berlage profile was not chosen. The preserved towers now contrast beautifully with the new urban blocks, which were built on the site of demolished parking garages.

Interestingly, not all areas underwent radical demolition. The most monumental part of the Bijlmer, around the metro line to Gaasperplas, was actually preserved. The metro line runs here on a structure rather than an embankment. Due to the high elevation and the significant span between the pillars, Gaasperpark passes underneath. This 'Bijlmermuseum' was designated as a protected cityscape in 2019. It is also where the memorial for the victims of the Bijlmerramp is located, with 'the tree that saw it all'. In the renovation of the flats, the parking buildings and internal streets were removed. The flats were now accessed from new streets at ground level, where parking is also allowed. This approach was essentially in line with Koolhaas' earlier proposal. One of the honeycomb flats, Kleiburg, was redeveloped as a 'DIY renovation flat'. The shell of these flats was renovated, and new owners could finish them according to their preferences.

Another variation can be found in the F-neighborhood, near the Amsterdamse Poort shopping center, according to a plan designed by Rein Geurtsen.[17] Here, the Bijlmerdreef retained its elevated position. The parking buildings were replaced by garages in two levels against the embankment. The public space above connects directly to the avenue. Residential blocks, ranging from six to eight floors, are accessed from this new ground level. On the opposite side of the avenue, the embankment was made into a monumental wide staircase leading to the lower Bijlmerplein. A market is held there, and in 2006, the new office for the Zuidoost district was opened. On the staircase stands a statue of the Surinamese writer and activist Anton de Kom. The separation of functions has been effectively broken.

The different approaches made the Bijlmer more varied and richer. Schaefer's 'photo from above' preserved the qualities of the 19th-century belt but also froze them. The diverse redesigns of the uniform Bijlmer idiom now give each section a strong individual identity.

Renewal of the Western Garden Cities

The renewal of the post-war garden cities in Nieuw-West began cautiously. Alongside the construction of new residential neighborhoods like Nieuw Sloten, De Aker, and Geuzenveld-West, the renewal in the early 1990s was limited to a few scattered projects, including the renewal of the shopping area around Plein '40–'45, the construction of residential neighborhoods Noorderhof and Oostoever, and new buildings at Koningin Wilhelminaplein.

As a first step in the renewal, the Amsterdam Federation of Housing Corporations organized a major event in 1992 at theater De Meervaart. How should the renewal be approached? In 1993, three so-called pilot projects were designated: Neighborhood 9 in Geuzenveld (connected to the redesign of the road layout of Geuzenbaan), the Zuidwestkwadrant in Osdorp, and Overtoomse Veld-North in Slotervaart. The Bos en Lommer district focused mainly on the renewal of the Bos en Lommerplein, with the iconic bridge buildings over the A10 and the new construction around the shopping square.

To coordinate the projects, the Steering Group Western Garden Cities was established in 1994, with representatives from the districts and the 'central city' (the municipal government). This group also commissioned a vision to be developed for the entire garden city area: *Parkstad. A Multidimensional Perspective for the Western Garden Cities (1995)*. A key notion in the vision, proposed by Anna Vos, is the principle of 'the Scottish Plaid'. The large water, bike, road, and parking elements (blue, yellow, black, green) in Nieuw-West form a highly differentiated network of public spaces with often beautiful profiles. This network serves as an excellent starting point for the renewal in *Parkstad*. The 'fields' within the network could take on a new shape during transformation, benefiting from their location relative to surrounding roads and green elements and, of course, depending on the desired program and the quality of the existing buildings.

Compared to the concepts of the 'photo from above' in the 19th-century belt and the redesigns for the Bijlmer, the Scottish Plaid concept focuses on the quality of the urban elements network. Within this network, variation is possible.

Starting in 2000, the first new and renovated homes in the pilot project areas were completed. However, significant numbers were only realized in 2009 and 2010, across many more locations. This was mainly the result of investments by the three new operating companies of housing corporations: Far West, Prospect, and Westwaarts.[18] In total, over 19,000 new homes were built in the Western Garden Cities (including Bos en Lommer) from 2000 to 2021: 11,000 after demolition and 8,000 at additional locations. Moreover, nearly 3,000 homes were added by transforming office buildings.[19]

The legal planning and spatial framework for the renewal was developed under the leadership of Bureau Parkstad. This project bureau was established in 1999 as a collaboration between the four involved districts and the municipality of Amsterdam, with the aim of formulating an integrated approach and then coordinating it. Based on the development plan *Richting Parkstad 2015* from 2001, a whole series of renewal and implementation plans were developed in the following years. A Quality Team and supervisors for each neighborhood ensured consistency and quality in the plans.

Bureau Parkstad was dissolved in 2007, and the leading role in the renewal approach was transferred to the involved housing corporations. The focus shifted to implementation.

Crucial to the success of the operation was the reorganization of housing ownership by the corporations. The operating companies were dissolved, and one corporation became responsible for the renewal of a specific neighborhood. The merging of the districts Geuzenveld-Slotermeer, Osdorp, and Slotervaart into one district, Nieuw-West, in 2010 also helped streamline the execution process.

A constant in the renewal process was the renewal of schools. A total of no less than 42 schools were extensively renovated or newly built: 29 for primary education, 10 for secondary education, and 3 for higher education.

1 Bijlmermeer, demolished buildings, respectively newly built, 1992–2012
2 Study for the renewal of Bijlmermeer, design OMA/Rem Koolhaas, 1985
3 F-district, urban planning design, Rein Geurtsen, 1998
4 Phasing of renewal, Development Plan Parkstad towards 2015, Municipality of Amsterdam, 2001
The renewal of phases 1 and 2 is nearly completed. Planning for the neighborhoods in phase 3 was abandoned during the real estate crisis. The renewal of the Roëll neighborhoods (Couperusbuurt, Dichtersbuurt, and Van Deysselbuurt, north of Roëllstraat) and the Wildemanbuurt in Osdorp is being prepared.
5 Urban renewal Nieuw-West, 2000–2021

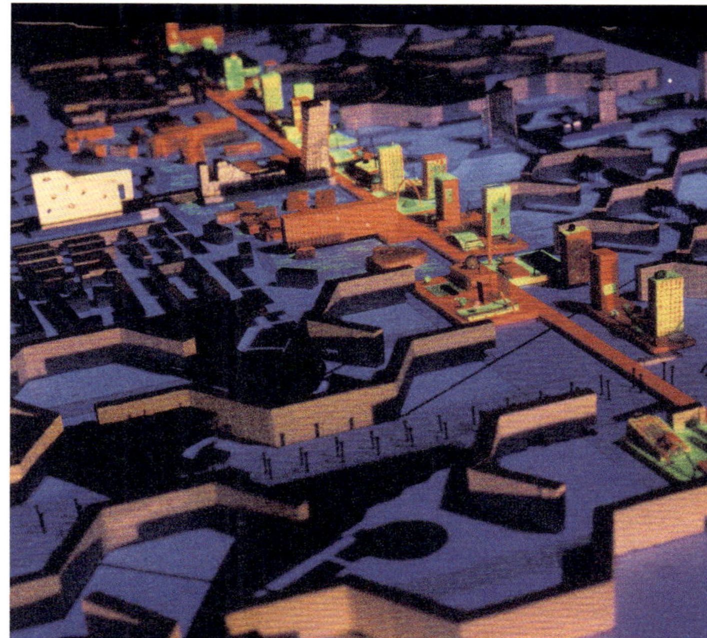

2

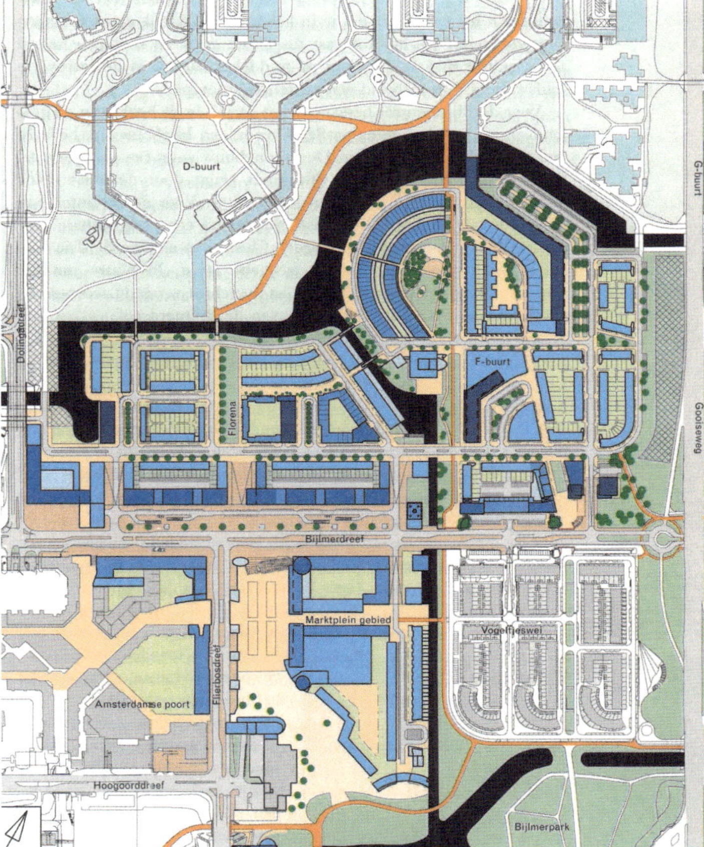

3

Change in Direction

After the real estate crisis of 2008, a notable shift occurred in the approach to urban renewal. In the Parkstad approach, demolition and new construction were central. The goal was to replace more than 13,000 homes with new buildings. It is difficult to determine exactly how many homes were demolished during the period from 2000 to 2021. An estimate based on available data on the development of the housing stock showed that around 5,100 homes were ultimately demolished since 2000.[20] This is much less than initially planned.

Across the different renewal neighborhoods, many blocks were not demolished but were renovated more or less extensively. In many cases, these were culturally and historically valuable complexes, such as the Airey homes and the A.H. Gerhardhuis in Slotermeer, the Knijtijzer buildings in Overtoomse Veld, the gallery block Seneca designed by architect Bodon at

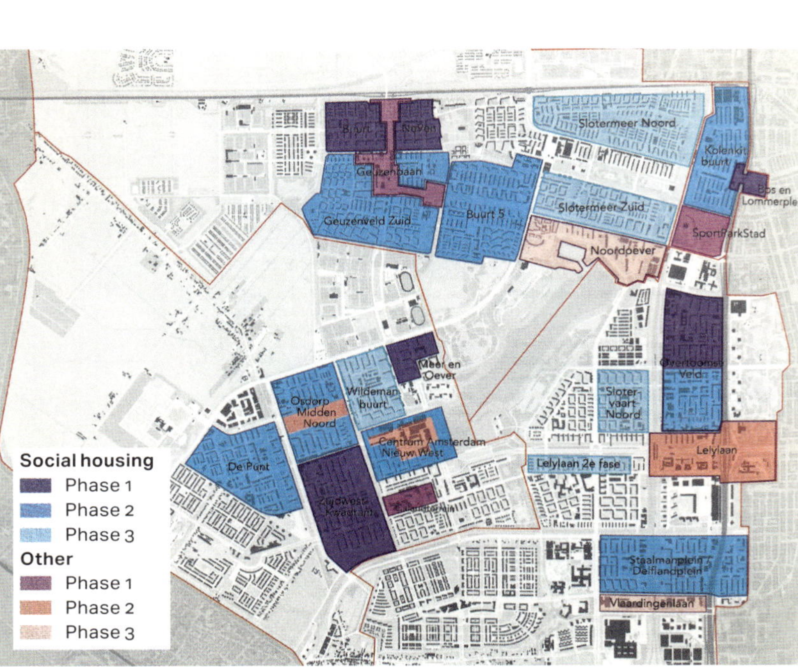

4

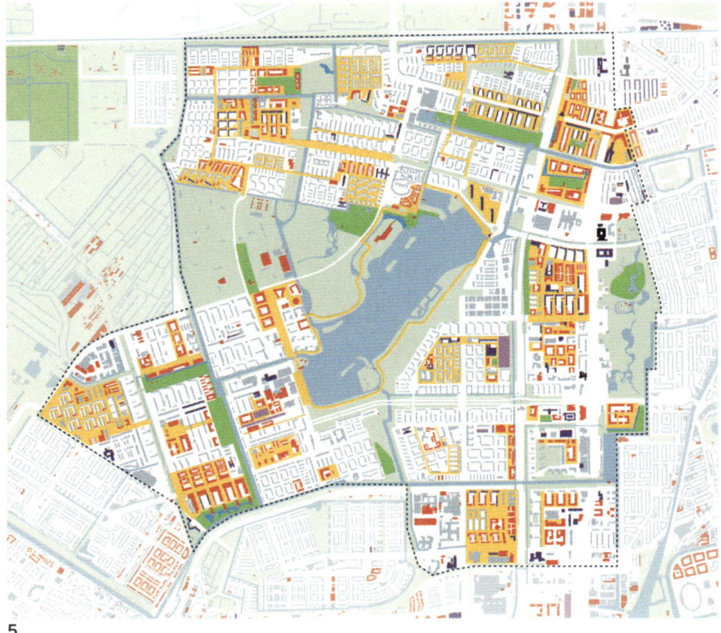

5

1

2

3

Confuciusplein, and the blocks by Jaap Bakema in Geuzenveld. For the renewal of the porch apartment blocks designed by architect Willem Dudok in Geuzenveld, renovation was the goal from the outset.

Staalmanpleinbuurt

One of the most successful renewal projects in Nieuw-West is the Staalmanplein neighborhood, located near the Slotervaart Hospital and Heemstedestraat Station on the Ring Line.[21]

The renewal started in 2001 and was approached in phases, allowing residents to 'move up' from their old homes to new ones. In the final phases, after much discussion and procedures, it was decided not to demolish the blocks around Staalmanplein, designed by Arthur Staal and Cornelis Keesman, with their characteristic kiosks, but to renovate them.

The number of homes in the neighborhood ultimately increased from 1,007 to 1,651 – a significant densification. Initially, the neighborhood only had social rental housing. Today, it is a highly diversified neighborhood, with 888 social rental homes (54%), 257 mid-range rental homes (16%), 296 private sector rental homes (18%), and 210 private sector owner-occupied homes (13%). 759 homes were renovated (30 of which are 'DIY flats'), 65 were created in an old office building, and the remaining 827 are new homes. The mixture of affordable and more expensive homes, as well as new and renovated homes, has made the Staalmanplein neighborhood a true urban neighborhood.

The program also contributes to this. In the new buildings around the new Staalmanpark with the large bear, designed by artist Florentijn Hofman, a primary school, mosque, sports hall, and nursing home have been included. The retained telephone exchange will have a cultural function. The ground floor of the renovated buildings around Staalmanplein and the kiosks are designated for restaurants and businesses.

Two spatial aspects are very decisive for the quality of the renewed Staalmanplein neighborhood. First, the decision to maintain the rows of mature street trees on the wide sidewalks gives the neighborhood an elegant identity. But the most important change is a subtle intervention in the renovation of the retained blocks: a high gate beneath one of the blocks has created a pleasant new walking route from the park to Staalmanplein and the tram stop.

The qualities of the renewed neighborhood seem to be proof of the effectiveness of the 'Scottish Plaid' concept. Within the retained network of large urban elements and the area around it, a neighborhood has emerged with its own identity and

1 Renovated kiosks at Staalmanplein
2 Widened and elevated gate during renovation, design by Arjan Gooijer Van Schagen Architects, 2020
3 Reconstruction Paperdome in K-district, design by Shigeru Ban, 2000
4 Isometric views of the existing and new Staalmanpleinbuurt, urban design by Stefan Bödecker, 2002 and Frits Palmboom, 2009

special qualities. However, many discussions and procedures could have been avoided if the qualities of the public space and the buildings had been considered in the planning from the outset. This might be the most important lesson: the quality of the city is less supported by a 'photo from above' or 'redesign,' but rather by 'processing' or 'enriching' the existing.

Broadening the approach

The city's renewal, in phases of reversing decline and recovery, concentrated on the renewal of the housing stock. Since the rapid growth of Amsterdam in 2007, new challenges have arisen, and different priorities have emerged.

In the garden cities, the task became broader. Many older office buildings turned out to be obsolete. Additionally, many schools became vacant due to the concentration in secondary and higher vocational education. Some of the vacant offices and schools were demolished, but a large portion turned out to be suitable for new programs, such as hotels, incubators, and student housing.

Across the Western Garden Cities, ten hotels and one hostel have been built, totaling 2,022 rooms and 330 beds, respectively.[22] After the success of Garage Notweg (2009) and De Vlugt (2010), fourteen 'incubators' have been established in vacant buildings. These incubators vary in size, but contain several hundred workspaces, in addition to studios. In most cases, this is temporary use with contracts ranging from five to ten years. Some incubators have since been demolished to make room for new buildings.

The available data doesn't provide an exact number of student and youth housing units built in the garden cities. If we look at the buildings specifically designed

1 Street restructuring Frans Halsbuurt
2 Spaarndammerhart

1

for this market, there are eighteen complexes, with a total of 5,584 often rather small units – an average of 310 units per complex. These are mainly located near the metro stations of the Ring Line. The largest are Little Manhattan next to Lelylaan Station, with 869 units; the former GAK building with 651 units; and the first Lieven complex in the Delflandplein neighborhood with 570 units.

The intensification in the Ring Zone is a result of the immense pressure on the housing market since the city's rapid growth. This is also true for the intensification of existing buildings in other, older parts of the city. Attics and cellars are being adapted for living, apartments are being split, or rooms are being rented out. The stagnation in construction during the real estate crisis only accelerated this process.

The stagnation also created opportunities for temporary use. The incubators established since 2009 in the garden cities are part of an extensive program throughout the city. Initially stemming from the artist studio policy, this has now expanded significantly. In addition to studios, many incubators contain workspaces, restaurants, and various facilities.

A recent example is the (re)construction of the Paperdome in the K-neighborhood in Zuidoost. The dome, made of cardboard tubes, was designed by Japanese architect Shigeru Ban in 2000 for dance performances in the newly developed first section of IJburg. After serving as an information center in the Vinex district of Leidsche Rijn in Utrecht and being stored for years, it was ultimately rebuilt as a temporary sports hall for 3x3 basketball.

A more structural initiative has been formulated in the 'Environmental Vision Amsterdam 2050: A Human Metropolis'. Emancipation of the suburbs and polycentricity are key themes in this vision. The renewal of the shopping and service centers at Buikslotermeerplein, Osdorpplein, and ArenA Poort is expected to contribute to a stronger self-awareness and a more complete range of facilities in North, Nieuw-West, and Zuidoost. The first housing projects in these centers have been completed, a mega-cinema has been built at Noord Station, and the construction of a Verhalenhuis (Story House) and new facilities for the De Meervaart theater are being prepared.

Experiments

A few hopeful experiments to conclude. In the Frans Halsbuurt in De Pijp, all streets have been made almost car-free and green over the past few years. Cars are now parked in a parking garage for 600 cars under the Boerenwetering canal. The spaces are primarily intended for permit holders in the area. What a relief! This experiment offers an attractive perspective for all other 19th-century neighborhoods: cars off the street and (still) placed in separate parking facilities.

In the Spaarndammerbuurt, a mistake from the early urban renewal period has been corrected. Building on the modernist idea of creating space in the old city by merging city blocks, the buildings on Krommeniestraat were demolished to make room for a school building. Forty years later, the school has found new accommodation, the street pattern of the housing blocks has been restored, and an attractive new residential courtyard has been created: Spaarndammerhart, designed by korthtielens and Marcel Lok. In form, material, and color use, it is a distinctive interpretation of the Amsterdam School experiments further along in the neighborhood. The project won the Amsterdam New Construction Award 2022. It is also a call to carefully consider how mistakes can be repaired during major maintenance and renewal of early urban renewal projects in the coming years.

2

RESIDENTIAL, BLOCK, AND PLOT LAYOUTS

Historically, the dominant housing type in Amsterdam's construction practice was the traditional 'Gothic townhouse': narrow, deep homes with two or three floors, arranged in a row, accessed from the street at the front, with a courtyard at the back, sometimes with a back house, and often including commercial space on the ground floor and an attic under a tiled roof. In the 19th century, this type was adapted to house multiple households, with each floor – often four or five – occupied by a different household. Sometimes a floor was split into two smaller units. After the introduction of the Housing Act in 1901, new buildings incorporated 'light' porches at the front, with each floor accessing two apartments. This type of apartment layout evolved further after World War II, with larger kitchens and bathrooms with showers, and the storage rooms were relocated from the attic to the ground floor.

After experimenting with gallery houses and maisonettes, the porch-apartment type became the dominant model for replacing substandard housing in the inner city and in 19th- and early 20th-century neighborhoods. The standard design was typically five stories tall, with storage units and one (elderly) apartment on the ground floor, two deep family units on the second, third, and fourth floors, and youth apartments on the top floor. The narrow streets, often 12-15 meters wide, were preserved. By introducing one-way traffic, space was created for angled parking and trees. The architecture was relatively simple.

This housing type was also applied in the Marcanti terrain and Venserpolder areas, where the main improvements were larger plots and wider streets. In other housing developments, different typologies were experimented with, such as residential towers at the Oranje-Nassau Barracks and detached apartment blocks on the GWL site, with multi-story homes, sometimes accessed by a central corridor.

In these additional locations, housing was often mixed with other programs, such as schools on the Marcanti terrain and a combination of senior housing and care homes along De Werf by the Kostverlorenvaart, on the old RAI site, and on sites where churches had been demolished. On the former RAI site, a petting zoo and a sports hall called 'De Pijp' were also built. The transformed tram depot, De Hallen, now houses a library, TV studios, a cinema complex, a food hall, and a hotel.

In addition to a greater focus on materials and detailing, several fundamental changes in construction practices occurred in the 1990s and 2000s, with more differentiation by sector: homes were now being built in the private sector and by investors. The higher returns allowed for the introduction of elevators and built-in parking facilities. The number of floors in these buildings increased to seven, eight, or nine, and sometimes short galleries were added to provide access to multiple homes per floor. The Olympic Quarter in the south, next to the Olympic Stadium, is an interesting example of this.

While the renewal of neighborhoods like the Bijlmer, Banne, and Nieuwendam-Noord primarily reused conventional housing types, there was much more experimentation in the renewal of the 1950s and 1960s neighborhoods in Nieuw-West. Laan van Spartaan, for example, offers a mix of housing types: in addition to back-to-back townhouses, there are porch apartments over eight floors, gallery homes over ten floors, and student housing accessed by a central corridor. The housing is also combined with football fields, a healthcare complex, schools, a sports hall, and various everyday services along Jan van Galenstraat.

The migration wave that accompanied the city's growth since 2014 has led to a significant rise in complexes with small homes for long- and short-term stays, both in new buildings and in existing ones. Key characteristics include hotel-style entrances and an increase in the number of floors, particularly in the Ringzone in Nieuw-West.

In recent years, urban renewal has also focused on sustainability: insulation, solar panels, connections to district heating networks, and reducing reliance on gas. This shift affects the entire housing stock.

→ **Next page:**
Bos en Lommerplein, Geurst and Schulze, 2008

1C ORANJE-NASSAU BARRACKS 1990

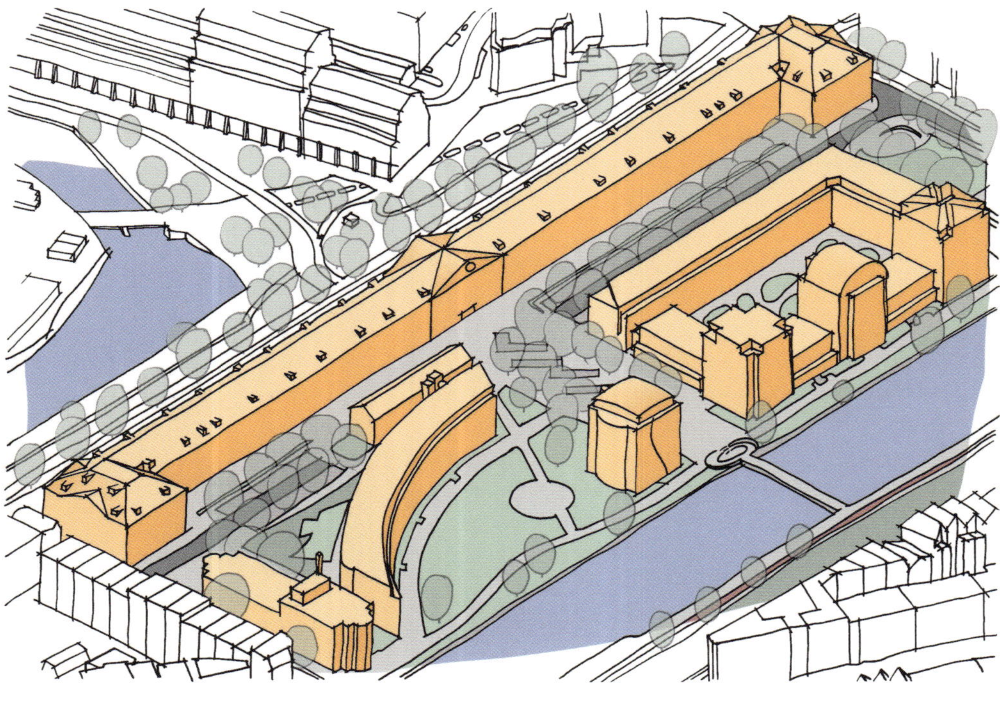

Features
Reuse of barracks, new residential blocks and towers of 9 stories

Urban planning – supervision
Hans van Beek (Atelier PRO), Hans van der Made (DRO)

Architects
Joop and André van Stigt, Hans van Beek, Cuno Brullman, Koji Yagi, Alexandros Tombazis, Patrick Pinnell, Tage Lyneborg, and Jeremy Bailey

Construction period
1987–1990

Houses per hectare
120

Average house size
75 m²

1D GWL SITE 1998

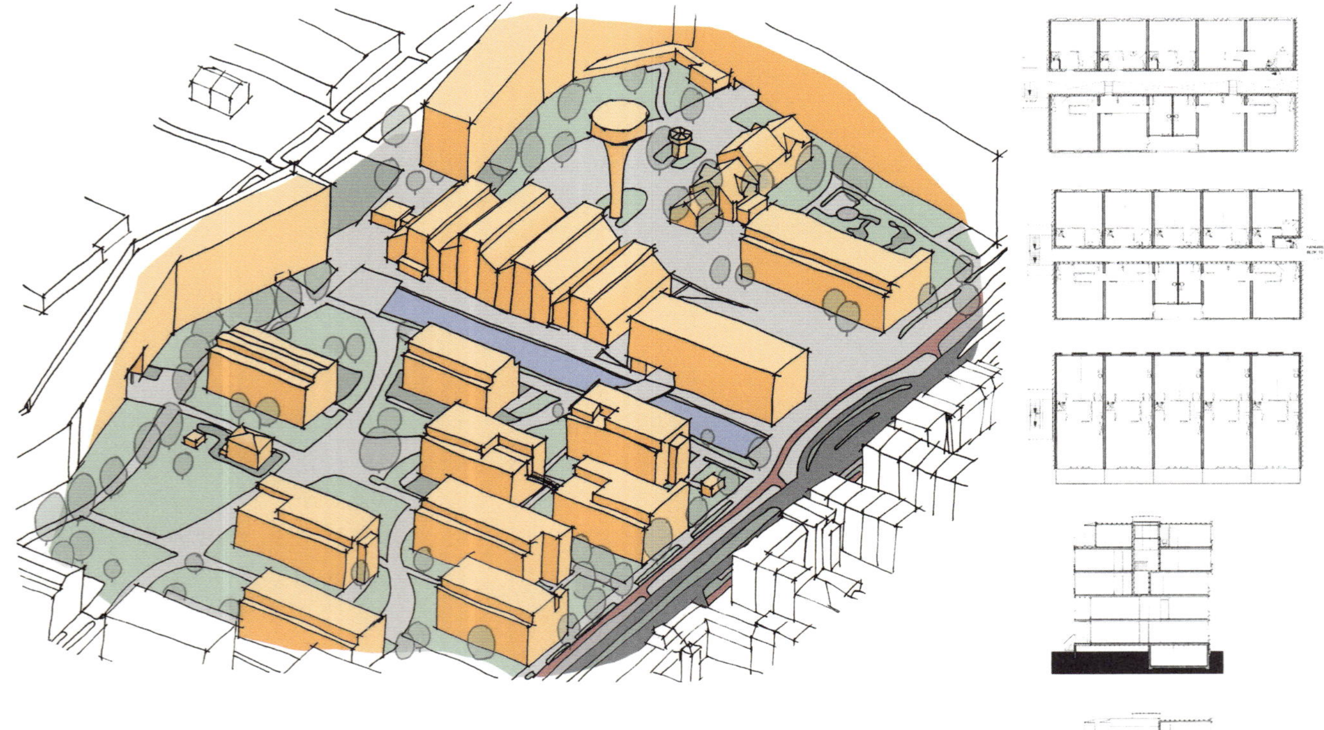

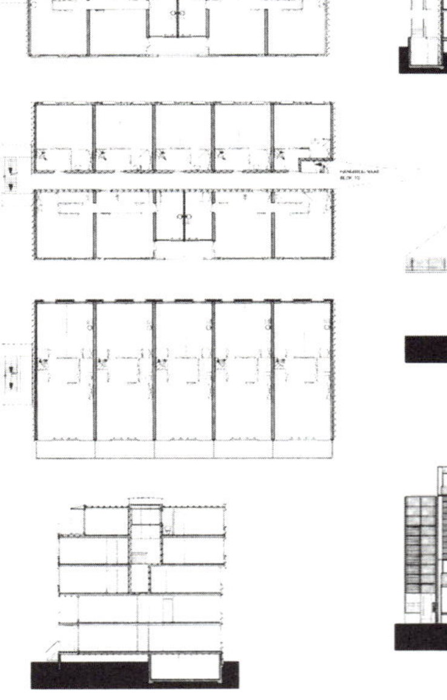

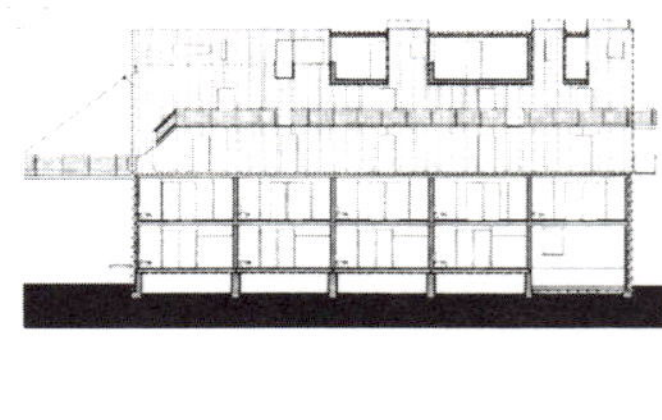

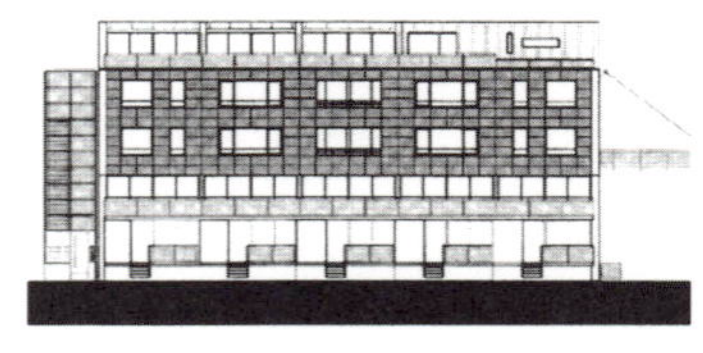

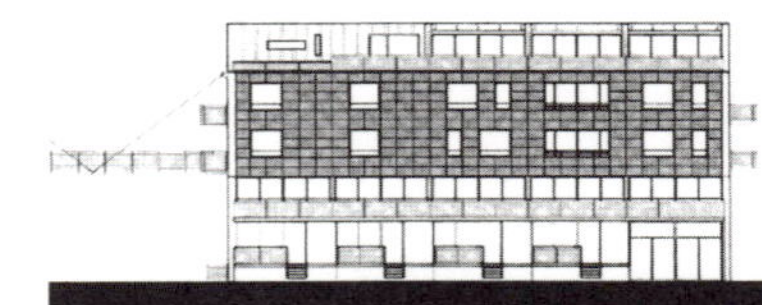

Features
Ecological neighborhood developed on former water supply land

Urban planning – supervision
Kees Christiaanse (KCAP)

Architects
among others, Neutelings Architecture, DKV architects, Liesbeth van der Pol, KCAP, Meyer & Van Schooten

Construction period
1995–1998

Houses per hectare
95

Average house size
87 m²

1A MARCANTI – KOP VAN JUT — 1984

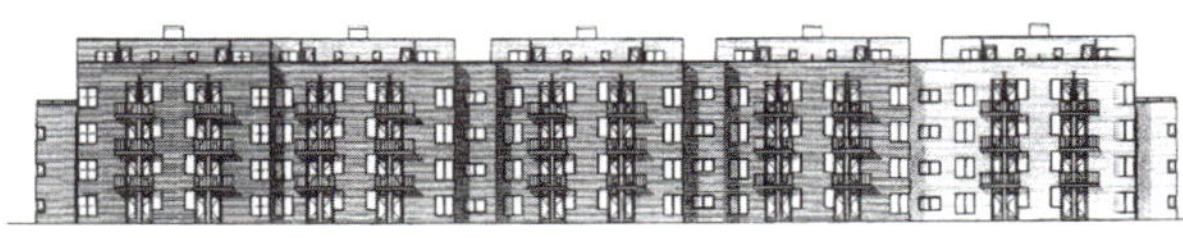

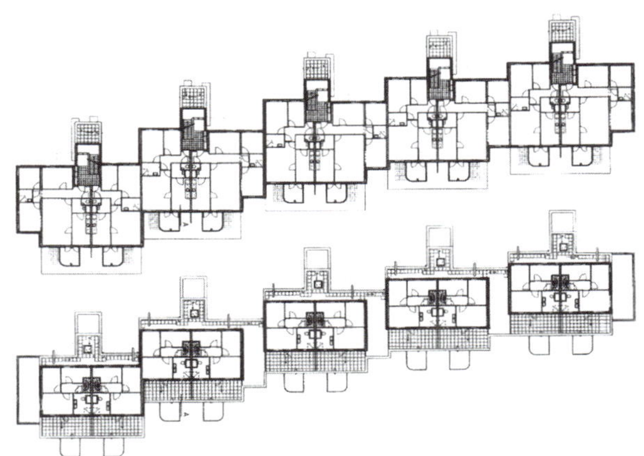

Features
Stacked flats in curved strip layout

Urban planning – supervision
City Development section PW Amsterdam

Architects
Sier van Rhijn

Construction period
1980–1984

Houses per hectare
150

Average house size
62 m²

1B VENSERPOLDER — 1984

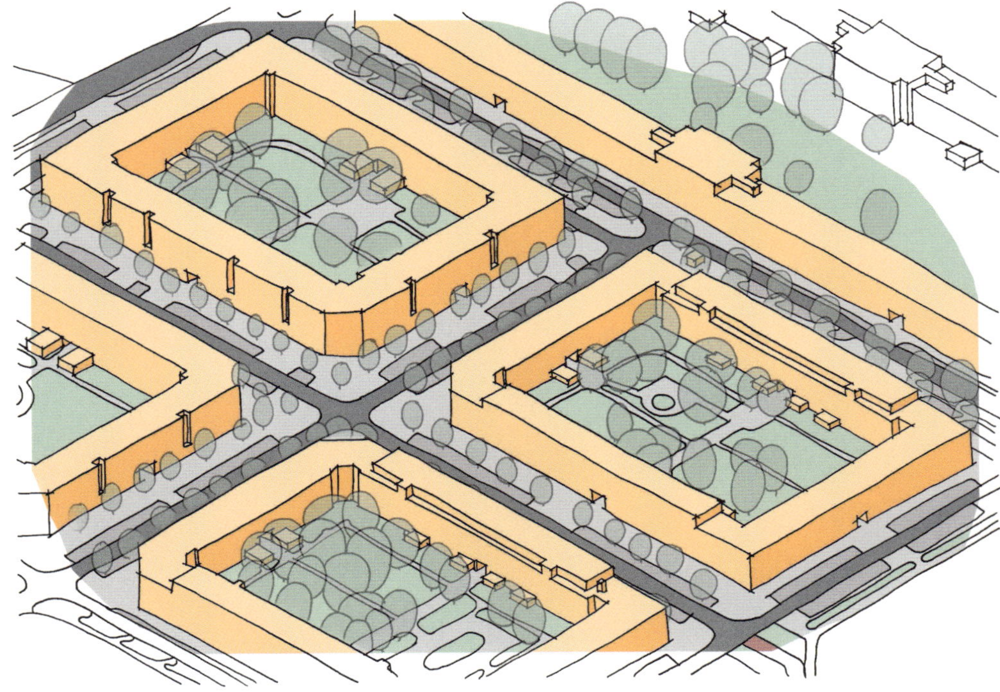

Features
Stacked flats in superblocks with public inner courtyards and on-street parking

Urban planning – supervision
Carel Weeber

Architects
among others, Carel Weeber, Hans Bosch, Hein van Meer, De Kat & Peek

Construction period
1981–1984

Houses per hectare
130

Average house size
61 m²

15 Station Sloterdijk
GVB
BENU Apotheek
55-BPL-2

Ring A10 s105
Rotterdam
Utrecht
s104
Slotermeer
Ring A10 s103
Zaanstad
Leeuwarden

1G LAAN VAN SPARTAAN 2013

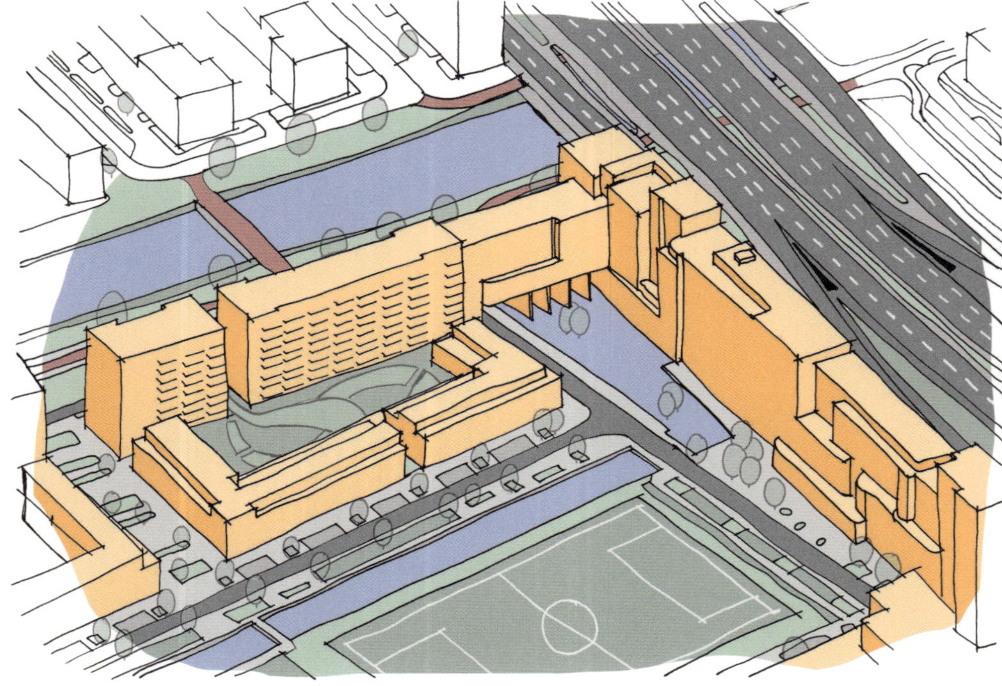

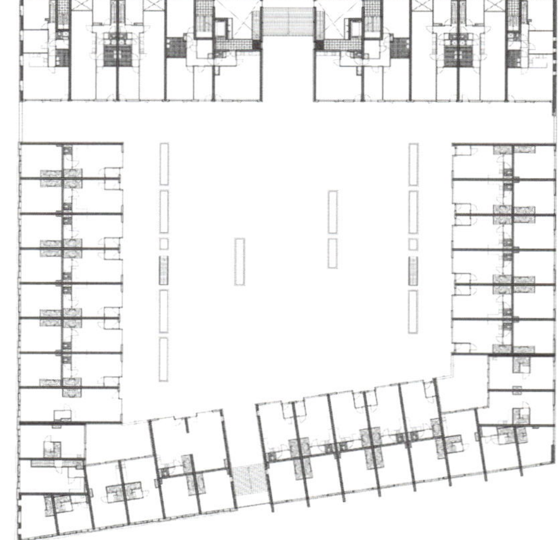

Features
City blocks in 3 and 8 stories with indoor parking around sports fields

Urban planning – supervision
Karen van Vliet (BGSV)

Architects
Ziegler | Branderhorst, Claus and Kaan Architects, Diederendirrix, Dick van Gameren, DP6 Architecture Studio, Studioninedots, KOW architects

Construction period
2011–2013

Houses per hectare
105

Average house size
82 m²

1H SPAARNDAMMERHART 2021

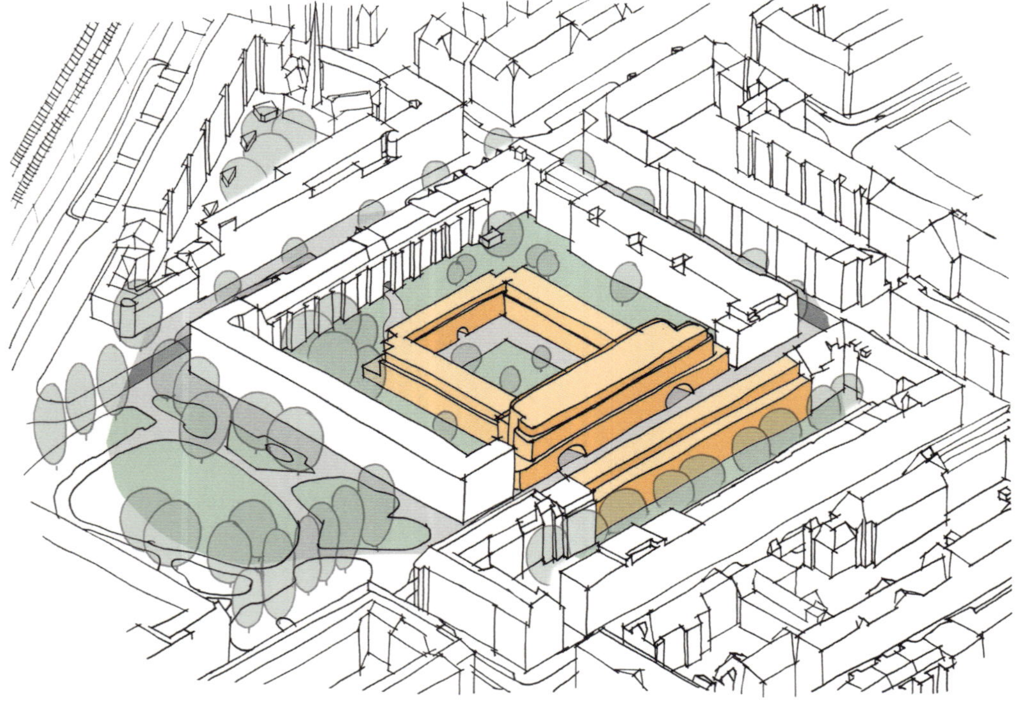

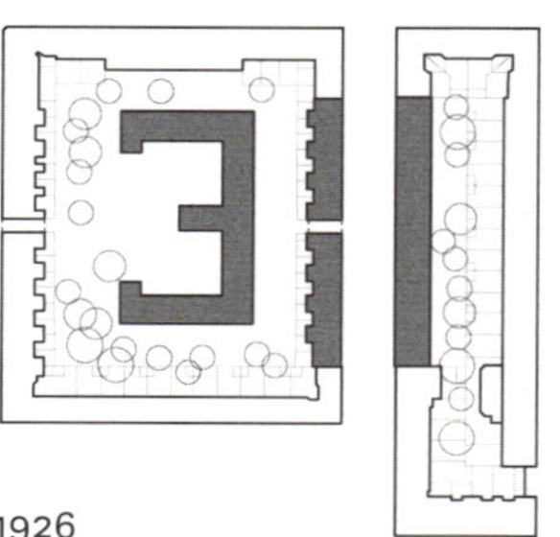

1926

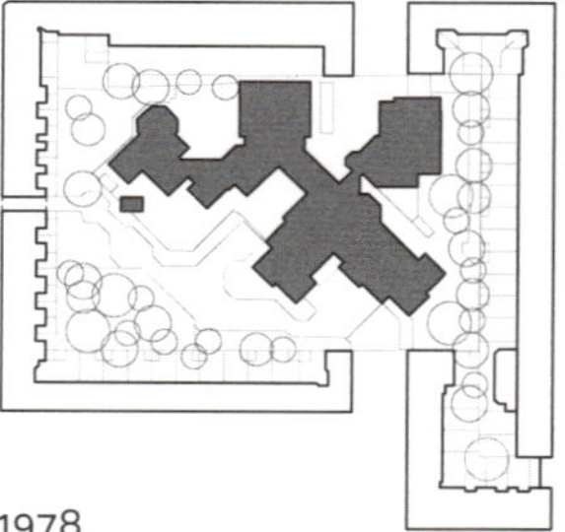

1978

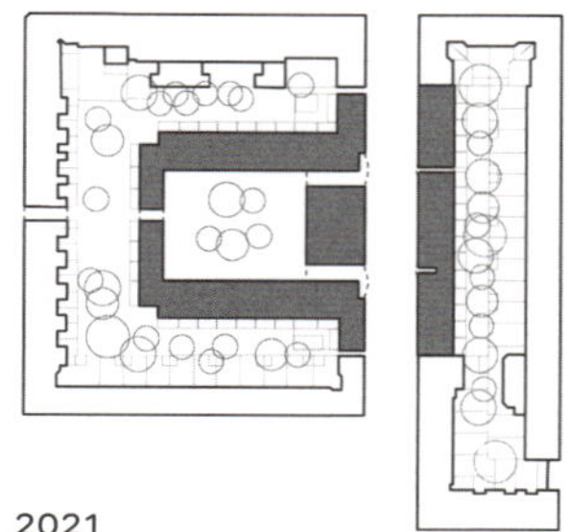

2021

Features
City block in 3, 4, and 5 stories with courtyard and underground parking

Urban planning – supervision
Joop Gerrits (West District)

Architects
korthtielens architects and Marcel Lok Architects

Construction period
2018–2021

Houses per hectare
92

Average house size
97 m²

1E OLYMPIC QUARTER — 2005

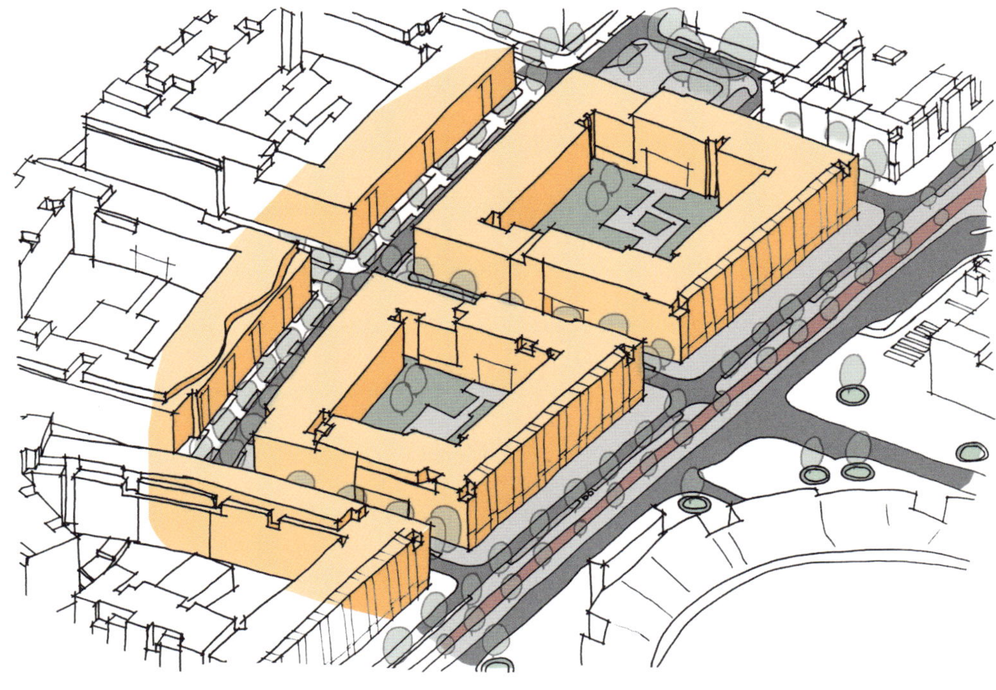

Features
Stacked flats in city blocks with shared inner gardens and underground parking

Urban planning – supervision
Hans Ebberink, Lafour and Wijk

Architects
Rudy Uytenhaak, Lafour and Wijk, Mulleners + Mulleners

Construction period
2000–2005

Houses per hectare
140

Average house size
99 m²

1F DELFLANDPLEIN — 2010

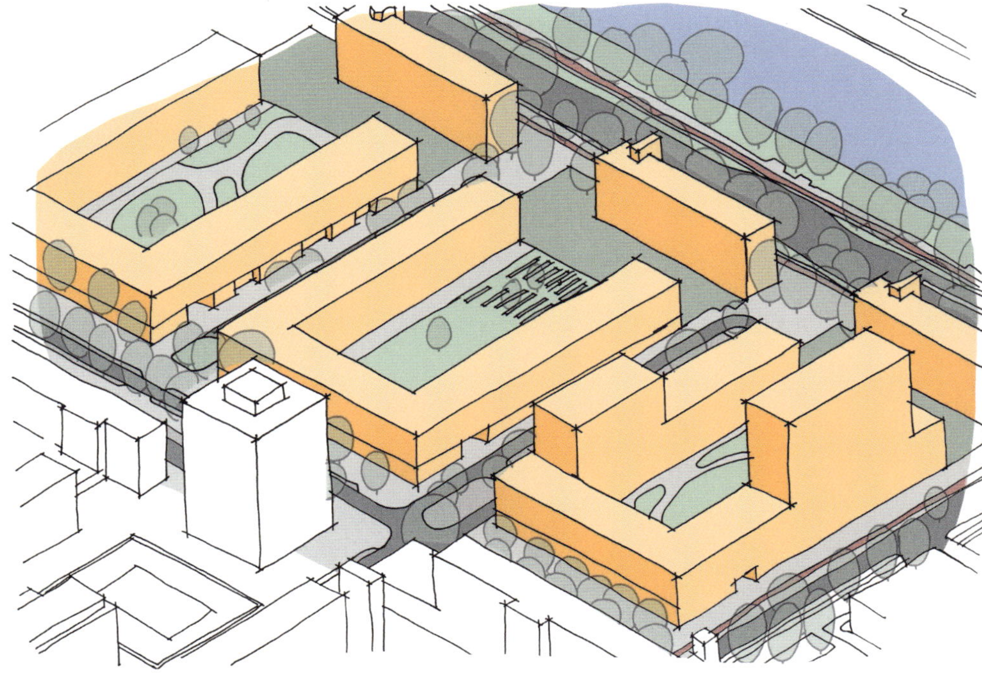

Features
City blocks with double-height plinth, above parking garage

Urban planning – supervision
Steef Buys, Marlies van Diest

Architects
Dick van Gameren, Marcel van der Lubbe (ANA Architects), Snitker/Borst Architects

Construction period
2008–2010

Houses per hectare
140

Average house size
80 m²

11 STOPERA

Since the 1930s, the city of Amsterdam had been searching for a location for a new city hall. After a design competition for a new building on the site of the burned-down *Palace of Industry* at Frederiksplein, the city chose the current location on Vlooienburg, by the Amstel River. In 1964, the municipal government issued an international competition for 'a democratic city hall, based on governance through persuasion, which would also serve as a meeting place for citizens'. The design by Austrian architect Wilhelm Holzbauer won. After discussions regarding co-financing with the national government, it was decided to combine the city hall with the new opera house (the 'Stopera'). Holzbauer worked on the plan together with the opera architects Bijvoet, Holt, and Dam. Construction finally began in 1982, after years of resistance.

In 1986, the opera house was opened, and in 1988, the city moved into its new city hall. The Great Hall is used by the Nationale Opera & Ballet, which also occupies various rehearsal studios and workshops within the building. In 2019, a major renovation of the Stopera complex began, aiming to make the building more sustainable, flexible, and user-friendly.

1 Muziektheater, viewed from the Blauwbrug
2 Aerial photo, 1978
3 Aerial photo, 2023
4 Main hall of the Muziektheater
5 Council chamber in 2018
6 Inner street Stopera, impression of the new situation
7 Inner street Stopera with photo studio
8 Aerial photo from the 1980s

1

2

3

4

5

6

7

8

1.9 CULTURAL PARK WESTERGASFABRIEK

At the end of the 19th century, four gas factories were built in Amsterdam to supply the city with energy. From the 1960s onwards, the city switched to Groningen natural gas, and the local gas factories were no longer needed. This was also the case for the Westergasfabriek on Haarlemmerweg. The Municipal Energy Company continued to use the site for storage until the early 1990s, but then it was decided to transform the area and buildings into a park, event space, and workspaces for the creative and cultural sectors. The soil was thoroughly remediated for this purpose.

In 1997, the Westerpark district issued an international design competition for the site, with the entry by American landscape architect Kathryn Gustafson being selected as the winner. Braaksma & Roos Architects were tasked with renovating the (monumental) buildings, including the gas holder (14 meters high, nearly 60 meters in diameter).

By 2003, the park was completed. It features elevation changes and a large new pond. The grass area in the central open space was reinforced to accommodate events. The adjacent 19th-century Westerpark effectively doubled in size with the expansion of the Cultuurpark (Culture Park) Westergasfabriek. The renovation of the gas holder was completed in 2007. Braaksma & Roos added 670 m² of space, and the buildings now house, among others, the youth theater De Krakeling and Fabrique des Lumières. The result is a multifunctional site that has proven its value to the city.

1 Design for the park extension, design by Gustafson, Porter + Bowman
2 Aerial photo, 2003
3 Aerial photo, 2023
4 Design sketch by Mecanoo
5 Adaptive reuse of the existing buildings
6 The new pond

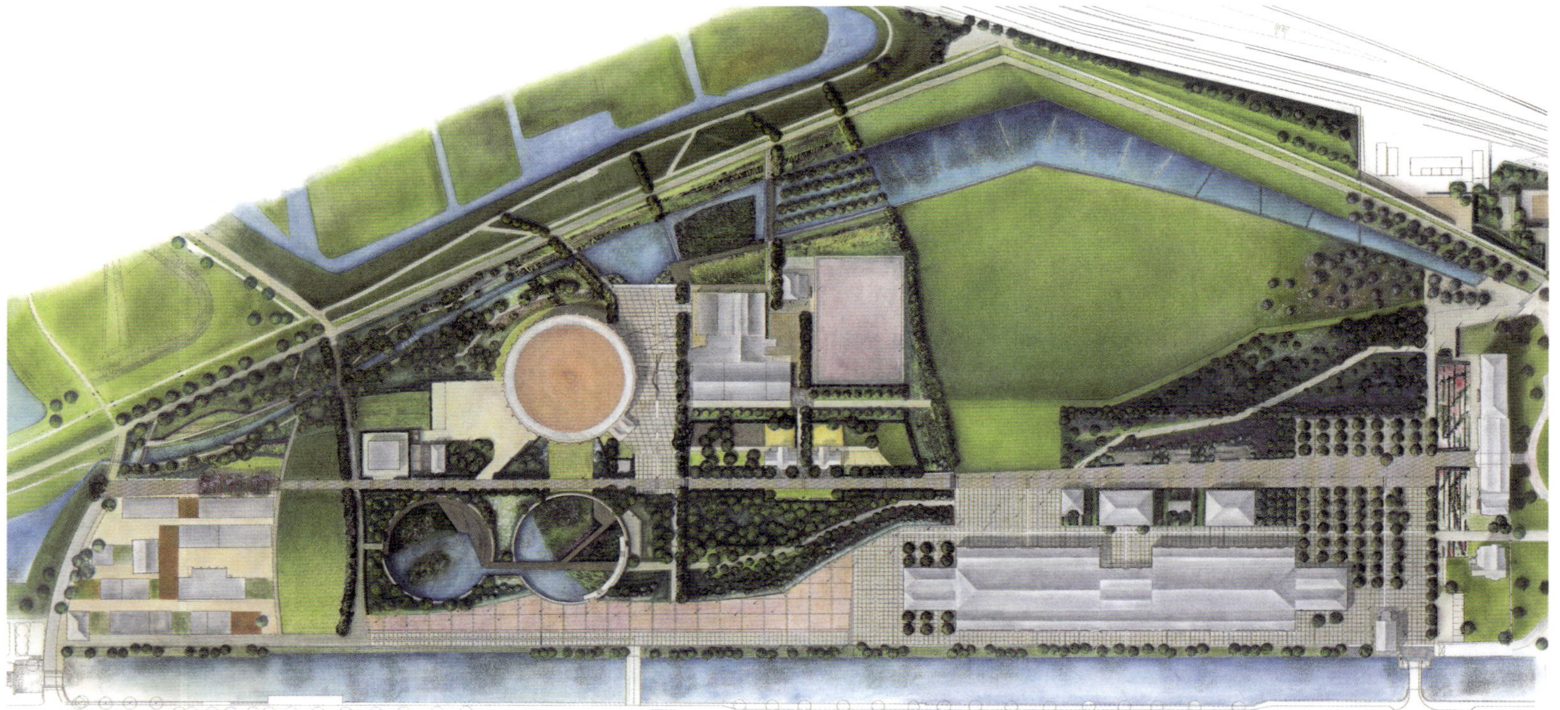
1

2

3

4

5

6

1K WIBAUTSTRAAT AND AMSTEL CAMPUS

In the mid-1970s, the Wibautstraat had a poor reputation: it was described as 'an almost impassable barrier between some dilapidated residential neighborhoods, which, due to years of neglect, are listed as urban renewal areas', wrote *NRC Handelsblad* in 1976. The street was dominated by large office buildings housing the Tax Office, the Labour Council, and various municipal services. The offices and printing presses of *de Volkskrant*, *Het Parool*, and *Trouw* were also located here. In the 1990s and 2000s, all these functions left the area, and the buildings were repurposed for temporary uses.

The 2001 Master Plan for the Wibautstraat set a new direction for the entire IJ Tunnel route. Ultimately, in 2012, only the Wibautstraat itself was redesigned. The plan to narrow the Weesperstraat to a single lane in each direction was (still) not carried out.

An open planning process involved close collaboration with residents from the surrounding neighborhoods, as well as representatives from various institutions and businesses, with different options being considered. Ultimately, the main desire was to transform the street into a city boulevard with bold buildings and a new layout from façade to façade, featuring wide sidewalks, a broad median, and rows of trees. This redesign made the street more pleasant and easier to cross. The rows of trees provide calm and structure. The only tree that can grow in this challenging location is the plane tree. To give them a chance to grow, the median was raised.

Almost all the large buildings have since been repurposed and renovated for

1

2

3

new uses. The buildings at the end of the Wibautstraat have been taken over by the Amsterdam University of Applied Sciences (HvA) and now form the Amstel Campus. The HvA developed plans to renovate the buildings (Benno Premselahuis, Koetsier-Montaignehuis, Kohnstammhuis) or to demolish and rebuild new ones. On the site of the Wibauthuis (demolished in 2007), which for many years housed numerous municipal services, you will now find the new Wibauthuis and part of the Muller-Lulofshuis. The construction of the Jakoba Mulderhuis was the final piece of the Amstel Campus development and, fittingly – architect 'Ko' Mulder worked for the Public Works Department – also houses urban planning students. Today, 27,000 people work and study at Amstel Campus, and nearly 300 student apartments are available.

The clustering of educational institutions led to many buildings across the city becoming available for other uses; the largest of these is the Leeuwenburg building near Amstel Station.

1 Jakoba Mulderhuis, atrium (photo: Sebastian van Damme)
2 Aerial photo, 2006
3 Aerial photo, 2023
4 Wibauthuis in 1994
5 Interior of the Wibauthuis
6 Jakoba Mulderhuis, design by Architekten Cie., Powerhouse Company, and Mark Koehler Architecten (photo: Sebastian van Damme)
7 Jakoba Mulderhuis, floor plan of the first floor
8 Overview map of the Amstel Campus

4

5

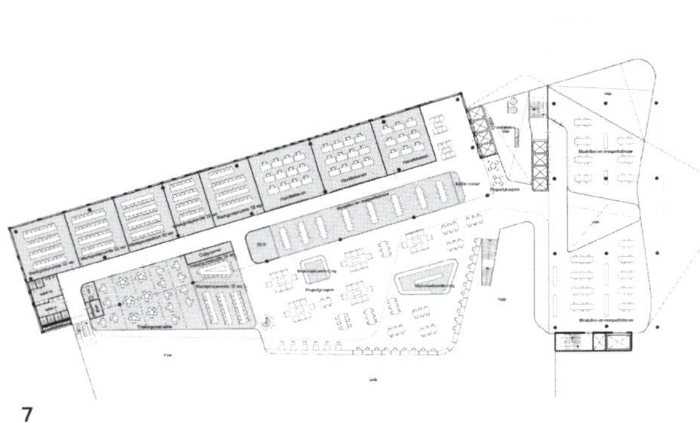

7

6

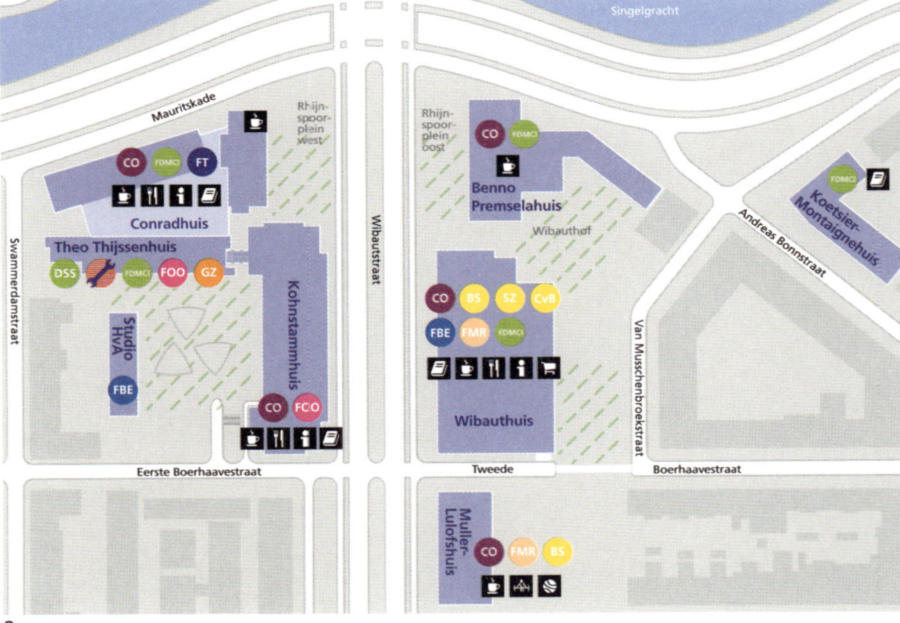

8

⓫ DE HALLEN

The complex now known as De Hallen was built between 1901 and 1928 as a tram depot for the Municipal Transport Company (GVB). Trams, and later buses, were stored and maintained here. Due to its function, the building was never open to the public. When the GVB ceased using the depot in the mid-1980s, it began a long period of vacancy, during which parts of the building were even squatted.

In 2007, the first renovation plan was created after the building was assigned a cultural purpose and designated as a national monument. However, this plan did not come to fruition. In 2011, a new plan by the 'Tramremise Ontwikkel Maatschappij' (TROM), with André van Stigt as the architect, was selected. The renovation was completed in 2014.

The complex, covering an impressive 22,000 m², houses a variety of neighborhood and urban functions, including a cinema complex, television studios, a library, a food hall, shops, and a hotel.

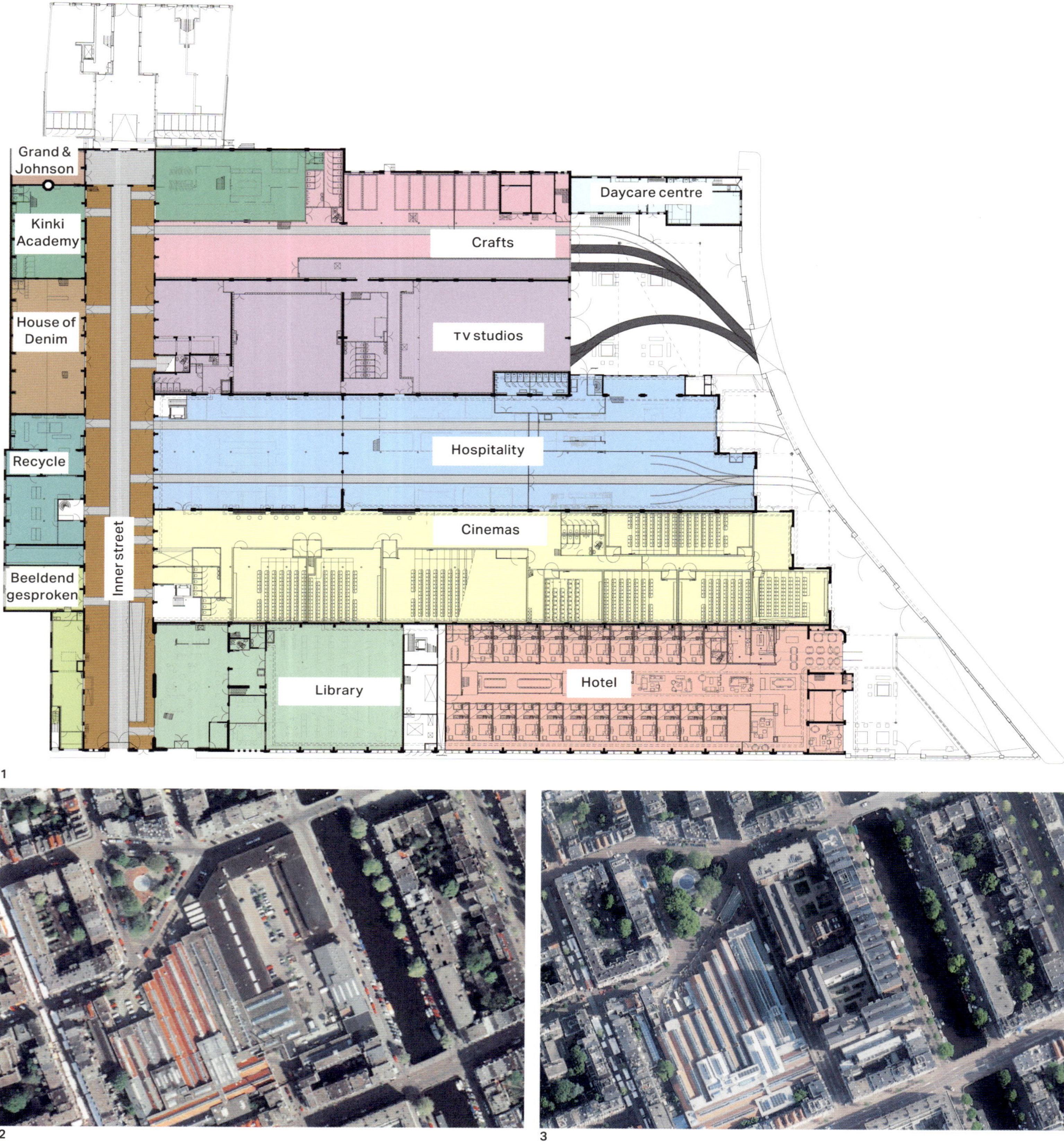

1

2

3

These are accessed via a public passage. In the vicinity of the depot complex, several residential buildings have also been added, including a complex for older LGBTQI+people.

1 Floor plan ground floor of De Hallen after renovation
2 Aerial photo, 2003
3 Aerial photo, 2023
4 Inner street in 1995
5 Inner street in 2014
6 Entrance to bicycle parking

4

5

6

1M OOSTERPARK

At the end of the 19th century and the beginning of the 20th century, a whole series of large buildings was constructed along the northern edge of Oosterpark, next to the 'dubbeltjeswoningen' (small and cheap apartments), including schools, an orphanage, university laboratories, and the KIT (Royal Tropical Institute) with the Tropenmuseum (now known as the Wereldmuseum). In the 1990s, the orphanage was transformed into a sleep-inn and event venue, Hotel Arena.

Around 2005, there was a desire to expand and renovate the KIT and Hotel Arena. This was seized upon by the Oost district to reconsider the entire northern edge of the park. This resulted in the vision 'Verdubbeling Oosterpark' (Doubling Oosterpark). The idea was to remove all the fences and hedges around the buildings and eliminate the messy parking lots throughout the northern edge of the park, which would lead to a doubling of the park's area. This would allow for a seamless connection to the southern part of Oosterpark with the beautiful, flowing lines from the design by L.A. Springer.

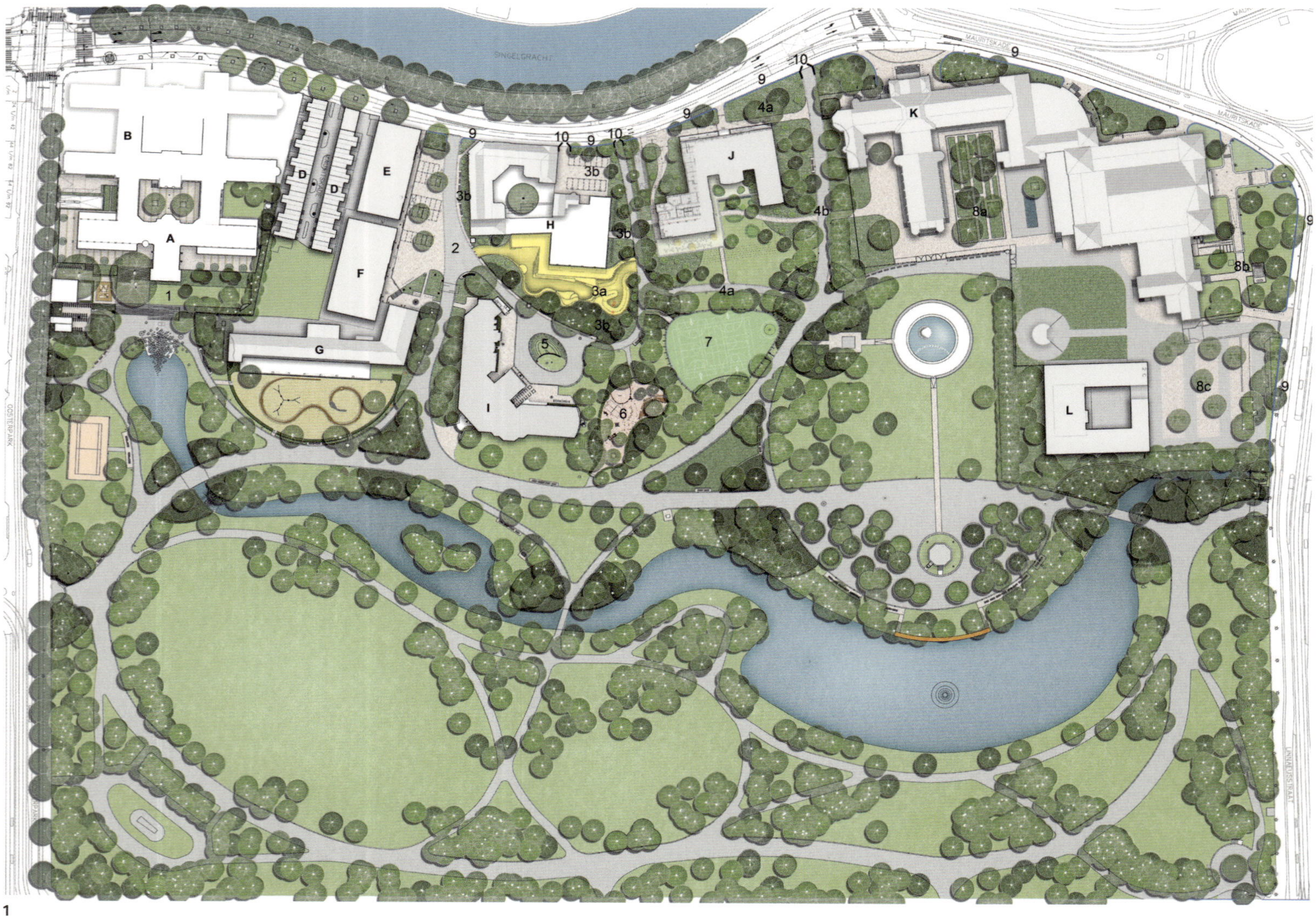

1

2

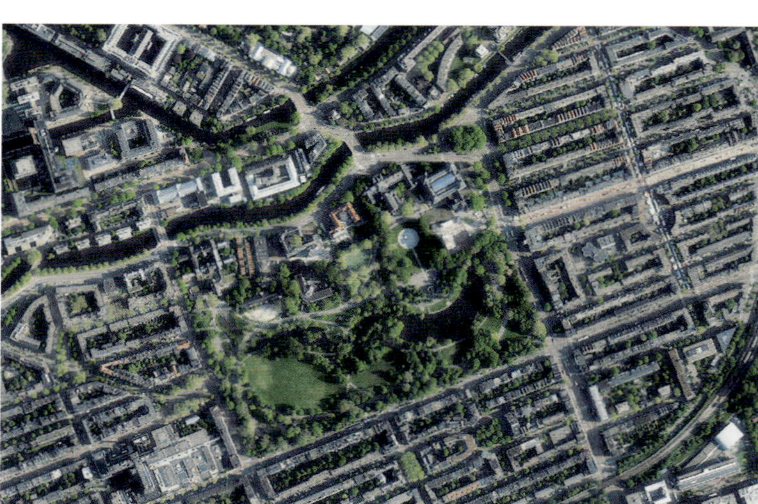

3

In 2015, the project was initiated based on a design by Buro Sant & Co. A new fence was constructed along the outer edge of the park, the path structure was adjusted, the planting was improved, and new play areas were created. Large stones were placed around a new pond near Hotel Arena where children can play. The buildings along the northern edge now mostly face the park, with entrances and large terraces on the park side. The latest addition to the park is a boutique hotel (also with a terrace facing the park) in the former Anatomical Laboratory building of the University of Amsterdam (designed in 1908 by Public Works architect J.B. Springer, the cousin of L.A. Springer).

1 Plan of Oosterpark renovation
2 Aerial photo, 2006
3 Aerial photo, 2023
4 Concept 'doubling' of Oosterpark
5 Oosterpark side of Hotel Arena, design by Team V Architectuur
6 Oosterpark in 1975
7-8 Play pond, design by Buro Sant en Co.

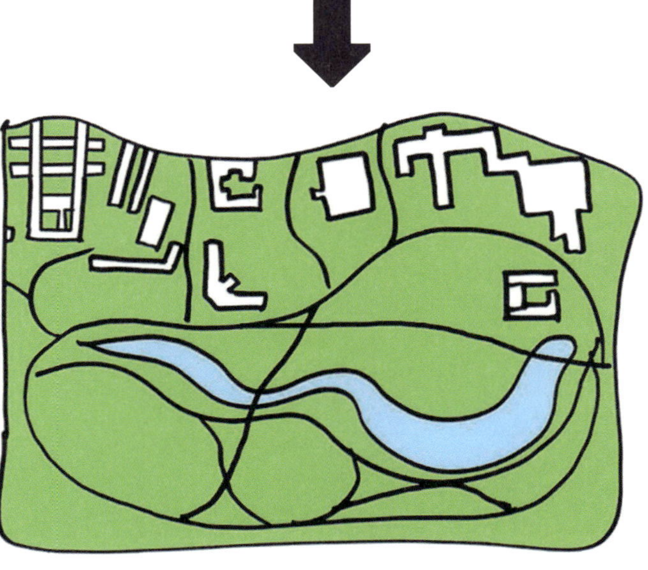

4

5

6

7

8

LOW-RISE HOUSING ON THE CITY EDGE — STOP THE EXODUS OF THE CITY

→ Julianapark East, 1975–2025

How could the departure of Amsterdam residents to the new towns be reversed? By the early 1970s, the dream of the 'city of the future' in Bijlmermeer had already faded. The honeycomb-shaped apartment blocks could not compete with the single-family homes in the new towns, complete with gardens and parking spaces right in front of the house.

The first response came in the late 1970s with a series of experiments featuring alternative block and plot layouts in Banne Noord, Nellestein, Holendrecht, and Reigersbos. While these projects addressed the desire for more architectural variety, they did not meet the demand for single-family homes. A new course was set in the early 1980s with the construction of Gein III and IV in Gaasperdam. The momentum continued into the 1990s with low-rise development in Sloten, Geuzenveld-West, Park Haagseweg, and De Aker in Nieuw-West, as well as Julianapark and Park de Meer in Oost. A wave of low-rise housing was also built across Noord, with De Bongerd and Elzenhagen-Noord as the most recent examples. To make space for these developments, agricultural businesses on the city's outskirts were bought out, allotment gardens were relocated, and sports parks were intensified – an intricate balancing act.

Around 2010, policy shifted. De Hoofdgroenstructuur (Main Green Structure) now protects sports parks and allotment gardens. As a result, in recent years, low-rise construction has been largely limited to smaller, former industrial sites such as Klein Kadoelen, Twiske-Zuid, and Papaverplantsoen in Noord. More often than not, these projects take the form of self-build housing.

MOVEMENT 2

To build housing on the city outskirts, you need to have control over the land. Amsterdam has a long history of annexing parts of surrounding municipalities for urban expansion. The largest annexation took place in 1921 when, after much pressure from the city, the national government added the municipalities of Sloten and Watergraafsmeer, the villages in Waterland, and parts of Nieuwer-Amstel and Oostzaan to Amsterdam. This made it possible to carry out large-scale urban expansions in the west and south and to develop Tuindorp Watergraafsmeer ('Betondorp') as well as the garden villages of Oostzaan, Buiksloot, and Nieuwendam. To enable this, all land was acquired by the municipality of Amsterdam and then leased out under the ground lease system.

Soon after World War II, it became clear that population growth and housing demand were far greater than anticipated when the General Expansion Plan was drafted. This made it necessary to consider expansions that had been deemed a step too far in the 1930s: in Noord, across the IJ, and in the Bijlmermeer, 'behind' Duivendrecht. A tunnel under the IJ and metro lines to Noord and the Bijlmermeer would connect these new developments to the city. However, this required further annexation of land from neighboring municipalities, which was no longer a given.

Ultimately, in 1966, the areas of Landsmeer and Oostzaan within the newly planned A10 Ring Road were incorporated into Amsterdam. At the same time, the municipality of Weesperkarspel, located southeast of the city, was dissolved, and its land was divided among four municipalities. The Bijlmermeer polder and the smaller surrounding polders were 'temporarily' assigned to Amsterdam.

This 'temporary' allocation of the Bijlmermeer to Amsterdam was the result of much debate. Instead of facilitating the further growth of large cities, the government explicitly focused on decentralization from the late 1950s onward. This culminated in 1966 with the Second Spatial Planning Report and the concept of new towns: the expansion of cities like Hoorn, Alkmaar, and Purmerend, villages like Zoetermeer, Spijkenisse, Nieuwegein, and Houten, and the creation of entirely new cities like Lelystad. Was this driven by fear of American-style suburbanization, or by a desire for more manageable, less anonymous urban

→ Movement – Relocation of horticulture, sports fields, and allotments for low-rise housing on the city outskirts

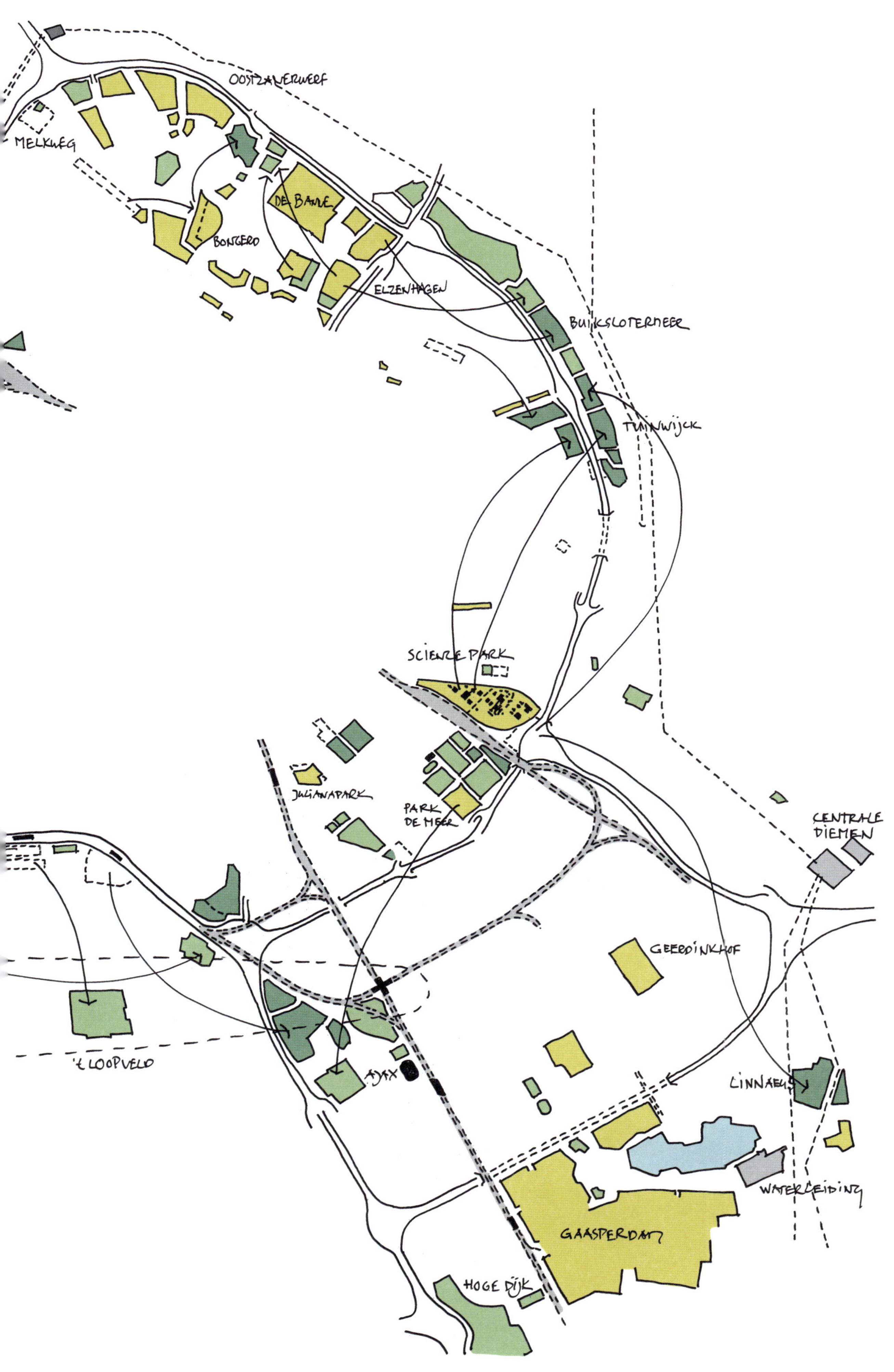
OOSTZANERWERF
MELKWEG
DE BANNE
BONGERD
ELZENHAGEN
BUIKSLOTERMEER
TUINWIJCK
SCIENCE PARK
JULIANAPARK
PARK DE MEER
CENTRALE DIEMEN
GEERDINKHOF
'T LOOPVELD
AJAX
LINNAEUS
WATERLEIDING
GAASPERDAM
HOGE DIJK

1

areas?[1] The report was prepared under the conservative Marijnen cabinet and released under the Catholic-Socialist Cals cabinet. The decentralization concept remained intact, but Amsterdam was granted the desired expansion opportunities in the north and southeast, with the latter being 'temporary'. Additionally, an unusual limitation was imposed: between the city and the new expansion in the southeast, Diemen and Duivendrecht (Ouder-Amstel) would remain independent. The Bijlmer would become an 'exclave'. After construction, the new city was to become independent, just like Amstelveen and Zaanstad. This would limit the size and the 'power' of Amsterdam.

In 1962, the Public Works Department published the *Structuurschema Agglomeratie Amsterdam 2000* (Structure Plan Agglomeration of Amsterdam 2000). The map dates back to before the annexations, and all the old municipal borders are clearly marked. The map provides a clear view of the concept for the development of the agglomeration, which had been agreed upon in previous years with the neighboring municipalities and the province. Existing cities and towns are shown in black, and in red are all the post-war neighborhoods under active construction at the time: the Western Garden Cities (Westelijke Tuinsteden), Buitenveldert, and North (Noord) in Amsterdam, the expansions of Amstelveen (Nieuwer-Amstel) and Weesp, and smaller neighborhoods in Badhoevedorp, Ouderkerk, Diemen, Landsmeer, and Zaandam. The areas shaded in pink are all the newly projected expansions: Poelenburg in Zaandam, new neighborhoods in North and on the territories of Landsmeer and Oostzaan, a doubling of Amstelveen, and the largest one, the Bijlmermeer, on the territory of Weesperkarspel.

This creates a pattern that is referred to in urban planning literature as a *finger city*. The expansions are laid out like the fingers of a hand in the landscape, with green wedges in between. The landscape is always nearby. On a smaller scale, this concept had already been experimented with in the Western Garden Cities. The Zaan region, Amstelveen, and the Bijlmermeer became large new 'fingers'.

New infrastructure

Part of the plan was a vast infrastructure program in the urban fringe. First, there was the port expansion around the North Sea Canal – marked in purple – on the western side. A large new industrial area was also planned in the southeast, between the A2 highway and the railway line to Utrecht, accessed by a canal extending from the Duivendrechtse Vaart.

Equally important was the expansion of the road and rail network. A ring road around the city was projected (the current A10), with a second ring (the A9) further out. The concept of a ring road wasn't new. In Movement 1, we already encountered an inner and outer ring in the Singelgracht zone. Not far off, in the 19th century, the Ceintuurbaan had been laid out as a central avenue connecting the city expansions from that time. The plans of Berlage and Van Eesteren also featured ring roads, though these were made up of broad lanes leading from square to square, such as Apollolaan in the South and Hoofdweg in the West. A remnant of the ring road designed by Van Eesteren is the Kennedylaan, between Europaplein and Berlagebrug.

In the 1962 plan, however, it was proposed that the ring road be part of the national motorway network, on an embankment, with grade-separated intersections, a limited number of on- and off-ramps, and direct connections to the sprawling highways in various directions – from the A1 to the A8. The breakthrough through the eastern city center connects to the north side via the IJ Tunnel and Leeuwarderweg to a motorway heading towards Purmerend and Hoorn. On the southern side, the Gooiseweg continues via the Bijlmer and Weesp towards Hilversum.

Parallel to the ring road in the North lies a wide new canal, appropriately named *Kanaal om de Noord* (Canal around the North), designed to relieve the heavy shipping traffic over the IJ. This also meant that the North Holland Canal through the North and the Willem locks lost their func-

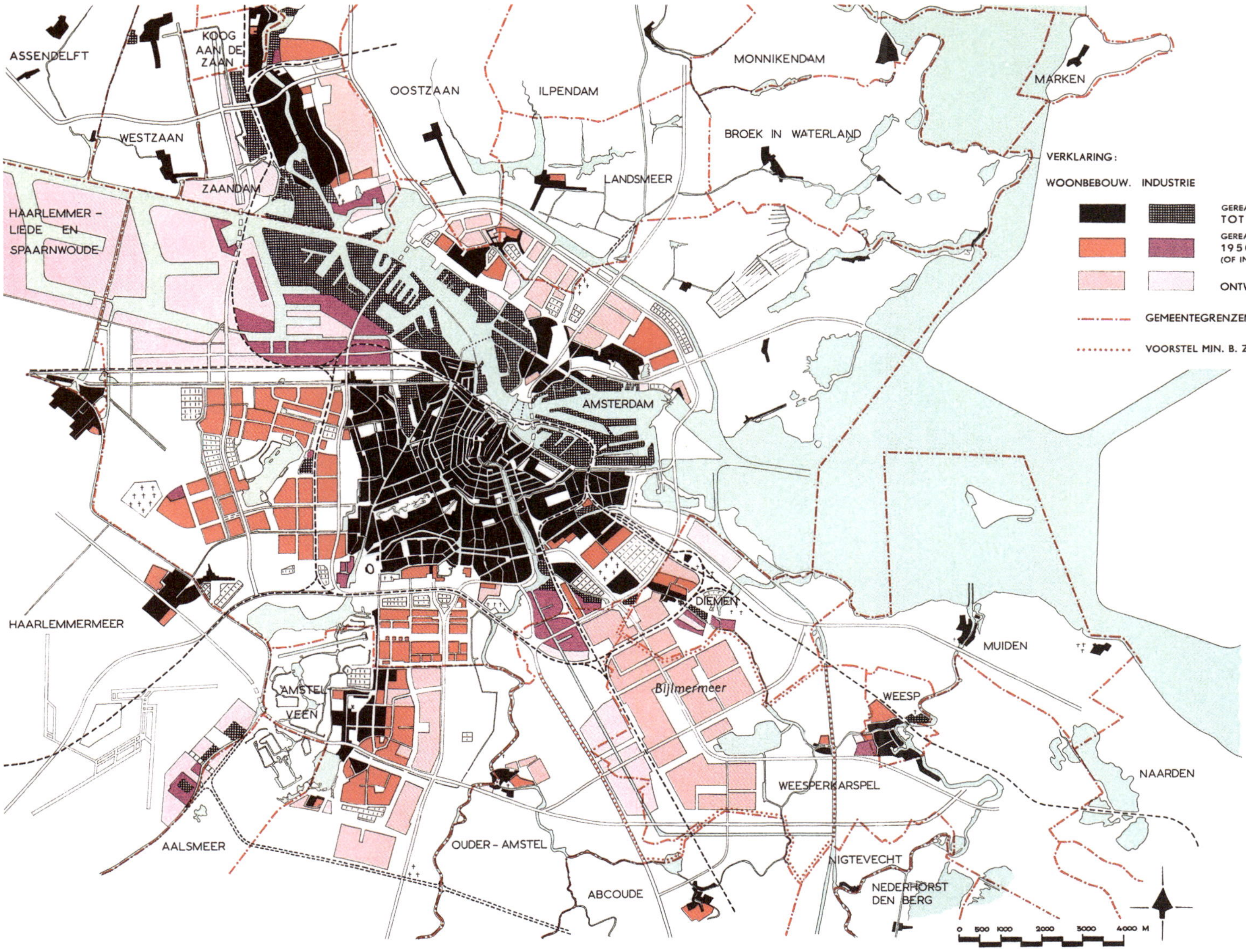

2

tion. The canal could be filled in. However, *Kanaal om de Noord* was not realized. What was constructed was a high-voltage power line, some distance from the A10 – along the northern bank of the planned canal – running from the new Diemen power plant to the north and towards Hoogovens (Tata Steel).

Ideas for new railway infrastructure on the west and south sides of the city date back to the 19th century. In the 1930s, in line with the AUP, work began on the embankment for the Ring Railway, but it wasn't until the 1970s and 1980s that the western and southern branches were completed. The catalyst for this was the Schiphol line, a fast connection to The Hague via the new terminal complex at the greatly expanded Schiphol.

Interestingly, the newly designed metro network is not shown on the map. As early as 1960, the Public Works Department published the study *Het stedelijk openbaar vervoer in de agglomeratie Amsterdam* (Urban Public Transport in the Amsterdam Agglomeration), outlining the contours of an extensive metro network, with the current Noord/Zuidlijn (North/South Line) and Oostlijn (East Line) as the central 'spine' connecting the new urban expansion in the Bijlmermeer to the city. The urban planning for the Bijlmer was entirely based on the metro line's route, the station locations, and the associated walking distances. However, the area being planned still did not fall under Amsterdam's jurisdiction in 1962, and metro funding had not been secured. It wasn't until 1968 that the plans for the 'city railway' were approved by the city council, including the final design for the Bijlmermeer and the government's commitment to covering 50% of the costs.

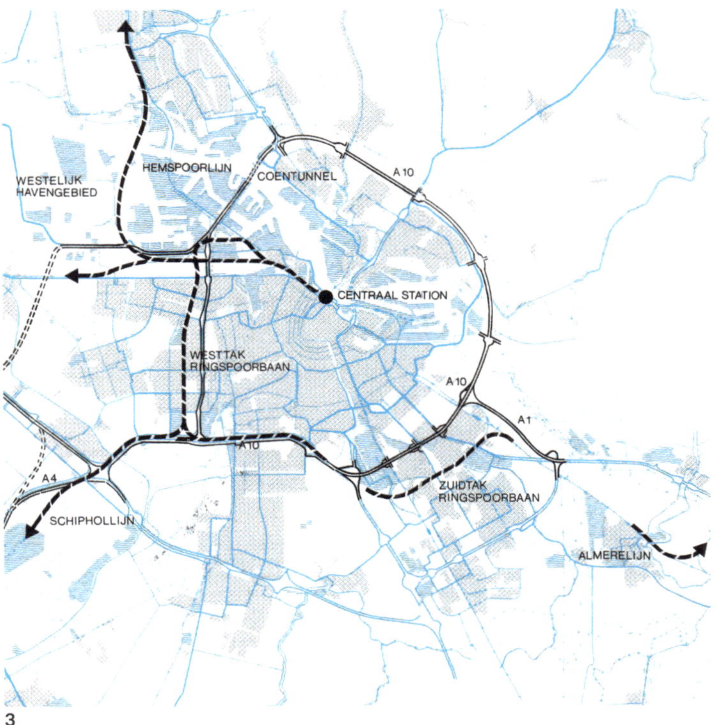

3

1 Sloten, 1975–2025
2 Structural diagram Agglomeration Amsterdam, 1964
3 Ring Road A10, west and south branches of the railway network (drawing from the Structural Plan 'The City Central', 1984–1986). The new infrastructure was realized in phases: the A10 between 1966 and 1990, the railway lines with the new stations between 1978 and 1993

1 Aerial photo construction allotment garden park Tuinwijck next to projected A10-North, seen in north-western direction, 1975

2 Sports parks and allotment gardens Amsterdam, 2025

From land reclamation and industrial construction to fitting and measuring

In the 1960s, work began in earnest on the implementation of the new perspective for the development of the agglomeration.[2] In the North, Nieuwendam-Noord, Banne Zuid, Het Breed, and Molenwijk were built before 1975. This continued the earlier developments of subdivisions around courtyards such as those implemented in the garden cities of Nieuw-West and Buitenveldert. At prominent locations, high-rise buildings were constructed, often with ten floors and accessed by galleries and elevators.[3] Industrial construction methods were experimented with for this type of building, where prefabricated floors and walls were assembled at the construction site.[4] The construction of Molenwijk and the Bijlmer further developed and applied these construction systems on a large scale. In Molenwijk, 1,200 homes were built using the Indeco-Coignet system. In the Bijlmer, more than 12,500 industrial homes were built, including the flats in the E-, F-, G-, H-, and K-neighborhoods; around 7,000 of these were built using the EBA-II system.

In 1975, the final honeycomb flats, Hakfort and Huigenbos, were completed. Nellestein was then a friendlier variant, but after that, the city definitively moved away from high-rise buildings. The South Bijlmer was named Gaasperdam. In Gaasperdam, and later also in Banne Noord and Oostzanerwerf, a combination of mid-rise buildings in three and four floors and low-rise single-family homes was chosen.

By this time, all areas that had become available due to the 1966 annexations had been used. There was no longer support for new annexations. New low-rise projects could only be realized by finding space within the municipal boundaries.

A relatively simple option was to use land reservations for the construction of new roads for low-rise buildings. For example, in the North, this occurred with the repurposing of land for the Zuiderzeeweg and the 'extension' of the Purmerweg. Housing was built on the latter route at the edge of Floradorp and at Buiksloterbreek. A whole series of industrial areas in the North were also converted into low-rise neighborhoods: the Nintemanterrein, De Bongerd, and more recently several smaller areas, such as the Marjoleinterrein, Twiske-Zuid, and Kiekensterrein, all with 40 to 100 single-family homes.

The main candidates for new developments were Landelijk West, the Watergraafsmeer in the East, and the Buikslotermeer in the North. Existing agricultural functions had to be purchased for housing construction, allotment gardens and sports parks had to be relocated. What followed was a long process of adjusting and redesigning – a slow reimagining of the urban fringe. In fact, this process continues to this day with the redesign of the Brettenzone and the Tuinen van West.

Looking at it now from a distance, three major developments can be identified. Firstly, nearly all the glasshouse horticulture businesses in the city were bought out. In addition, many sports parks and allotment gardens were moved 'outward', sometimes literally outside the municipal boundaries, sometimes within the municipality: at Driemond and in the transition zone to Waterland along the A10. Moreover, the use of sports fields was greatly intensified by the use of artificial grass and the merging of clubs. This freed up much space for housing.

The three major developments are discussed in more detail below. In the last ten years, a shift in direction has been observed, with an increasing focus on integrating sports complexes and allotment parks into new urban areas.

Horticulture

Landelijk West had undergone a major transformation since the annexation of the municipality of Sloten. A large part of the polders had been peat bogs and were used in the 1950s and 1960s to relocate horticultural businesses in order to make space for the construction of the garden cities Overtoomse Veld and Slotervaart. Field crops were replaced by greenhouse horticulture. Supported by a significant subsidy from the government, the businesses around the Louwesweg and in the Akerpolder were bought out in the late 1980s. These areas were raised and then developed. Around 5,400 homes were built both in Nieuw Sloten and De Aker, mostly as single-family homes.

Outdoors

A significant number of 'Amsterdam' sports clubs play in sports parks outside the city limits. Traditionally, hockey, rowing, and horseback riding have been done in the Amsterdam Forest, which is on Amstelveen's land. In the early 1990s, a large tennis complex was added to the Vietnamweide, relocated from the old site on the Zuidas where the ABN AMRO headquarters was built. During the same years, Sportpark 't Loopveld opened in Amstelveen. The municipality of Amsterdam purchased the land, set up the fields, and then rented them out to associations, such as Nautilus on Valentijnkade in the East. Amstelveen made the sports park possible through a zoning plan. With Ajax's move from Middenweg to the Amsterdam Arena, the

2

1

1 Buiksloterbanne North, 1975–2025
2 Food garden IJplein, established 2014

2

youth team relocated to sports complex De Toekomst just west of the Arena; later, the women's team also played there. On the old Ajax site, the residential neighborhood Park de Meer was built. The police sports fields at the Police Academy on Sloterweg were relocated to Overamstel, making room for the residential neighborhood Park Haagseweg.

In the case of allotment garden parks, the movement to the outskirts was even more pronounced. In the 1960s, three allotment garden associations had already moved to Duivendrecht to make room for the construction of Buitenveldert. In the 1980s and 1990s, nearly all the allotment garden parks from Watergraafsmeer were moved to Driemond and to the strip along the A10 in the North, in the transition to Waterland. Sports and allotment garden parks from North itself also moved to this strip, with Tuinpark Buikslotermeer relocating in 2004. This made the construction of Elzenhagen-Noord possible. Further along, the allotment garden association De Bongerd had already moved to Kadoelen in the 1990s. On the old site, the new low-rise neighborhood De Bongerd was built.

On the west side of the city, allotment gardens had to be reduced to make room for the construction of the A4. In compensation, Tuinpark Ons Buiten was expanded, and new gardens were established along Osdorperweg, such as the Nieuwe Bijenpark. Several attempts were also made to relocate Ons Buiten entirely. This would have allowed for housing to be built near Nieuwe Meer at the Oude Haagseweg, but this plan was eventually abandoned.

A similar process occurred around the construction of new railway lines near Sloterdijk. The Sloterdijkermeer allotment garden association was downsized. In compensation, new gardens were created further west: De Bretten and Groote Braak. Some utility gardens from Nieuw-West were also relocated.

A few smaller garden parks were closed down: Julianapark, Molukken, Blijkmeer on Zeeburgereiland. By the early 2020s, around 6,000 allotment gardeners were active across 29 parks.

Artificial grass and mergers

The area of sports fields in the city in 2025 is much smaller than in 1975, while the number of athletes in club associations has actually increased. The main reason for this is that the use of fields could be much more intensive with the introduction of artificial grass. On natural grass, a maximum of 350 hours of play per year is possible, and not too often in succession; on a mix of artificial and natural grass, 700 hours of play is possible, and on 100% artificial grass, play can happen at any time.

With the increased use of fields, numerous mergers of clubs took place. In 1975, there were more than 100 football clubs – the largest organized sport in Amsterdam – now there are 57.[5] The number of football players increased: from 25,000 to 35,000! Women's football grew, and now instead of starting at the age of 10, you can start playing football as young as six. There are many youth teams, and they also play on smaller fields. Various sports have also changed in character or are being practiced less; 11-a-side football is increasingly becoming 6-a-side. Korfball is also played on smaller fields; handball has mainly become an indoor sport. The number of participants in athletics, baseball, and cycling has remained fairly stable, but tennis, for example, has declined. The greyhound racing track at Sportcentrum Ookmeer was closed in 2003.

Due to the intensification and mergers, several sports parks could close, such as sports park De Aker and more recently Melkweg and Riekerhaven. The 'densification' of Sportpark de Eendracht created space for the low-rise neighborhood Geuzenveld-West; part of the Buiksloterbanne sports park became the Banne Zuidcost neighborhood. The partial availability of this last sports park also played a role in the experiment with a second professional football club, next to Ajax. FC Amsterdam was formed in 1972 by merging the top teams from DWS, Blauw-Wit, and De Volewijckers. The experiment at the Olympic Stadium lasted until 1982. However, De Volewijckers never became as large as it was in the 1960s. Ultimately, the club even merged with its eternal rival, DWV, in 2013.

Integration

In recent years, there has been an increasing focus on integrating sports complexes into new urban areas, following the model of the Olympiaplein in Amsterdam-Zuid. An interesting example is the Laan van Spartaan. After the relocation of the baseball players of Amsterdam Pirates to Ookmeer, sportpark Jan van Galen was reduced in size. The football fields of VVA/Spartaan are now situated in the central area of the new residential neighborhood. A similar concept was long in development for Zeeburgereiland. The idea was that football club Zeeburgia would play there, but now instead, a skate park has been created in that location. The old athletics track at Elzenhagen has been rotated and integrated into the urban planning for the new neighborhood.

A special form of integration is the sports fields on the roof of the Smart Mobility Hub at the Johan Cruijff ArenA. Construction began in 2025.[6]

An example of integrating allotment gardens is the Klein Dantzig garden park. It is part of the new Park Frankendael, located on the site of the old city nursery in the Watergraafsmeer. An open public walking route runs through the garden park, which is closed at night. This idea is now being further developed in many other allotment parks, such as the garden parks near Westerpark. Public routes expand the Westerpark, creating new connections from West to the newly developing city neighborhoods in Haven-Stad.

In various locations, experiments are being conducted with other forms of gardening. This is happening on a large scale in the Tuinen van West. In North Amsterdam, smaller forms of 'urban farming' can be found at IJplein, NoordOogst, and Sixhaven.

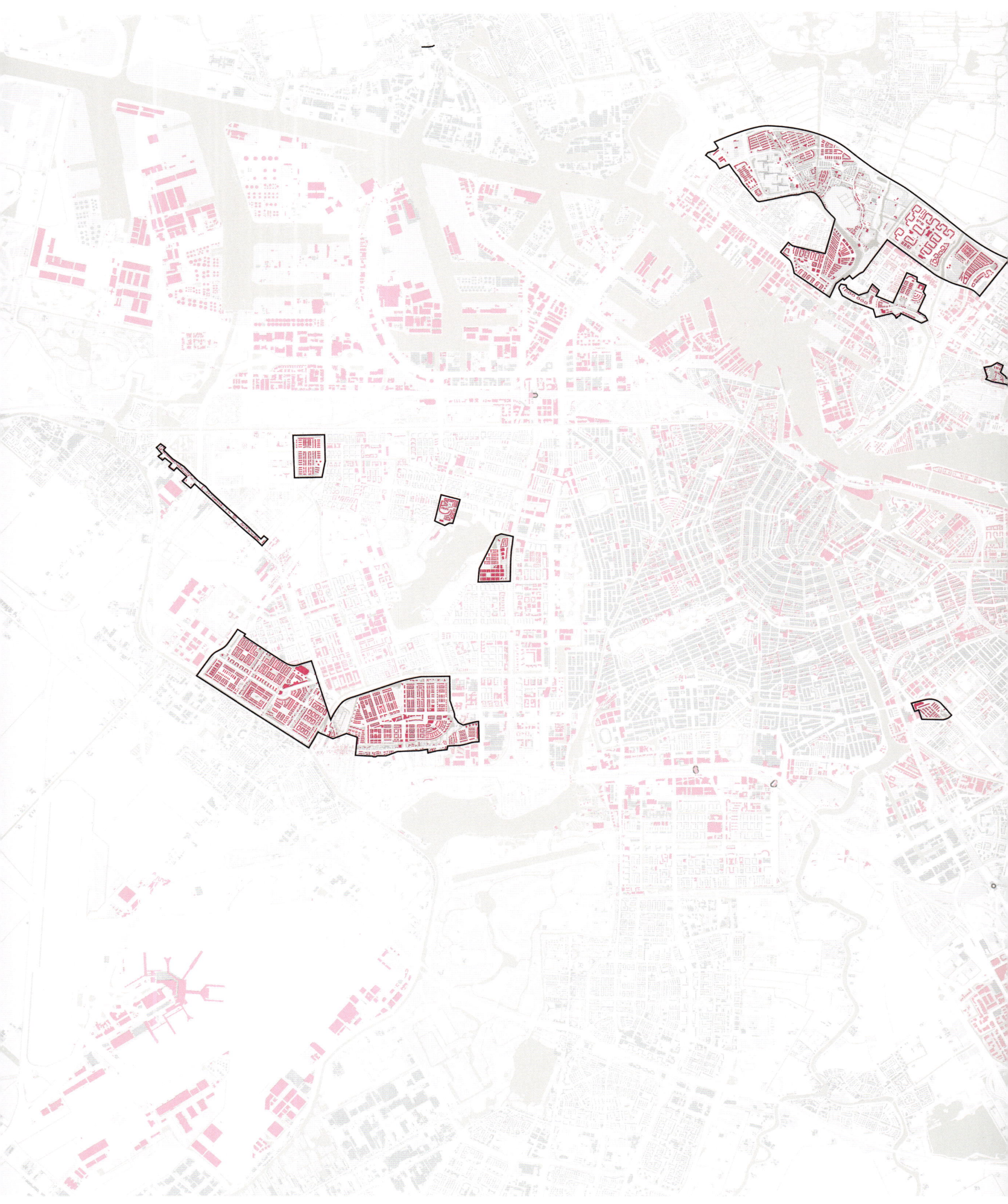

The concept of a 'compact city' doesn't typically evoke the construction of low-rise neighborhoods. Instead, it often brings to mind intensive building in urban densities. However, the Structuurplan 'De stad centraal' (Structural Plan 'The City Central') of 1986 fully embraced low-rise development, with the idea that it could prevent more Amsterdammers from moving to the new towns. A substantial supply of single-family homes with gardens in an attractive, quiet residential environment at the edge of the city was considered crucial. An additional argument was that this would help avoid extra commuting and prevent further damage to the landscape. These considerations were revisited a few years later in the national VINEX policy. The Vierde Nota Extra (Fourth Supplementary Report) of 1991 identified several new locations for large-scale housing construction near cities, accessible by stations and, in many cases, new tram lines. Amsterdam's policy had already anticipated this.

In total, around 20,000 low-rise homes were built in the city between 1975 and 2025, including approximately 1,000 on individual self-build plots, but excluding IJburg and low-rise development in urban renewal areas. The size, design, and methods of access to the low-rise neighborhoods vary significantly.

Gaasperdam is still a classic urban expansion. In the new garden cities of Landelijk West, there was ample experimentation with compact low-rise buildings. Recent neighborhoods showcase a wide variety of building forms.

Gaasperdam

The development of the southern part of the urban expansion of Zuidoost followed a classical method: agricultural land in the 'outer area' was purchased, raised, and made suitable for construction (including the creation of water channels, roads, sewage systems, metro) and then carried out in phases. The subsoil was less unstable than in the Bijlmermeerpolder, and the sand for the raising came from nearby, from what is now the Gaasperplas. The entire process ultimately took twenty years, starting with the first groundworks in the late 1960s.

In the layout of Gaasperdam, the characteristic zoning principle of the Bijlmer around the metro lines and the elevated

← Built in the urban fringe, 1975–2025

avenues was gradually abandoned. This can clearly be seen in the plans for the three consecutively built neighborhoods around the stations Holendrecht, Reigersbos, and Gein.

Holendrecht still has a strict layout with stacked buildings in the 400-meter zone from the metro and low-rise buildings in the adjacent zone up to 800 meters, with an extension leading to a park. The neighborhoods are accessed (and separated) by elevated roads with parking lots alongside them.

In Reigersbos, you will find many more mixed forms of construction, but the most characteristic feature is the central car-free shopping street on both sides of the station with housing above the shops, as well as a market square, a sports hall, and a secondary school. The roads are built halfway up, with tunnels for pedestrians and cyclists. The low-rise buildings in the southern edge have a nice flow towards the newly developed recreation area around the Hoge Dijk, with the nature organization De Ruige Hof.

Around Gein Metro Station, almost only low-rise buildings were constructed, extending to the municipal and provincial borders. The main roads here are also built halfway up, but parking mostly takes place in the residential streets. In the transition to the open meadows around the Gein river, there are walking and cycling routes. The transition to the Gaasperpark around the lake is less attractive. Although the extension of the Gooiseweg to Weesp and the Gooi was abandoned, the layout still gives a temporary and fragmented impression.

The housing densities in the low-rise neighborhoods are around 30 homes per hectare, comparable to the densities in the new towns.[7]

New garden cities in Landelijk West

Under the leadership of the Steering Group for Additional Housing Locations, new housing locations were sought starting in 1978.[8] Reports identified the polders in Landelijk West as the most suitable large locations: the Middelveldse Akerpolder, the Lutkemeer, and the three Osdorper polders. Sloten was initially not included, mainly due to the expected high buy-out costs for the gardeners. Three models were drawn up and compared in terms of the number of homes and land costs. The model with the most homes – 27,000! – was the favorite: a series of neighborhoods in the polders around a tram line from Stadionplein to a new railway station near Geuzenveld. The proposal elicited various comments, not least because the cherished finger structure of the city would be affected. The green wedge of Sloterpark, through Ookmeer and the Osdorper polders to the outskirts, would be transformed into a central park. A condition for construction was the rotation or closure of the fourth runway at Schiphol, the Zwanenburgbaan. However, in 1982 it was determined that this was not feasible. Only the Middelveldse Akerpolder and, in fact, Sloten fell outside the noise contours of the airport and were suitable for housing construction. The decision was made to 'widen' the southwest finger of Amsterdam.

Design studies and calculations, however, showed that much higher densities than usual would need to be achieved to make the plans work. Even then, a substantial national contribution per home would be required. A solution came in 1986 with Amsterdam's bid for the 1992 Olympic Games. Nieuw Sloten became the Olympic village in the bid book for Amsterdam's 'Compact Games.' It was agreed to achieve a density of 55 homes per hectare with 80% low-rise; the national government offered a subsidy of 20,000 guilders per home. Ultimately, Barcelona won the Games, but Amsterdam gained Nieuw Sloten (and the Arena).

A broad north-south traffic road was originally planned through the Sloten area. This was scrapped, and after an agreement was reached on a much smaller traffic system, preparations for execution could begin. Design workshops and study assignments showed that the high densities might be feasible, but this assumed a carefully designed public space, smart use of corners and edges by the water, and the application of different housing typologies than the

1

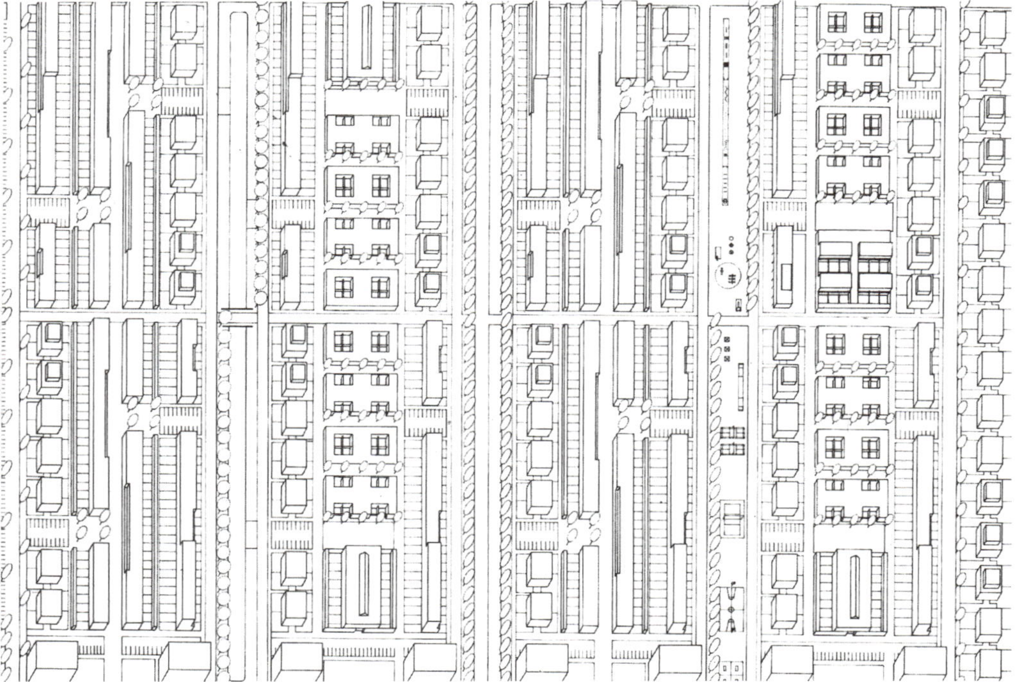

2

3

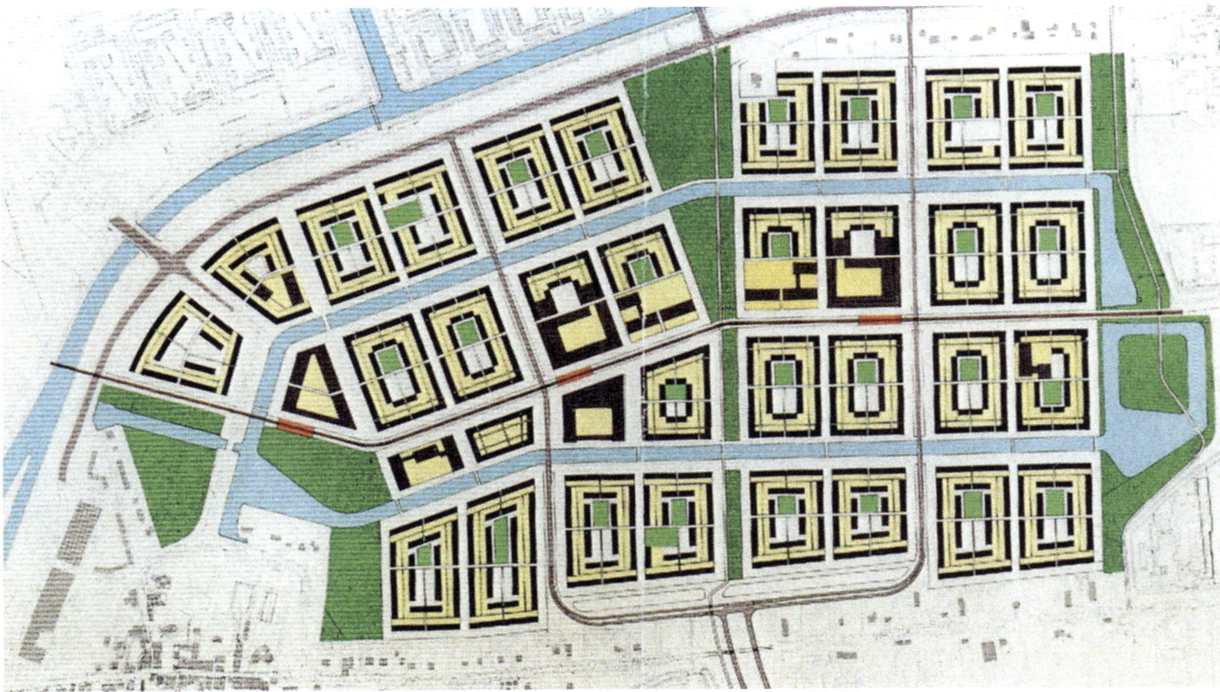

1 Gaasperdam
2 Plotting study for Nieuw-Sloten, design by DKV architects, 1987
3 Central park model Landelijk West, new garden cities around a park, design by DRO, 1983
4 Urban design of Nieuw-Sloten, with low-rise housing in double courtyards, design by DRO-Hans Davidson, 1985

4

traditional single-family row houses from the new towns. To make this possible, a development model was chosen in which architects and developers were assigned building strips with space for 300-500 homes. A supervisor oversaw the coherence and could allocate a budget of 2,000 guilders per home from a quality fund for specific solutions for the transition between private and public spaces. Landscape architect Alle Hosper and later Lodewijk Baljon excelled in the role of supervisor.

In the neighborhoods ultimately developed in Nieuw Sloten, a range of new housing typologies was applied: traditional single-family homes, but also narrow three-story homes, duplex apartments, quadrant homes, patio houses, and homes with terraces by the water instead of gardens. In addition, great attention was paid to transitions with hedges, pergolas, and garden walls. By 1995, nearly 5,000 homes had been completed, with a density of 50 homes per hectare and 70% low-rise.

In the following years, De Aker followed, where approximately the same number of homes were built, and the same development formula was applied. A referendum blocked the extension of the tram line from Sloten to the new neighborhood. The green area of the Vrije Geer near the village of Sloten was preserved. An alternative was the extension of the tram from Osdorp along the Calandlaan. A new center was built at the Verlengde Calandlaan and the Ecuplein. The low-rise neighborhoods in De Aker derive their quality mainly from their location along the wide green strip by the Ringvaart of the Haarlemmermeerpolder, the Groene As.

1

2

Urban landscape

Most of the other low-rise locations developed in the city over the past decades are much smaller, ranging in size from 2 to 1,000 homes. A whole series of these can be found in Amsterdam-Noord: larger ones, such as Oostzanerwerf, Twiske-Oost, the Walvisbuurt, Buiksloterbanne, Jeugdland, De Bongerd, and Elzenhagen-Noord, as well as smaller ones, often on former industrial sites like 't Twiske-Zuid and Klein Kadoelen.

In the east, these include Julianapark, Park de Meer, and housing at the end of Zeeburgerdijk, all with a mix of low-rise and apartment buildings. In Landelijk West, around the Osdorperweg and Sloterweg, there is a special form of intensification. On former industrial plots, and sometimes on the site of demolished annex buildings, hundreds of mostly detached homes have been added.

During the real estate crisis, this segment of the housing market was also recognized at the policy level. While developers and housing corporations were struggling, individual 'self-builders' managed to construct around 1,000 homes on 'found land' across the city since 2011.[9]

The most beautiful low-rise neighborhood in recent years is Klein Kadoelen. On the Wilmkebreek, a new neighborhood with 50 homes has been built on the former factory site of the Kiekens company. DELVA designed the urban plan. In addition to the houses, which feature architecture referencing Waterland barns, a triangular square has been created with a view of the low-lying polder of the Breek. There, geese and sheep wander around, and you can watch the sun set.

1 Klein Kadoelen
2 Papaverplantsoen

RESIDENTIAL, BLOCK, AND PLOT LAYOUTS

In addition to the honeycomb flats, three low-rise neighborhoods were also developed in the Bijlmer in the early 1970s: Geerdinkhof, Kantershof, and Kelbergen. The latter two are characteristic examples of woonerven (car-free residential streets) inspired by early experiments in Emmen. Rows of eight family homes, with storage sheds in the front yard, are located along wide, car-free residential paths around sunken parking courtyards. Through generously planted green strips, you can easily walk to the surrounding green areas.

Examples of what were named 'cauliflower neighborhoods' from a few years later can be found not in Amsterdam, but in Diemen, Duivendrecht, and Landsmeer. The low-rise neighborhoods built in Amsterdam after 1980 all have a more structured design, drawing from successful pre-war low-rise neighborhoods, such as in Watergraafsmeer, with tree-lined avenues and canals and front doors facing the street. This approach was first applied in Gein and later most explicitly in Nieuw Sloten, the Middelveldse Akerpolder, and Geuzenveld-West. Parking is provided on the street. Corners and block ends are used for special housing types. Over time, the houses become taller – ranging from two to three and sometimes four stories – and sometimes narrower. Scattered throughout are playgrounds, incorporated into the layout.

Density is further increased by experimenting with housing types. On the Oostoever, the architectural firm Duinker-van der Torre ingeniously interwoven upper-lower homes with rear houses and patios. The architecture firm Mecanoo solved parking in an innovative way at Park Haagseweg. In the first phase of De Bongerd, Rudy Uytenhaak built a distinctive type of quadrant homes in three stories along residential paths, with parking on private land.

Self-builders often maximize the allowable floor area within the spatial and functional guidelines of the building envelope. The most interesting experiments take place on 'difficult' plots. One of the first self-build projects in Noord, on Bosrankstraat, for example, was built against a blank wall of an adjacent commercial building. The high and relatively shallow homes are oriented toward front gardens and a quiet residential courtyard. A little further along at Papaverplantsoen, very deep plots were available, and an inner street was created. Most of the homes are built in four stories and also have large rear houses along the inner street. Parking is integrated inside, but there are also studios and workspaces, which are sometimes rented out as complete, independent homes.

Scattered across the neighborhood in Noord are several hidden plots where semi-detached houses and detached homes have been built; for example, at the bottom of Nieuwendammerdijk around Meerpad and Die, or the new Waterland barns of Klein Kadoelen. Parking is often provided on a small plot at the edge. The homes are accessed by residential paths with hedges along the way, creating a very intimate streetscape.

This trial and error resulted in a variety of more urban forms of low-rise housing, with expressive architecture.

→ **Next page:**
Nieuw Sloten, design
Hans Ruijssenaars, 1995

2C PARK HAAGSEWEG 1992

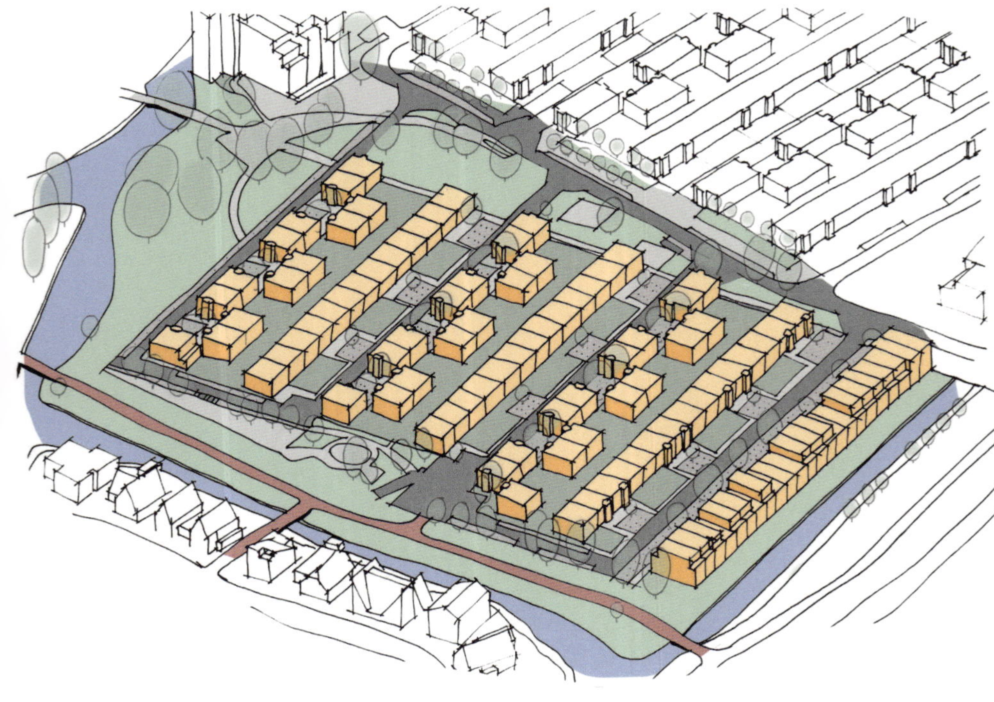

Features
Single-family homes with compact parking solution

Urban planning – supervision
Mecanoo

Architects
Mecanoo

Construction period
1990–1992

Homes per hectare
45

Average home size
111 m²

2D OOSTOEVER 1996

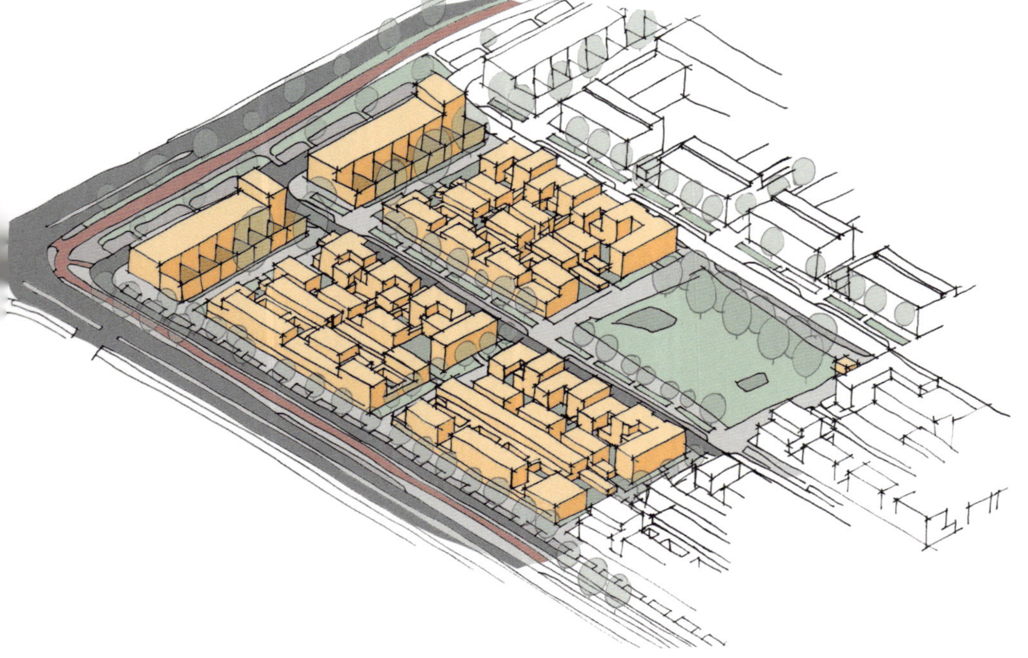

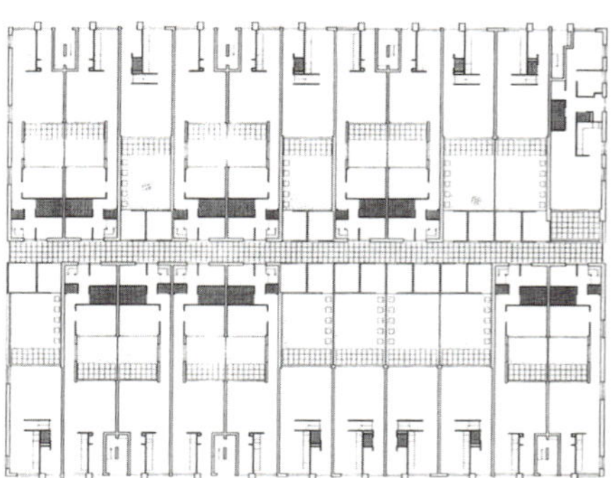

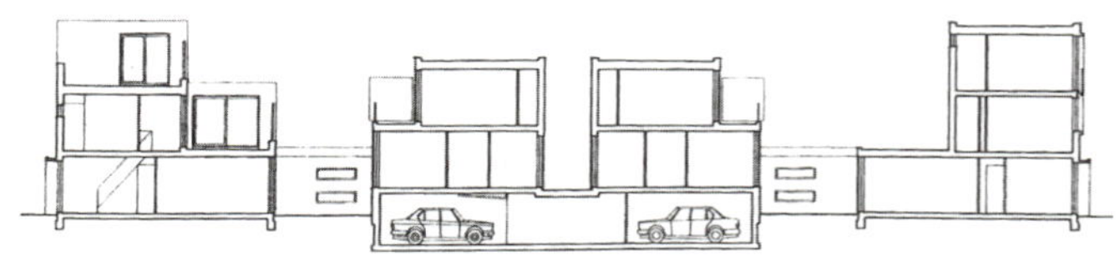

Features
Linked, deep upper-lower homes in street layout with rear paths

Urban planning – supervision
Mark Eker, Maurits de Hoog
(De Hoog ontwerp en onderzoek)

Architects
Duinker-van der Torre

Construction period
1994–1996

Homes per hectare
65

Average home size
95 m²

2A KELBERGEN 1975

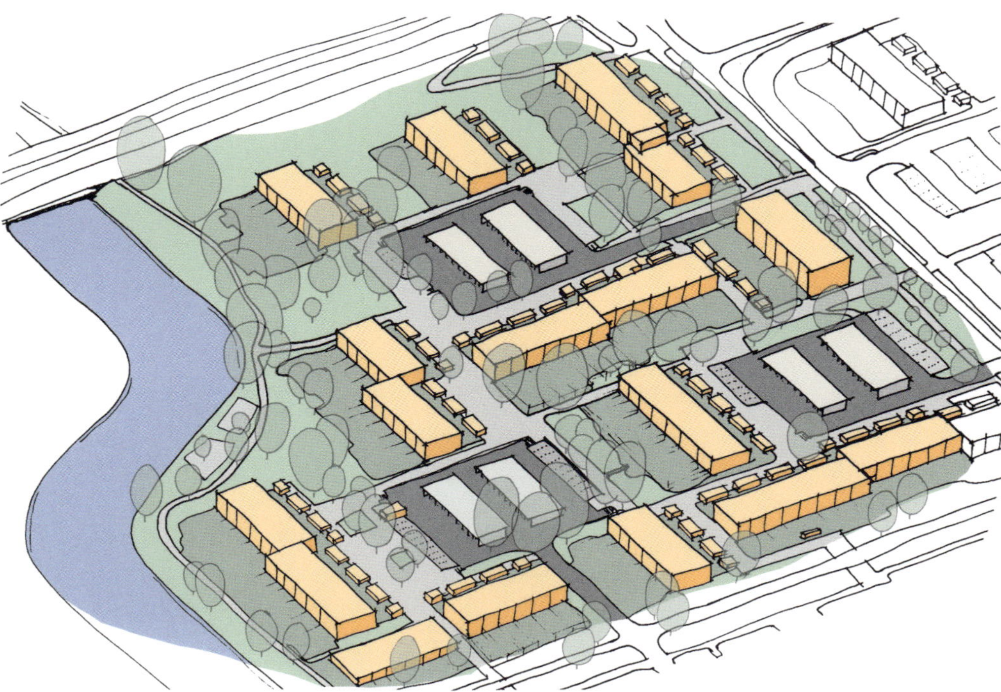

Features
Single-family homes on residential courts around sunken parking squares

Urban planning – supervision
City Development section PW Amsterdam, Jan Sterenberg

Architects
Jan Sterenberg

Construction period
1972–1975

Homes per hectare
25

Average home size
90 m²

2B GEIN 1987

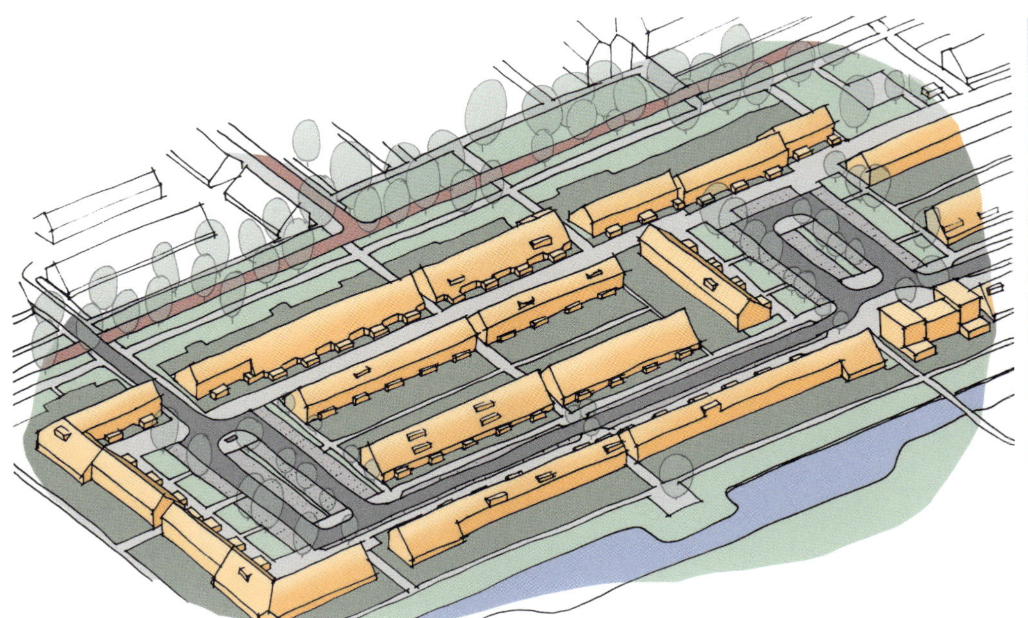

Features
Single-family homes on streets and canals

Urban planning – supervision
Marjati Pratomo (DRO)

Architects
including Marge Architects

Construction period
1985–1987

Homes per hectare
35

Average home size
87 m²

LAAN VAN VLAANDEREN
ZONE
30

2G PAPAVERPLANTSOEN 2017

Features
Self-build houses and apartments on deep plots with back houses along an inner street

Urban planning – supervision
Steven Delva (DELVA)

Architects
Self-build with various architects

Construction period
2015–2017

Homes per hectare
85

Average home size
90 m²

2H KLEIN KADOELEN 2020

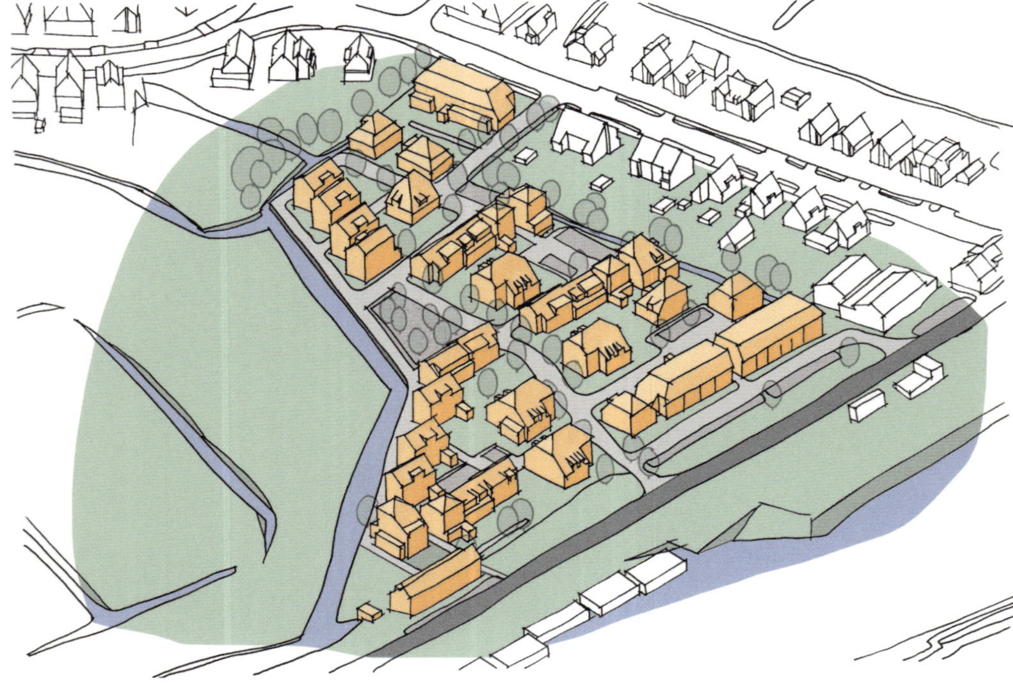

Features
Residential neighborhood with detached houses, car-free paths, and oriented towards the polder

Urban planning – supervision
Steven Delva (DELVA)

Architects
Houben / Van Mierlo architects

Construction period
2017–2020

Homes per hectare
20

Average home size
159 m²

2E NIEUW SLOTEN 1997

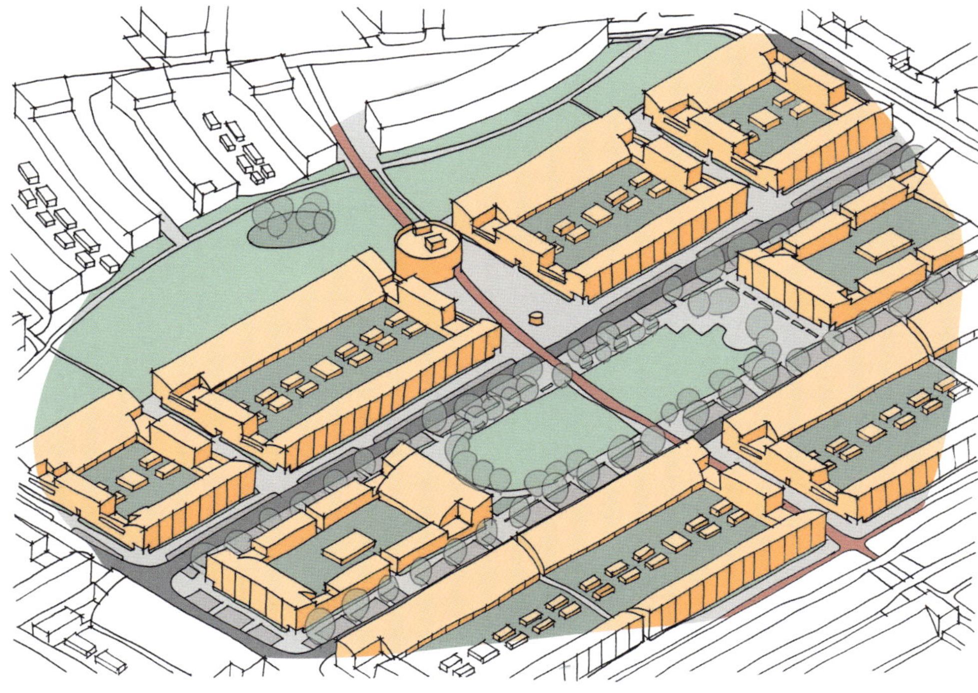

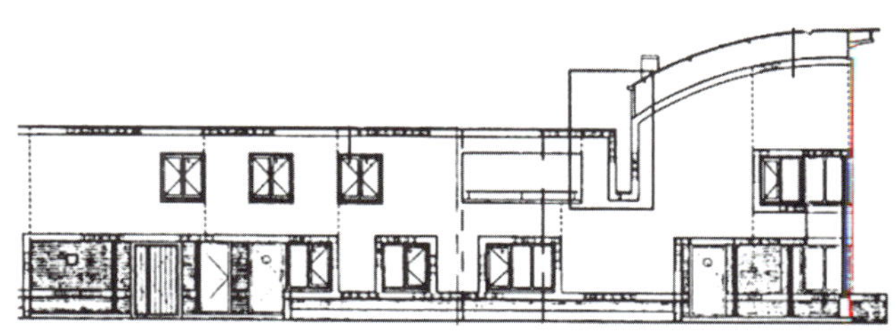

Features
Single-family homes in lane layout

Urban planning – supervision
Lodewijk Baljon, Jan Brouwer, Kees van Ruyven, Wil Val (DRO)

Architects
Hans Ruijssenaars

Construction period
1990–1997

Homes per hectare
50

Average home size
101 m²

2F DE BONGERD 2007

Features
Quadrant homes in three floors along small streets, parking on own property

Urban planning – supervision
Rudy Uytenhaak

Architects
among others Rudy Uytenhaak Architectenbureau, Van Sambeek & Van Veen Architecten, Heren 5 Architecten, Architectenbureau Paul de Ruiter

Construction period
2006–2007

Homes per hectare
60

Average home size
119 m²

21 CENTER DE AKER – DUKAAT

In the design of De Aker, almost all the amenities were included in a long building block of nearly 400 meters along Pieter Calandlaan. Dukaat, as this building is called, was one of the first superblocks not only meant for residential use but also mixing homes and amenities. The building contains not only 250 homes in six stories but also shops, offices, a health center, a daycare center, and a primary school on the ground floor. The building was designed by TANGRAM Architekten and completed in 2001.

Due to the scale and orientation of the block, there was a risk of an unattractive and unsafe 'backside' on the northern side, mainly consisting of logistics and storage areas. This was solved by building amenities on this side and internalizing the freight street. On top of this, a long-elevated square was constructed. From this 'upper street,' the homes could be accessed. The response to this new type of superblock was positive, with NRC *Handelsblad* calling it an 'exemplary urban building.'

1 Sketch of the public deck on the first floor at the rear side of the building, design by Tangram Architects
2 Topographical map, circa 1998
3 Aerial photo, 2023
4 Rear view of building block with deck and school, design by Tangram Architects
5 Cross-section of Dukaat with deck and internal expedition street, design by Tangram Architects
6 Residential floor plans of Dukaat
7 Front facade of Dukaat, design by Tangram Architects

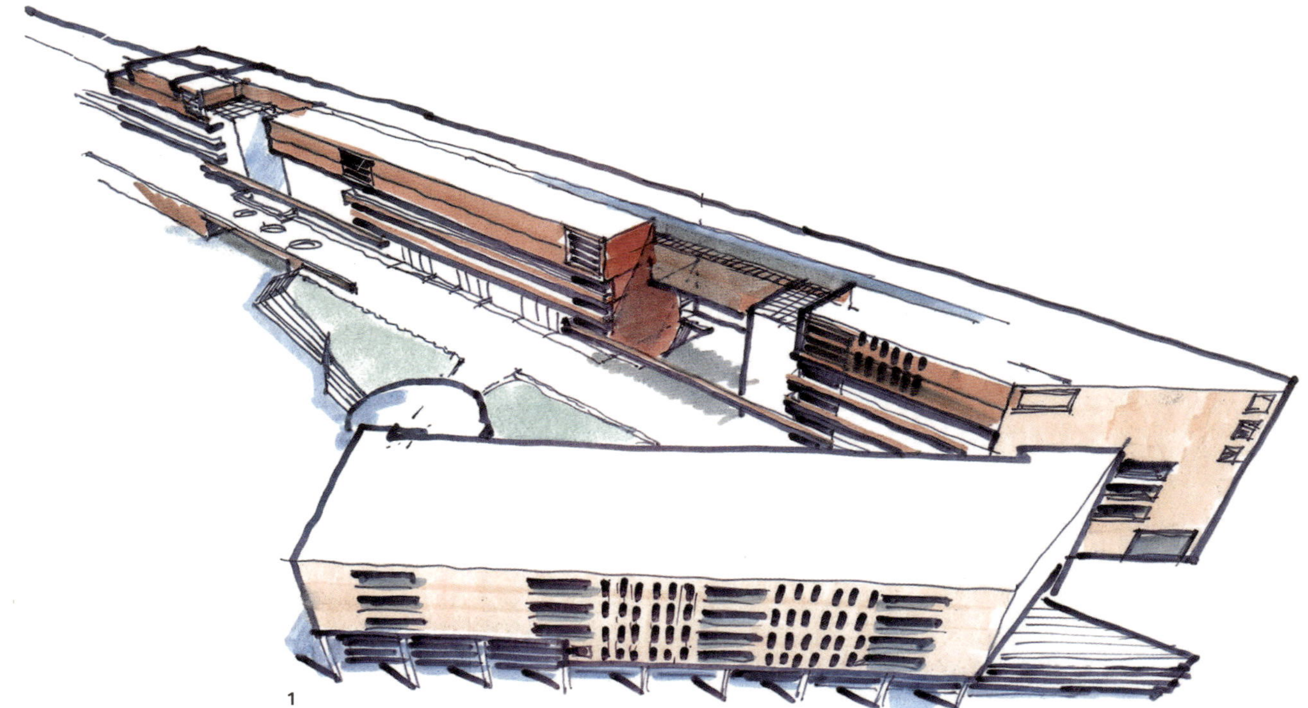

1

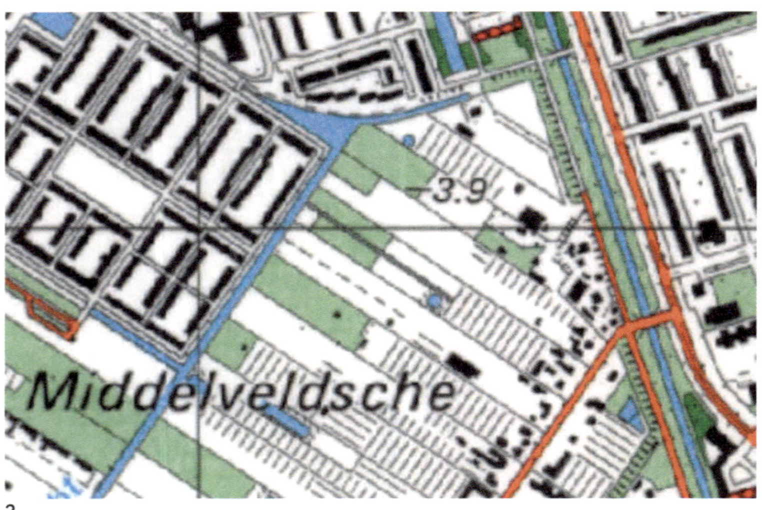

2

3

4

woningtype G
woningtype F
woningtype A
woningtype E
woningtype E
woningtype F
woningtype A
cultureel-maatschappelijke voorziening
1000 +
expeditie
straat
winkel
galeria
bergingen
1500 +

5

6

DUKAAT

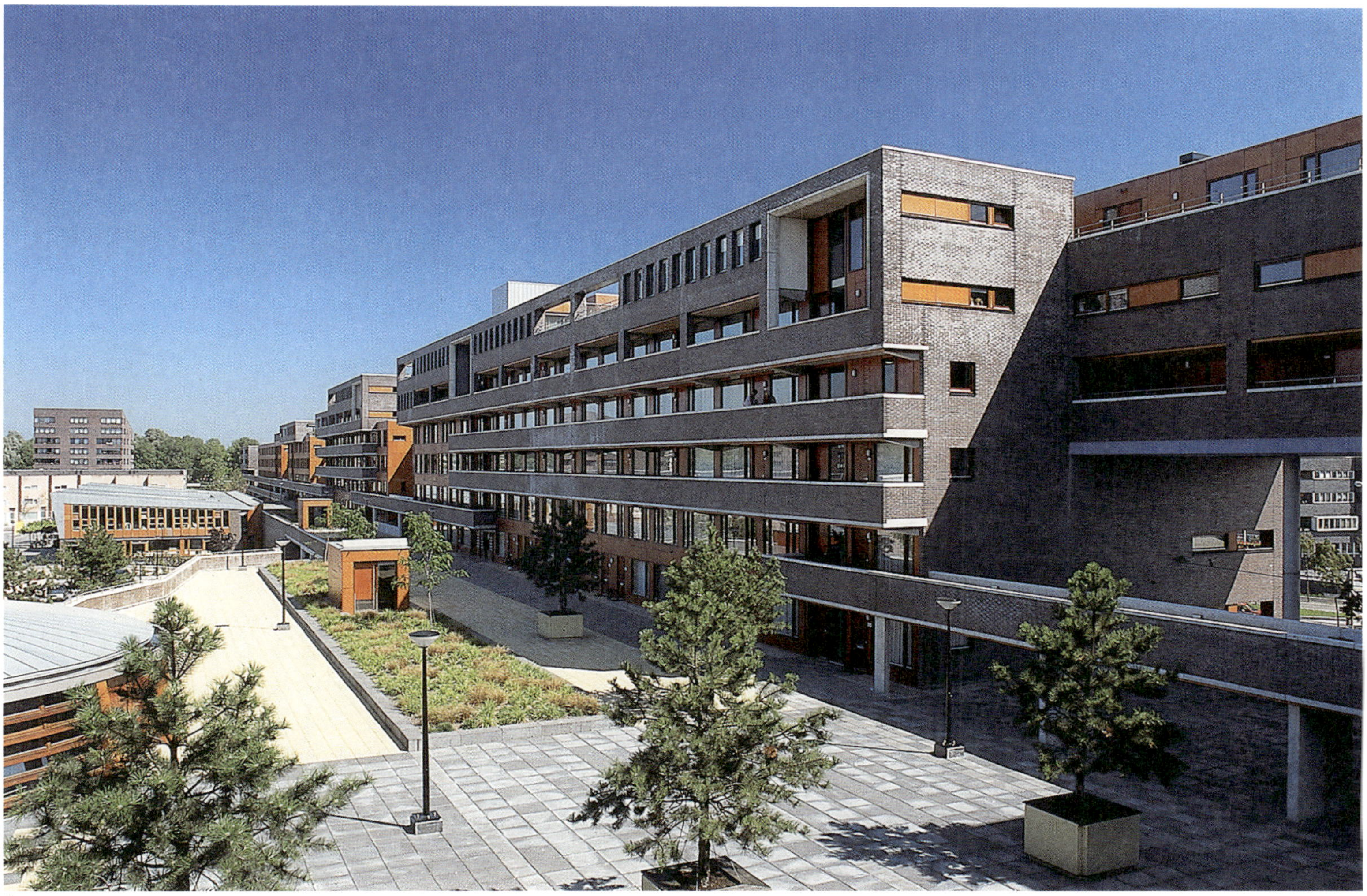

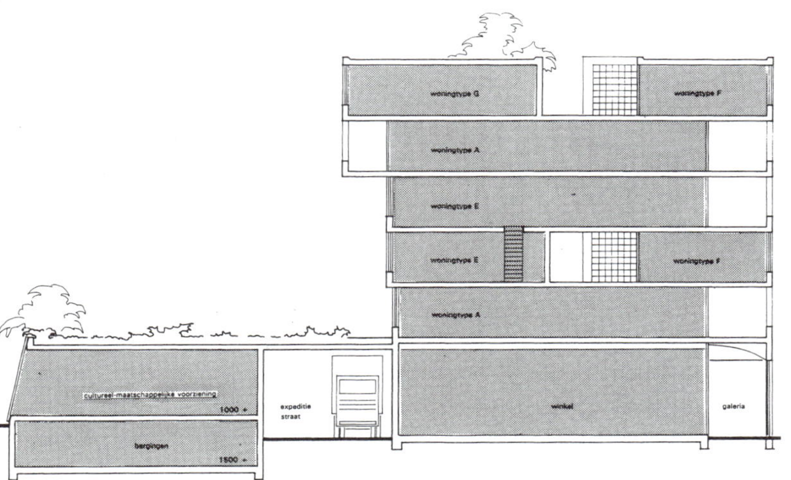

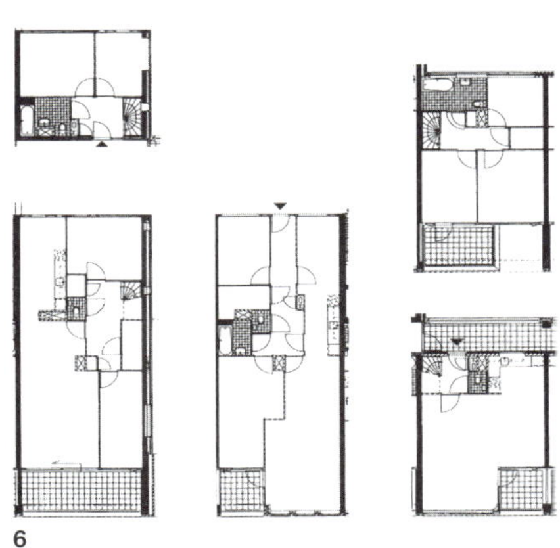

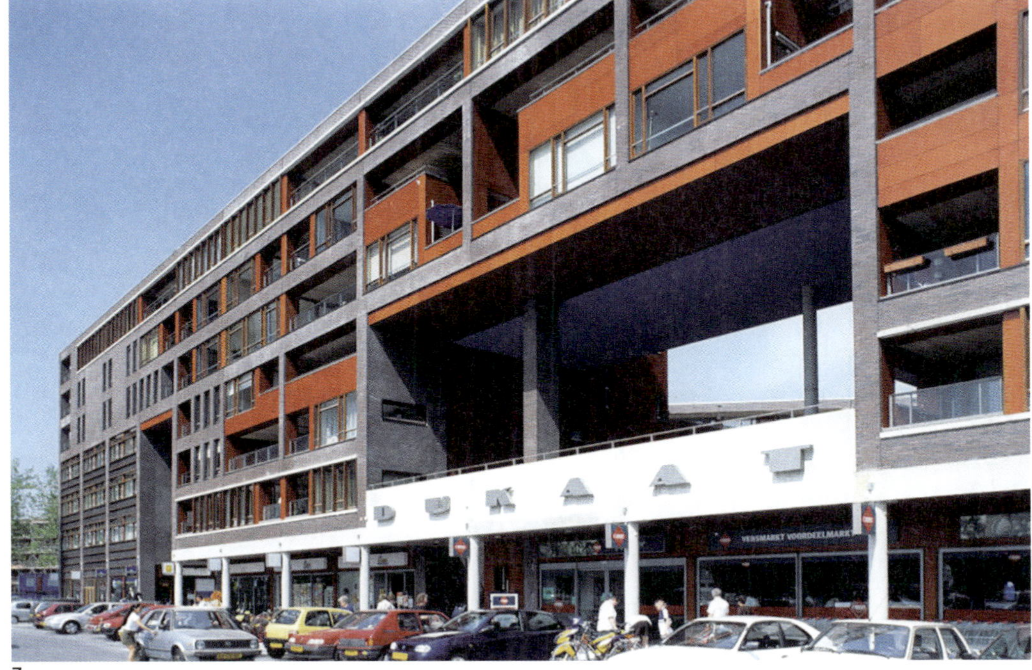

7

2J TRAM NETWORK EXPANSION

In 1875, the Amsterdamsche Omnibus Maatschappij (AOM) introduced the first (horse-drawn) tram in the city, running between the Plantage and Leidseplein. In 1900, the municipality took over AOM and began electrifying the tram lines. With the urban expansions, the network developed significantly, albeit only on the south side of the IJ. Amsterdam-Zuidoost received a metro line.

Since 1975, the tram network has been further expanded, always linked to housing development at the city's edge. Line 2 was extended in 1975 to Louwesweg and the new Slotervaart Hospital. In 1991, the route was extended further to Nieuw Sloten. The tram arrived even before the new residents did.

Line 1 to Osdorp operated in a two- to three-minute service in the 1970s. This decreased with the aging of the Western Garden Cities until, with the construction of, among others, De Aker, the number of passengers increased again. In 2001, the line was extended from Meer en Vaart (Osdorp Centrum) to the rear of De Aker (Matterhorn stop).

Line 5 ran for a long time between Haarlemmerplein and the Dam, but in 1978 a new Line 5 was introduced, connecting the new NS Zuid Station with Central Station (CS). In 1990, the line was extended through Buitenveldert and Amstelveen, with the final stop at Binnenhof. During the same years, express tram 51 also began running, partly along the same route, to the Amstelveen extension in Westwijk. The trams had different entry heights, which made the stops in Buitenveldert and Amstelveen long and unclear. This was solved by eliminating the express tram and introducing a regular tram line 25, which has been running since 2024 between Zuid Station and Uithoorn. In Amstelveen, many intersections were made grade-separated for traffic safety.

For the access to IJburg, a metro line was originally planned, but a tram was ultimately chosen. Tram line 26 opened in 2005, running from Central Station to Theo van Goghpark on Haveneiland. The line will be extended in the future to connect Centrumeiland and Strandeiland.

Until 1990, tram 9 ran from Central Station to the Ajax stadium De Meer and later to the center of Diemen. After the opening of the North/South line in 2019, the line was renamed line 19. This line now runs across the city from Sloterdijk to the new extension of Diemen: De Sniep. This is the longest tram line in Amsterdam.

1 Aerial photo, 2003 (IJburg Stop)
2 Aerial photo, 2023 (IJburg Stop)
3 Metro (left) next to rapid tram (right) at Amstel Station
4 Stop at center Nieuw Sloten near Kasterleepark
5 Tram 26 running through IJburg under construction
6 Tram network extensions, situation 2024

1

2

3

4

5

Route tram 1, 2024

Route tram 2, 2024

Route tram 5, 2024

Route tram 13, 2024

Route tram 19, 2024

Route tram 26, 2024

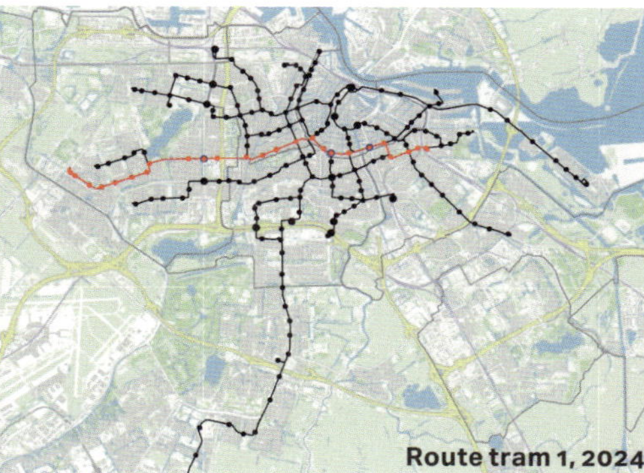

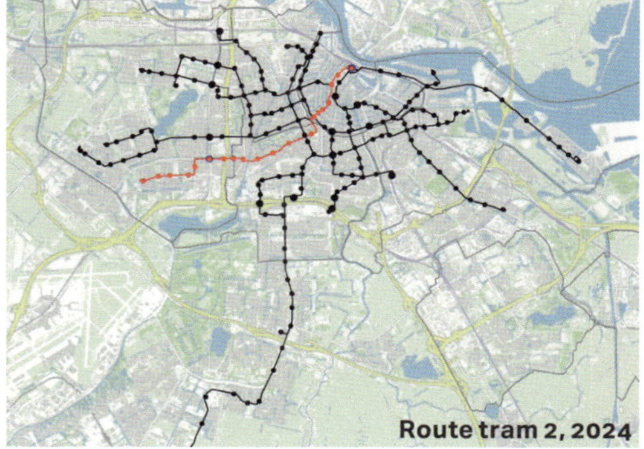

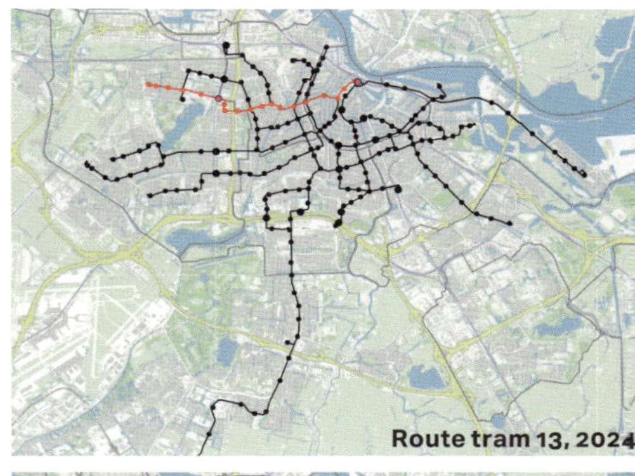

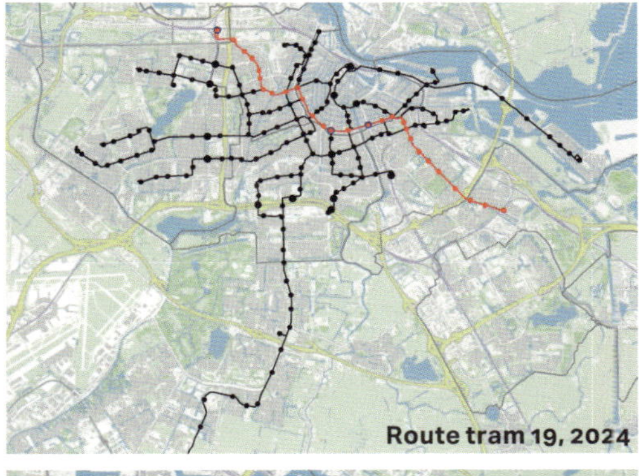

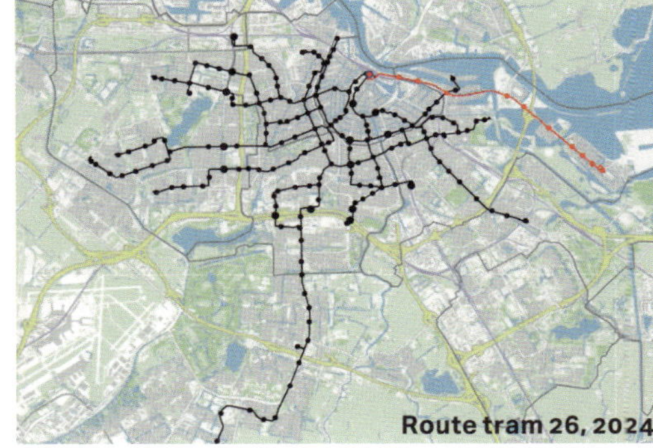

6

2K SPORTPARK SLOTEN

Sportpark Sloten was established in the mid-1950s and was initially used only for football and baseball. Over time, the usage of the park has become much more intense and diversified, largely due to the construction of the low-rise neighborhoods Sloten and De Aker, which have many young families.

The introduction of artificial grass made it possible to play on the fields more intensively. This created space for clubs that had previously played at Sportpark De Aker and Sportpark Riekerhaven to move to Sportpark Sloten, allowing for different uses of those areas.

Sportpark Sloten has become a very diversified area. For example, a cycling circuit has been built around the park, a wide asphalt path 2.5 kilometers long. At the entrance to the park, a viaduct has been constructed to prevent cross traffic, but it also adds a slight incline to the circuit. The Amsterdam Cycling Club and ASC Olympia use the circuit and organize races, such as the annual Driedaagse and since 2018, the '100 van Sloten'.

Additionally, space has been made for many other sports, such as hockey, handball, and American football. The large sports hall used to house Turnace, which moved from Jan van Galen Sportpark to Sloten in 1998. The hall is now used by other gymnastics clubs and for combat sports like judo, boxing, and karate.

The highlight of the sports park is the Amsterdam Velodrome, an indoor cycling

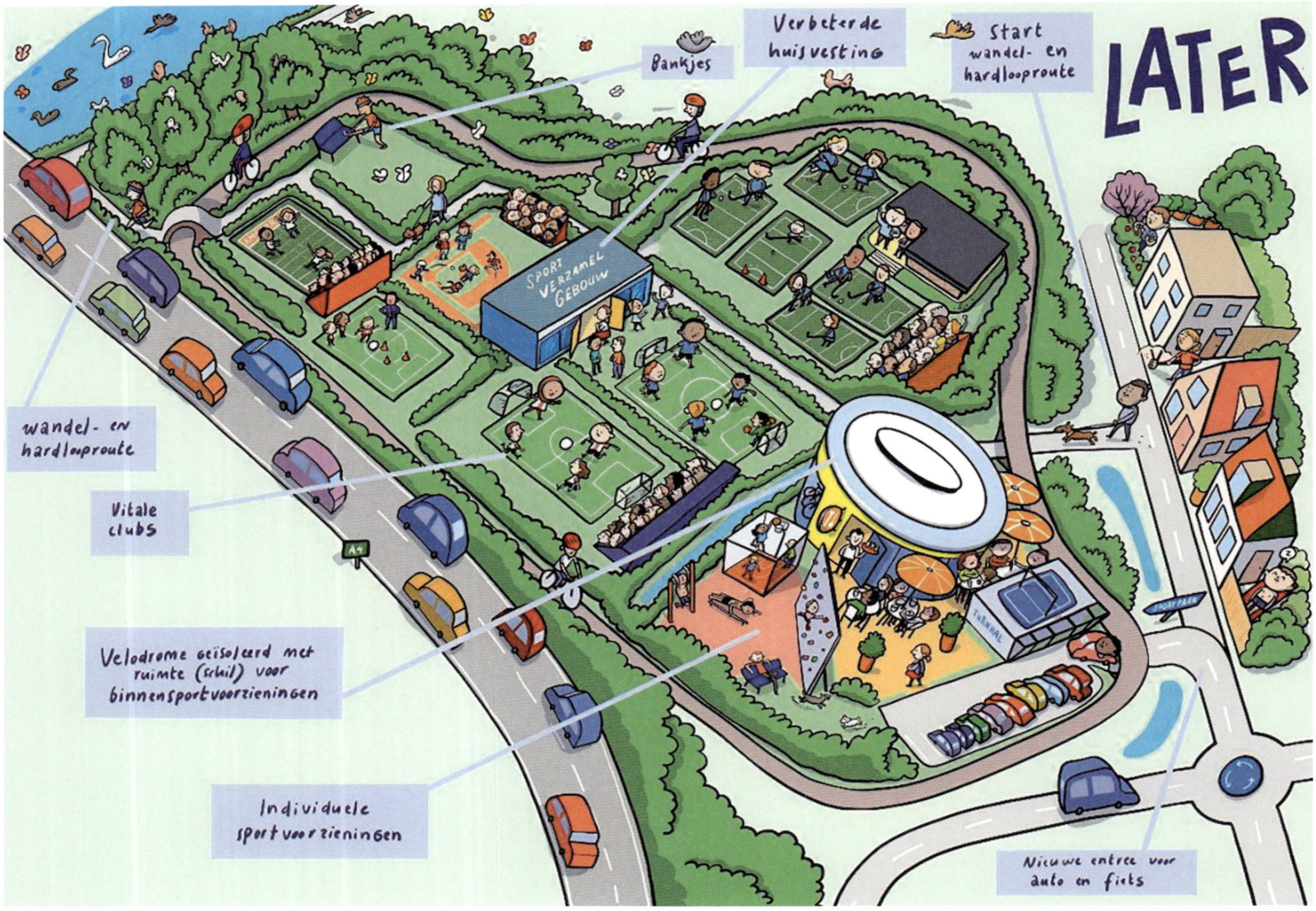

1

2

3

track suitable for all disciplines. The first wooden track, 200 meters long, was built in 1972. In 2001, the track was fully covered and renovated.

In 2017, a project was started to renew and intensify the sports park. Hockey is a rapidly growing sport in Amsterdam. The merged club Xenios moved from Sportpark Sloten-West to Sloten in 2019 and now has five water-based fields there. Several outdated clubhouses were demolished and replaced. The new clubhouse for Xenios opened in 2022. Since 2024, the central area of the cycling track has been used for 3x3 basketball. The number of parking spaces has also been expanded.

After the construction of 11,000 homes in the nearby Schinkelkwartier, the sports park will see even more intensive use.

1 Illustration of the future Sportpark Sloten
2 Aerial photo, 1972
3 Aerial photo, 2023
4 Clubhouse of the Xenios hockey club, 2024
5 Velodrome Sloten in 1972, still uncovered (photo: © c/o Pictoright Amsterdam, 2025)
6 Velodrome now

4

5

6

2L NELSON MANDELAPARK

The Nelson Mandela Park was originally an integral part of the greenery in the Bijlmermeer and was simply called Bijlmerpark. The design of Bijlmerpark, by H.J. Laumans in 1971, featured a finely structured green space with a 'human scale' but was executed in a simple and relatively rough manner due to budget constraints.

Around 2009, the park was in need of major maintenance, and there was also a need to make space for sports facilities. While the Bijlmer area had a lot of greenery, it strangely lacked sports amenities. Additionally, the groundwater issue in the park had to be addressed. As a result, the park was raised, and new water features were added. All of the trees had to be felled for this. The architectural firm Mecanoo was tasked with redesigning the park, incorporating sports facilities, a butterfly hill, a tree garden, and a magnolia valley. The park was completed in 2011.

The plan for residential construction along the edge near the Gooiseweg was abandoned during the credit crisis. In 2025, the construction of the first blocks began. All 700 homes will be built using timber construction.

In 2014, the park was renamed Nelson Mandela Park. In 2021, a memorial artwork for Mandela was added to the park. Created by South African artist Mohau Modisakeng, the sculpture consists of seven fragmented faces representing the residents of the Bijlmermeer and carries a quote from Nelson Mandela: 'We are human only through the humanity of others'.

1 Plan of Nelson Mandelapark, design by Mecanoo Architects, 2004
2 Aerial photo, 2006
3 Aerial photo, 2023
4 Bijlmerpark in 1976
5 Bijlmerpark connection to Brasapark on top of Gaasperdammertunnel
6 Entrance to Nelson Mandelapark
7 Sculpture, design by Mohau Modisakeng
8 Kwaku festival, 1992

1

2

3

4

5

7

8

6

2M TUINEN VAN WEST

In the Nieuw-West district lies the multi-functional recreational area Tuinen van West. The area was originally agricultural land and was redesigned according to the principles of the General Expansion Plan of 1935. In the decades that followed, it was considered both a site for housing development and an industrial area. However, the proximity to an incoming flight path from Schiphol and disputes with the government over accessibility made these purposes unfeasible. In 2009, a decision was made to construct the A5 highway on the edge of the area, and the polders were designated for recreational use. Only the Lutkemeer polder was assigned an industrial designation.

The area consists of four former polders: the Lutkemeer polder, the Osdorper Bovenpolder, and the Osdorper Binnenpolder North and South, and covers approximately 700 hectares. Each former polder now has its own distinct character, ranging from culture and festivals to urban farming and quiet natural spaces. Sustainability is a central theme in the area. During the construction of the A5, a number of (nature) compensation projects were carried out.

1 Fruittuin van West (Fruit Garden of West)
2 Aerial photo, 2006
3 Aerial photo, 2023
4 Fruittuin van West (Fruit Garden of West)
5 Chin Chin Festival, 2018
6 Vision map Tuinen van West, 2010

1

2

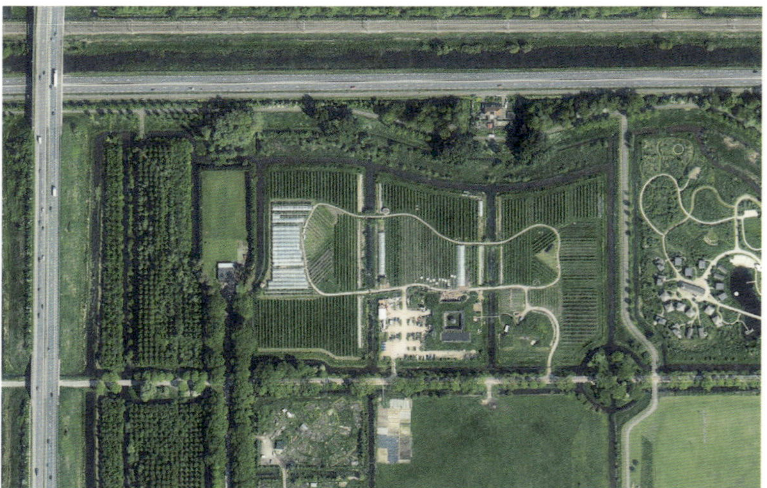

3

4

5

6

WATER CITY —
CITY ISLANDS

In August 1975, photographer Jusopo Arsath Ro'is captured a stunning series of images during Sail Amsterdam. His photos show ships arriving and departing, the admiral sailing tradition, and quaysides packed with visitors. Some spectators even climbed onto a floating grain elevator. Meanwhile, the Amsterdam Philharmonic Orchestra performed *Watermusic* by Händel.

Looking at the city surrounding the event, the industrial character of the waterfront is striking. Warehouses and cranes still dominate the landscape, especially on Java-eiland, while across the water, the massive dock of the ADM (Amsterdam Drydock Company) is still in full operation.

Just five years later, ADM had shut down, and its former site became the venue for the Festival of Fools. Another five years after that, its harbor basin was filled in, and the first homes of the new IJplein neighborhood were completed. Since then, the IJ waterfront has undergone a dramatic transformation. Nearly 50,000 homes[1] have been built on the harbor islands of the new Waterstad (Water City), along with office spaces, cultural venues, hotels, creative hubs, and popular restaurants and cafés. The ferries crossing the water are packed. The IJ has become part of the city.

1 During Sail 1975, the Amsterdam Philharmonic Orchestra performs
2 Fleet review Sail 1975

1

2

MOVEMENT 3

The transformation of the ports and industrial areas around the IJ into a 'water city' was made possible by the closure of the old metal and shipbuilding industries, as well as the relocation of many businesses to the Western Port Area). Several large water-related companies moved to the new dock basins, while smaller businesses relocated to industrial zones near Sloterdijk and Cornelis Douwesweg. Many of these companies came from the Eastern Port Area, including OBA's coal terminal and Cornelder's transshipment terminal.

In fact, much of the city's core infrastructure was also relocated to the Westelijk Havengebied. The Hemweg power plant underwent several expansions, taking over the function of Elektriciteitscentrale Noord (North Power Plant) on Papaverweg, along with the AEB (Afval Energiebedrijf, Waste-to-Energy Plant, also originally from Papaverweg), and RWZI-West (sewage treatment facilities, relocated from North and the Oostoever, and later from Zeeburgereiland and Spaklerweg). The municipal yard, the bike depot, and, in 2023, Liander (also previously on Spaklerweg) all followed. The Dutch Railways (NS) also opened large new marshalling yards near Hemweg.

Various logistical functions made a similar move. The Bodecentrum site in Dapperbuurt, Van Gend & Loos on Het Funen, and the PTT postal sorting center on Oosterdokseiland all relocated westward.

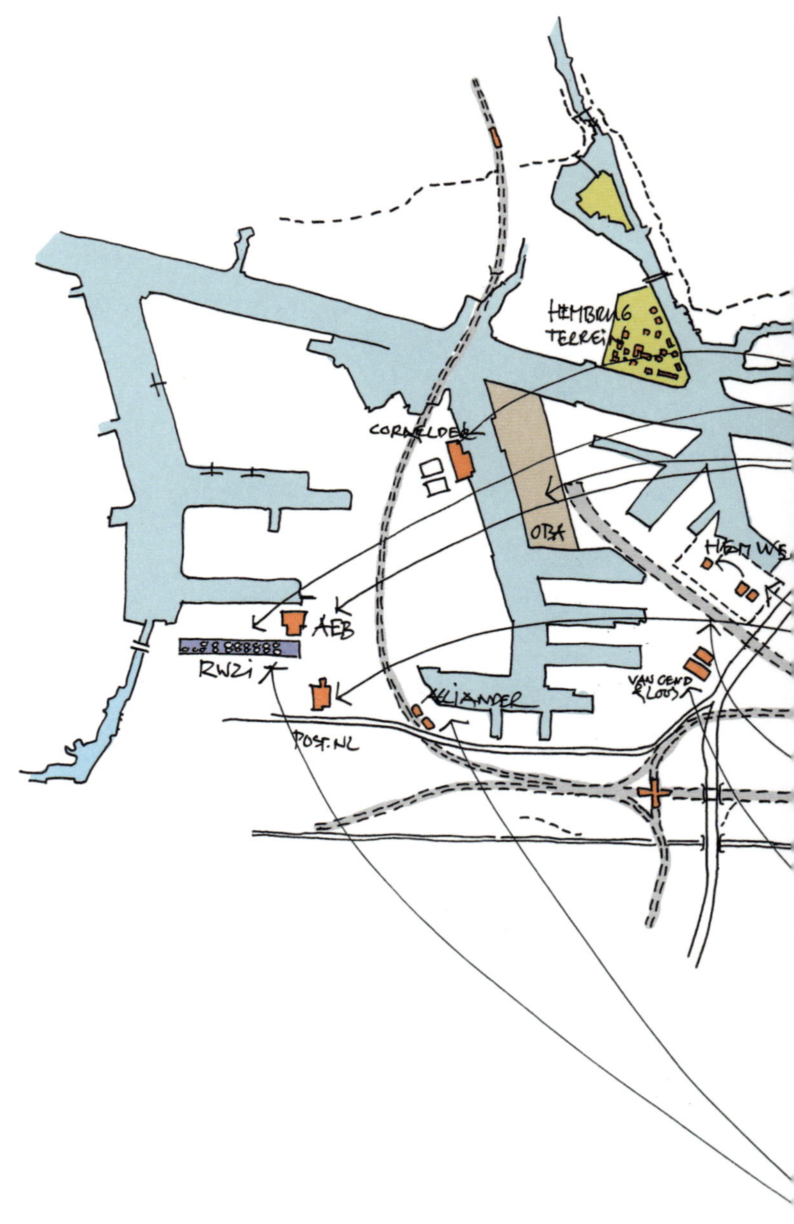

Three development phases of the port

The shift to the Western Port Area represents the third phase in the development of the Port of Amsterdam. The first took place in the seventeenth century, with expansion onto reclaimed islands east of the old city, while the second occurred in and around the IJ during the nineteenth and first half of the twentieth centuries.

Located in the vast lagoon behind the North Sea coast, Amsterdam has always been oriented toward waterborne trade. Though its name derives from the Amstel, it was the IJ that connected the city to the world through a remarkable network of waterways: via the Buiten-IJ and the Zuiderzee to the Wadden and the North Sea.

The Buiten-IJ and the Zuiderzee were treacherous bodies of water. A north wind combined with a spring tide could cause massive surges. The irregular course of many dike segments and a name like Nieuwendam ('New Dam') suggest that the earliest dikes frequently overflowed and had to be rebuilt. It is assumed that this was also the case around the original settlement at the mouth of the Amstel.[2] Major storm surges in the late Middle Ages forced the construction of stronger, more inland dikes along the eastern side of the city. In contrast to the relatively straight trajectory of the Nieuwendijk, Haarlemmerdijk, and Spaarndammerdijk on the city's western flank, the Zeedijk bends sharply southward near Olofspoort. From there, the Sint Antoniesdijk curves gently eastward before reconnecting with the presumably older Diemerzeedijk near the inn at Zeeburg, at the far end of the Zeeburgerdijk. After these great storms, a vast, shallow marshland formed in the IJ just outside the dikes on the city's eastern side – often referred to on later maps as the Stadsrietlanden.

↑ Movement – relocation of companies to the Western Port Area creates space for new city islands

The large water body of the Nieuwe Diep, located within the present-day Flevopark, may also be a remnant of one of these breaches.

Over time, this marshland was gradually reclaimed through landfilling, forming a labyrinthine part of the city full of surprises, beginning with the Lastage and the Groenburgwal area in the sixteenth century. The seventeenth-century series of islands, however, is particularly striking: from Vlooienburg, Uilenburg, Valkenburg, Rapenburg, and Marken, to Waalseiland, the Kadijken, Kattenburg, Wittenburg, and Oostenburg, extending all the way to Het Funen. The western islands in the IJ – Bickerseiland, Prinseneiland, Realeneiland, and Bokkinghangen – form a smaller archipelago but share the same distinctive character.

Interestingly, the shipbuilding and storage facilities of the rapidly expanding trading city grew in tandem with these islands. Each new generation of cargo and warships required the construction of new shipyards on ever-new islands. The same applied to the ropewalks and warehouses of the VOC, WIC, and naval fleet. As a result, older sites became available for urban development, often retaining their original lot divisions – still clearly visible in the Lastage area.

A similar process of upscaling took place in the nineteenth century, driven in part by the introduction of steam engines and the use of cast iron and steel as construction materials. Expanding on the traditional port areas in the eastern inner city, new harbor islands were reclaimed throughout the nineteenth century on the city's eastern side. The KNSM and Java islands became home to the terminals of the KNSM and SMN shipping companies. By 1900, shipbuilding and the metal industry had crossed the IJ, with companies such as ADM, Kromhout, Draka, and Verschure establishing operations there.

The construction of the Noordzeekanaal (North Sea Canal) and the land reclamation of the IJ in the 1870s gradually shifted Amsterdam's orientation. The sea – its gateway to the world – was no longer to the east but now lay west of the city. However, the full impact of this shift on urban development unfolded very slowly. Far beyond the city, the Petroleumhaven was completed in 1889, followed by the Coenhaven in 1924.[3] It was not until the 1930s that new dock basins were planned farther west, in the IJ polders along the Noordzeekanaal. From 1958, development accelerated with the expansion of the Westhaven, large-scale raising of the IJ polders, the construction of the Amerikahaven, and the establishment of the Mobil refinery in 1968. Over the following decades, transshipment terminals and industrial facilities gradually followed.

Once the Oranjewerf – Amsterdam's last major water-related industry on the city's eastern side – relocates in the next five to ten years, the reorientation of the city, nearly 150 years in the making, will be complete.

1

1 Entrepotdok, 1975–2025
2 Houthaven-Pontsteiger, 1975–2025

Transformation in the water city

Within the broader perspective of the water city – the area beyond the dikes in the IJ – the new development at IJplein was not the first transformation project. That distinction belongs to the redevelopment of Kattenburg in the 1970s, followed closely by the renewal of Wittenburg, Oostenburg, and the Kadijken. Just as with the early urban renewal plans within the dike ring, nearly all existing buildings on Kattenburg and Wittenburg were demolished, making way for an entirely new beginning. The new development on Kattenburg drew most literally from English precedents: stacked maisonettes in meandering blocks, accessed via residential decks above parking garages and galleries on the third floor. The approach to the Kadijken, in contrast, exemplified the preservation-and-restoration strategy that emerged a few years later, with the conversion of deep warehouses along the Entrepotdok, the renovation of the Sibbelwoningen, and lot-by-lot new construction on vacated industrial plots.

By the early 1990s, the transformation of the nineteenth- and early-twentieth-century harbor islands was underway. 'Living on an urban island' turned out to be a gap in the market: there was renewed interest in city living, particularly close to

2

the inner city. Both existing and newly developed islands in the water city became ideal testing grounds for innovative urban housing concepts. Following the redevelopment of the Abattoir and Entrepot-West, the next decade saw the emergence of residential districts on KNSM, Java, Borneo, Sporenburg, and the Oostelijke Handelskade.

Building on the redevelopment of the Eastern Port Area and expanding upon the so-called Pampus Plan by the architecture firm Van den Broek and Bakema (1964), early concepts emerged for further urban expansion to the east, toward the new Flevopolders and Almere.[4] Though beautifully situated along the IJmeer, this area was difficult to access – it lay 'behind' the Amsterdam-Rhine Canal – and the banks of the Diemerzeedijk were heavily polluted. During the 1950s, a waste incineration site had been established there, which the municipality took over in 1969 but did not fully close until 1982. The remediation and capping of the site – along with the creation of Diemerpark – cleared the way for the expansion of the water city with the new islands of IJburg.

Thus, a completely new urban district took shape on the eastern side of the city, extending into the IJ and the Buiten-IJ. It was connected to the city by extended and newly constructed tram lines, the Piet Heintunnel, and a series of distinctive new bridges: the Jan Schaefer Bridge, the Enneüs Heerma Bridge, and the Nesciobrug.

On the western side of the city, the closure of NDSM in 1984 also freed up a large site. However, it long remained a peripheral location, far to the north of the IJ. Precisely because of this remoteness, it became an attractive experimental space for theater performances and the city's first large-scale music festivals.[5] The vast shipbuilding hall was partially occupied by squatters and, following a design competition in 2000, was converted into a creative hub providing space for 250 artists and craft-based enterprises.

Apart from the redevelopment of the Silodam, little new construction took place in the central and western sections of the IJ in the early years. This changed in the 1990s when redevelopment opportunities arose around Central Station due to the relocation of the postal sorting center on Oosterdokseiland and the removal of railway sidings on Westerdokseiland. Both islands were redeveloped with highly compact, mixed-use urban programs that differed significantly from the Eastern Docklands. The transformation of the central IJ area took a decisive turn in 2001 when Shell announced plans to consolidate its large research facility in Noord onto the northern part of its site. This allowed the southern portion – near the ferry landing, with its old laboratories, tower, and canteen – to be redeveloped.

Numerous institutions that had outgrown their premises in the inner city found a new home in this central IJ area: NEMO, De Appel, ARCAM, the Muziekgebouw, BIMHUIS, the OBA (Public Library), the Palace of Justice, the Eye Filmmuseum, and Paradiso. In 2014, the Marineterrein also became publicly accessible, effectively expanding the inner city.

A crucial factor in this expansion was the complete redevelopment of Central Station, in conjunction with the construction of the North/South metro line. Major east-west traffic flows of cars and buses were shifted to the IJ side, freeing up the old Open Havenfront on the city side of the station for pedestrians. A tunnel was built on the IJ side for vehicular traffic, while the bus station was elevated. As a result, the ground level became a domain for pedestrians and cyclists. New bridges and passages through the station now connect the inner city to the IJ and the urban islands on either side.

Following the redevelopment of the central IJ area, subsequent projects emerged further west, including the NDSM shipyard, the Houthavens, Buiksloterham, the Danzigerkade, and the Minervahaven. These areas also attracted significant new employment. The former NDSM site on the northern bank of the IJ became a hub for creative industries, while a fully-fledged fashion cluster took shape around the Minervahaven.

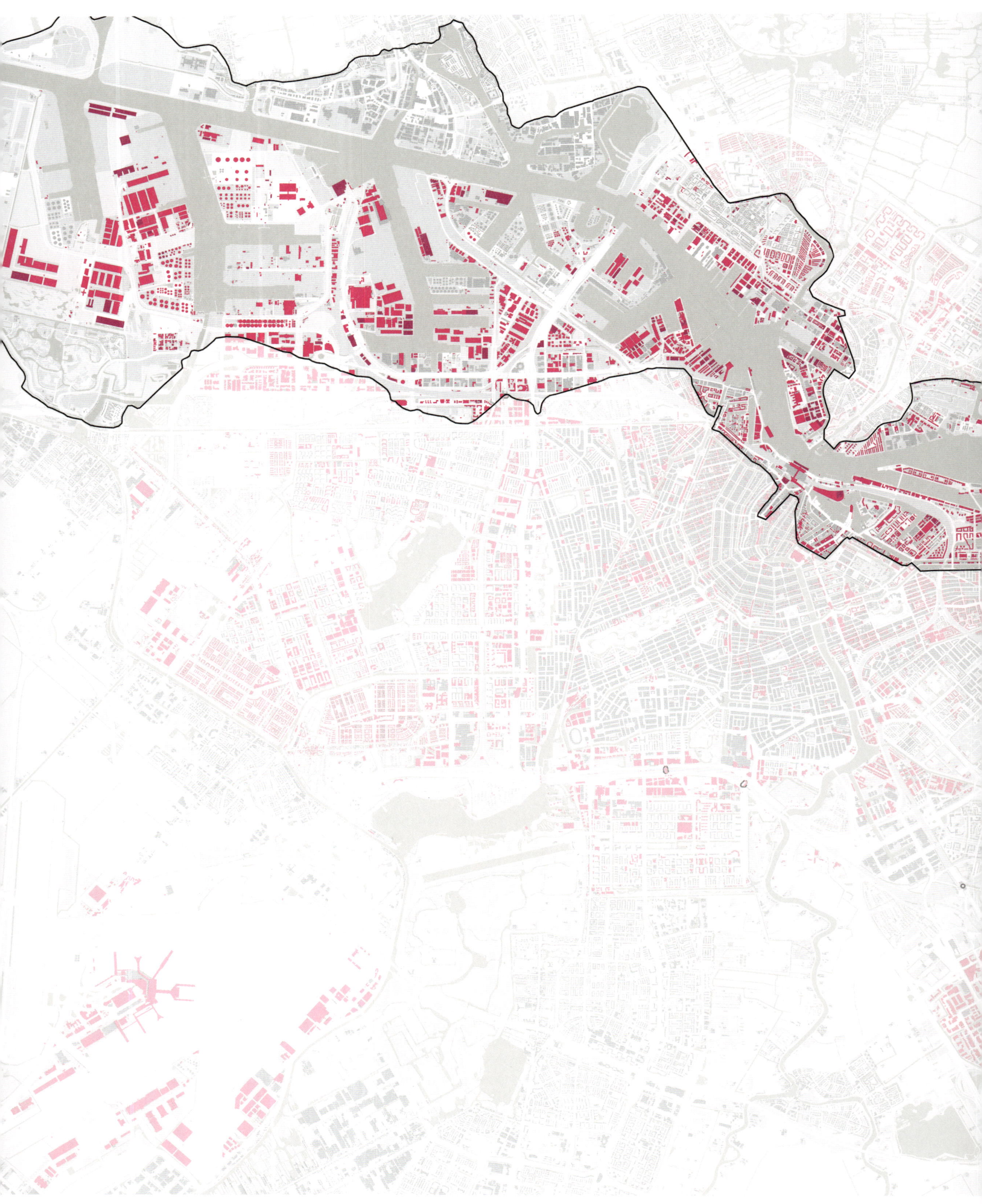

Old cityscapes provide a beautiful depiction of the orientation of the 'wijdvermaarde koopstadt' (widely renowned merchant city) on the IJ.[6] Such panoramas were not abstract constructions. From the Volewijck promontory across the IJ, one could actually see the city in this way. At the tip of the promontory near the Tolhuis, gallows stood where the corpses of the executed were hung as a deterrent – or should one say for instruction and amusement? What is certain is that the trip across the water and the view back toward the city became a popular outing, just like in many other cities situated by the water.[7] In the garden of the current Tolhuis, built in 1859, a playground was later created, and summer concerts were regularly held.[8]

With the construction of Central Station in 1889 on an island at the mouth of the Amstel, the view of the city disappeared. However, in the painting *Een zomeravond bij het Tolhuis* (A Summer Evening at the Tolhuis) from 1891 by Nicolaas van der Waay, one can still see that the garden by the water was still in full use. There was little interest in developing the plots on the IJ side of the station. When new platforms and a second steam canopy were built around World War I, only a few buildings had to be demolished. A handful of buildings remained at the corners of the Ooster- and Westertoegang, used by shipping companies as lodging houses and restaurants.

The 'overkant' (opposite shore) received another boost in those same years due to two major public exhibitions: the ENTOS in 1913 and the ELTA in 1919.[9] The latest airplanes and the airshows during the ELTA attracted no fewer than 500,000 visitors. The municipality constructed the entrance building, designed by the young architects Joan van der Mey and Piet Kramer.[10] It was later converted into a restaurant and named the IJ-paviljoen. The terraces offered a fantastic view over the water. However, interest in the location waned, and in 1938, the Bataafse Petroleum Maatschappij – a subsidiary of Shell – took over the bankrupt pavilion and the Tolhuistuin from the municipality. The IJ-paviljoen continued to function as a canteen for the KSLA, Shell's laboratory, until 1977.[11] That year, a new canteen, designed by Arthur Staal, was opened, and the IJ-paviljoen was demolished. Despite the construction of the Havengebouw, completed in 1960, De Ruijterkade became a desolate area

← Map Built in the Water City, 1975–2025

1

2

3

'behind' Central Station. The Buiksloterwegveer and Valkenwegveer (to Meeuwenlaan) continued to operate, but the IJ as a public space disappeared from the collective memory of Amsterdammers.

This first changed with the five-year spectacle of Sail starting in 1975. However, from 1980 onwards, the IJ once again became a part of daily life in the city. In that year, the ADM merged with the NDSM, and the business activities were relocated to the NDSM site. In the summer of 1980, the large warehouse of the ADM served as the setting for the Festival of Fools, until a short circuit caused a major fire, prematurely ending the festival.

To somewhat soften the blow of the merger and the loss of many jobs in the northern part of the city, the municipality purchased the land and designated it for housing for residents from the adjacent neighborhoods. At that point, there were no plans for the future of the harbor area. The housing development on what would come to be called the IJplein was therefore designed as a relatively autonomous project. The proposal by the designers of OMA, Rem Koolhaas's firm, to build high-rise residential towers alongside a new garden village, was derailed by discussions with future residents about the service fees for the elevators. The new neighborhood was ultimately designed on a relatively small scale.[12]

Around the *Structuurplan 'De stad centraal'* (Structural Plan 'The City Central') from 1986, the first ideas emerged for what was then called the IJ-as, or IJ-axis: a cohesive transformation of the city islands along the IJ shores and the area surrounding Sloterdijk Station on the west side, extending to a new city expansion in the IJmeer: Nieuw-Oost.[13] Inspired by the plans for the Docklands in London and the Kop van Zuid in Rotterdam around the same time, the redevelopment of the abandoned harbor areas was seen as an opportunity for the city to reinvent itself both economically and spatially. In the first explorations, one sees the filling in of harbor basins, similar to what had been done during the redevelopment of the Surrey Docks in London, housing construction on piers and in a new polder in the IJmeer, and large-scale infrastructure: an IJ-boulevard for car traffic and an IJ metro for public transport. The new metro line could become part of a 'large ring,' a ring line around the city that would also connect the new work areas on the southern side of the city.

To get a concrete idea of what the transformation could mean, a competition was organized for the *Oosterdok*.[14] Many of the participants, as well as the jury, broadened their scope and submitted proposals for a larger area. The winners, Henk de Boer and Alle Hosper, focused on the head of the Eastern Handelskade, while second-place winner Teun Koolhaas proposed a radical redesign of the entire IJ shore and the Eastern Port Area, including the filling in of the IJhaven (IJ harbor).

The planning for the IJ-axis was then divided into large chunks and began with the preparation of *Nota's van Uitgangspunten* (Report on Objectives) for the different sections, starting with the *Nota van Uitgangspunten* for the Eastern Port Area in 1985. This was thoroughly revised in 1989 and finalized in 1990 after an agreement had been reached with the government regarding the coverage of costs for the *Piet Heintunnel*, the extension of tram lines, and the financial deficit per housing unit.[15]

The memorandum focused on the main lines of development: the method of access, the mix of functions, with a general indication of the building forms, building heights, the number of houses in different sectors, and the locations of facilities (shopping center *Brazilië*, schools). A new generation of designers within the municipality, Hans Ebberink, Ton Schaap, and Jan de Waal, advocated building on the existing qualities of the water landscape. The plans for filling in areas and a new 'Kompaseiland' were abandoned, and existing quays and some characteristic buildings were retained. Initially, the focus was on 100% social housing, partly as compensation for the loss of housing in urban renewal areas. In the revised version, it was determined that 50% of the housing would be built in the free or lightly subsidized sector. This shift targeted a different demographic: 'new city dwellers.' Part of the *Nota van Uitgangspunten* was also that built parking facilities would be provided. This was a significant step. Unlike in urban renewal neighborhoods, the streets and quays would not be filled with cars.

By the late 1980s, planning had already started for the sites of the now-closed *Veemarkt* (Cattle Market) and the relocated *Abattoir* (Slaughterhouse). The remaining islands would follow over time. The already acquired *KNSM-eiland* (KNSM Island) was the starting point. A partnership was formed with the housing corporation *Het Oosten*. In addition, an external urban designer was appointed: Jo Coenen. The first homes were completed in 1993: the robust residential block *Piraeus*, designed by German architects Hans Kollhoff and Christian Rapp. The chosen development model for KNSM Island and the surprising architecture of this first residential block set the tone for further development on the other islands.

The *Nota van Uitgangspunten* for the IJ shores, *'Amsterdam naar het IJ'* (Amsterdam towards the IJ), was published in 1990 and revised and finalized in 1991. The changes addressed the main points raised in the discussions in the city council and

1 A summer evening at the Tolhuis, Nicolaas van der Waay, 1891
2 IJ Pavilion, 1936
3 Festival of Fools at the ADM site, 1980
4 Model of the western part of the urban plan for IJplein with characteristic urban villas, OMA, 1981
5 Structural sketch of the IJ-axis, Department of Spatial Planning, 1987
6 Urban plan for KNSM Island by Jo Coenen, 1989

the city itself.[16] The final *Nota van Uitgangspunten* focused solely on the Southern IJ shore, the area around Central Station (CS). The planning for the area around the Sixhaven near the Tolhuis in the North was delegated to the North district, and a reservation for a pedestrian bridge from Java Island was removed. For integrating the new infrastructure (IJ-boulevard, IJ-metro, bus station), underground options were chosen.

A notable element in the *Nota van Uitgangspunten* was the proposal to place the execution in a public-private joint venture. The idea for such a public-private partnership (PPP or PPS) had been adopted from the United States and England. A well-known example is the London Docklands Development Corporation (LDDC). The government provided the land and ensured favorable tax regulations. The LDDC created a broad urban planning framework for a mixed-use residential and work area and then made an agreement with the American developer Olympia & York for the construction of the iconic office complex Canary Wharf. Successful infrastructure projects by the LDDC included the construction of the Docklands Light Railway, London City Airport, and the building of The O2 Arena.

For the development of the IJ shore, the municipality chose to collaborate with the Nederlandse Middenstandsbank (Dutch Bank for Medium sized Companies) and its subsidiary MBO.[17] The collaboration took shape in 1991 with the establishment of the Amsterdam Waterfront Financieringsmaatschappij (AWF).

Rem Koolhaas was commissioned to create a master plan. The plan was presented in the fall of 1992 and widely discussed. However, the Business Plan that the AWF would create based on the master plan was never finalized. ING, formed after the merger of NMB with Postbank and Nationale Nederlanden, withdrew in 1993. The risks were deemed too high. The municipality then took over the planning for the area itself. Agreements were made with developers for each sub-area, sometimes for an entire island, as with MAB for the Oosterdokseiland (Eastern Dock Island), and in other cases per plot, as on the Oostelijke Handelskade (Eastern Handelskade). The development of infrastructure was financed by the municipality and the government. While the PPP may not have been successful, Koolhaas's master plan had a significant influence later on.

From Jettys to Anchors

In the *Nota van Uitgangspunten* for the Southern IJ bank, the municipality had chosen a highly developed spatial concept, the so-called Jettys model, designed by urban planner Gert Urhahn,

4

5

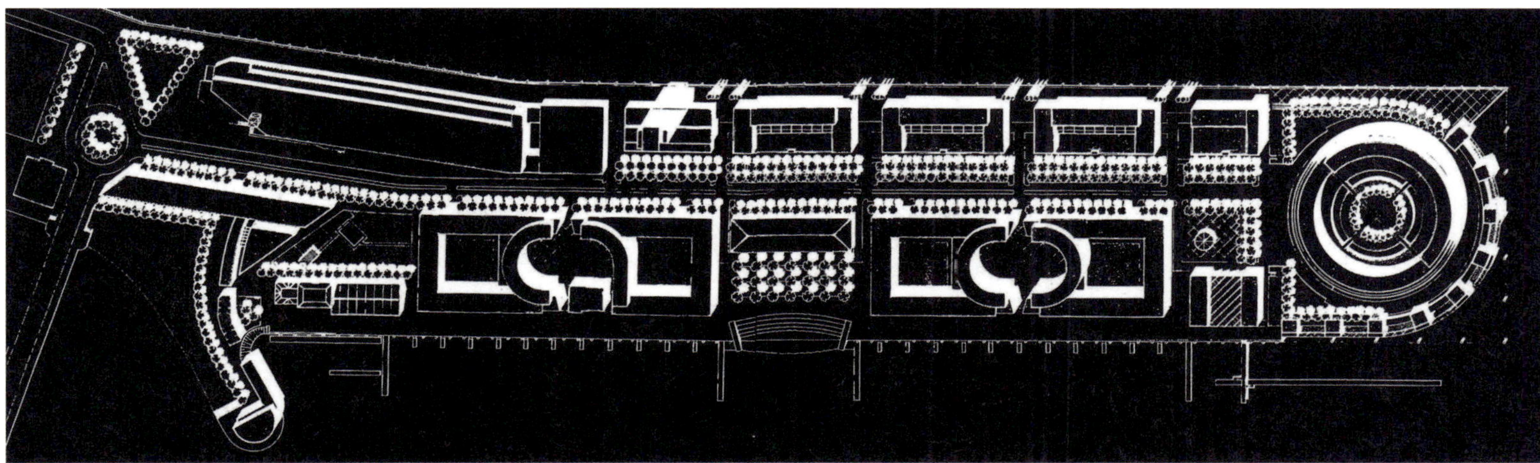
6

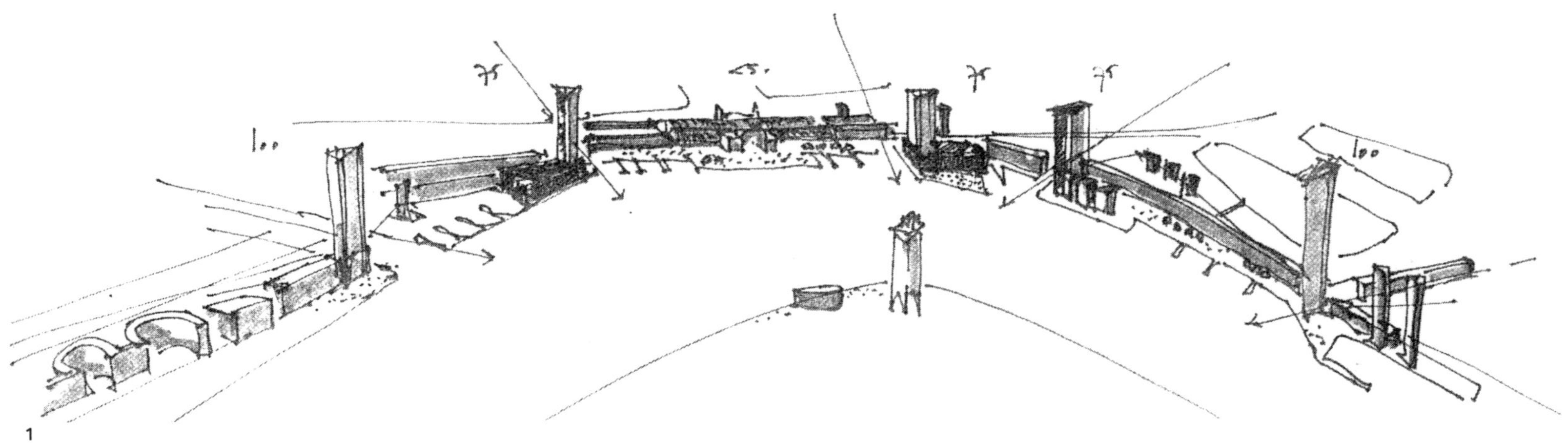
1

who was still working for the municipality at the time. To re-establish a relationship between the city center and the IJ, new public spaces along the IJ were proposed at all the underpasses beneath the railway, accompanied by large towers, increasing in height from 60 meters at Central Station to 100 meters at the Kop van de Oostelijke Handelskade and Barentszplein. This concept built upon the way Willem Dudok had designed the new Harbor Building at De Ruijterkade in the early 1960s and the winning ideas from the Oosterdok competition. The bend in the IJ was thus given a new, unified spatial form.

Koolhaas challenged this concept and advocated for an approach that focused on the opportunities and qualities of the individual islands. The shape of the IJ as a whole would then be a result and full of contrasts. In his vision, one or more tall towers would fit at the Westerdokseiland, while a very compact new work area had been designed at the Oosterdokseiland, built on a deck over the rail bundling. At Central Station, a 'reversed steam cap' would house various cultural facilities, such as a new branch of the Public Library and De Ysbreeker.[18] This approach offered much more flexibility and aligned with the first experiences in the Eastern Port Area, which took an island-by-island approach: no general model, but rather an exploratory journey full of surprises.

A crucial step was then taken in 1995 with the introduction of the concept 'Anchors in the IJ' in a municipal note. The new cultural facilities, which had been concentrated in Koolhaas's master plan on Station Island, could also be spread across the various islands.[19] They could become attractive public spaces and breathe new life into the IJ banks. The organizations that had developed a platform for modern classical music at De Ysbreeker were later joined by the improvising jazz musicians from BIMHUIS, finding a new place in the Muziekgebouw aan 't IJ on the Oostelijke Handelskade. The Public Library and the Conservatory moved to the Oosterdokseiland, and the Palace of Justice to the Westerdokseiland.

The successful formula of the 'anchors' actually fit very well with how public buildings functioned in the 17th-century water city. In daily use, the Waag, the Zuiderkerk, the synagogues, and the Arsenal (now the National Maritime Museum) are not only important public spaces, but also landmarks in this labyrinthine part of the city.

Variants of this are the 'motherfuckers' or 'meteorites' in the urban planning design that Adriaan Geuze from West 8 created in 1995 for Borneo-Sporenburg. The majority of the new buildings on the peninsulas in his design were conceptualized as deep city houses in three layers – a sea of houses. A few large and tall city blocks stand out from this. They are located at prominent sites. In the architectural designs by Koen van Velsen (Pacman, 1998) and Frits van Dongen (The Whale, 2000), they have also taken on a distinctive shape.

The theme of anchors and meteorites reappears in all subsequent projects in the water city, from Eye and the Pontsteiger to the Sluishuis and Jonas on IJburg.

IJburg

The *Nota van Uitgangspunten* for IJburg was published in 1996. Unlike the polders, piers, and platforms in the study plans for Nieuw-Oost, the urban planning proposal by Frits Palmboom opted for a differentiated layout with larger and smaller reclaimed islands around a large inner water body: the IJburg Bay.[20] In a referendum in 1997, more Amsterdam residents voted against than for the construction of the new district, but the threshold for the vote was not met. In 2002, the first homes were completed on the Haveneiland.

Due to the natural values in the IJmeer, various compensation projects were carried out, including the Hoeckelingsdam for the Waterland coast towards Uitdam. Furthermore, the number of homes was capped at a maximum of 18,000.

Compared to most other Vinex locations, IJburg has a fine, high housing density.[21] However, it is still not high enough to justify the construction of a metro line.

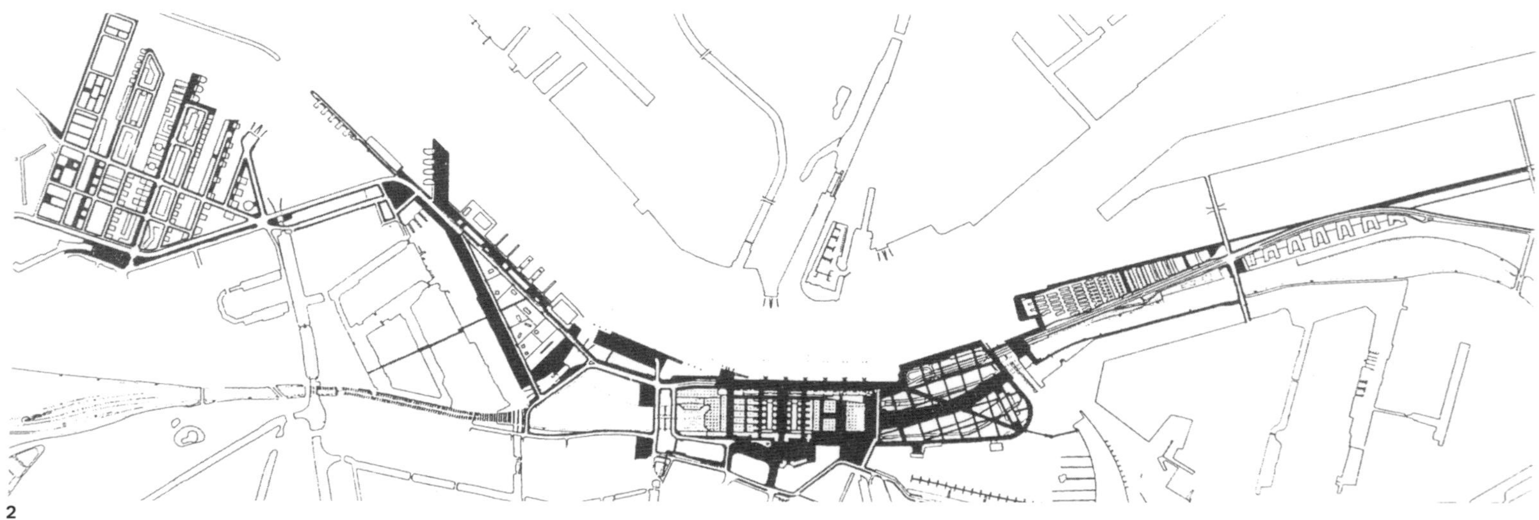
2

3

1 Public spaces along the IJ at the railway underpasses from the old city, with towers rising in height: 60 meters at Central Station, 100 meters at the head of the oostelijke Handelskade and Barentszplein, design by DRO-Gert Urhahn, 1991
2 Masterplan IJ waterfront AWF, design OMA/Rem Koolhaas, 1992
3 Sketch of cultural facilities in an inverted steam cap on the IJ side of Central Station, design by OMA/Willem-Jan Neutelings, 1992
4 Aerial view drawing of the urban design for IJburg, Frits Palmboom, 1996

The idea for a 'large ring' – a metro ring line around the city from the earliest IJ-axis plans, which would connect IJburg to Central Station as well as to the southern parts of the city – did not come to fruition. The IJtram now connects the new district to the city. However, the plan does include a reservation for a metro connection towards Almere, the so-called IJmeerlijn.

Haveneiland is the most urban neighborhood, with the long IJburglaan, the Theo van Gogh park, and the marina surrounded by compact buildings and various amenities. Construction started in 2002, and the last homes – in the Jonas project by the harbor – were only completed in 2023. The inner canals and the series of bridges give it a strong, unique identity.

Construction on Steigereiland and the Rieteilanden began in 2004. These are smaller neighborhoods with lower densities and experimental typologies: DIY housing projects, water homes, and villas.

The long construction timeline was primarily caused by the real estate crisis of 2007. Housing sales stagnated, and investors withdrew. As a result, the reclamation of Strandeiland and Buiteneiland was delayed and only resumed in 2015. The beach with the successful Blijburg pavilion was able to remain longer as a result. In the meantime, work continued on housing development at Centrumeiland, primarily by DIYers and housing cooperatives.

In the plans for the final islands, an important change has been made: housing development will be concentrated in the Muiderbuurt and Pampusbuurt on Strandeiland. Buiteneiland will be used as a soil depot and will gradually be developed into a park-like area with sports fields, recreational facilities, and new nature. The first construction plans on Strandeiland were started in 2024.

After the decision in 2003 to move the wastewater treatment plant from Zee-

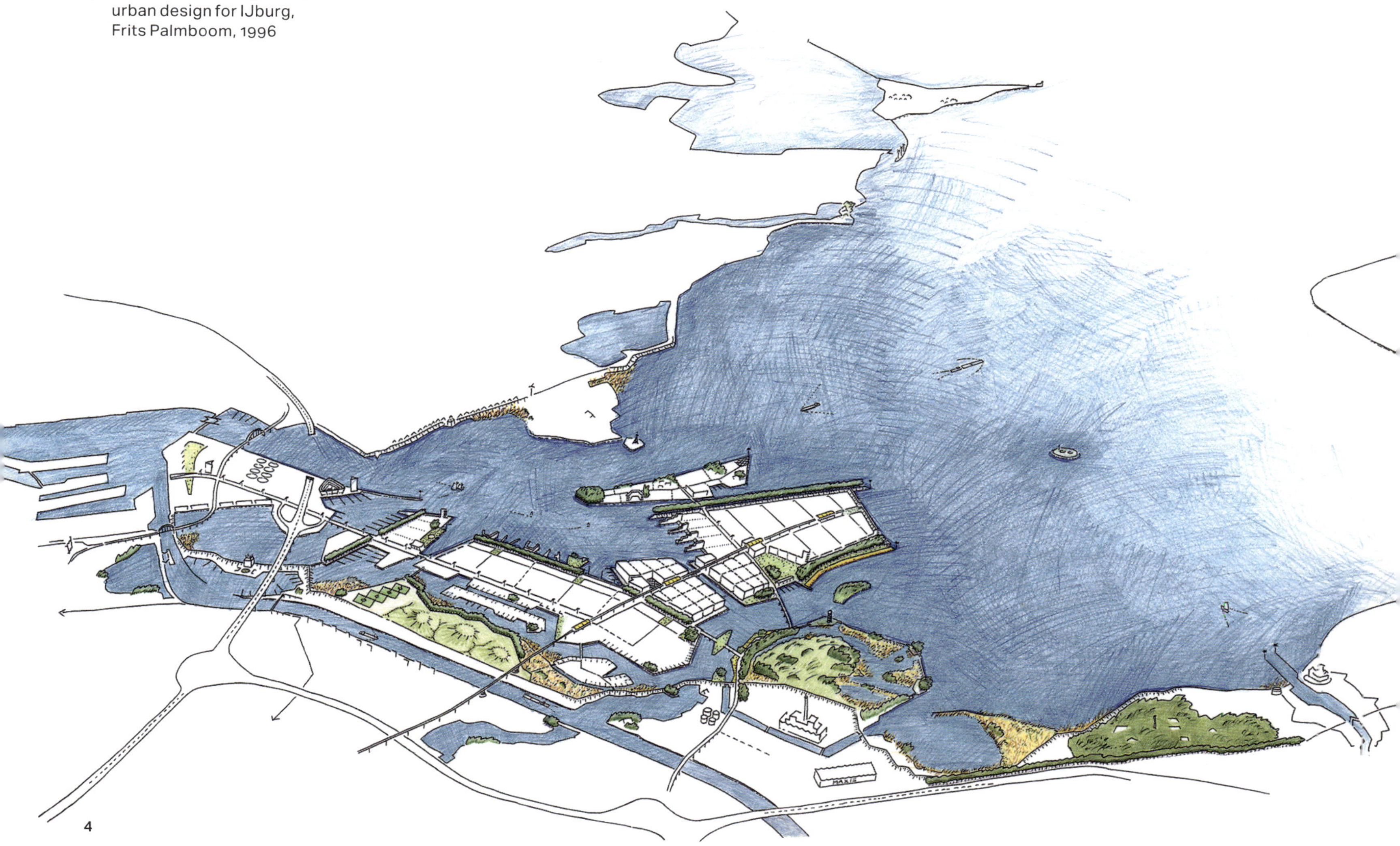

4

1

2

1 Aerial view Sluisbuurt, seen in eastern direction
2 Aerial view of Overhoeks, 2024 (Sant and Co).
3 Kop Grasweg Buiksloterham, 2018
4 Side view design Vertical Sloterdijk (NL Architects)

burgereiland (RWZI-East) to the Western Port Area, planning for this island also began. It is the old harbor sludge depot, located at a strategic point between the city and IJburg. Initially, relatively low housing densities were planned, but in the Sportheldenbuurt and recently in the plans for the Sluisbuurt, densities have been significantly increased. In the Sportheldenbuurt, compact city blocks have been built around sports fields and a spectacular skate park. In the Sluisbuurt, the density has increased from 1,500 to 5,000 homes. The first 100-meter-high residential tower in a series was completed in 2024. Once the two Baaibuurten on the southern side of the island are built, Zeeburgereiland will accommodate more than 12,000 homes in total.

Unlike other major area developments in the water city, no *Nota van Uitgangspunten* was established at the start of the planning for the Northern IJ shore (and more recently for Haven-Stad). Given the long realization times and the highly variable societal conditions, greater flexibility was needed. After Shell's decision in 2001 to build a more compact new laboratory along the IJ, a master plan was created in collaboration with BVR, the spatial development consultancy of urban planner Riek Bakker, for the western part of the Northern IJ shore, including NDSM and the adjacent industrial areas along Cornelis Douwesweg.

This master plan was never formally adopted, but the so-called *Public Space Framework* has been closely followed over the past decades. The main additions to the existing street network include bridges over the Van Hasseltkanaal and Zijkanaal I, as well as a continuous park strip along the IJ. The bridges open up the area for car traffic and enable direct and pleasant cycling routes. Eventually, it should be possible to cycle along the entire green shore, but as long as not all businesses along the shore have moved, the route remains discontinuous. The *Oeverpark* near Overhoeks, with its collection of typical Amsterdam city elms, is already a lovely spot to catch the breeze and – on the sunny side of the IJ – enjoy the view over the water.

The sub-areas have very different emphases. From the vast former Shell laboratory complex at Overhoeks, only a few buildings have been preserved: the tower, the canteen, the entrance building, and the *Groot Lab*. All others were demolished because the soil was heavily polluted and required extensive remediation. The construction plans have been adjusted several times under the influence of the real estate and banking crisis. ING Real Estate, together with Ymere, formed the development combination Overhoeks but was hit hard by the crisis and sold its position in 2012 to Amvest. Ultimately, around 3,500 homes will be built, including 1,000 apartments in the towers behind the A'DAM Tower, the spectacularly (by Felix Claus) renovated former Shell tower. In addition to the Eye Filmmuseum and A'DAM, a faculty of the Amsterdam University of the Arts, the Maritim conference hotel, a hostel, and a high school have also found a place in the area.

3

The differentiation on the NDSM site is much larger, especially due to the gradual development. Many of the buildings and slopes in the eastern part have been preserved and designated as national monuments. Besides larger and smaller companies and STRAAT, a museum for street art and graffiti, the area is used for various festivals, demonstrations, and events. The monthly flea market is one of the largest in the region. On the western part of the site, around 2,500 homes have been built since 2015. A similar number will follow in the coming years. Notably, a substantial office program has also been realized, such as the long glass building on the old crane track. The headquarters of HEMA and the publisher VNU Media have settled in a rugged city block. Marinas, museum ships, a yacht shipyard, and the ferry landing create a vibrant cityscape on and around the water.

In Buiksloterham, the contrasts are still very large at this point. The industrial area is gradually transforming, plot by plot, into a mixed urban district. Most traditional industrial companies and garages are moving out, but modern industries (such as stroller manufacturers), large-scale retail, and many creative companies have settled here. Temporary functions (vintage shops, incubators, restaurants) and experiments such as DIY housing projects and the off-grid water homes at Schoonschip have driven the transformation. In the coming years, it will become clear whether it is possible to naturally mix living and working and (still) create sufficient parks and green spaces.

4

Haven-Stad

The development of Haven-Stad further west is also a long-term project. In 2013, a Transformation Decision was made, stating that the entire harbor area within the A10 ring will eventually be transformed into a mixed urban area, potentially with 40,000-70,000 homes and tens of thousands of jobs. For well-functioning businesses, this is not an attractive prospect. The development of Haven-Stad will therefore proceed step by step. The first steps have been taken around Sloterdijk Station, the Minervahaven, and the Transformatorweg.

The redevelopment of the Houthavens also has a difficult history. In the early 1980s, many of the wood transshipment and processing companies located here closed or relocated. This was partly linked to the closure of large companies in Zaandam such as Bruynzeel and William Pont. The zoning plan for the Houthaven, created in the 1990s, focused on housing, but it stalled in legal proceedings at the Council of State due to objections from nearby port businesses. Only after mediation was an agreement reached on measures to reduce noise nuisance, both in the industrial processes and by the construction of a high noise barrier: Block 0.[22] The measures were partly financed through land exploitation.

The real estate crisis then caused further delays. During this period, only Block 0 was realized, not by project developers or housing corporations, but by CPOs – in collective private commissioning. Only from 2015 onwards did work accelerate on the realization of buildings on the various piers. In total, about 2,700 homes were built.

The construction of a tunnel for car traffic – a remnant of the ideas for the IJ boulevard from the early 1990s – allowed for a park-like connection between the Houthavens and the adjacent Spaarndammerbuurt. Schools and neighborhood facilities are located along the park. Retail and hospitality in Spaarndammerstraat benefit from the new construction in the Houthavens. The last new homes will be delivered in 2025.

Even in the further development towards the west, the noise nuisance from businesses plays an important role. The harbor is a zoned industrial area where businesses can be established in high environmental categories 4 and 5. However, the permitted and actual nuisance from businesses is often less than in the zoning decision. Therefore, the actual nuisance was carefully mapped out in the early 2010s. This made a huge difference. The Provincial Implementation Plan (PIP) from 2015 then made the first developments possible around Sloterdijk Station and at Transformatorweg. Since 2015, several residential towers have been built around the station. The one-sided office area has thus become more mixed and urban. For housing on the adjacent industrial areas at Transformatorweg, the first tenders have now been issued.

For the success of Haven-Stad, new infrastructure and green spaces, like on the eastern side of the IJ, are of great importance. Major projects include the extension of the metro ring line towards CS, with new stations near Transformatorweg and Nassauplein, and the relocation of the NS Zaanstraat yard to a location further in the Western Port Area. There is still no clear timeline for execution and full coverage of costs.

Just like for the Northern IJ shore, a *Public Space Framework* has been drawn up with new road profiles, new cycling routes, further expansion of Westerpark, and connections to the city.

A flexible strategy seems wise. Unexpected developments can lead to entirely new perspectives. Who would have thought that such a unique cluster of fashion industry businesses would emerge on Danzigerkade and in Minervahaven? Not the municipality, but the Port of Amsterdam was the driving force behind this development. Together with developer Heren 2, they cleverly responded to the demand for space from Gaastra and PVH, the owner of fashion brands Calvin Klein and Tommy Hilfiger. A whole series of other companies followed.

City around the IJ

The islands of the outer-dike water city form a complete archipelago, with a strong identity: wide vistas, water, and a whole collection of remarkable water engineering artworks.[23]

The movement of business activities to the west offered the opportunity to give the IJ new meaning as a landscape element in the city. A central role in this is played by the new water square at Central Station. This water square is not a classic square but a large open body of water, with the Anchors in the IJ surrounding it. The IJ here is 280 meters wide; much wider than the Amstel, which varies in width from 80-130 meters. The distance between the Muziekgebouw and the Palace of Justice is nearly 1,300 meters. For comparison, Sloterplas is much larger: 370 meters wide and nearly 2 kilometers long. The central water square, therefore, feels more intimate. At the same time, looking along the Muziekgebouw and the Palace of Justice, you can see far into the distance. From the 'balcony on the IJ' at CS, the view towards the Oranjesluizen is almost 4 kilometers; the distance to NDSM and Shipdock is 3 kilometers. You can still just make out some of the harbor activities.

The contrast between the two shores of the IJ is enormous. On the outer bend of the Southern IJ shore, islands with hard quays and street walls run parallel to the IJ. The long canopies of the station emphasize the longitudinal direction even more. The inner bend on the northern shore, however, is characterized by deep inlets and buildings perpendicular to the IJ. On the southern shore, cars drive along the stone quays; behind them, you can also see trains and buses coming and going. This is where all the movement happens.

The sunny northern shore is becoming increasingly greener and radiates calm. Initially, you only saw the trees of the Tolhuistuin and, in the distance, the trees near the Willemsluizen, but now the trees of the Oeverpark on Overhoeks are also growing significantly. People walk and cycle here. The attractive contrast between the shores, as we know it from the painting by Nicolaas van der Waay, reappears in a new form. If the Oeverpark at Shell is extended to NDSM and the shore at the Hamerkwartier also becomes accessible and green, a long park along the IJ will be created.

Due to the large size and the distinctive architecture of the series of Anchors in the IJ, the water square somewhat resembles the Bacino of Venice, the wide basin in the lagoon with the promenade at the Molo and the Riva degli Schiavoni, the view of Giudecca and San Giorgio, the long sightlines towards the Lido and the lagoon, surrounded by the Venetian 'anchors': the columns, the Palazzo Ducale, the church of Palladio on San Giorgio, Punta della Dogana, and the domes of Il Redentore and the Salute.

In Amsterdam, the Muziekgebouw faces directly onto the water square with its large overhanging roof and high glass foyer. The Palace of Justice is part of the IJ Dock, a robust complex, but light in color and autonomously positioned in front of the continuous facade of the dark residential buildings on Westerdokseiland. The detached objects along the IJ promenade on the northern shore, the iconic Eye Filmmuseum, the cheerful A'DAM Tower, the terraces of THT next to it, with the tall towers of 'the Strip' in the background, form a beautiful contrast with the long, glass station canopy on the southern side.

RESIDENTIAL, BLOCK, AND PLOT LAYOUTS

Since the late 1980s, the transformation of the water city has involved experimentation with a wide range of housing, block, and subdivision forms. For each island, the development formula has varied: together with one or more market parties, a specific program was chosen, responding to the housing demand of the moment, along with an urban designer who could exploit the qualities of the location and realize the challenges of the program. This ultimately resulted in a fantastic series of projects, with unique innovations and strong, very different identities.

The renewal of Kattenburg from the 1970s still aligns with the modern tradition. Stacked maisonettes had been used earlier.[24] However, here they were built on a semi-submerged parking garage, accessed from galleries and grouped around green courtyards.

The urban design for IJplein from 1980 is the first postmodern plan, paradoxically with various references to early modern designs from the 1920s, such as the layout of Tuindorp Nieuwendam in the north, with narrow streets and public inner gardens, the 'bleekveldjes.' The western part is inspired by a study plan by German architects Hans and Wassili Luckhardt from 1927, *Stadt ohne Höfe*, combining long blocks with detached urban villas. With a collage-like technique, a variety of urban elements were added: a walking promenade, an athletics track, ditches, a willow lane, the ferry square.

In almost all later plans for the islands, references are made to classical urban planning principles and model plans from the period up to 1920. Sometimes, foreign examples have been used, such as the large urban blocks in Berlin and Paris in the plan by Jo Coenen for KNSM Island, the courtyards in those cities in the design by Peter Defesche for Westerdokseiland, or the London superblocks with mews and inner streets in the design for Haveneiland by the design team Felix Claus, Frits van Dongen, and Ton Schaap, or the sturdy 19th-century city blocks in New York and Chicago (NDSM). Much more often, Amsterdam examples have been used: the 17th century canal belt blocks with courtyards (Java Island), the Jordaan (Borneo-Sporenburg), the hospital pavilions on the WG site (Overhoeks), and brick architecture at the Olympiaplein (Zeeburgereiland). Various islands also feature references to the classic Amsterdam back house: in Valkenburgerstraat, on Java Island, and more recently in the plans for Block 0 in the Houthavens and the first new residential blocks in Buiksloterham along Ridderspoorweg.

If you take a broad view at the housing on the series of city islands, the most striking common features are: seven to nine floors, internal parking solutions for cars and bicycles, and access via elevators. You hardly find any stair-access apartments here anymore. Elevators provide access to two, three, or four apartments per floor, sometimes more through a short gallery, a corridor, or a light well. This principle has been most thoroughly implemented in the apartment complexes in Overhoeks. Elevators access, from the underground parking garages and central entrance halls, up to fourteen apartments on a single floor in some cases. A major advantage of internal parking is that the street scene is not dominated by cars. This applies to the entire water city.

Another common feature of the housing on the city islands is the strong differentiation; not only in architecture and sector but especially in apartment size and living form.

This began in the planning for Java Island with the distinction of diverse urban lifestyles, ranging from transient newcomers to luxury dual-income households and large urban families. Based on this, the building blocks experimented with back houses, as well as palazzos in the inner courtyards and individually self-developed four- and five-story houses on the new cross-canals.

The blocks on Haveneiland-West also feature a strong mix. All forms of housing and financing categories from the overall program for IJburg are represented in each building block: senior housing, small and larger family homes for sale, studios for young people and students, and mid-priced rental apartments. As a result, the blocks also have a highly differentiated structure. Each architect and client came up with new types of homes and combinations.

← Balcony on the IJ, collage for presentation proposal in B&W Amsterdam, 2015

→ **Next page:** Oostenburg

3C BORNEO-SPORENBURG 2000

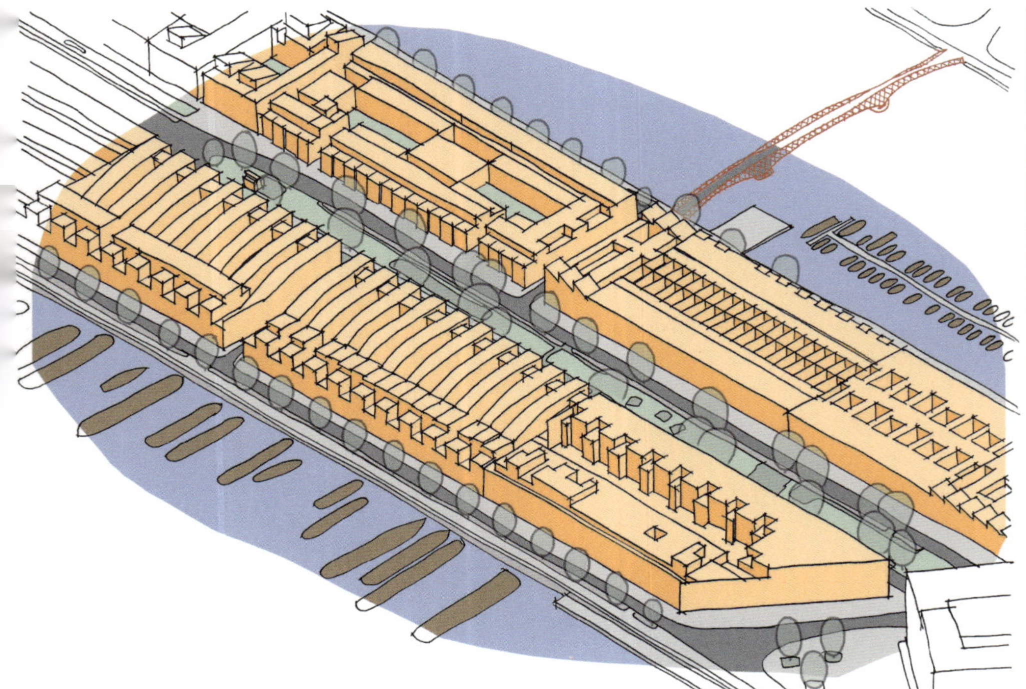

Features
Closed blocks with deep townhouses in three layers and indoor parking

Urban planning – supervision
Adriaan Geuze, Wim Kloosterboer (West 8), Wim Hendriks, Ton Schaap (DRO)

Architects
including Rudy Uytenhaak, KENK, MVRDV, HRH architects, KAAN architects, CASA, M3H, Heren 5, Rapp + Rapp, Ruth Visser, Liesbeth van der Pol, Steven Sorgdrager, Tupker & van der Neut

Construction period
1996–2000

Houses per hectare
100

Average apartment size
92 m²

3D HAVENEILAND – WEST 2003

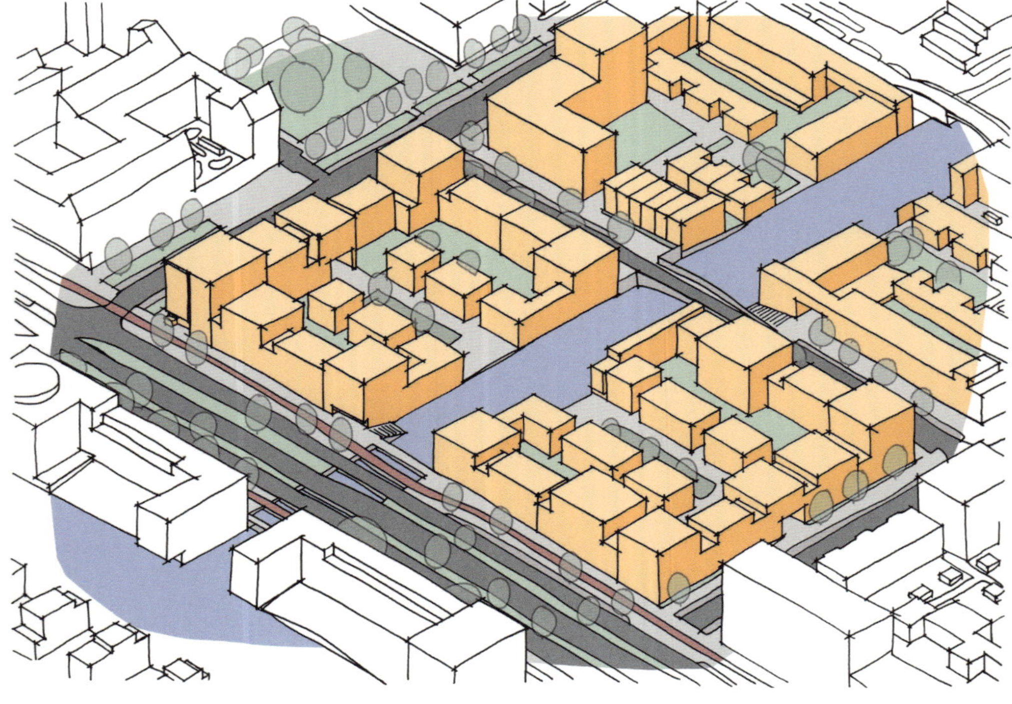

Features
Urban blocks with a variety of housing typologies and indoor and underground parking

Urban planning – supervision
Felix Claus, Frits van Dongen, Ton Schaap, Jan Stigter, Kees Rijnboutt (chair)

Architects
KCAP (block 11 a-b)

Construction period
1999–2003

Houses per hectare
85

Average apartment size
121 m²

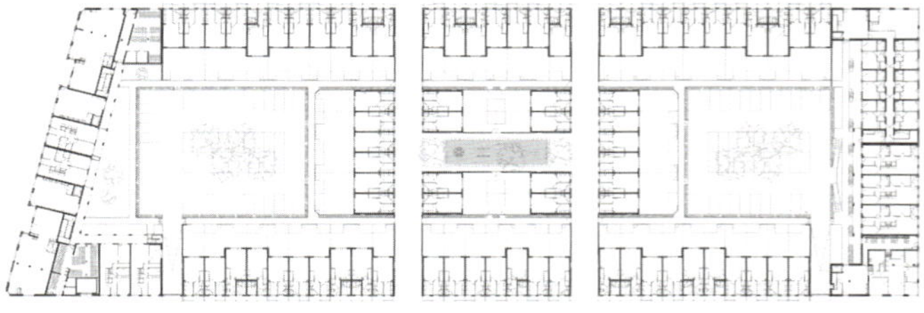

3A KATTENBURG — 1975

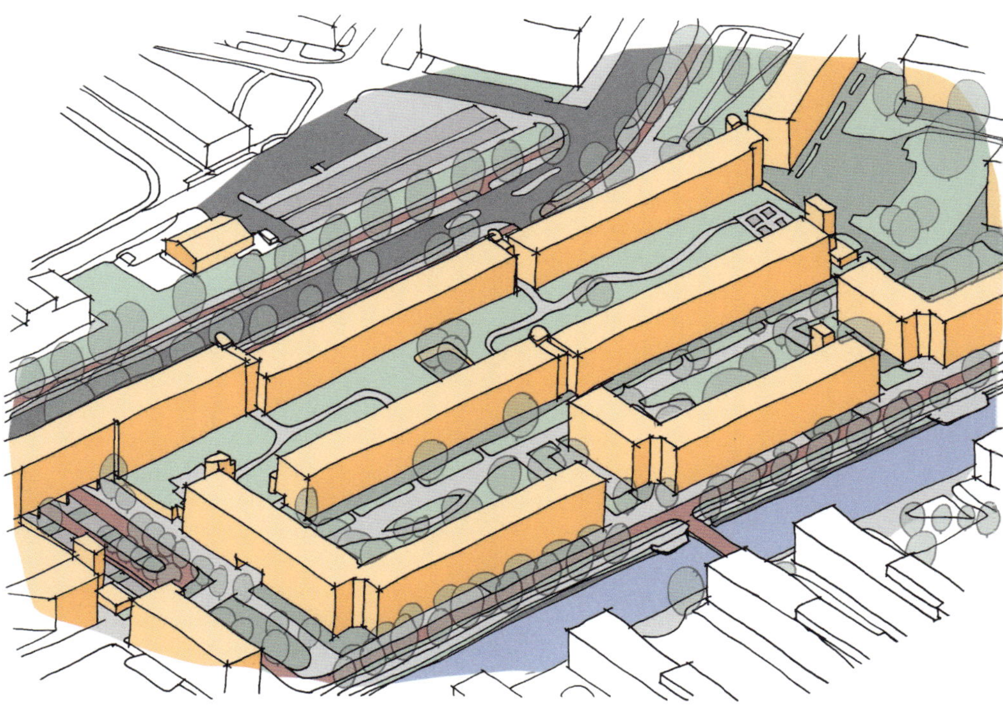

Features
Courtyard layout with stacked maisonettes on a parking garage

Urban planning – supervision
City Development section
PW Amsterdam

Architects
Apon, Van den Berg, Ter Braak, and Tromp

Construction period
1973–1975

Houses per hectare
90

Average apartment size
84 m²

3B JAVA-EILAND — 2000

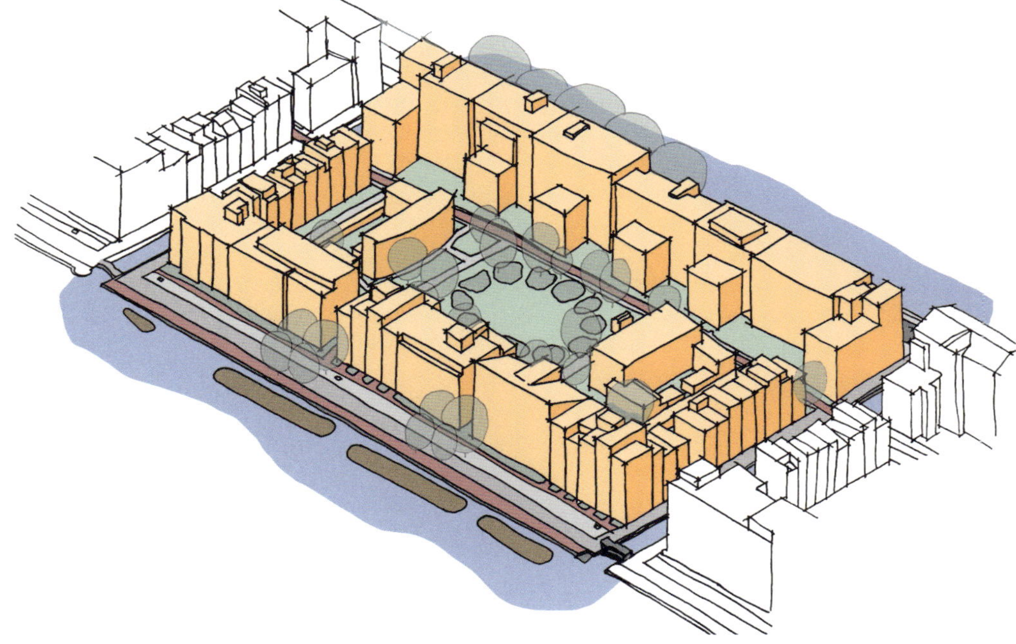

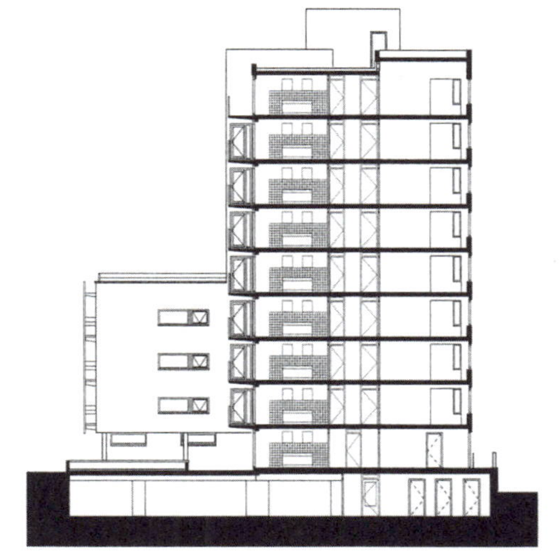

Features
Superblocks with a variety of housing typologies, partly on a semi-underground parking garage

Urban planning – supervision
Yttje Feddes, Ton Schaap, Sjoerd Soeters, Jan Stigter, Rudy Uytenhaak

Architects
including Sjoerd Soeters, KCAP, Rudy Uytenhaak, Marcel Lok, Architecten Cie., Mecanoo, Claus en Kaan Architecten, Geurst and Schulze

Construction period
1993–2000

Houses per hectare
140

Average apartment size
88 m²

ERKSPOOR

3G OVERHOEKS 2016

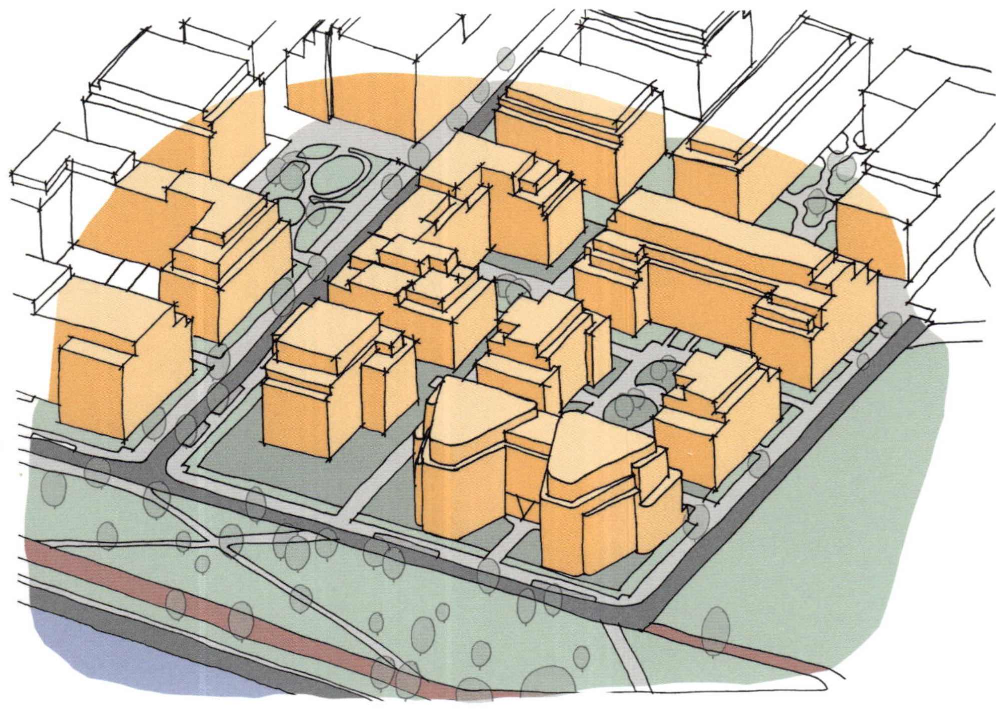

Features
Detached apartment complexes, 6-9 stories, underground parking

Urban planning – supervision
Bram Breedveld, Jaap van de Bout, Jeroen Geurst, Ton Schaap, Kari Stötzer

Architects
including Jo Coenen & Co Architekten, Álvaro Siza, Van der Hoeven Architekten, Tony Fretton Architects, and Geurst & Schulze architecten

Construction period
2009–2016

Houses per hectare
190

Average apartment size
94 m²

3H HOUTHAVENS 2023

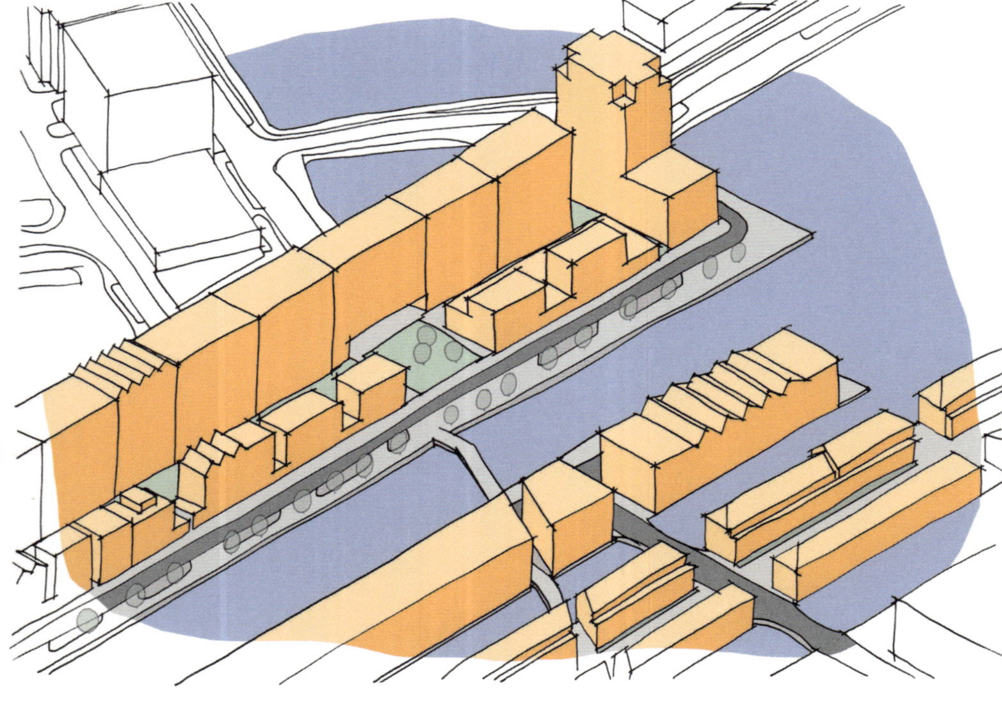

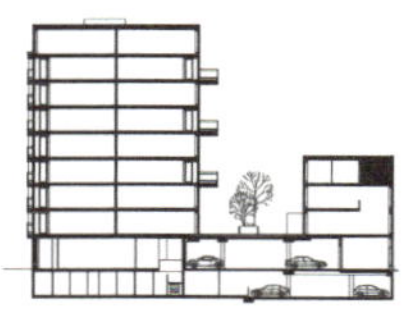

Features
Piers with various housing typologies. Block-0: CPO development with built-in parking

Urban planning – supervision
Jan Brouwer, Wim Hendriks, Ton Schaap, Sjoerd Soeters

Architects
including Heren 5 Architecten, Marc Koehler Architects, Thijs Asselbergs architectuurcentrale, de Architekten Cie., Architektenburo Brink & Fleer

Construction period
2012–2023

Houses per hectare
155

Average apartment size
98 m²

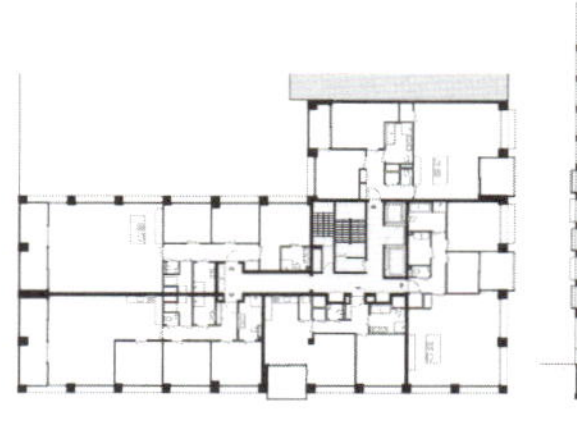

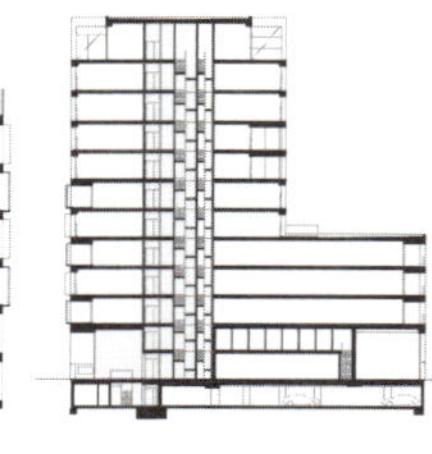

FUNEN 2005

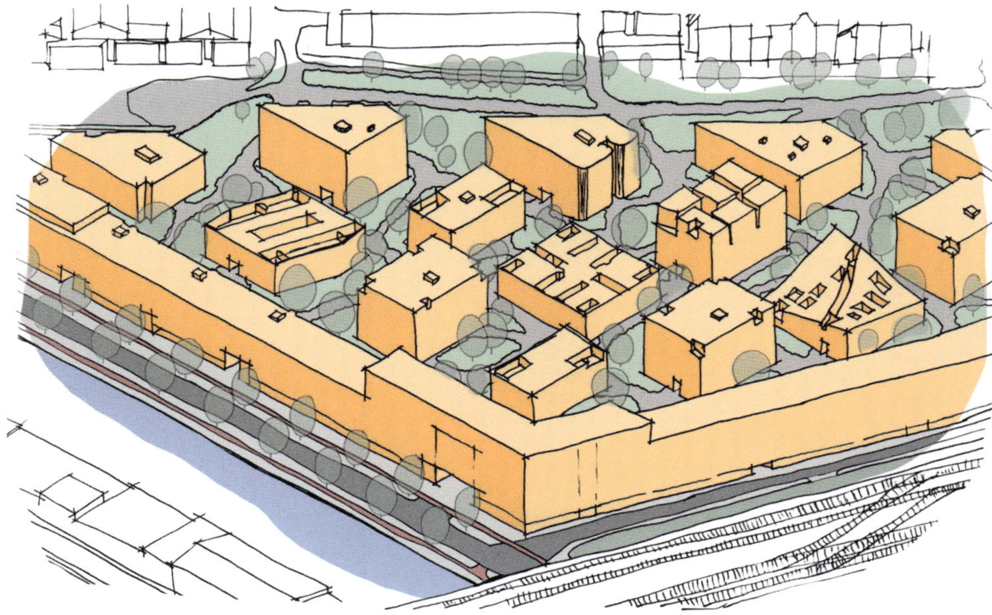

Features
City villas in a car-free and green interior area, shielded by an 8-story high wall with gallery apartments

Urban planning – supervision
Frits van Dongen, Pieter van Wesemael (Architecten Cie.)

Architects
including Architecten Cie., Van Sambeek & Van Veen Architecten, NL Architects, Lafour & Wijk, Architectenbureau Kuiper en Co, Geurst & Schulze Architecten, DKV Architecten, De Architectengroep, Claus en Kaan Architecten

Construction period
1998–2005

Houses per hectare
85

Average apartment size
99 m²

3F WESTERDOKSEILAND 2009

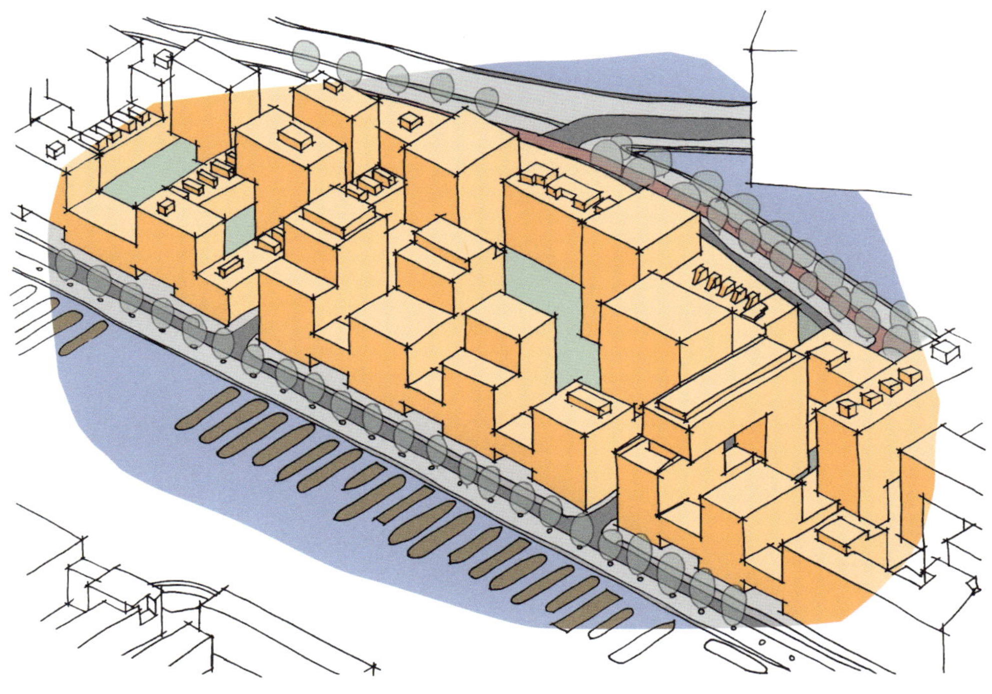

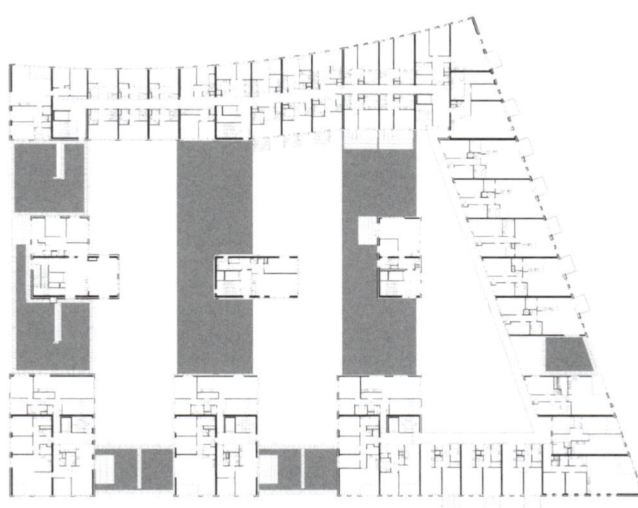

Features
Apartment blocks around inner courtyards with 2 levels of underground parking

Urban planning – supervision
Peter Defesche (OD 205), Tjeerd Dijkstra (chair), Jan Brouwer, Toine van Goethem, Ton Schaap

Architects
including Architecten Cie., Heren 5 Architecten, Meyer en Van Schooten Architecten

Construction period
2001–2009

Houses per hectare
190

Average apartment size
99 m²

31 IJBURG – LAND RECLAMATION, NATURE, BRIDGES

In the late 1980s, the planning process for the construction of new islands for housing in the IJmeer began. After a referendum (negative, but with too low a turnout to be valid), the construction of the islands began in 1999. As of 2025, more than 25,000 people live on IJburg.

The new residential area was not traditionally reclaimed but land was pumped up. Sand was brought from the shipping channels in the Markermeer, which was pumped in layers – like a stack of pancakes – to create the islands, due to the unstable underlying soil. For the first islands (Steigereiland, Haveneiland, Rieteilanden), 25 million cubic meters of sand were required. Three years later, the first residents moved into their homes. The construction of Centrumeiland, focused on DIY housing, began in 2013. The development of Strandeiland started in 2018, with the first homes there being built in 2024.

For the construction of Buiteneiland, a different method is being followed. The island will serve as a soil depot and will be gradually formed by earth excavated from construction projects in the city.

Compensating the lost nature was an important condition for the development of IJburg. The establishment of a nature development fund provided money to invest in expanding and strengthening nature. For example, mussel beds were created, and the Diemerpark (after remediation) and the Diemervijfhoek were developed. The Hoeckelingsdam was built in front of the Waterland coast.

Bridges play a crucial role on IJburg.

1

2

3

The largest ones open up and connect the islands. The most famous is the Enneüs Heermabrug, which is 230 meters long and was designed by British architect Nicolas Grimshaw. The Nesciobrug is a 780-meter long bicycle bridge over the Amsterdam-Rijnkanaal. For the various islands, 'families' of bridges have been designed. For instance, Erna van Sambeek designed the fourteen distinctive brick bridges for Haveneiland.

1 IJburg Beach, 2023
2 Aerial photo, 2003
3 Aerial photo, 2023
4 Nescio Bicycle Bridge
5 Enneüs Heermabrug Bridge
6 Building a bridge on IJburg
7 Bridge family Haveneiland, designed by Sambeek and Van Veen Architects

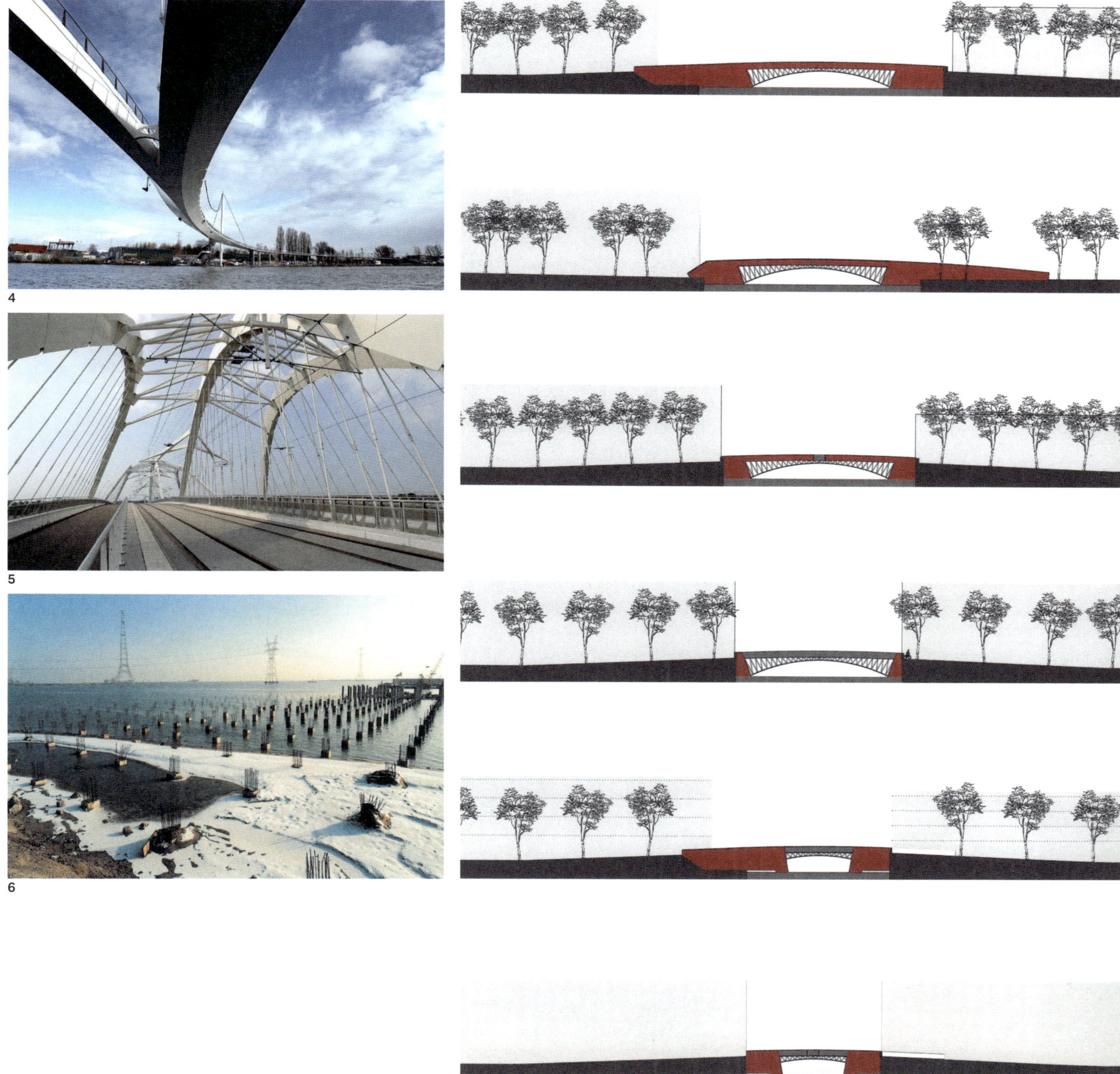

4

5

6

7

3J RWZI WEST

In 2006, Waternet opened a new large sewage treatment plant in the Western Port Area. This facility replaced two old sewage treatment plants, one on Zeeburgereiland and the other on Spaklerweg. Housing development was then possible on these locations.

The replacement was a massive operation. In addition to the new sewage treatment plant itself, 49 kilometers of sewer pipes had to be laid, and four booster pumping stations were built to transport the wastewater from the city to the Western Port Area. The booster technique comes from the dredging world. The wastewater is pumped through the sewers under high pressure.

The four booster pumping stations have a unique, almost futuristic design. Booster station West is integrated into the greenery of the Rembrandtpark. The station was designed by BUROBEB and is only partially visible. Booster station East on Zeeburgereiland was designed by Bekkering Adams Architecten. The sculptural structure is made from cobalt blue and green concrete, adorned with various decorative patterns. The pumping station in the North at Klaprozenweg was designed by Bonnemayer Architecten. It's a large tube that appears to float in the evening due to special lighting. Booster station South is the most spectacular design. GROUP A created a building on Spaklerweg with matte silver panels that resemble a spaceship or a large engine block. At night, the seams between the panels light up.

The new construction in the Harbor Area also features remarkable architecture. Architecture studio Herman Hertzberger designed the new office building. A distinctive feature of the façade is a water screen that provides cooling in the summer. DS landscape architects integrated the new basins into a dune landscape with pools and pines. The area is rarely accessed, creating a unique habitat for flora and fauna.

1 RWZI-West (Wastewater Treatment Plant), designed by Architectuurstudio Herman Hertzberger
2 RWZI-West, designed by Architectuurstudio Herman Hertzberger
3 Aerial photo, 2003
4 Aerial photo, 2023
5 Booster Pump Station East, designed by Juliette Bekkering Architects
6 Booster Pump Station West
7 Map of adjustments in the sewer system
8 Booster Pump Station South
9 Booster Pump Station North

1

2

3

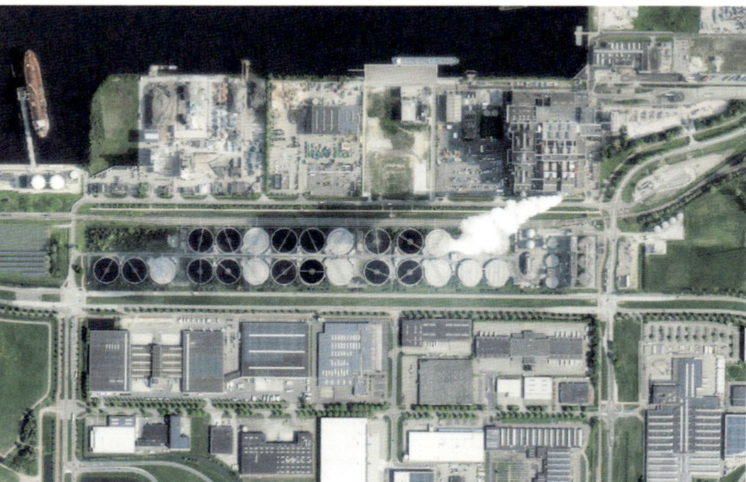
4

5

6

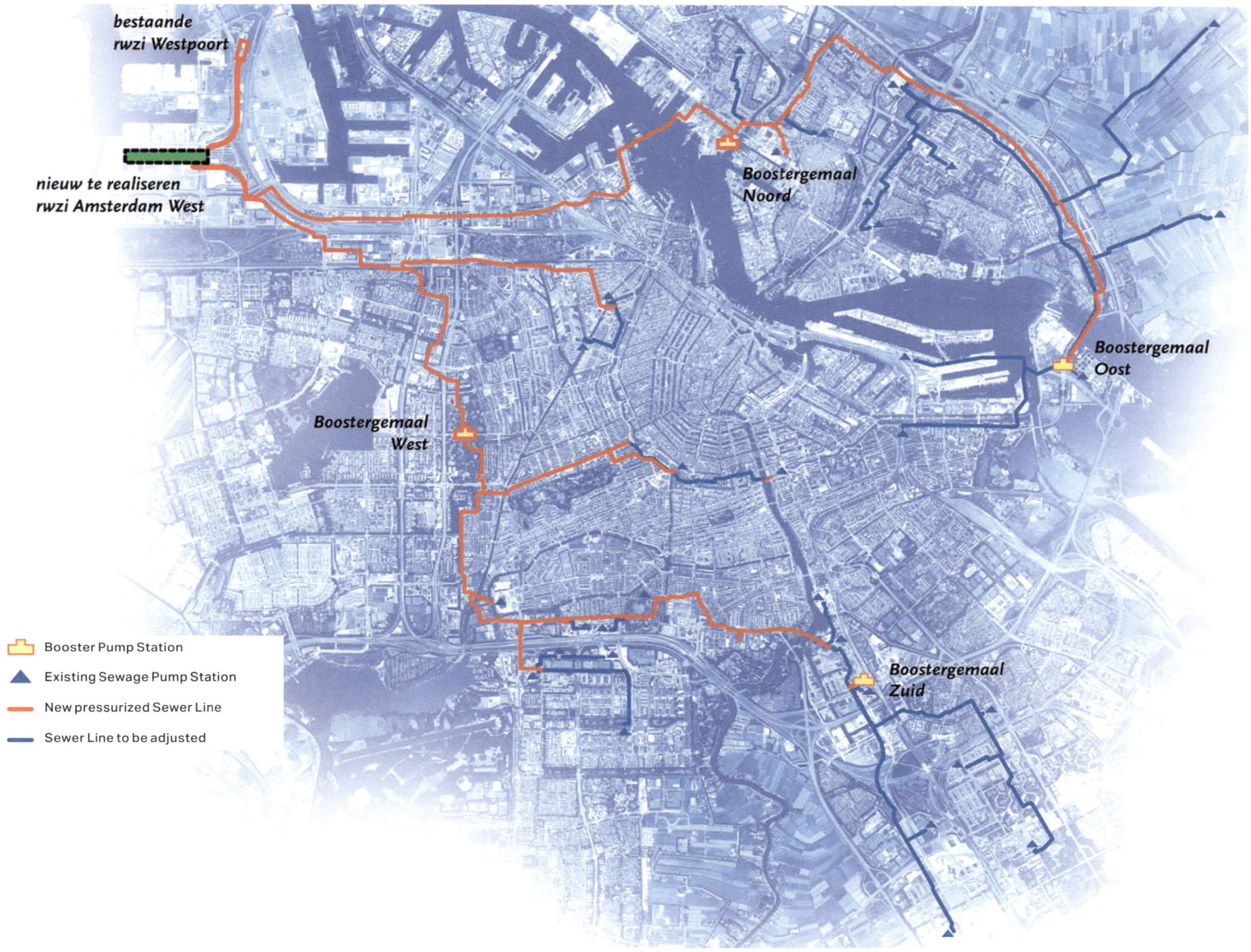

bestaande
rwzi Westpoort

nieuw te realiseren
rwzi Amsterdam West

Boostergemaal
Noord

Boostergemaal
Oost

Boostergemaal
West

Boostergemaal
Zuid

Booster Pump Station

Existing Sewage Pump Station

New pressurized Sewer Line

Sewer Line to be adjusted

7

8

9

3K NDSM SHIPYARD

Since the beginning of the 20th century, shipbuilding and repair yards were established along the IJ in the northern part of Amsterdam. In 1946, these merged into the Nederlandsche Dok en Scheepbouw Maatschappij (NDSM). During the economic crisis of the 1980s, NDSM went bankrupt, and a large part of the site was left vacant. It quickly became a haven for squatters, and artists found the location to be ideal for their activities, making it famous for dance parties and theatrical performances, including those by the Dogtroep. It became a valuable place, a fringe area full of experimental art and culture.

Starting in 2000, the municipality began developing the area of the NDSM shipyard. The western part of the yard was designated as a mixed-use residential and work area. The eastern part was declared a monument in 2007. The ensemble of slipways, rails, cranes, the large shipbuilding hall, the forge, the carpentry hall, and the welding hall, together with the surrounding water, gives a fascinating insight into the original functioning of the yard. The large shipbuilding hall has been converted by Kinetisch Noord into a center for studios and small businesses. Both slipways have been renovated. The open space regularly hosts a large flea market and various festivals. It is being explored whether there could also be space for sports and green areas in this location. The industrial and rugged character of the site remains intact.

Kraanspoor was the first prominent new building in the western part of the area (completed in 2007). It is 270 meters long and sits on the concrete structure that once supported a crane. The new part of the building is simple in form and material. Existing elements such as stairs have been reused wherever possible. Since then, around 2,500 homes have been built in NDSM-West. Additionally, the new headquarters of HEMA and publisher VNU Media are located here, along with a branch of the ROC. The plans include space for an additional 2,500 homes.

1 Crane track in 2008
2 Café Noorderlicht
3 Aerial photo, 2003
4 Aerial photo, 2023
5 The Y-Slope, renovation design by Dynamo Architects
6 The Concertgebouw Orchestra performs on the Y-Slope, 2024 (photo: World Wide Wendel / Nathan Reinds)
7 The skyline of NDSM West in 2024
8 Plan of the big Shipbuilding Hall, design by Dynamo Architects
9 Interior of the Shipbuilding Hall, 2020
10 Cross-section of the Shipbuilding Hall, design by Dynamo Architects

1

2

3

4

5

6

7

deelproject : NOORDSTROOK
deelproject : KUNSTSTAD
deelproject : ZUIDSTROOK / VRIJE KAVELS
8

9

optie 3e laag
optie 3e laag
7
type A
type A
type B
type B
type B
type A
type A
type B
type B
kruisspoor
optie vide
1
A8
deelproject : ZUIDSTROOK
E1
E2
E3
deelproject : KUNSTSTAD
E4
E5
deelproject : NOORDSTROOK
C8
10

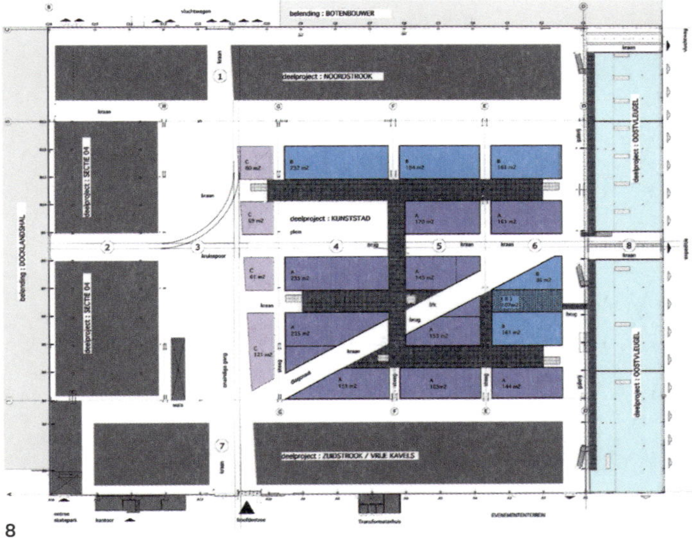

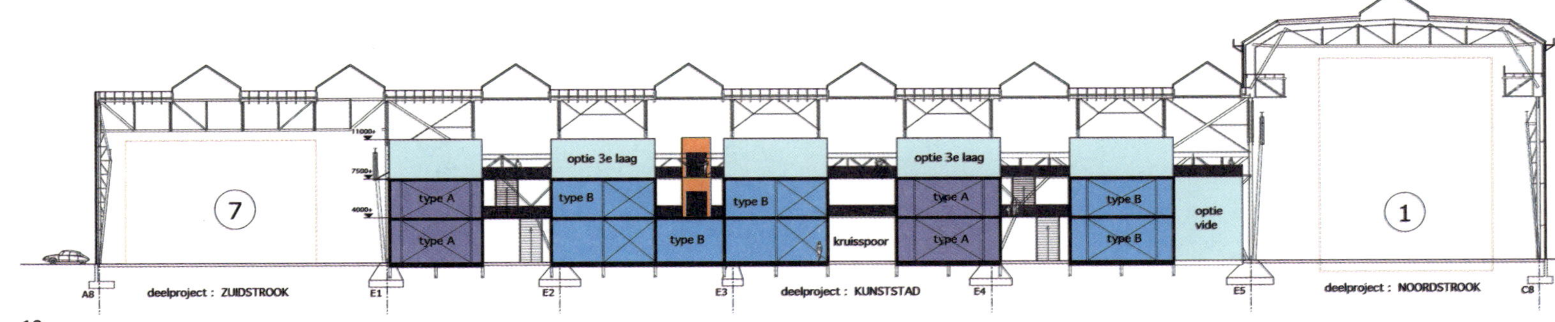

3L IJPROMENADE

As early as the late 19th century, the old gallows field at the Buiksloterweg ferry landing in Noord was used for the storage and transshipment of oil products. After one of Royal/Shell's subsidiaries acquired the Dordtse Petroleum Maatschappij in 1911, laboratories were also built here, including the Groot Lab in 1929. In the following decades, Shell acquired various plots of land, and the KSLA, the Royal Shell Laboratory Amsterdam, grew into a complete city with 46 buildings on a 27-hectare site. Notable new construction projects included the Overhoeks tower (1971) and the staff restaurant (1972), both designed by architect Arthur Staal. These buildings marked the 'opposite' side in the curve of the IJ, but the site and buildings were not publicly accessible.

Shell's decision in 2001 to build a compact new laboratory on the edge of the site opened up a new perspective. The vacated area could be developed into an urban district of more than 20 hectares, located right in the city and close to Central Station. In 2003, the municipality purchased the land.

The new laboratory opened in 2009. ING and Ymere then began the remediation and redevelopment. The plan consists of three parts: a compact residential neighborhood with around 3,000 homes, a series of high residential and hotel towers in what

1

2

3

4

5

is called 'the Strip,' and a cluster of urban amenities along the IJ. The most prominent developments include the newly built Eye Filmmuseum (2012), THT in the old staff restaurant with a large new restaurant and a branch of Paradiso (2014), and the renovated Overhoeks tower with hospitality, offices, a hotel, and the observation terrace above (now A'DAM Tower, 2016).

The cluster is centered around a new public quay along the IJ, called IJpromenade, which is directly connected to the ferry square via a new bridge.

On the other side, the promenade connects to Oeverpark, which has a beautiful collection of Amsterdam elms, and to Schegpark, which lies between the new residential area and 'the Strip.'

In 2026, the final new construction projects and Schegpark will be completed. The closed laboratory complex will have made way for a lively and highly mixed urban area.

1 Aerial photograph of the Shell site in 2003
2 Impression of the Schegpark
3 Overview drawing of Oeverpark and Schegpark
4 Aerial photo, 2003
5 Aerial photo, 2023
6 Eye and the A'DAM Tower in 2019
7 THT, former Shell staff restaurant
8 Eye, interior

6

7

8

3M SPAARNDAMMERTUNNEL AND HOUTHAVENPARK

In the design of the new construction plans for the Houthavens in 2006, emphasis was placed on social and spatial connections with the neighboring Spaarndammerbuurt. The new residents could strengthen the support for the retail and catering facilities on Spaarndammerstraat. Conversely, new facilities, such as schools, would be established in the new development to serve the existing neighborhood. However, it soon became clear that the Spaarndammerdijk formed a dangerous barrier between the old and new areas. Although relatively little destination traffic passed through the road, there was a lot of through traffic, especially faster vehicles traveling to and from the city center. As a result, it was decided in 2013 to tunnel a large portion of Spaarndammerdijk.

The tunnel design was created by contractor Max Bögl. Ultimately, 800 meters

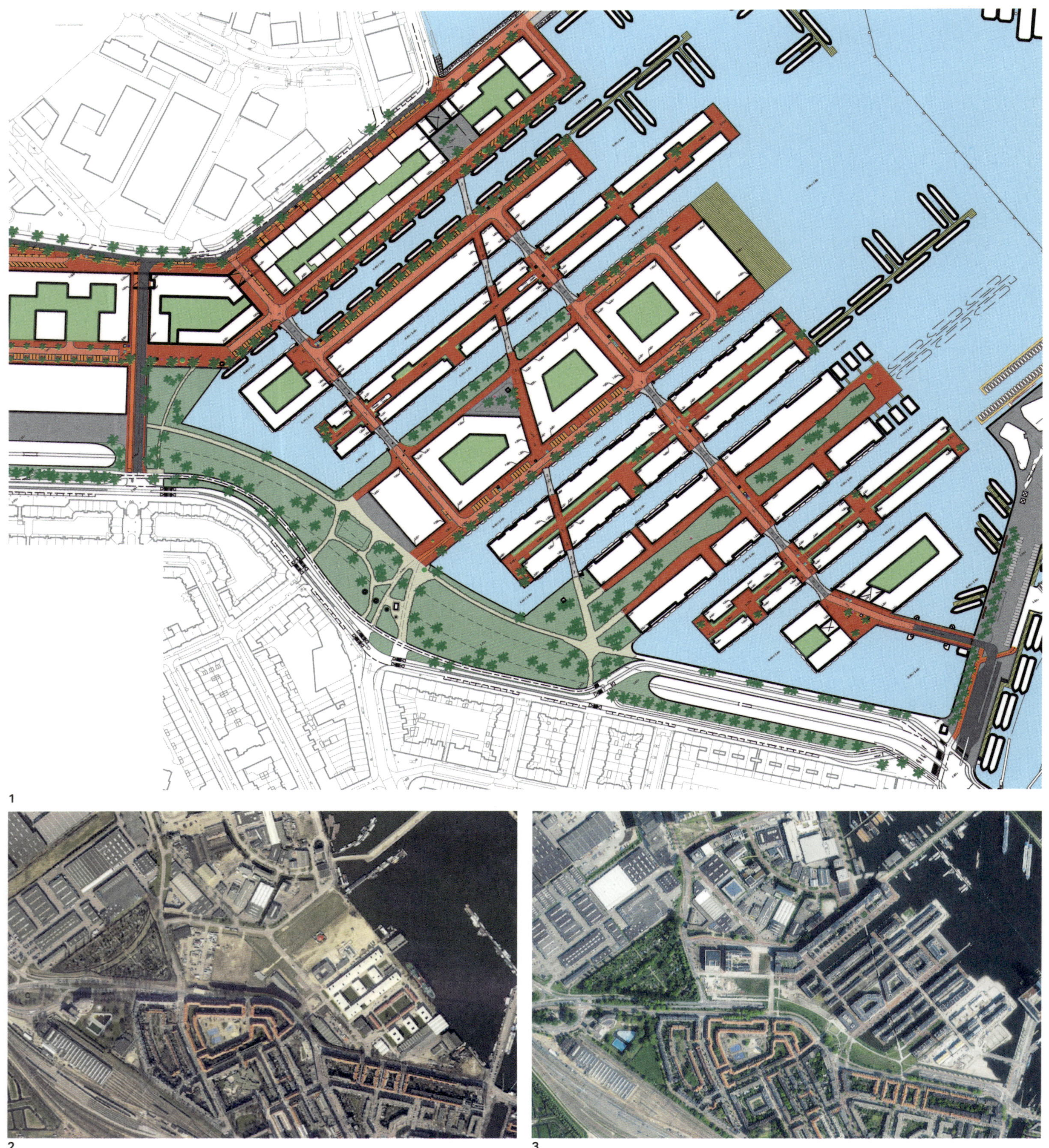

1

2

3

of the road were constructed as a lowered passage, with 470 meters fully underground. After the tunnel opened in 2018, work began on the development of the Houthavenpark on top of it. This park is specifically designed to serve both the Spaarndammerbuurt and the Houthavens.

It offers plenty of opportunities for sports and recreation. Additionally, the schoolyards of two elementary schools and a secondary school are located next to the park. A busy, through road has been transformed into a green connection between two neighborhoods.

1 Excerpt of the Master Plan map Houthavens, 2016
2 Aerial photo, 2009
3 Aerial photo, 2023
4 Bench Houthaven Park, 170 meters long
5 Houthaven Park
6 Houthaven Park
7 Intersection Spaarndammerstraat-Tasmanstraat, 1982
8 Entrance to Spaarndammertunnel

4

5

6

7

8

SOUTHWARD — INTEGRATION OF XL BUILDINGS

Would it work this time? After long preparations and difficult negotiations, a contract was finally signed at the end of 2024 to move the A10 Zuid underground (Zuidasdok). Work on the expansion of Zuid Station is already in full swing. By 2036, the tunnels and station should be completed.

In 1975, the District Court moved from Kleine-Gartmanplantsoen in the city center to a new building on Parnassusweg, bringing with it a wave of law firms. A little further down the road were the RAI convention center and the first buildings of Vrije Universiteit, but who could have imagined what was about to unfold here? It wasn't until 1981 that the A10 Zuid was completed, and the Schiphol Railway Line began running to the airport and Leiden. In 1985, the WTC opened, and from that moment, things moved fast, not just around Zuid Station but across the entire southern city edge. The Binnengasthuis and Wilhelmina Gasthuis hospitals relocated to AMC, the science faculties moved to Science Park, Ajax to the Arena. The RAI expanded.

But how do you build a pleasant, well-functioning city around these massive structures? The integration of XL buildings into their surroundings will remain a pressing issue for the decades to come. Already, a different kind of city is taking shape, with a new residential typology: towers!

→ NMB bank building
Parnassusweg, 1975–2025

MOVEMENT 4

The development of Zuidas over the past decades is a remarkable phenomenon. After the construction of the WTC in 1985 and the completion of the new road and rail infrastructure on the city's southern edge, a key moment in Amsterdam's development came in 1993 when land near NS Zuid Station was allocated to ABN AMRO.

ABN and AMRO Bank had numerous branches in the city center. The construction of the new headquarters for the merged bank at Zuidas implied a significant shift – the city center would lose an important part of its function. More banks and financial institutions soon followed, attracting a wave of accounting and consulting firms. This cluster then became an ecosystem where many other internationally operating Dutch companies, such as AkzoNobel and Arcadis, also chose to establish their headquarters, relocating from Arnhem to Amsterdam. Several international business service providers, including EY, Accenture, and Uber, also set up offices here.[1]

Philips initially stood out by moving its headquarters from Eindhoven to the Breitner Tower near Amstel Station. However, in early 2025, the company also opened an office at Zuidas in a thoroughly renovated building on Prinses Irenestraat, originally constructed in 1974. The succession of tenants in this building offers a clear picture of the area's evolving dynamics. The law firm Klynveld Kraayenhof & Co was the first to occupy it before merging into KPMG and relocating to Amstelveen. NautaDutilh also occupied the building for many years until moving in 2016 to a new development on Beethovenstraat. From 2003 until its relocation to the former prison on Amstelveenseweg, part of the building was used by The British School of Amsterdam.

Sarphati

The southward movement has a remarkable parallel in the city's 19th-century development. The earliest railway, built in 1839 to Haarlem, faithfully followed the towpath of the old trekvaart canal. However, the Rhijnspoorweg to Utrecht, Arnhem, and the Ruhr area took an entirely new route. The opening of Weesperpoort Station in 1843 sparked a wave of construction in the southeastern part of the inner city in the years that followed.

Samuel Sarphati initiated the construction of the Palace of Industry (1853–1864), an exhibition hall made of cast iron and glass, crowned by a massive dome on Frederiksplein. He also oversaw the development of the highly modern Amstel Hotel (1867). In 1860, together with Cornelis Outshoorn, Sarphati designed the first expansion plan for the city beyond the dismantled fortifications, covering what is now the Weesperzijde neighborhood and the northern part of De Pijp. The plan included the construction of a museum and a university complex, as well as the relocation of the livestock market and the city's waste dump to sites far outside the old city.

In 1867, city architect Jacob van Niftrik elaborated on these ideas in a more comprehensive proposal for urban expansion. The old fortifications and a 500-meter-wide zone beyond them provided space for growth. The central feature of this plan was the construction of a new central station on the city's southern edge. Unlike in many other Western European metropolises – such as London, Paris, and Berlin – Amsterdam and the national government opted to replace the old terminus stations and connect the railway lines from Utrecht and Amersfoort to those from Haarlem and the northern part of North Holland. However, Amsterdam and

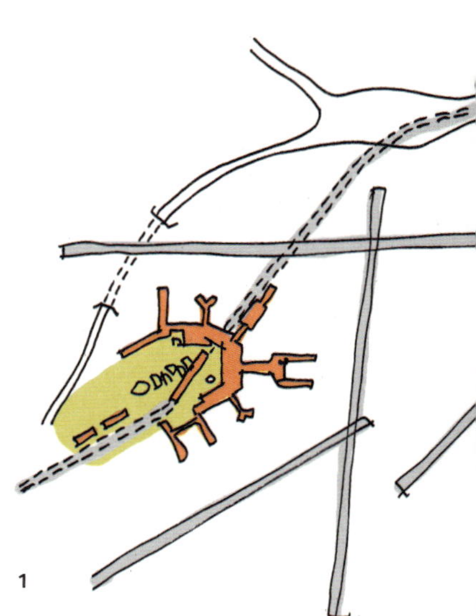

1 Movement of financial services to the station areas on the outskirts of the city and towards Schiphol

2 Palace of Industry Frederiksplein, seen from the Amstel, circa 1880

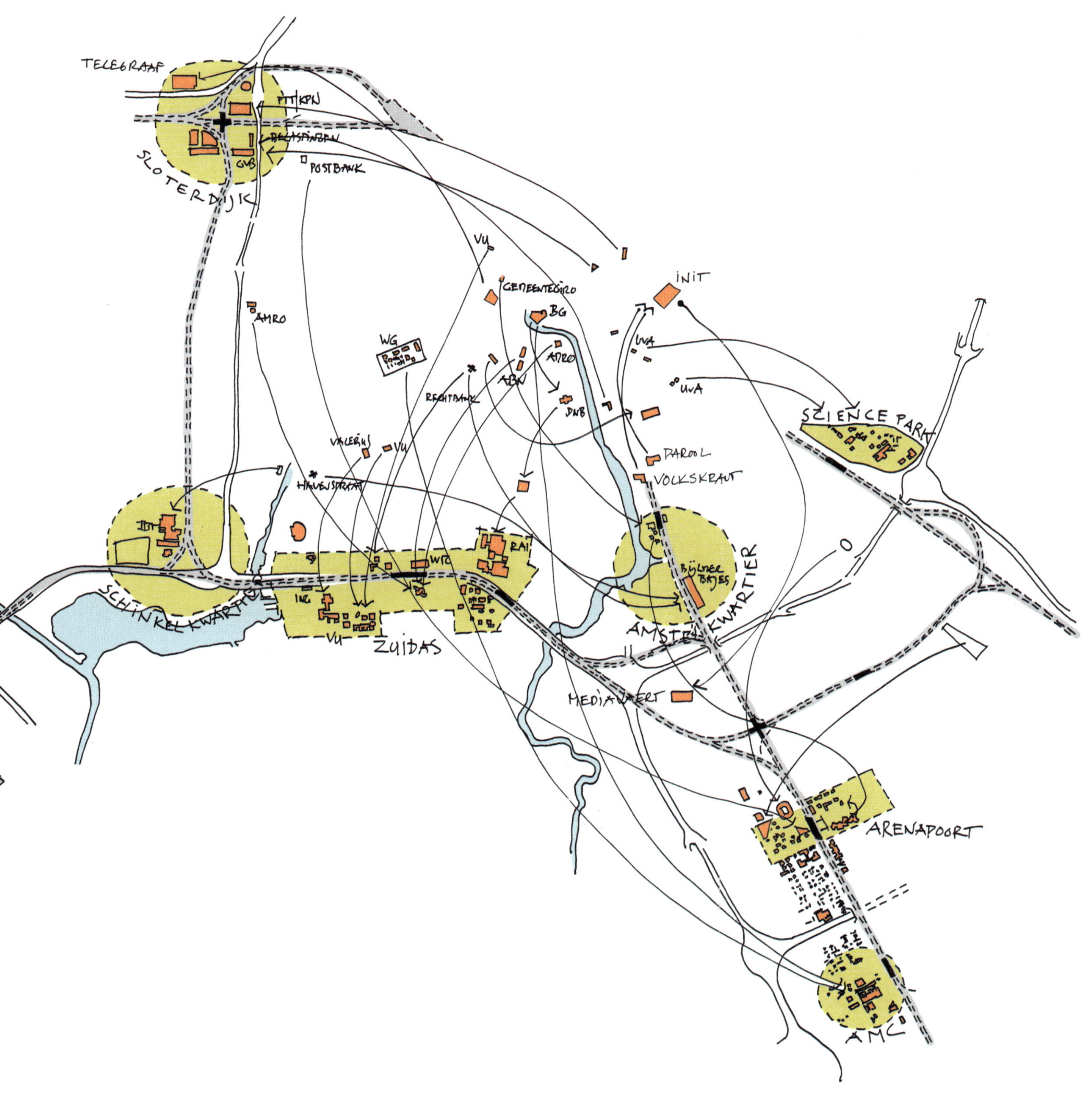
TELEGRAAF
PTT/KPN
GVB
POSTBANK
SLOTERDIJK
AMRO
VU
GEMEENTEGIRO
BG
INIT
WG
AMRO
ABN
RECHTBANK
DNB
UvA
UvA
SCIENCE PARK
VALERIUS
VU
PAROOL
VOLKSKRANT
HAVENSTRAAT
RAI
WTC
ING
VU
ZUIDAS
SCHINKELKWARTIER
BIJLMER BAJES
AMSTELKWARTIER
MEDIAWERF
ARENAPOORT
AMC

1

1 Amsteldijk with a view of the Omval, 1975–2025
2 World Trade Center, 1985
3 RAI Station, 1985

2

3

the national government fundamentally disagreed on the ideal location for the new central station: should it be on the southern edge of the city or on an artificial island at the mouth of the Amstel in the IJ? The national government won the debate, and in 1869, the city council approved the current location. The new Central Station opened in 1884.

The station completely cut off the inner city from the IJ, but one could also argue that it actually *saved* the historic city center. Over the course of the 19th and early 20th centuries, the inner city evolved into a lively fusion of a 17th-century merchant city and modern metropolitan amenities – including the new stock exchange, department stores, restaurants, theaters, and hotels.[2] Space was also made for large office buildings, such as the Nederlandsche Handel-Maatschappij – later ABN – on Vijzelstraat and the Amsterdamsche Bank on Rembrandtplein.

Southward

A century later, integrating modern office buildings, a new generation of urban amenities, and – above all – cars into the old city proved to be far more challenging. The diagram illustrates just how significant the southward shift has been.

Key projects from the early 1960s include the construction of the Burgerweeshuis (1960, relocated from Kalverstraat), the RAI convention center (1961, relocated from Ferdinand Bolstraat), and the VU hospital (1963–64, partially moved from the Valerius Clinic and the VU laboratory on De Lairessestraat).

From the mid-1970s onward, the area around Zuid Station saw further developments, including the previously mentioned District Court, the NMB headquarters (1974, relocated from Herengracht, later moving again in 1986 to the Zandkasteel in Amsterdamse Poort), and the VU main building (1973, relocated from Keizersgracht). The UvA also moved several laboratories and institutes from the Plantage neighborhood to Watergraafsmeer (Nikhef, AMOLF). Starting in 1979, the various departments of the Wilhelmina Gasthuis and the Binnengasthuis gradually relocated to the new AMC, followed by the Emma Children's Hospital in the late 1980s.

Around Station Bijlmer, a series of large office complexes opened in the following years: Fokker's headquarters, Atlas (1983), the HEMA and Bijenkorf headquarters at Frankemaheerd (1986), the Zandkasteel (1986), and AMRO Bank's back offices at Foppingadreef (1988). In the adjacent Bullewijk district, numerous smaller multi-tenant office buildings quickly appeared. Further west, IBM constructed its Dutch headquarters on Johan Huizingalaan in 1978, aligning with the typewriter factory already built there in the 1960s.

The opening of the World Trade Center in 1985 marked a new phase in the southward movement as well as in the city's overall development. The years 1985–2006 have previously been described as a period of economic recovery and internationalization. The construction of the WTC at Zuidplein, near the entrance to Zuid Station, was a key milestone in this transformation. Initially, the WTC was conceived as a multi-tenant office building with approximately 80,000 m^2 of floor space. Through a series of expansions, it has since grown into a 156,000 m^2 complex with a range of facilities and around 250 tenants. Many of the businesses housed in the WTC have international roots.

A rail shuttle service between Zuid Station and Schiphol had already been in operation since 1978. In 1981, the line was extended to Leiden and connected to RAI. The 'southern link' was completed in 1993 with further extensions toward Duivendrecht and Weesp. In 2006, the opening of the Utrechtboog provided direct connections from Zuid Station to Utrecht and Arnhem.

During the city's prolonged economic recovery phase, the southward movement focused on five areas, each of which was given a distinct name, profile, and development strategy: Zuidas, the area around Amstel Station, the ArenA district, Science Park, and Riekerpolder. An exception to the southward trend was Sloterdijk. Although not located in the southern part of the city, it shared the same characteristics: a transport hub on the city's periphery where major offices relocated from the inner city in the 1970s and 1980s – including *De Telegraaf*, SFB, KPN Telecom, the Tax Office, and the GVB.

Schiphol

The rapid development of Schiphol has been a key factor in this movement. The number of passengers transported grew from nearly 8 million in 1975 to 72 million in 2019 – a ninefold increase! How is it possible that an airport with a relatively small home market has grown so significantly?

Starting in the late 1940s, the airport – then still part of the Amsterdam Port Authority – began preparing for a major expansion in both capacity and quality. An international comparison (Chicago, New York, London, Paris) led, in 1949, to a proposal from a research group led by aviation pioneer Jan Dellaert for the construction of a tangential runway system. This plan envisioned multiple runways aligned with different wind directions surrounding a central area containing the piers and terminals.

Between 1950 and 1968, four new runways were built: the Aalsmeerbaan, the Kaagbaan, the Buitenveldertbaan, and the Zwanenburgbaan. The central terminal area, including the new passenger terminal, officially opened in 1967. By 1975, the terminal complex had already doubled in capacity. In 1978, Schiphol was connected to the national rail network via the Schiphollijn.

From the early 1990s onward, the airport experienced a period of rapid growth. The *Open Skies* agreement with the United States, signed in 1992, allowed for direct flights to and from all U.S. airports. This agreement provided a strong foundation for the development of the joint network between KLM and its American partner Northwest Airlines and reinforced Schiphol's role as a hub, offering seamless connections between intercontinental and European flights. The percentage of transfer passengers at Schiphol increased significantly during these years, rising from 27% in 1990 to 44% in 1996.

Table Development of Schiphol 1975–2025

	Passengers	Flight operations	Transfer	Cargo	Employment
1975	8 m	143.700		0,3 m tons	22.500
1990	16,5 m	246.500	27%	0,6 m tons	35.900
1996	27,8 m	342.600	44%	1,1 m tons	43.401
2006	46,1 m	423.000	42%	1,5 m tons	61.691
2016	63,5 m	479.000	37,8%	1,7 m tons	65.000
2019	71,7 m	498.000	36,1%	1,6 m tons	68.000

Sources: Annual Reports Schiphol Group starting from 1980, Regioplan, TU Delft[4]

The 2003 merger between KLM and Air France, the expansion of cooperation with other airlines within the so-called *SkyTeam* alliance (from 2004), the opening of the fifth runway (2003), and the new Departure Hall 3 (2005) all contributed to Schiphol's continued growth. In 2006, the airport handled just over 46 million passengers; by 2019, that number had risen to 71.7 million, with a total of 496,747 flight operations. KLM accounted for half of these passengers, followed by EasyJet, Transavia, and Delta Airlines.

Compared to other European airports, Schiphol performs exceptionally well. While it ranked fifth or sixth in the early 1990s, by 2019, only London Heathrow (80.9 million) and Paris Charles de Gaulle (76.1 million) had higher passenger numbers in Europe. Frankfurt, Madrid, Istanbul, and Moscow trailed at a considerable distance.

A crucial factor in this success is the airport's network. Schiphol offers direct connections to 332 destinations – the second highest number among European airports, surpassed only by Frankfurt.[3]

A closer look at recent data reveals that, since 2006, *transfer traffic* has grown by approximately 25%, whereas *O-D (origin-destination) traffic* has surged by an impressive 47%. This growth can be attributed to the increase in leisure travel, as well as Amsterdam's rising popularity as a business and tourist destination. In this regard, the success of the airport-city combination is most clearly visible.

Schiphol provides employment for a large number of people. There are approx-

1

1 Central area Schiphol with terminals, offices, and parking facilities
2 Buikslotermeerplein

2

imately 68,000 jobs – for comparison, Amsterdam's inner city has 103,695.[5] Nearly half of these jobs are linked to companies in the air transport sector, while about a quarter are with suppliers. Just over 20% of the jobs fall outside the aviation industry, with companies such as Microsoft, Cargill, and Hilton.

At the same time, the central airport area has developed into what is often referred to as an *Airport City* – a 'city' with 7,500 hotel rooms, retail establishments, and a substantial office employment base.[6] Schiphol Real Estate manages 217,561 m² of office space at the airport (as of 2016), including the Schiphol WTC, completed in 1996 (52,000 m²).

Equally important to the economic significance of the airport is the business activity surrounding it. A 2011 study by BCG/McKinsey, commissioned by Schiphol Group, estimated Schiphol's contribution to the Dutch economy at approximately €30 billion per year – or 4.5% of GDP. Aviation activities, both directly and indirectly, generate around 300,000 jobs.[7]

A 2015 study by Decisio, commissioned by the Ministry of Infrastructure and the Environment, further mapped Schiphol's economic impact. According to their analysis, in 2013, Schiphol-related employment – both on and off the airport premises – involved 113,900 people (94,100 FTEs) and represented an added economic value of €9 billion per year. Decisio also highlighted Schiphol's importance for European headquarters (accounting for nearly 9,000 jobs in North Holland) and for the establishment of distribution centers (7,500 jobs in North Holland). However, they noted that quantifying this impact remains challenging.[8]

What is clear is that the presence of the airport is a key factor in attracting internationally operating companies, particularly those in the logistics and distribution sectors. The Schiphol hub is crucial for companies such as Canon, Nissan, Intel, Caterpillar, and Yamaha. Their *nuts and bolts* can be easily flown in via the cargo holds of frequent passenger flights and then quickly distributed across Europe.

Conversely, Schiphol's arrival and departure routes cause significant noise pollution, including during the *edges of the night.* This results in sleep disturbances and health issues not only around the city but also in areas like Zuidoost and Nieuw-West.

Centers

The construction of stations and highways transformed the southern part of the city from a peripheral area into the best-connected location in the region. Zuid Station quickly grew into the city's second major railway hub, offering direct connections to all other major Dutch cities. From 2025 onward, international trains will also depart from here, and this number is expected to increase rapidly. As a result, the Zuidas is no longer just an Amsterdam phenomenon – the area is increasingly functioning as the metropolitan business center of the Dutch metropolis as a whole.

Notable is the relocation of banks to Zuidoost. ING has built a complete campus there, and ABN AMRO is renovating *de Fop.* This development is turning the ArenAPoort into a center that is at least as diverse as the Zuidas.

Including the inner city, Amsterdam now has three major clusters of urban and regional functions. The Zuidas and ArenAPoort might best be described as *nevencentra* – secondary centers. There is also a clear distinction between these areas and other centers in the region. The Stadshart in Amstelveen, Inverdan in Zaandam, the Buikslotermeerplein in Noord, and the Osdorpplein in Nieuw-West primarily serve local needs.

In the 1986 Structural Plan 'The City Central', a new category of employment areas was introduced: not industrial estates, but office districts. All of these were planned around the newly projected stations at the city's periphery and along the A10 ring road, ensuring excellent accessibility.

What would these new business areas look like? The World Fashion Centre (1968–1978) along the A10, designed by Hugh Maaskant, still had a façade and entrances facing Koningin Wilhelminaplein, but the RAI and the AMC were little more than massive building complexes surrounded by vast parking lots. The architecture of the first major office buildings was also far from inspiring. The IBM headquarters (1976), the WTC (1985), and the large KPN Telecom office at Sloterdijk (1986) were all massive structures dominated by reflective glass. Brutalist buildings such as Leeuwenburg, the main VU building, the District Court, and the Bijlmerbajes evoked mixed reactions. Meanwhile, Aldo van Eyck's Burgerweeshuis and the first new university laboratories in Watergraafsmeer had a more welcoming, small-scale appearance, but were also highly inward-looking.

The Rembrandt Tower (1992–1995) set a new tone. It introduced a different shape – not a large and bulky mass, but a tower – with a more distinctive, metropolitan architectural style, and it stood on a new square. This Amstelplein also featured a reconstructed remnant of the old Blooker complex, repurposed as a hospitality venue. But how could the other 'XL buildings' be transformed into a city? That term had been used in a study on integrating large-scale building projects into the historic city center, such as the Stopera, the Maupoleum, and the P.C. Hoofthuis.[9] Now, the question was essentially reversed: how could these inward-facing and often uninviting complexes regain meaning in the everyday life of the city?

Integration of XL Buildings

A great opportunity arose in the planning process for the *Arena*, the new Ajax stadium near Bijlmer Station and the Amsterdamse Poort shopping center. As part of the bid book for Amsterdam's candidacy for the 1992 Olympic Games, a proposal had been made in 1985 to build a new stadium there. After the Games, the old Ajax

➔ Built Southwards, 1975–2025

stadium and the Olympic Stadium could be demolished to make way for housing.

Various American examples also showed how stadiums had become multifunctional: usable for different types of events, not just football and not just on weekends. The highlight was the inflatable and retractable roof of the new stadium in Indianapolis. Combined with a convention center, the new stadium in that city made a year-round calendar of events possible, providing a boost to the local economy.

The new Ajax stadium was given a retractable roof, and the broader leisure concept was incorporated into the planning for the surrounding area, including a mega cinema, an event hall, and a concert venue (first Heineken Music Hall, later AFAS Live), as well as retail. Large-scale retail in the periphery of cities was not popular in the Netherlands; it was considered a threat to downtown shopping areas. The *Maxis* and the furniture boulevard in Diemen, near the A1, were seen as cautionary examples. However, by relocating the furniture boulevard to a well-connected location like Bijlmer ArenA Station and combining it with other amenities, these concerns were mitigated. Decathlon and MediaMarkt also joined the development. The multifunctional approach thus applied not only to the stadium but to the entire collection of facilities. The large parking garage beneath the *Arena* served all these amenities and became the region's first *P+R* (Park and Ride) garage. The metro provided quick access to the city center. Later, the Ziggo Dome was added, further expanding the venue offerings.

A crucial element was the clustering of all these facilities around a new public space: the *Arena Boulevard* (renamed *Johan Cruijff Boulevard* in 2018). Supervisor Pi de Bruijn and urban designer Dick Bruijne designed a wide and long square, stretched diagonally between the station and the entrance of Villa Arena, the multi-level furniture boulevard. Around it, the other facilities were positioned with addresses facing the new boulevard. Unfortunately, one of the larger plots remains undeveloped to this day.[10] As a result, the boulevard feels incomplete and lacks a sense of enclosure.

One particularly successful intervention was the complete renovation of Bijlmer ArenA Station (2007), initiated by alderman Duco Stadig and designed by the British firm Grimshaw. This firm had previously worked on the access bridges to IJburg.[11] The bright station hall and the stairways to the platforms connect directly to the underpass, which is just as wide as the Arena Boulevard. The paving materials used in the simultaneous redevelopment of the boulevard continue underneath the station and were also used in the redesign of Hoekenrodeplein. This created a seamless connection between both sides of the

1

1 RAI complex Europaplein, 1961
2 Bijlmer ArenA Station, design by Grimshaw Architects, 2007
3 ABN AMRO headquarters, 1999
4 Amsterdam-Zuid Station, design by ZJA, 2023
5 Stationsplein Sloterdijk

station. The Arena area and Amsterdamse Poort were subsequently combined under the name ArenA Poort.

The same strategy was followed in the integration of the WTC. The first step was the creation of a new station square, Zuidplein, during the expansion of the WTC in 2002. This square provides access to the existing offices and the new tall WTC tower on the other side of the square, and there are dining facilities. Beneath the square, a large bicycle parking facility was created. A special type of paving was used for the square, and trees were planted. On the south side of the station, another square was created, Mahlerplein, at the entrance to the large new ABN AMRO headquarters. The Ito office complex opposite the bank has a high ground floor with dining facilities. A temporary pavilion, Circl, was built in front of the ABN AMRO office for events and also with dining options. It has recently been demolished. Once the bank has moved and the office complex is redeveloped, the ground floor will hopefully have a more public character.

But the most important intervention was yet to come. At the beginning of the 1990s, a project organization for the Zuidas was established with a project director from outside the municipal organization and a direct line to alderman Stadig. From the start of the planning process, it was clear to all involved that the broad infrastructure bundle of the A10, the railway line, and the metro formed a barrier that would hinder the proper functioning of the Zuidas. Throughout the 1990s, numerous plans were drawn up for gradually moving the entire infrastructure underground, including off-ramps and parking garages, and partially with buildings on top. Such a mega-operation was only conceivable in a PPP arrangement. ING, the State, NS, and ProRail all played important roles here, of course.

However, the massive investment turned out to be unrealistic as a result of the banking crisis. Therefore, alternatives were sought. Eventually, an option was developed where the tracks and metro remain at the embankment and only the highway lanes go underground.

Part of the plans, which were implemented in 2019, includes wide pedestrian passages under the tracks. The new station was designed by a combination of ZJA, Team V Architecture, and BoschSlabbers landscape architects. The tracks remain at the same level – lower than at Bijlmer ArenA Station – but due to the width of the passages, high canopies, and light strips between the tracks, the station is still expected to play a pleasant and connecting role. The space that becomes available after the A10 is moved underground will feature tree-lined avenues, and bus and tram stops will be created. Travelers will be able to easily transfer from the station. A reservation for a third platform with a fifth and sixth track also makes future growth of international train traffic possible.

At the other major new work areas, the interventions are smaller in scale but comparable in intent. At the RAI, the above-ground parking lots were removed, and in 2009, the so-called Elicium was opened at Europaplein, featuring a whole series of flexible meeting and conference rooms and a large hall, the 'ballroom.' The square and the pedestrian area leading to RAI Station were made more compact and redesigned. Next to the station, the striking tower of the nhow hotel was built.

For the AMC, a glass entrance pavilion was completed in 2020. From the new Holendrecht Station and the bus stops, you now walk through a park to the hospital. A much more pleasant entrance than before, which used to be via the parking garage or the dry corridor.

Similar interventions were made at Science Park and at Sloterdijk Station. Karres and Brands created a new, integrated design for the public space at Science Park, emphasizing walking paths, pleasant lighting, and abundant greenery. The bus stops at the front square of Sloterdijk

2

3

4

5

Station were relocated, allowing the square to be redesigned with a green layout and plenty of flowering plants. Just like the Döner stall and the Annahoeve at Science Park, the restaurant Brett at the station square in Sloterdijk adds to a more lively street scene.

The redesign around Amstel Station is halfway through. Amstelplein near the Rembrandt Tower was the earliest example of the approach to public space around the new large office complexes on the edge of the city. By now, tram and bus stops have been moved and redesigned at the front of the station. In the coming years, a large operation will follow on the Amstel side. This will not only create space for new offices, but primarily for residential buildings.

Mixing

After the opening of the new ABN AMRO building at Mahlerplein in 1999, preparations began for a series of 90-100 meter high office towers in the Mahler complex. The first were designed by foreign architects Rafael Vinoly and Toyo Ito and were completed in 2005. The others followed in the years after, each more spectacular than the last.

However, when the real estate crisis broke out in 2007, followed by a crisis in the banking sector, the perspective of the office market changed. For the first time, vacancies occurred. Many office buildings from the 1970s and 1980s did not meet modern standards for flexibility, climate control, and ICT facilities. In 2009, KPN moved into a new office in Sloterdijk. The enormous, old mirror office of 40,000 m^2 from 1990, also in Sloterdijk, remained empty for years and was only put back into use in 2018, as a hotel. Renewal and repurposing of office buildings became major new challenges.

But a more significant course change followed. Housing had already been part of the plans for the area around the Rembrandt Tower in the early 1990s, and a strip of housing was also included in the first plan for the Zuidas. The pressure on the housing market in the new growth phase of the city from 2007 accelerated the thinking about mixed functions. The quality of the work areas themselves also played a role. A work environment with a wide range of amenities and a lively street scene, even outside regular office hours, is far preferable to a sterile office park. The same applies to a university campus. In addition to the new beta faculty and various facilities related to the internet hub, the Science Park also saw the creation of the Matrix buildings for start-up companies, the new construction of the University College, and housing. It had already been decided earlier to move the University Sports Centre from the Zuidas to the Science Park.

In the 2011 Amsterdam Structure Vision 2040, this idea of mixing was incorporated into the policy for 'the rollout of the central area'. The leading principle for large new projects became the mixing of urban functions at high densities, well connected by public transport and bicycle routes, and with attractive public spaces. In strategic documents, such as the Development Strategy Road Map 2025, this was further elaborated in the approach to the Ring Zone.[12] Under movement 1, this concept was already addressed with the intensification of the transitional zone between West and Nieuw-West around the A10 and the ring line from 2005. Now, the entire, highly fragmented area between the pre-war city and the post-war expansions was included, including the Zuidas and Sloterdijk, and a series of new projects started, such as the Amstelkwartier and Schinkelkwartier.

Zuidas

Since the start of the Zuidas project in 1995, a total of 900,000 m² of office space has been completed and 3,000 homes have been built by 2023.[13]

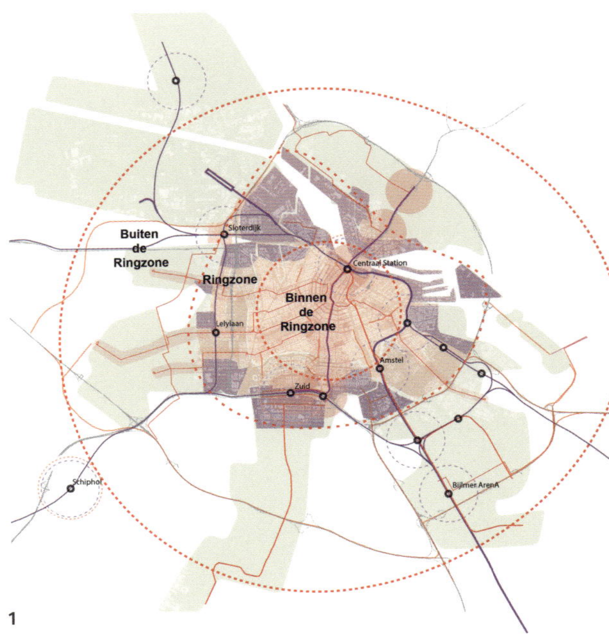

1

2

1 Ringzone, diagram Development Strategy Road Map 2025, 2016
2 Sciencepark, 1975–2025
3 Diagrams Masterplan Zuidas Pi de Bruijn 1998 and recalibration Masterplan Zuidas Ton Schaap, 2018

The initial Zuidas Master Plan, drawn up under the leadership of urban designer and supervisor Pi de Bruijn and adopted in 1998, focused on the area around Zuid Station and the undergrounding of the infrastructure. A central element was the extension of Minervalaan from Berlage's Plan Zuid to the station, with the termination of this 'Minerva axis' in striking towers – the later Symphony Towers – at Mahlerplein.

In the revision of the master plan in 2018, under the supervision of urban designer Ton Schaap, the undergrounding of the railway and metro was abandoned, and the connections to the surrounding area, the relationships with Buitenveldert and the Prinses Irenebuurt, and the areas on both sides were considered more broadly. Essentially, a more comprehensive and neutral urban plan was created that builds upon and enriches the orthogonal pattern of Van Eesteren's Buitenveldert.

The basic scheme of the building blocks around Mahlerlaan has been further extended to the flanks, towards Amstelveenseweg and RAI. The broad Mahlerlaan has effectively become the central element.

Within the grid, there is a stronger mix. In addition to a high school, various hotels, the headquarters of the European Medicines Agency EMA, and the new Amsterdam Court of Justice (designed by KAAN Architects), a whole series of residential plans have been realized. First in the previously planned Gershwin project, but also the striking Valley by MVRDV, and the winner of the Zuiderkerk Award 2024, the youth housing tower Stepstone, designed by LEVS Architects. The transformation of the 1970s office strip on Prinses Irenestraat also contributes to making the Zuidas a more vibrant part of the city.

In the coming years, much is still planned. The new neighborhoods will take on a greener character, the AFC sports park and the VU will be more strongly integrated, and – if things go well – even Sporthallen Zuid and the RAI will change in character. The most recent ideas for the RAI include moving logistics and supply underground. The edges will take on a more open character and could possibly be combined with residential construction. The real 'proof of the pudding' will be the completion of the Zuidasdok, planned for 2036.

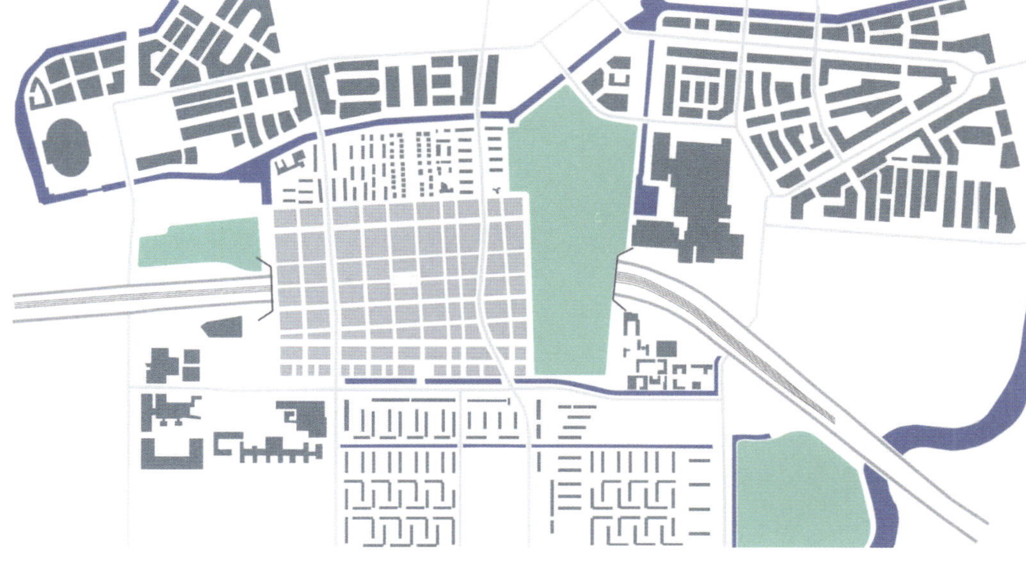

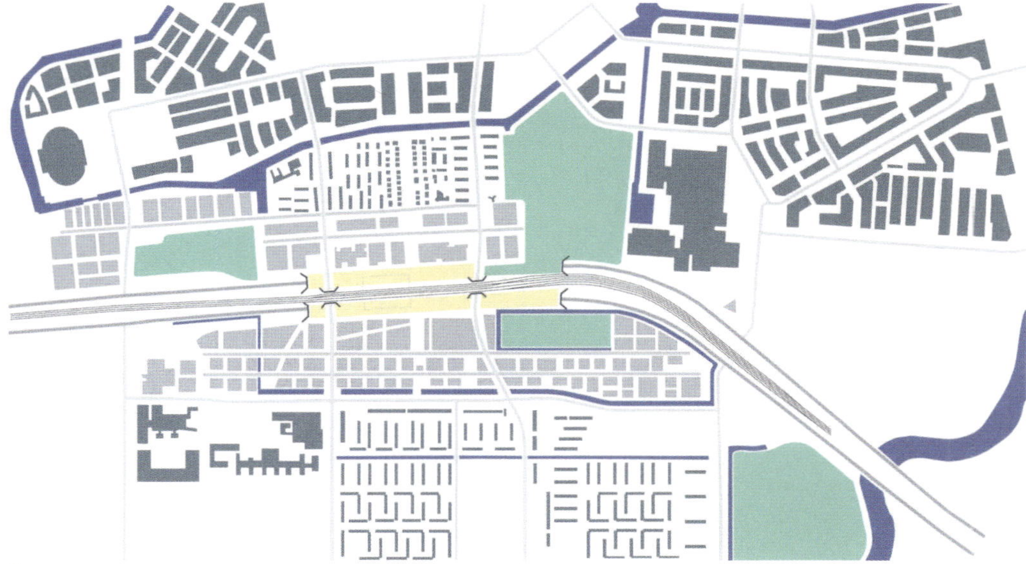

3

From Overamstel to Amstelstad

When the Rembrandt Tower and the surrounding area were built at Amstel Station, it was already clear that the former Zuidergasfabriek site would eventually be developed as well. The gasworks factory was demolished in 1992. After the departure of the water treatment facility and the construction of the new headquarters for Waternet in 2006, it took a long time before the successors of GEB, Nuon, and Liander, moved to other locations, and the land could be cleaned.

The construction of the planned Amstelkwartier here would then mark the beginning of a long-term transformation process further south. Initially, there were incubators, self-build projects, and student housing, followed by regular housing construction. Eventually, the redevelopment would reach the AMC after decades.

However, the transformation process has proceeded much faster, in leaps and bounds. The entire zone up to the AMC is now referred to in explorations as Amstelstad. The long-term housing capacity here seems comparable to that in Haven-Stad. Amsterdam still has years of development ahead. What is on the agenda? Let's go from north to south.

Around the Treublaan near the Berlagebrug, demolition of various post-war office buildings and schools has started, and the Van der Kunbuurt is being renewed. The strip development with porch apartments is mostly making way for intensive and mixed-use buildings. Around Amstel Station, there were initially one, then three, and later four towers; soon there will be seven. The Leeuwenburg office complex is being renovated, but the former offices of Delta Lloyd will be demolished. The station entrance and the Amsteloever are being redesigned. The area as a whole is essentially becoming the entrance to Amstelstad. New buildings at the tip of the Weespertrekvaart and commercial spaces and studios under the tracks should make the public space more accessible and lively.

The Amstelkwartier has had a restart in recent years. The new park at the bend of the Amstel was discovered during the COVID-19 pandemic by large groups of young people. Around the nearby Bella Vistapark by the old water tower, attractive residential complexes have been built, and the first new homes in the Bajeskwartier have been completed. New bridges over the Weespertrekvaart and Duivendrechtsevaart, as well as an underpass under the railway, now make the Amstelkwartier easily accessible from the Rivierenbuurt and the Watergraafsmeer. Preparations are underway for the next round around the business complex De Kauwgomballenfabriek and Overamstel Metro Station.

A little further down, since 2020, several

new headquarters have been built near the A10, including for the jeans company G-Star RAW and for DPG Media. The latest building opened in 2024 and houses (at 40,000 m²) all the 'brands' of DPG, such as radio station Qmusic, NU.nl, *Het Parool*, and the *Volkskrant.* The printing press had already been established there, but now the editorial offices have also moved from Oostenburg. While the editorial office of NRC 'returned' from Rotterdam to Rokin in the city center, the editorial offices of *Parool and Volkskrant* now moved 'out of the city.' The business area where DPG is located is now referred to as Amstel Business Park. It lies on the land of the municipality of Duivendrecht and also houses various food and logistics companies. It is likely that this will remain the case for the foreseeable future.

Cross Duivendrecht Station still looks abandoned, but a plan has been in the works for some time to build 5,000 homes near the station in the municipality of Ouder-Amstel: De Nieuwe Kern. This is also the name of the first building that will be built within the plan starting in mid-2025. It had previously been called the Smart Mobility Hub. It is located on the site of Sportpark Strandvliet and will house 2,100 parking lots for cars, 700 for bicycles, and space for tour buses on two floors. Football fields will be reinstated on the roof, along with various other urban sports facilities. The building has now been tendered. The design is by architectural firm Cepezed, in collaboration with Buro Sant en Co and Goudappel Coffeng. It is the first time – at least in the Netherlands – that such a concept is being realized. Due to the efficient land use, all the current parking lots at the ArenA can be removed and then used for the housing project.

Earlier, ArenAPoort was mentioned. Here, too, a process of intensification is underway, and a series of new construction projects are being prepared. So far, the focus has been on the reuse of existing buildings. Vattenfall has moved into the renovated offices at Hoekenrodeplein, ABN AMRO is renovating 'de Fop', the old back office on Foppingadreef, and ING has built a complete campus on the site where HEMA and Bijenkorf once had their offices. The Zandkasteel in the middle of ArenA-Poort has thus become available. The building by the Alberts and Van Huut architectural firm from 1986 was designated as a municipal monument in 2017. The various parts have since been converted into apartments, offices, a school, and an art lending service. Wouldn't this also have been a nice spot for a library?

Recently, the transformation of the office area in Bullewijk has accelerated. This is the most unexpected development. In the 1980s and 1990s, dozens of office complexes were built here in the form of 'urban villas', with four to five stories, parking around them at ground level and later on parking decks. Immediately after construction, they were very popular, but have since become 'out of demand', leading to high vacancy rates. Offices have a very different, much shorter lifespan compared to residential buildings; a maximum of twenty-five years seems to be the limit.

Since 2021, there has been a metamorphosis, with a significant number of office villas replaced by six residential towers reaching up to 110 meters. Most of them are located along Hondsrugweg. The wide road profile is being transformed into Hondsrugpark and will eventually become the central green space of the new neighborhood. In total, including the Paasheuvelweg area, around 15,000 homes are planned, with various amenities and the preservation of the current amount of office space.

The most notable development was the construction of Our Domain in 2021, a residential complex with nearly 1,000 student homes and 650 private-sector rental apartments across from the AMC. Who would have thought that such a compact housing project would appear in such a peripheral location? The apartments are being managed by Greystar, a globally operating American housing rental company in the private sector, which leases astronomical numbers of 'units'. How sustainable will this project be?

Schinkelkwartier

On the other side of the city, in the southern part of Nieuw-West, a similar development is underway. Since the privatization of the Slotervaart Hospital in 1997, there has been ongoing debate and turmoil about the future of the hospital, which was built in 1975 and was once extremely modern. Ultimately, in 2018, the hospital was declared bankrupt and taken over by the real estate company Zadelhoff. The renovation of the hospital is well underway. The building has been 'topped off' and now provides space for various new healthcare concepts, a health center, clinics, training facilities, and workspaces. Under the banner of De Plantijn, 1,300 homes will be built around the Slotervaart Center for Healthcare, the Antoni van Leeuwenhoek and blood bank Sanquin. The area will feature a central green square and better connections to the surrounding area, following the proven recipe for integration.

De Plantijn is part of a much larger area development, called Schinkelkwartier. More than 11,000 homes will eventually be built here, but it will also remain an important work area with the renewed headquarters of IBM and the Riekerpolder Business Park. The main feature of the area will be a slow-traffic connection between Sloterweg and Stadionplein, with a new bridge over the Schinkel. The fragmentation caused by the large infrastructure of railways and highways will be broken, and the area will become part of the city.

As a catalyst for area development, vacant offices have been repurposed as incubators. In the former ACTA building, you'll find a mix of 400 student units, studios, and the Radion venue. In offices of IBM and the former headquarters of Mexx (later Nissan), B.Amsterdam has been established, offering space for startups. A vacant office in Riekerpolder has been converted into homes.

In 2021, the municipal council approved the new *Omgevingsvisie Amsterdam 2050* (Environmental Vision Amsterdam 2050): *'A Human Metropolis'*. In this vision, previous choices were reaffirmed and placed within a regional context. Alongside further development towards Zaanstad and Almere, there is a focus on the connection with Schiphol, the Haarlemmermeer, and Utrecht, within the 'inner ring' of the Randstad. Studies like *Enter [NL], International Gateway of the Netherlands* from 2017 had already advocated for extending the North/South metro line towards Schiphol, which would provide substantial public transport access to areas like Schinkelkwartier (and within that, the Riekerpolder Business Park). In the series of work environments along the airport corridor, the Schinkel area could develop as an innovation district.

RESIDENTIAL, BLOCK, AND PLOT LAYOUTS

In the early years of the southward movement, large-scale office complexes and facilities were primarily developed: Atlas, AMC, 'de Fop', and the Arena in Zuidoost, as well as the WTC, Rivierstaete, the Court House, ABN AMRO headquarters, and the RAI expansions in Zuid; in West, IBM and the Slotervaart Hospital opened, and in Oost, the Bijlmerbajes, Leeuwenburg, and the UvA laboratories in the Science Park. Some of these buildings are located in parks or gardens, but most were accessed from elevated roads and parking garages, which isn't ideal and leads to fragmented public spaces. When the first truly tall Rembrandt Tower (135 meters, 1992–1995) was built at Amstel Station, it was combined with the creation of the Amstelplein square in front of it. Other complexes also received new contexts in the 1990s through the design of new public spaces around them, such as Arena Boulevard, Zuidplein, and Mahlerplein on either side of Zuid Station. The buildings were oriented towards these public spaces.

However, there was still no real urban fabric in the sense of streets, alleys, canals, and squares that anchor buildings to the city, where building masses can be oriented and from where they are accessible. The first attempts at 'parceling' work areas in this sense occurred around 2000 in Sloterdijk, on the southeast side of the station, and in the Mahler-4 project at Zuid Station. In Sloterdijk, a simple street pattern and buildings in four to eight layers were chosen. The streets are not very lively because the ground floor, often just entrances, sometimes even houses parking garages. The Mahler project also has a simple street pattern and continuous building masses in four to eight layers. The street pattern is cut through by the diagonal, car-free Debussylaan, with restaurants along it. Beneath the ground, a large two-level parking garage was built. Above this, five towers were built, ranging in height from 70 to 100 meters – lower than the Rembrandt Tower and more integrated within the building masses. This integration happened in different ways: some architects placed the towers directly on top of the basement, while others chose to raise the towers starting from the ground level. The classic theme of the distinction between the upper building and the crown is missing in most cases, and the ground floors are not accessible everywhere.

After the Mahler project, the Zuidas started the Gershwin project in 2010. This marked the introduction of high-rise residential towers in Amsterdam. Although the so-called Wolkenkrabber (the Skyscraper) at Victorieplein in Zuid dates back to 1932 – designed by J.F. Staal – it is only 40 meters tall and serves as a prominent landmark in the predominantly four- to five-story Plan Zuid. Gershwin, however, features a whole series of residential towers arranged in a grid pattern, adjacent to the office towers across Mahlerlaan and combined with lower residential buildings that often decrease in height towards Gershwinlaan and the nearby Boelegracht. The towers have two to five apartments per floor (e.g., 900 Mahler), but recently, experiments have been made with more segmented building masses, like in the Valley tower, and more apartments per floor (five to twelve in Stepstone). In recent years, around fifteen residential towers of 70–100 meters in height have been built in the Amstelkwartier, Sloterdijk, Bajeskwartier, and around Hondsrugpark. Will there be a hundred of them soon? There is a big challenge ahead to add architectural and urban qualities with this new type of development!

→ **Next page:**
RAI with NHOW hotel

4C AMSTELKWARTIER PHASE 1 — 2020

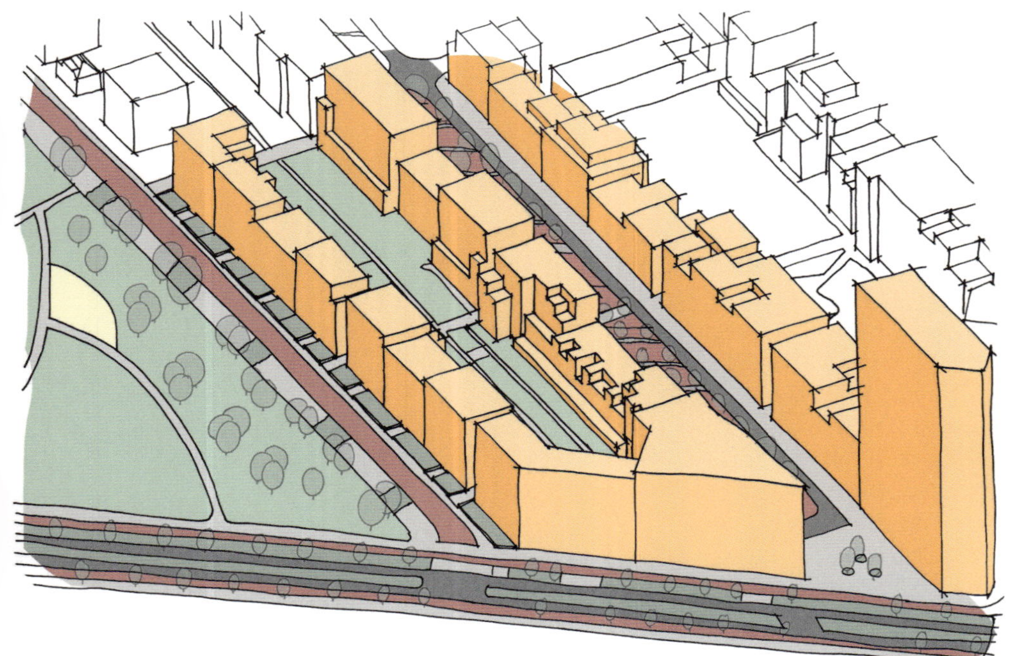

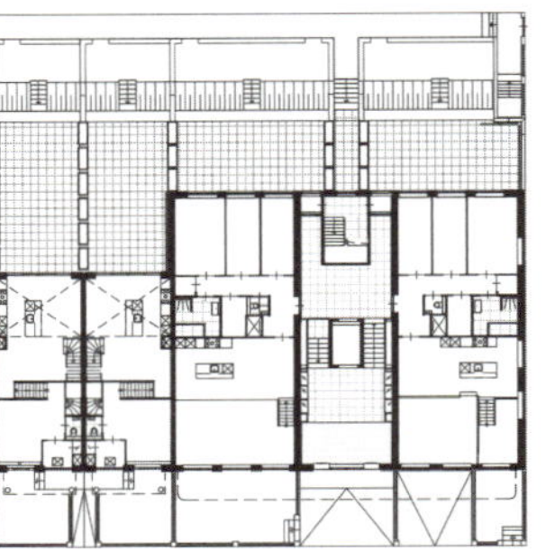

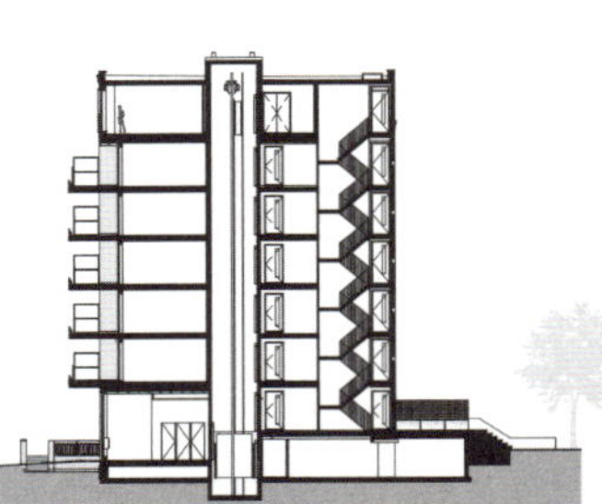

Features
Apartment complexes in closed building blocks with 5 - 9 floors and indoor parking, oriented towards Bella Vistapark; three hotel and residential towers up to 22 floors (70 meters)

Urban planning – supervision
Ellen Monchen, Bart Vlaanderen (DRO-R&D)

Architects
Mulderblauw Architects, Paul de Ruiter Architects, Kampman Architects, SeARCH, oz Architects, Inbo, OeverZaaijer Architecture and Urban Planning, and Geurst & Schulze Architects

Construction period
2012–2020

Houses per hectare
200

Average house size
80 m²

4D AMSTEL III – OUR DOMAIN — 2020

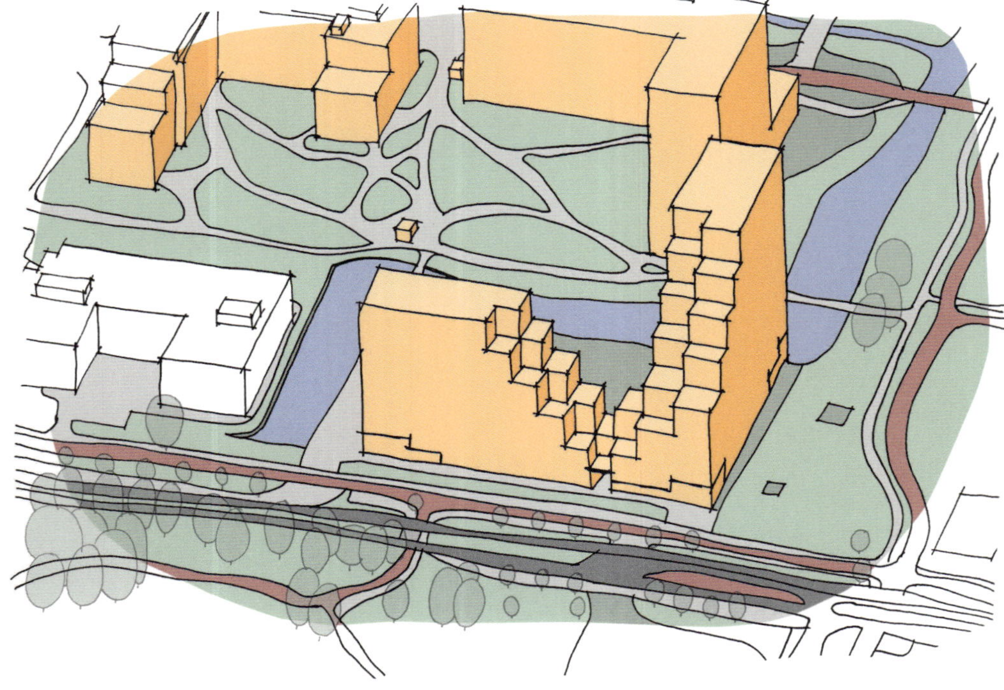

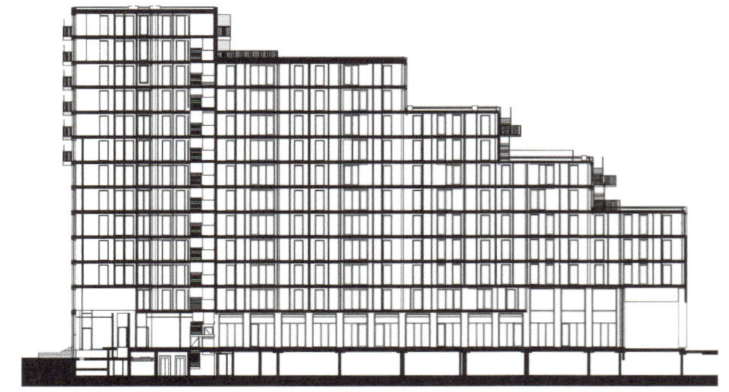

Features
Three buildings combining student housing, apartments, and commercial spaces around an inner courtyard

Urban planning – supervision
Don Murphy (VMX), Arjan Snellenberg (DRO-R&D)

Architects
oz Architects

Construction period
2018–2020

Houses per hectare
470

Average house size
34 m²

4A OMVAL – AMSTELPLEIN 2001

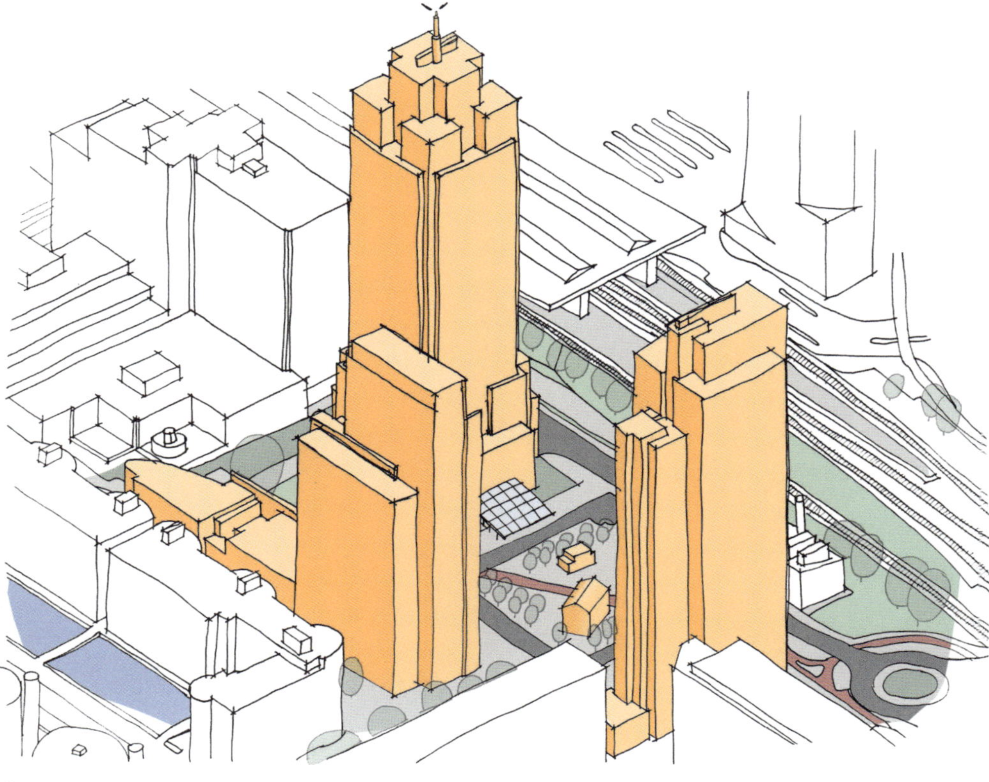

Features
Three office towers around Amstelplein (Rembrandttower 135 m, Breitnertower 95 m, Mondriaantower 120 m)

Urban planning – supervision
Hans Epskamp (DRO)

Architects
ZZDP Architects in collaboration with SOM, ZZ+P Architects

Construction period
1991–2001

Houses per hectare
n/a

Average house size
n/a

4B ZUIDAS – GERSHWIN 2020

Features
Office and apartment complexes in various typologies, 2-29 floors, indoor and underground parking

Urban planning – supervision
Pi de Bruijn (Architecten Cie.), Cees Geldof, Hans van der Made (DRO)

Architects
including Architecten Cie., LEVS Architects, UN Studio, DOK, Claus en Kaan architects, SeARCH, KENK, KCAP, Bedaux de Brouwer, Inbo

Construction period
2006–2020

Houses per hectare
155

Average house size
88 m²

rai
AMSTERDAM
nhow
elevate your stay
DAF
Heineken
fuzetea
LAVAZZA
MX
GRAND CAFÉ

HOBEKA
Entrance K
AREA

4G AMSTEL III – SPOT 2025

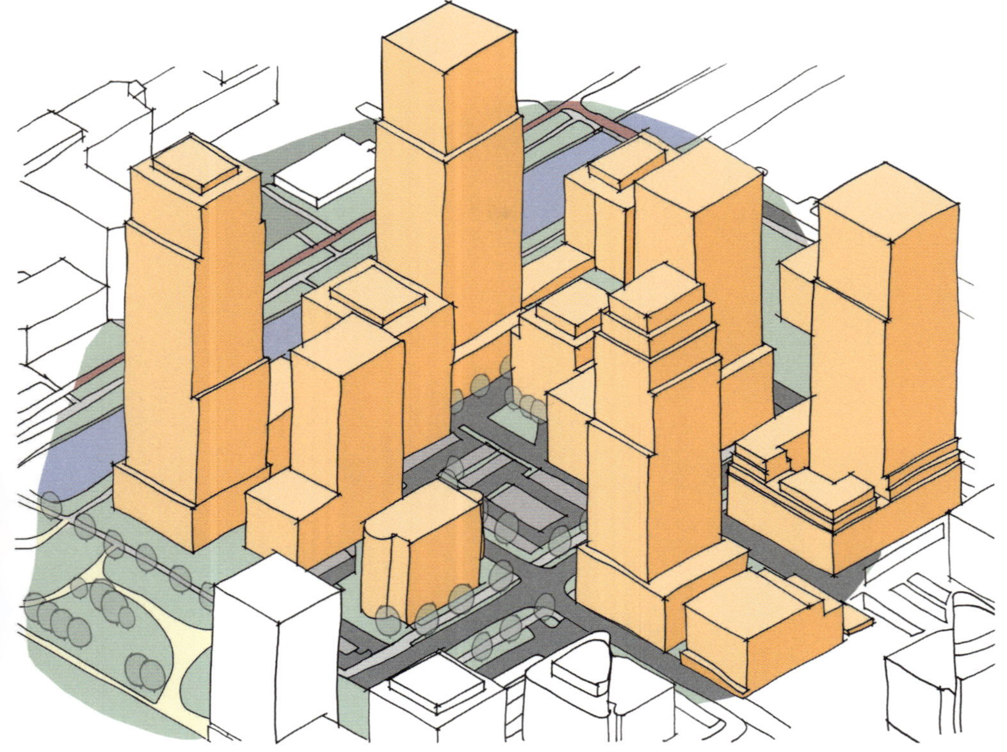

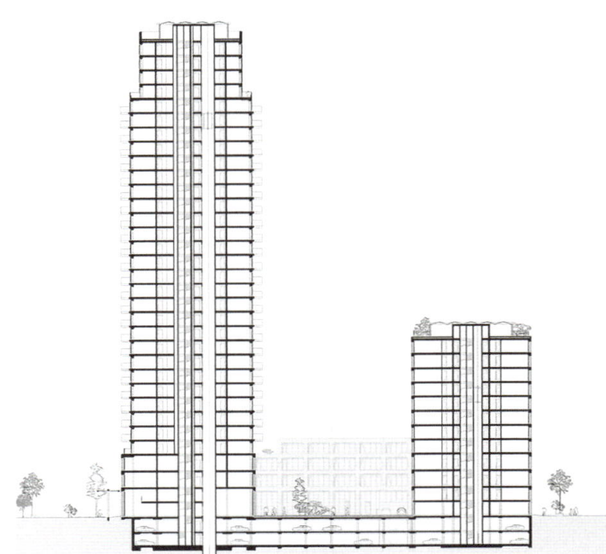

Features
Residential towers in a transformation area, oriented towards the future Hondsrugpark

Urban planning – supervision
Don Murphy (VMX),
Stephan Sliepenbeek (DRO-R&D),
Aldo Trim (KAAN Architecten)

Architects
KAAN Architecten,
ZZDP Architecten

Construction period
2021–2025

Houses per hectare
430

Average house size
67 m²

4H BAJESKWARTIER 2025

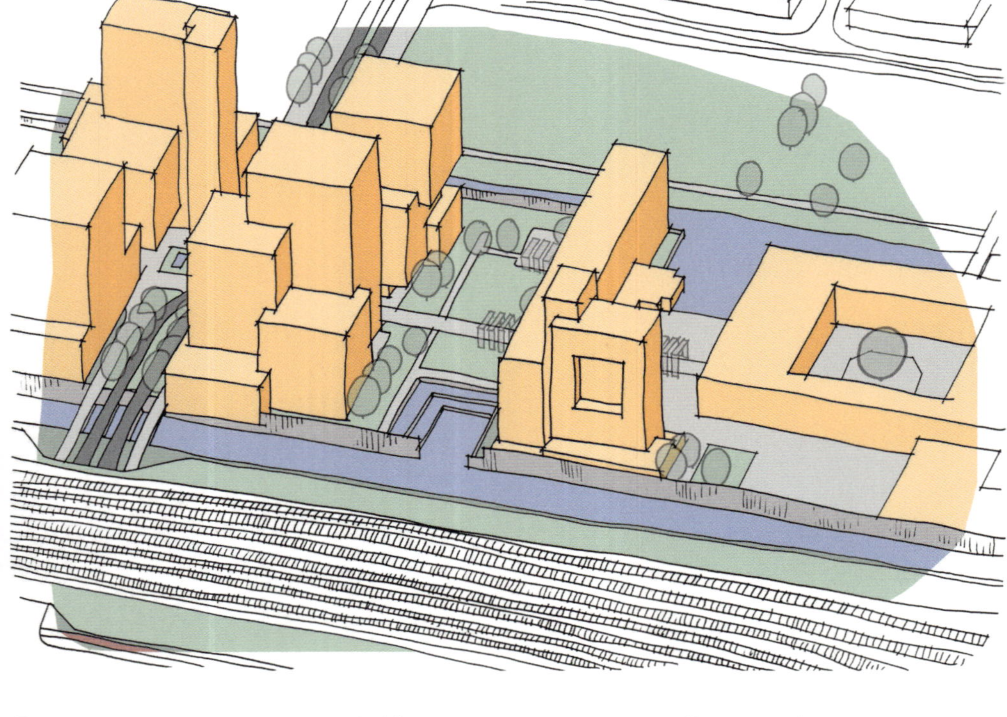

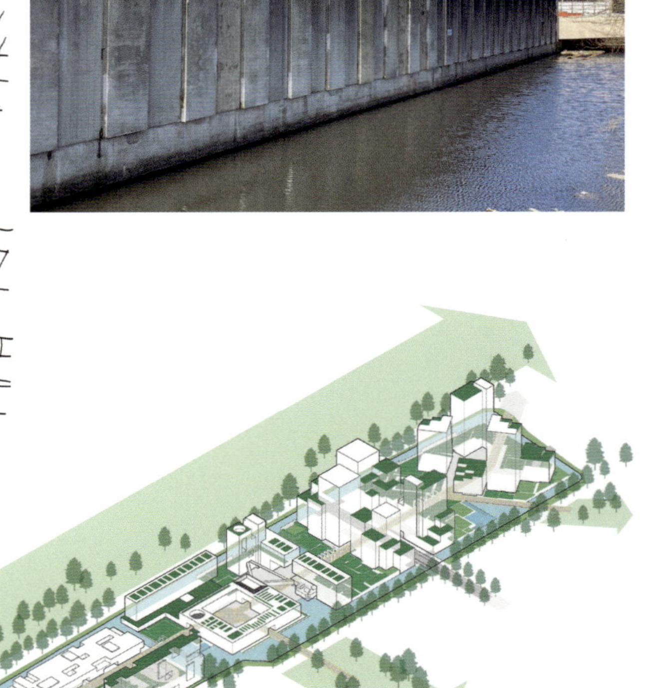

Features
Residential towers, apartment complexes, and a hotel on the site of the former Bijlmerbajes

Urban planning – supervision
OMA

Architects
Moke Architecten,
Arons & Gelauff Architects,
Civic Architects

Construction period
from 2019

Houses per hectare
165

Average house size
60 m²

4E ZUIDAS – VALLEY 2021

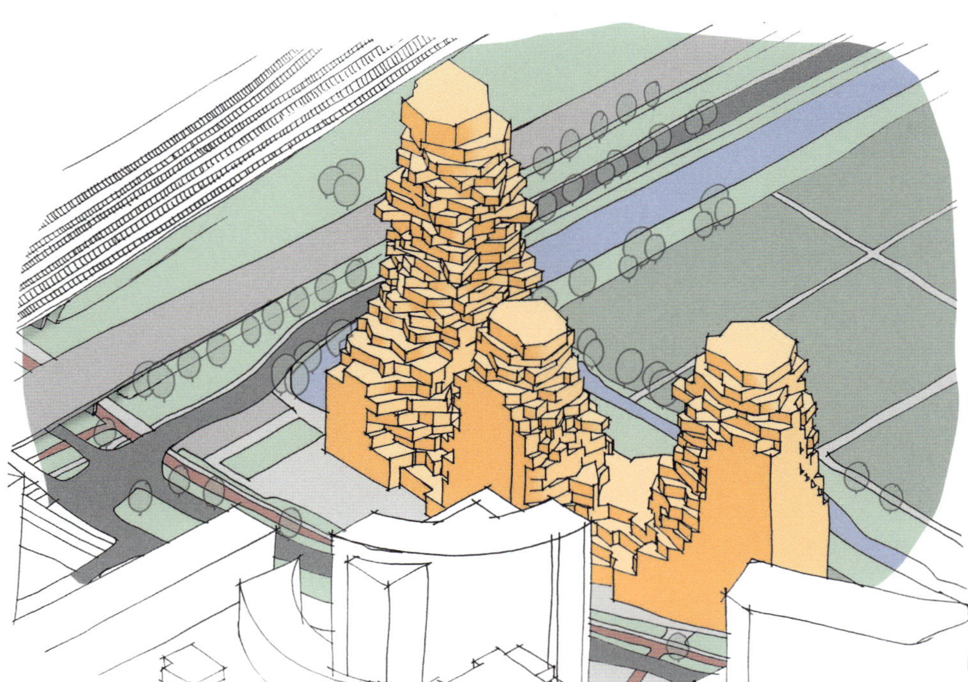

Features
Three residential towers on a podium with offices and restaurants, featuring an internal atrium and public rooftop gardens accessible from the street, along with a three-level underground parking garage

Urban planning – supervision
Paco Bunnik, Ton Schaap, Martijn de Wit (DRO-R&D)

Architects
MVRDV, Arup, and Piet Oudolf

Construction period
2017–2021

Houses per hectare
195

Average house size
100 m²

4F STATIONSKWARTIER SLOTERDIJK 2024

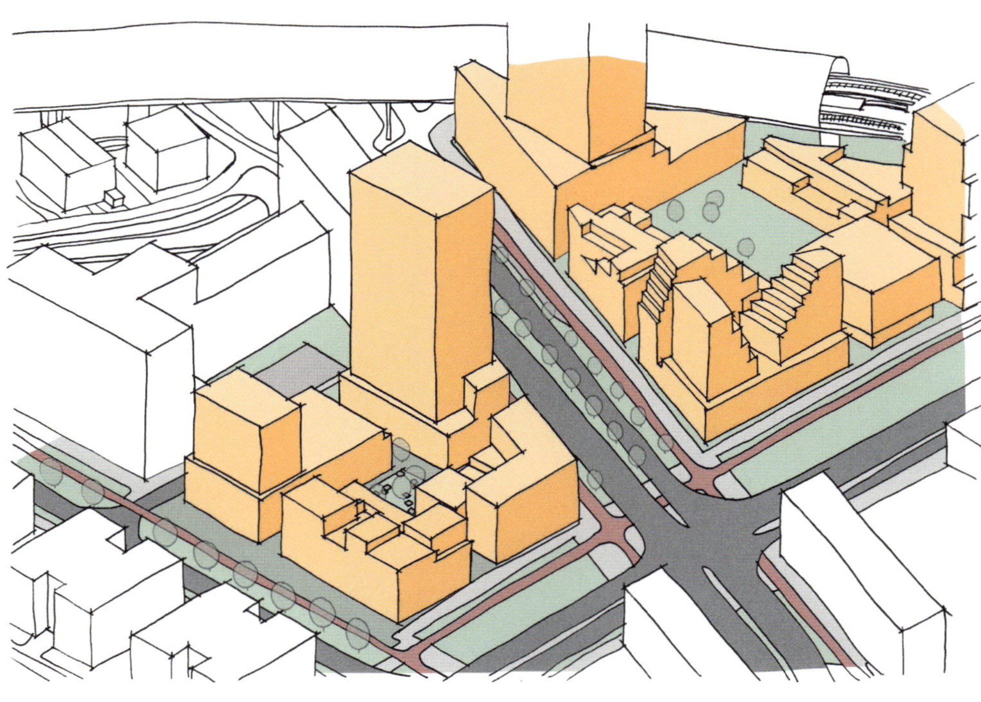

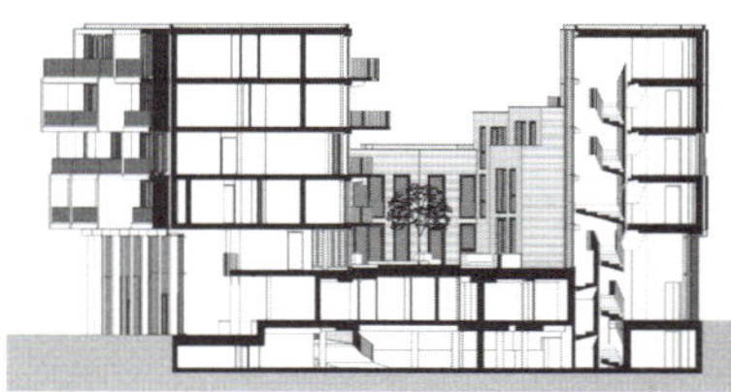

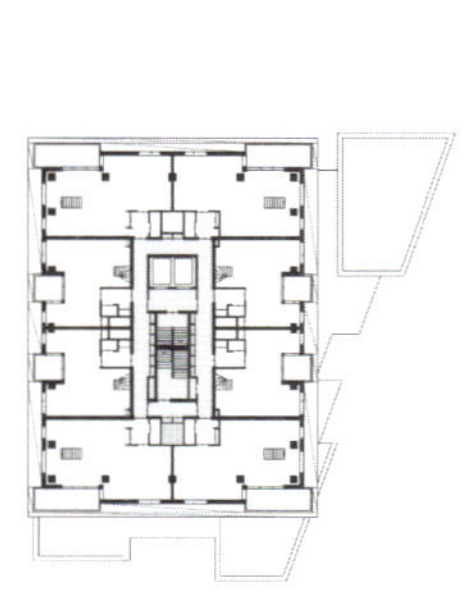

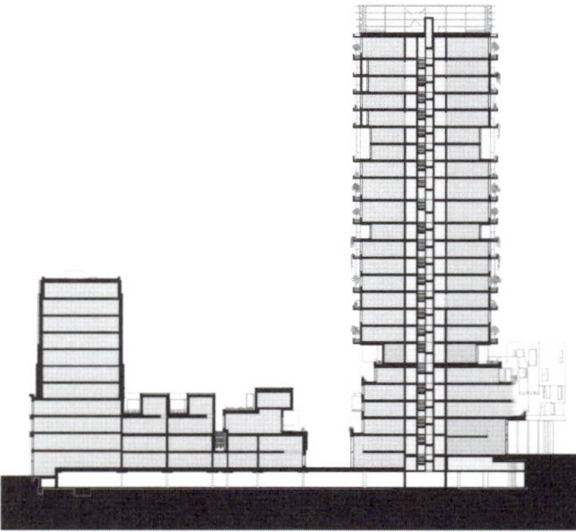

Features
Residential towers and apartment complexes in the transformation area around the station

Urban planning – supervision
Jurgen Krabbenborg (DRO-R&D), Don Murphy (VMX), Marjolein Peeters (Studio Scale), Joram Schaap (DRO-R&D)

Architects
including Engel Architects, NL Architects, De Zwarte Hond, Space Encounters, studio Donna van Milligen Bielke, i29 Architects, and VDNDP

Construction period
2018–2024

Houses per hectare
150

Average house size
95 m²

41 SCIENCE PARK

The Science Park in the Watergraafsmeer is located in a hidden spot in the city, 'behind' a large NS railway yard. The area originally housed various allotment gardens, and in the 1960s, research institutions from the University of Amsterdam (UvA) were established: the biology faculty and the experimental 'particle accelerator' of Nikhef. In the 1970s and 1980s, all the allotment gardens were relocated, and institutes such as AMOLF, CWI, and SARA settled in the area. Around these institutions, the successful internet hub AMS-IX developed. Based on this success, the UvA decided in 2005 to move its entire science faculty and the University Sports Centre to the area, which was then named the Amsterdam Science Park.

The area development is a collaboration between the University of Amsterdam, the Dutch Research Council (NWO), and the City of Amsterdam. The master plan for the development of the Science Park was created in 2003 by KCAP and Karres en Brands landscape architects. The plan divides the space into building strips running parallel to the original structure of the polder. To improve the area's accessibility, a new NS station was built in 2009, and a new avenue, the Carolina MacGillavrylaan, was created from Molukkenstraat. The aim was to extend it towards the A10, but this has not yet been realized.

After years of preparation, partly due to concerns about the habitat of the natterjack toad, the project officially began in 2005. In addition to new buildings for scientific facilities, the sports center, and University College, nearly 2,000 homes have been built in the area. The so-called Matrix buildings provide space for (start-up and growing) businesses. The data towers near the internet hub highlight the special character of the area. The public space has been completely redesigned.

In 2022, a new development phase started in the Science Park, focusing on densification, sustainability, diversification, and integration with the city.

1 Amsterdam Sciencepark Station
2 Polder Restaurant
3 Aerial photo, 2004
4 Aerial photo, 2023
5 Matrix One
6 Data center AM4, design by Benthem Crouwel Architects
7 Diagram showing the layering of the design
8 Masterplan Sciencepark, 2003, design by Karres en Brands, KCAP

1

2

3

4

5

6

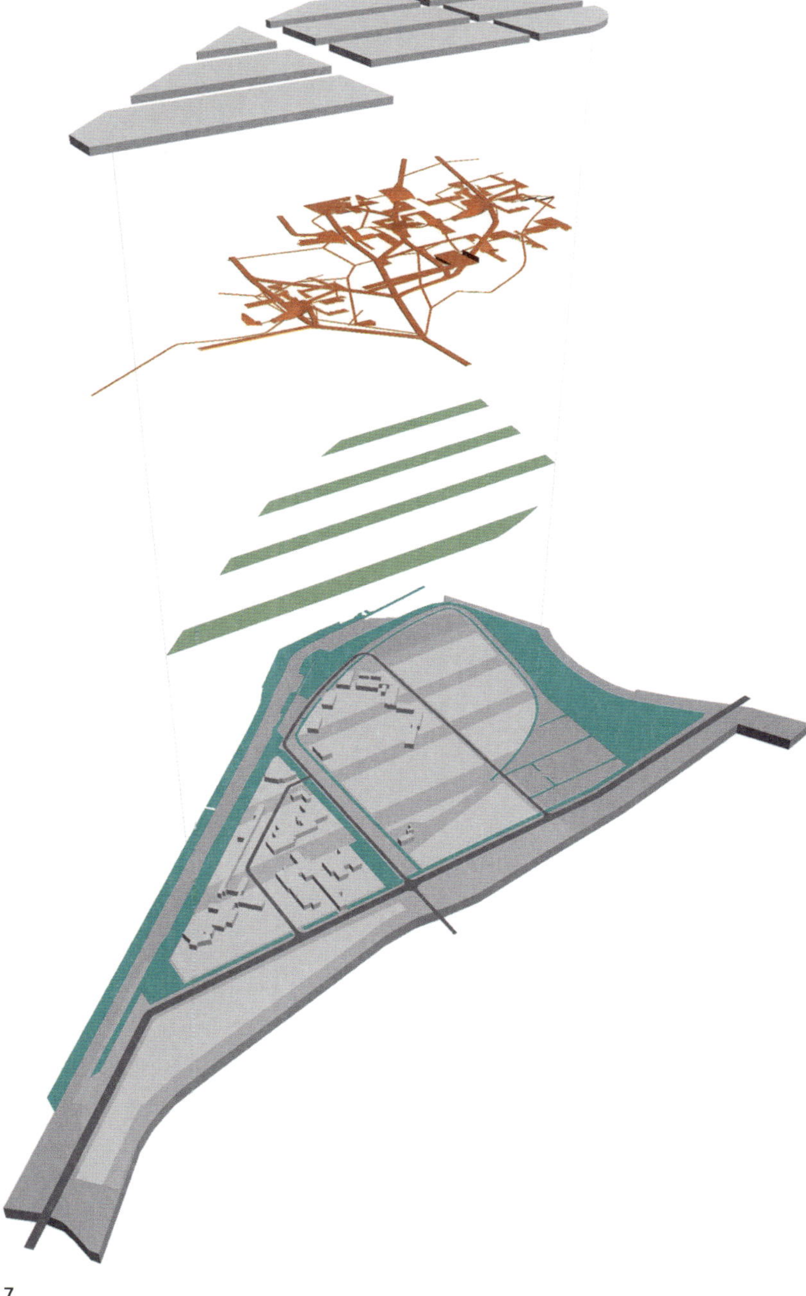
7

8

4J BIJLMER ARENA STATION

In 1971, the first temporary Bijlmer Station was opened on the then-ground-level railway line Amsterdam-Utrecht. A few years later, a new station was opened on the elevated railway connection (1976) and the new metro line (1977).

When the Amsterdam Arena opened in 1996, the station became dangerously crowded before and after football matches. This situation was further exacerbated by the development of Arena Boulevard, which brought several major attractions. The doubling of the tracks on the Amsterdam-Utrecht route provided an opportunity to replace the station.

The new station needed to handle the much larger number of passengers. Additionally, a better connection had to be made at ground level between the Arena area on the west side and the Amsterdamse Poort shopping center on the east side.

The new Bijlmer ArenA Station was designed by Nicolas Grimshaw and Arcadis. The four train tracks and two metro tracks are located 10 meters above the ground. The Arena Boulevard running beneath the station and the station hall create light and pleasant spaces. The design of the roof also helps dampen the sound from passing trains. The station was completed in 2007 and won two architecture awards in 2008.

1 Site plan for the redesign of ArenAPoort, design by Karres en Brands
2 Aerial photo, 2003
3 Aerial photo, 2023
4 Amsterdam Bijlmer Station in 1988
5 Entrance to the station from Johan Cruijff Boulevard
6 Hoekenrodeplein after redesign, design by Karres en Brands
7 Longitudinal section of Amsterdam Bijlmer ArenA Station, design by Grimshaw Architects
8 Construction of station canopy, design by Grimshaw Architects

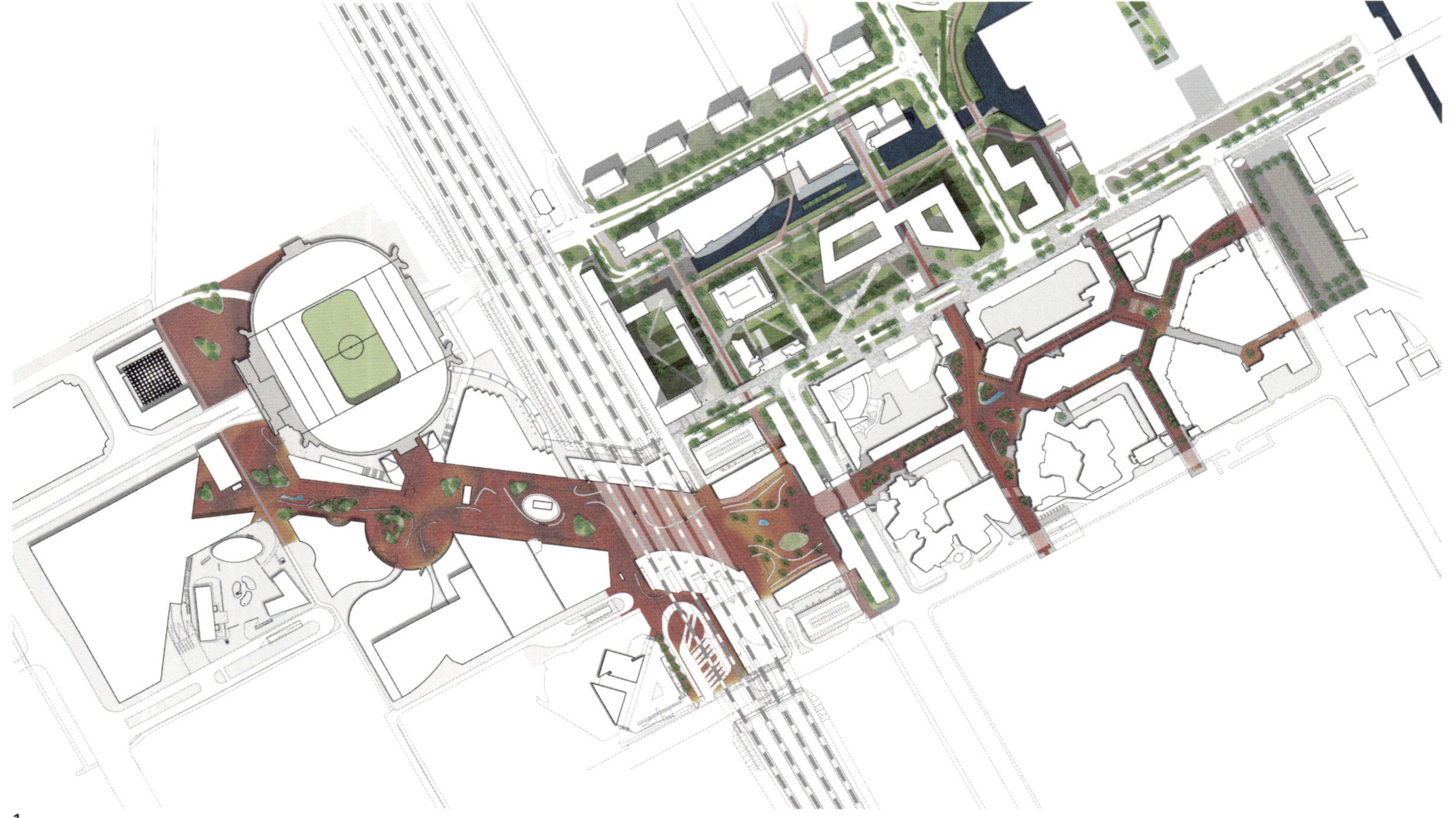
1

2

3

4

5

6

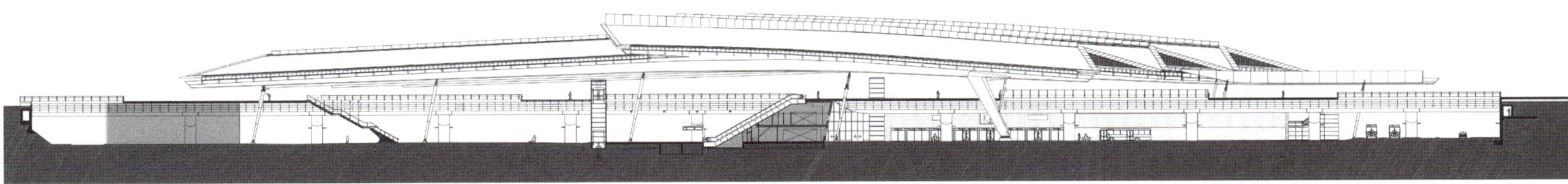
7

8

4K OLYMPIC STADIUM AND STADIONPLEIN

Since the 1928 Olympic Games, Stadionplein has never been much more than a stony parking lot with a few kiosks on it. These kiosks were originally intended for purchasing tickets for the Olympic Games. This is also the image many Amsterdammers have had for a long time: a large parking lot where tour buses would depart and fairs were held. Citroën operated the garage buildings on the opposite side of Amstelveenseweg. With the exception of major Ajax and Oranje matches and the short period when FC Amsterdam played there, the Stadium itself was a relatively uncomfortable place in the city.

When Ajax moved from De Meer to the Arena, new possibilities emerged. Initially, the plan was to demolish the Olympic Stadium entirely and build a large number of homes. After campaigns led by Piet Kranenberg, it was decided to preserve the Stadium and only remove the later-added concrete second ring. The Stadium was excellently restored. Underneath the field and the athletics track, a large P+R parking garage was built. The space under the stands was repurposed for offices and restaurants. The garages also began a new life with a highly mixed-use program. Residential construction was limited to the area north of the stadium, on the former grounds of tennis park Frans Otten.

Around 2001, the desire emerged to address the square itself and transform it into an attractive and multifunctional public space with room for housing, shops, terraces, and more greenery. OMA created the urban plan; West 8 designed the public space.

On the new square, the original sales kiosks were rebuilt. Greenery and art were added, and two residential blocks with a total of 100 homes and an underground supermarket were built on the square. The blocks have a double-height base along the Amstelveenseweg axis, with community facilities and shops, including the familiar FEBO. A market is regularly held on the square.

1 Olympic Stadium in 1991, still with concrete second ring
2 Olympic Stadium, 2020
3 Aerial photo, 2012
4 Aerial photo, 2023
5 Aerial view redesign Stadionplein, 2008, design by OMA
6 Stadionplein concept, design by OMA
7 Stadionplein in 2001
8 Stadionplein

1

2

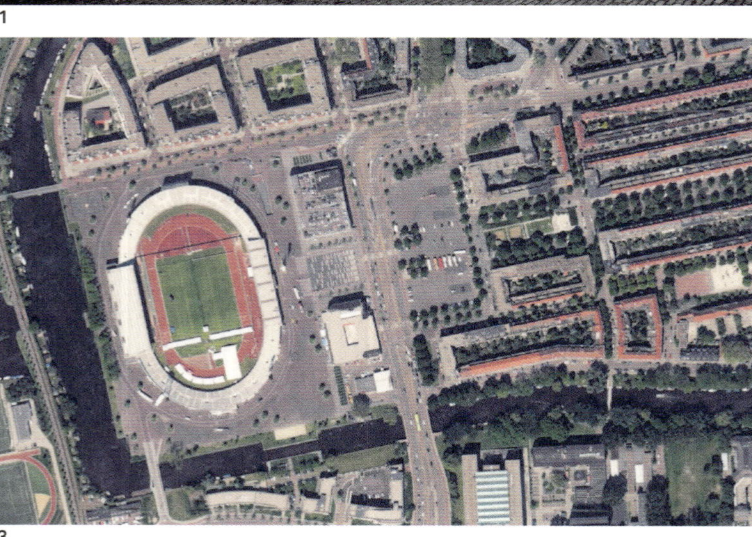

3

4

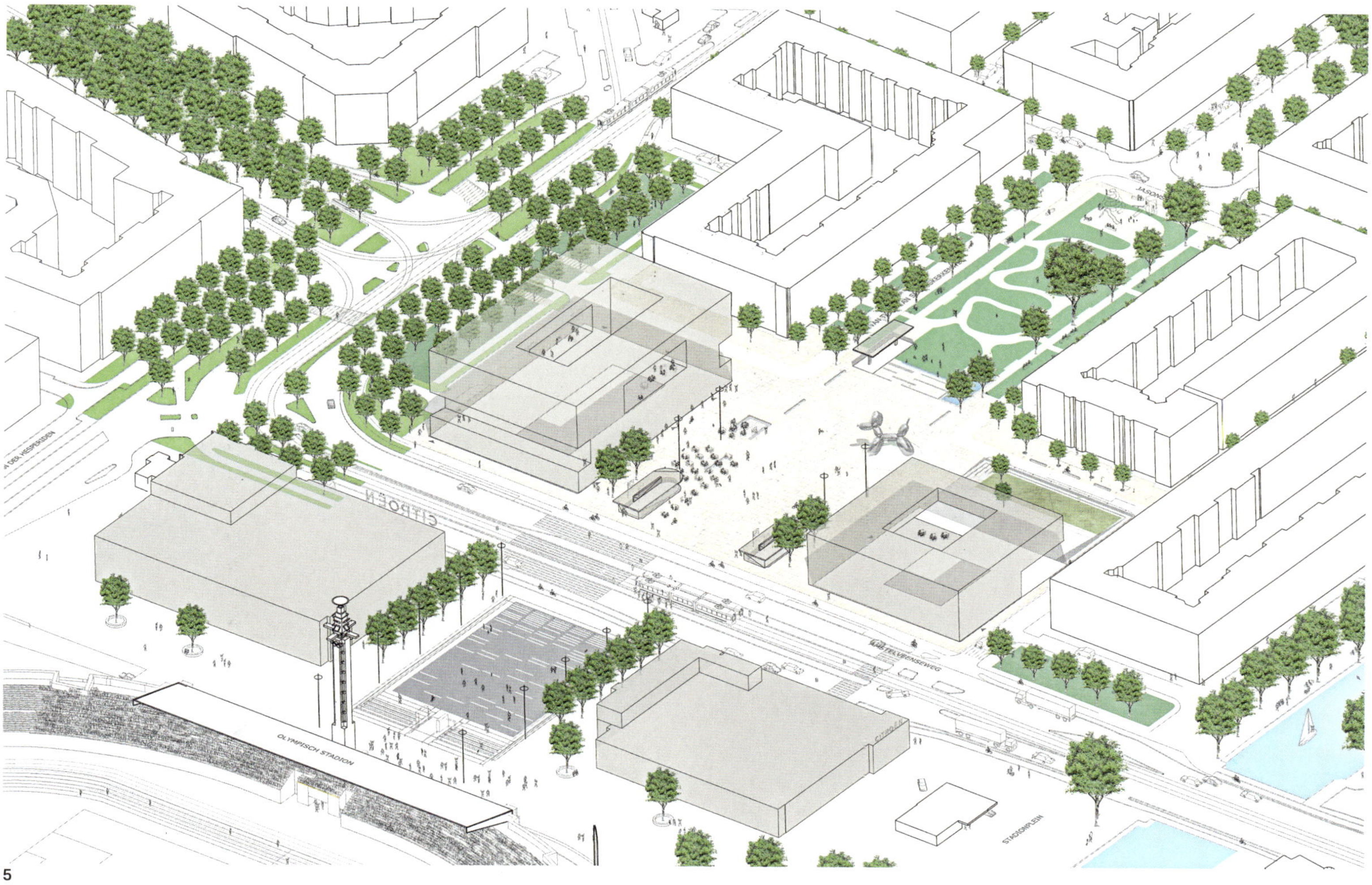

5

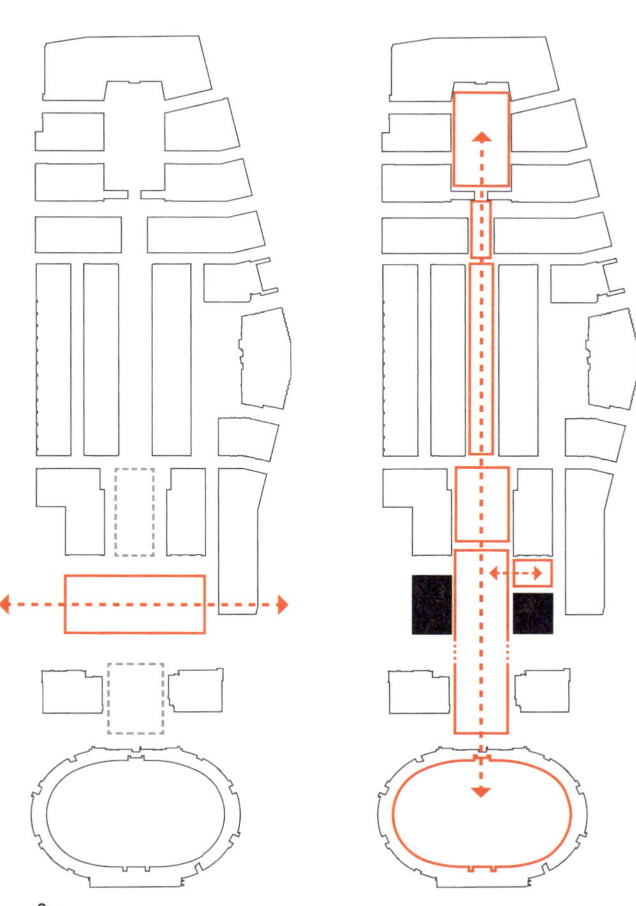
6

7

8

4L COURT BUILDING

By 1999, the old Court building on Parnassusweg from 1975 no longer met the requirements, but it wasn't until 2010 that a decision was made to build a new court next to the old building. A temporary court was established on Ferd. Roeskestraat. KAAN architects (part of the NACH consortium) designed the building with more than 60,000 m² of program space on behalf of the Dutch Government Real Estate Agency.

The building, completed in 2021, is located at the junction between the residential neighborhoods of South and the towers of the Zuidas. A large square, which covers almost a quarter of the plot, connects with the avenue that runs toward Zuid Station after the A10 has been tunneled. Since the judiciary is an inherently public matter, the building is not a closed bunker but features a transparent façade facing the square. At the same time, it exudes authority through its material use and clean detailing.

On the square stands a five-meter-high artwork by New York artist Nicole Eisenman, *Love or Generosity*. The figure is bent forward, holding a small owl, an arrow, and an acorn in her hand. These symbols represent wisdom, perseverance, and protection against evil, respectively.

1 The old Courthouse in 1990
2 Aerial photo, 2005
3 Aerial photo, 2023
4 Sculpture 'Love or Generosity'
5 Cross-section, design by KAAN Architecten
6 New courthouse viewed from the south, design by KAAN Architecten (photo: FG+SG Architectural Photography)

1

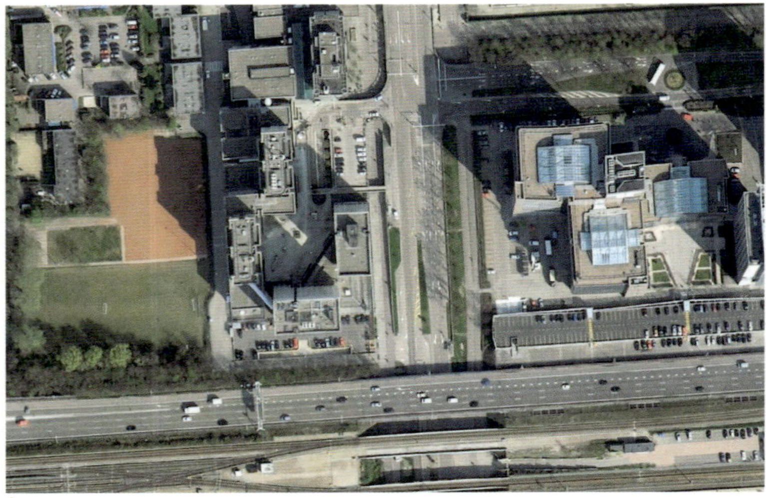

2

3

4

5

6

4M ENTRANCE AMC

The two largest hospitals in Amsterdam, the Binnengasthuis and the Wilhelmina Gasthuis, merged in 1983 to form the Academic Medical Center (AMC). Along with the Emma Children's Hospital, they occupied a large hospital complex on the outskirts of Amsterdam-Zuidoost, which at the time was the largest hospital in Europe. In 2018, the AMC merged with the VU University Medical Center to form Amsterdam UMC.

Although the hospital was connected directly to Holendrecht Metro Station via a pedestrian bridge and walking path, the hospital entrance was perceived as unclear, as it was somewhat located within the parking garage. In 2017, the hospital organized a design competition for a new entrance and better integration with the surrounding area. The team of Temp. architecture.urbanism, Studio Nuy Van Noort, and Studio BLAD won with their proposal for the construction of a new glass entrance pavilion and the creation of a park. A ramp across the park leads visitors to the entrance. It was completed in 2022. The park clarifies the routes between the neighborhood, the metro station, and the hospital, providing a pleasant green space for patients and staff to take a walk. The pavilion itself offers a warm welcome to patients and visitors. A terrace connects the entrance, the ramp, and the park.

1 Overview of entrance AMC and park, design by Temp.architecture & studio Nuy van Noort
2 Aerial photo, 2015
3 Aerial photo, 2023
4 Entrance to the AMC in 1981
5 Cross-section of the entrance pavilion, design by Temp.architecture & studio Nuy van Noort
6 New entrance to the AMC (photo: Katja Effting)

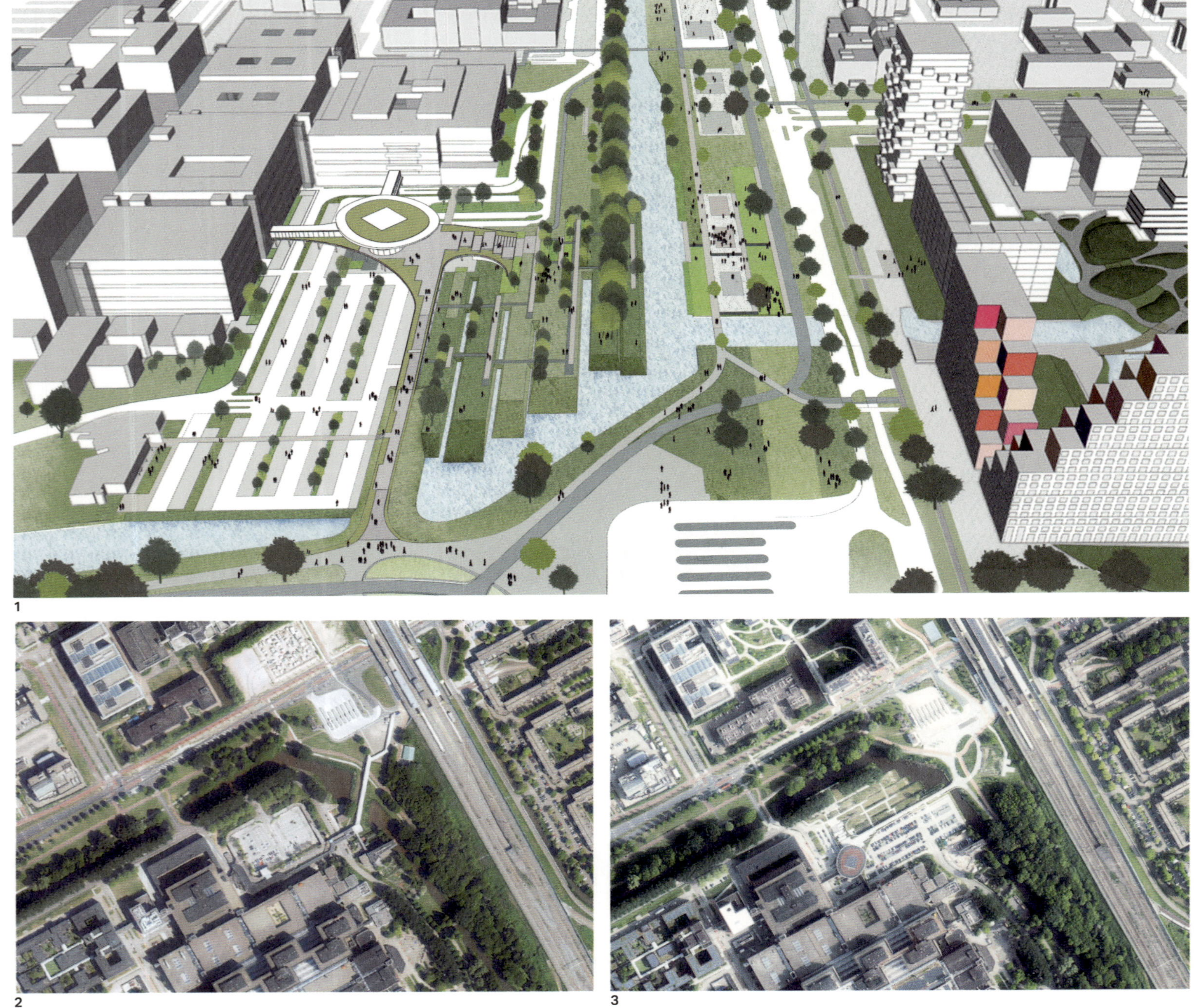

4

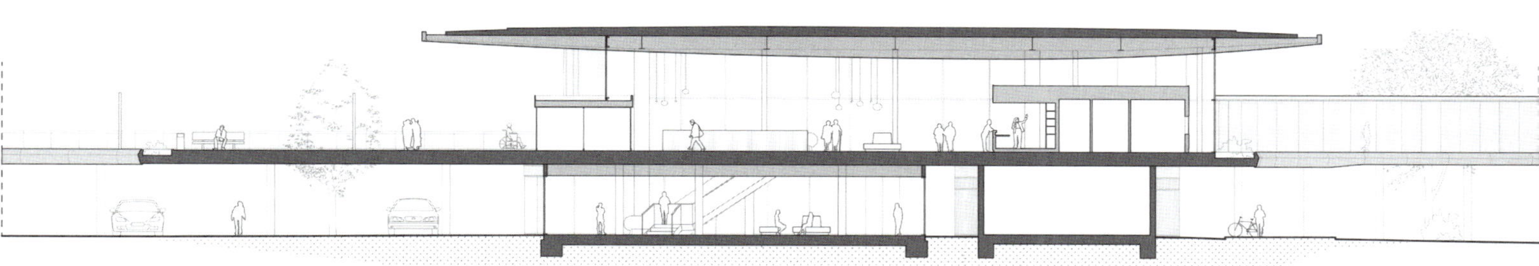

5

6

MOVEMENT 5

SUPERCLUSTER CITY CENTER — INTERACTION

Due to the southward movement, many buildings in prominent locations in the city center became available for new functions. The clustering of educational institutions and the relocation of the city hall and the OBA reinforced this process. Some vacated buildings were repurposed for cultural uses, such as the Beurs van Berlage and De Bazel, but most became hotels. The city center thus developed into a concentration area for cultural and tourist facilities, hospitality, and education. It became a metropolitan meeting place.[1]

→ Rokin, 1975–2025

Notably, many companies from the creative and tech sectors also prefer to establish themselves in the city center. In this regard, Amsterdam fully aligns with the image of a modern global city that Richard Florida evoked in the late 1990s.[2]

Many streets and squares have been made car-free or low-traffic and redesigned for a pleasant stay, starting with the shopping streets. The canals and most squares followed. The crowning achievement is the redevelopment of the area around Central Station, including the Open Havenfront and the new quay along the IJ.

Other metropolitan meeting places are more dispersed across the city, such as ArenAPoort, De Hallen, the Westergasfabriek, and NDSM – not to mention all the festival venues, often far outside the city!

LACOSTE
Shop alles lokaal op peddler.com
PULL&BEAR

Since 1975, the city center has undergone a major shift in function. Many financial sector companies merged and moved south. Newspapers left, the post office closed, the municipality built a new city hall, and higher education institutions clustered in unprecedented ways. As a result, many buildings became available for new purposes.

One of the most significant changes was the departure of newspaper companies and their printing presses from Nieuwezijds Voorburgwal: *Het Handelsblad* merged with *NRC* in Rotterdam (1970), *Het Vrije Volk* and *De Tijd* ceased to exist, *De Telegraaf* relocated to Basisweg in Sloterdijk, and *de Volkskrant* (1965), *Het Parool* (1970), and *Trouw* (1976) moved to Wibautstraat.

The relocation of the banking sector to the south was already extensively covered. Large buildings that became vacant in the city center included the former ABN headquarters on Vijzelstraat and the AMRO offices on Rembrandtplein. The canal-side building of the Gemeentegiro on Singel was also vacated in the late 1970s following its merger with the Postbank. In 1985, the last stock exchange activities left the Beurs van Berlage. A few years later, in 1987, Fortis constructed an unsightly new office on the site of the Rotterdamsche Bank at Rokin, but this was demolished in 2015 after ABN AMRO acquired Fortis.

In 1975, 39,262 people worked in Amsterdam's banking and insurance sector, most of them in the city center. By late 2023, that number had increased to 43,127, but only 3,217 remained in the center. In Zuid, 8,645 people worked in the sector, while the majority – 23,500 – were now based in Zuidoost.

At the same time, the number of employed people in the city center has never been higher. In early 2024, the city center had just over 115,000 people working in jobs of at least 12 hours per week. Including part-time jobs under 12 hours, the total number of employed persons was nearly 140,000. In addition to around 30,000 jobs in tourism, most employment is now in business services, creative industries, and ICT – 70,000 jobs in total, in sectors that barely existed in 1975.[3]

The new way of working is far more compact, organized in flexible office spaces and coworking locations such as Capital C, Spaces, and The New Base.

This new employment landscape consists of many small businesses, often freelancers working from home and communicating with the world. But these sectors have also produced large companies, such as the payment service Adyen. In 2020, Adyen, with 2,000 employees, moved into the former department stores on Rokin, on the old site of Fortis. Other rapidly growing companies, such as Booking, Vodafone, and TomTom, established themselves in new developments on Oosterdokseiland. Guerrilla Games moved into the former *De Telegraaf* headquarters on Nieuwezijds Voorburgwal in 2021, while Tommy Hilfiger relocated to the Atlanta building at Leidsebosje in 2024.

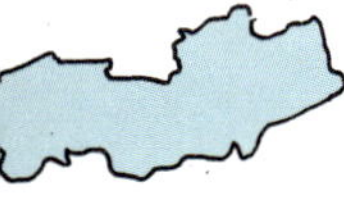

↑ Movement – expansion of the city center into a supercluster with cultural facilities, hotels, and restructured, car-free public spaces

Culture

Parallel to the transformation of the business services sector, the mid-1980s saw the beginning of a complete cultural makeover in the city center.[4] This renewal aligned with the Amsterdam 700 initiatives and the construction of the Muziektheater (now Nationale Opera & Ballet), which ultimately opened in 1986 as part of the Stopera.

A long list of institutions underwent renovation and expansion: De Nieuwe Kerk (1965–1980), the Anne Frank House (1987–1999), the Concertgebouw (1985–1988), the synagogue complex on Nieuwe Amstelstraat, the new home of the Jewish Historical Museum (1987), the Van Gogh Museum (1999 and 2015), Carré (2004), and the Stadsschouwburg (2009). The extensive renovations of the Rijksmuseum (1995–2013), the Stedelijk Museum (2003–2012), DeLaMar (2005–2010), the Scheepvaartmuseum (2007–2011), and Felix Meritis (2017–2020) marked the final stage of expanding and modernizing existing institutions.

That said, the renewal of Artis may be the longest-running project of all. In 1988, Artis celebrated its 150th anniversary and opened its Planetarium. The following year, the zoo expanded with a strip of land along the Entrepotdok, launching an impressive series of new construction and renovation projects, including the Groote Museum, the elephant and lion enclosures, and the Artis Library. The reopening of the Aquarium is planned for 2026.

But a whole range of new cultural facilities also opened, often as existing institutions outgrew their previous locations. The Allard Pierson Museum (1976) and the Special Collections department of the University of Amsterdam (2007) moved into the buildings on Oude Turfmarkt, formerly home to De Nederlandsche Bank. The Amsterdam Philharmonic Orchestra took up residence in the Beurs van Berlage (1985), Madame Tussauds relocated from Kalverstraat to the Peek & Cloppenburg building on Dam Square (1991), and the NINT moved from Marnixstraat, via the Asscher complex on Tolstraat, to NEMO (1997). The Resistance Museum relocated from the Lekstraat synagogue to Gebouw Plancius opposite Artis (1999), the BIMHUIS moved from Oude Schans, and the performers of the Muziekgebouw relocated from the Ysbreeker on Weesperzijde (2005). The City Archives moved from Amsteldijk to De Bazel (2007), and the OBA (Amsterdam Public Library) relocated from Prinsengracht to Oosterdok (2007).

The success of large exhibitions in De Nieuwe Kerk laid the foundation for the Hermitage in Amstelhof (2004, reopening after renovation in 2009), which later rebranded as H'ART Museum. The Netherlands Filmmuseum, too cramped in the Vondelpark Pavilion, concentrated its activities at Eye and the Collection Center on Asterweg (2012). Paradiso opened a second venue in Tolhuistuin, the former Shell canteen (2014). Finally, in 2024, the National Holocaust Museum opened in the former Reformed Teacher Training School on Plantage Middenlaan, directly across from the renovated Hollandsche Schouwburg.

All of these renovated, expanded, and newly built cultural venues attract far more visitors than they did in 1975. That year, theater, opera, and music performances drew 871,000 visitors. There are

no recent totals, but in 2018 alone, the ten largest venues attracted 4.8 million visitors. Museum attendance jumped from 3.2 million in 1975 to 10.5 million in recent years. Attractions and events have seen similar surges.[5]

Education

Almost all higher education institutions in Amsterdam underwent mergers in the 1980s and 1990s. The first was the founding of the Amsterdam University of the Arts (AHK) in 1987, created through the merger of the Academy of Architecture, the Academy for Visual Education, the Netherlands Film Academy, and the Reinwardt Academy. Later, the Theatre School and the Conservatory also joined. The new Theatre School (1997) and Film Academy (1999) buildings were constructed around Mr. Visserplein, forming a cluster of arts education institutions. Later, the new Conservatory was built on Oosterdokseiland (2008), and the Academy for Visual Education relocated to Overhoeks (2016), reopening as the Breitner Academy in A Lab, the former Shell Groot Lab. The Reinwardt Academy moved into a vacant building at Hortusplantsoen. In 2023, the National Ballet Academy opened a new facility in Overamstel.

The consolidation in other areas of higher professional education was even more extensive. Prestigious institutions such as the technical college (hts), the social academy, the teacher training college (pabo), the School of Economics (HES), and the Maritime Academy merged in 1993 to form the Amsterdam University of Applied Sciences (HvA). A strong clustering of programs was pursued at the head of Wibautstraat, initially in the former Tax Office building and the old Amstel Brewery headquarters, later expanding into the former Labour Council building and new developments on the site of the Wibauthuis and Rhijnspoorplein. With the opening of the Jakoba Mulderhuis in 2022, the Amstel Campus was completed. Only a few specialized programs remain at other locations, such as Sportpark Ookmeer and the AMC. By 2024, the HvA had an enrollment of 46,764 students.

The VU (Vrije Universiteit) opted for faculty clustering in Buitenveldert as early as the 1960s, with the new main building gradually coming into use between 1970 and 1973. The UvA (University of Amsterdam), however, followed a less consistent strategy. After abandoning large-scale development plans around the proposed traffic breakthrough at Valkenburgerstraat, a major new humanities faculty building was completed in 1984: the P.C. Hoofthuis on Spuistraat, designed by Theo Bosch on the site of the former Twentsche Bank. Ultimately, in 1998, the UvA settled on three main clusters (or four if including the medical faculty at the AMC): humanities in and around the Binnengasthuis complex, sciences at the Science Park in Watergraafsmeer, and social sciences on and around Roeterseiland. This restructuring remains an ongoing process. A key milestone will be the opening of the new University Library in 2025 in the former Surgical Clinic and Nurses' House at Binnengasthuisterrein. The future of the vacated P.C. Hoofthuis, the Maagdenhuis, and the existing library on Singel remains undecided.

The Gerrit Rietveld Academy (and its graduate school, the Sandberg Institute) remained independent of these higher education mergers. Its campus on Fred. Roeskestraat was renovated and expanded in 2004 and 2018. Alongside the HvA, InHolland University of Applied Sciences also offers higher education in Amsterdam. In 2024, InHolland relocated from Diemen to its new campus at Pina Bauschplein in the Sluisbuurt on Zeeburgereiland.

← Jodenbreestraat, 1975–2025

Tourism and hotels

Most of the vacant buildings in the city center were transformed into hotels. The old city hall (Prinsenhof) on Oudezijds Voorburgwal was converted into The Grand, with 177 rooms, but there are many more: the Conservatorium Hotel, Soho House in the Bungehuis, Amrâth in the Scheepvaarthuis, the W Amsterdam in the former Kas Bank and the National Government Building for the Money and Telephone Company, Andaz in the former library on Prinsengracht, and Banks Mansion in the Incassobank at the corner of Vijzelstraat-Herengracht – all luxury four- and five-star hotels. In 2025, Rosewood will open in the Palace of Justice on Prinsengracht.

The list of new hotels is even longer. Early examples include the construction of the Sonesta Hotel on the former site of *Het Vrije Volk* at Hekelveld and the Marriott, built after the demolition of the Koepelkerk at Leidsebosje. Many new hotels have been built especially around Central Station (CS). Since 2000, the Passenger Terminal Amsterdam (PTA) for ocean cruise ships has also been located there, along with new piers for river cruise ships.

The numbers speak for themselves. In 1975, a total of 1.6 million guests stayed in Amsterdam, of which 1.3 million were in hotels. The remaining 300,000 stayed in hostels, guesthouses, and campsites (and quite a few in Vondelpark). Hotel guests accounted for 2.8 million overnight stays. In 2023, 9.4 million visitors came to Amsterdam, also staying overnight in the city. In total, they made 22.1 million overnight stays.[6] The number of hotels increased from 316 in 1975 to 544 in 2024, with 277 located in the city center. Even more striking is the number of hotel beds. It was just over 20,000 in 1975, and now there are 92,000. The city center alone has nearly 32,000 beds. In the peak year of 2019, nearly 30,000 homes or rooms were offered at least once through Airbnb in Amsterdam. However, this number has significantly decreased due to new regulations.

Events

The city has long been a stage for the exchange of all kinds of knowledge, information, and goods. The Palace of Industry and later the RAI provided spaces for large, often annual congresses, fairs, and conventions, frequently with a national scope. Famous events include the Huishoudbeurs and the Landbouw-RAI. Since 1947, the Holland Festival has provided a platform for various cultural disciplines. In recent years, universities, conference hotels, and many smaller halls and venues have also played an important role, and the range of offerings has become much broader and more international, covering everything from vintage furniture, graphic works, and denim to heart surgery, cello, and green tech. Most congresses and conventions are multi-day events. Participants stay for a few days and combine the event with visits to museums, concerts, and restaurants. A popular festival is the IDFA, focusing on documentary films. In 2024, it attracted 260,000 visitors.

King's Day and the annual fairs are recurring events in public spaces. During Amsterdam 700, several large events were added: Sail (every five years), the Marathon, and Kwaku; soon followed by the Uitmarkt (1978), the Prinsengracht-concert (1982), and the Dam to Dam run (1985). Highly popular events include the annual Canal Parade (1996) and more recently, the Amsterdam Light Festival (2012).

A new outdoor phenomenon are the one- or multi-day music and dance festivals in almost all the city parks, at specialized festival locations (NDSM, Thuishaven, Riekerhaven, Ruigoord), and in the large regional parks (Spaarnwoude, Twiske, and the Amsterdam Forest). The Amsterdam Dance Event (ADE) is a mix of performances, demonstrations, and conferences centered around electronic music. In 2024, 500,000 visitors participated in more than 1,000 events at 200 locations over one week.

POLICY, STRATEGY, AND DESIGN

In the 1970s and 1980s, after the large-scale city reconstruction plans were abandoned, the policy for the city center initially focused on preserving and strengthening the residential function in neighborhoods like the Jordaan, Nieuwmarkt, and the islands. Between 1975 and 1985 – the period of 'reversing the decline' – 1,600 homes were improved, and 4,300 new ones were built, spread across 160 projects. Major projects included new construction on Kattenburg and Wittenburg, along the metro route in the Nieuwmarkt district, at the site of the traffic breakthrough at the Haarlemmer Houttuinen, and the repurposing of warehouses at the Entrepotdok. In the old city and the Jordaan, many smaller projects were carried out, including the improvement of a series of squats that were purchased and legalized around the inauguration of Queen Beatrix in 1980, and about 1,000 'homes above shops'.[7]

In the core area of the old city and the canal belt, the policy focused primarily on public space: how to curb traffic chaos, solve the parking problem, and fight crime?

The first parking meters were installed in 1964 with a rate of 25 cents per hour, and the number of 'amsterdammertjes' (small bollards) was also greatly expanded during these years. The story goes that by the mid-1980s, about 100,000 of these bollards had been placed around the city to prevent illegal parking along the streets and sidewalks and to give pedestrians more space.

One of the first policy documents of the new municipal executive, which took office in 1978, was the Traffic Circulation Plan. It contained detailed maps of what were called 'main networks' for cars, parking, bicycles, and pedestrians. This created a hierarchy and functional specialization within the street network. Major interventions in public space stemming from this plan included the closure of Leidsestraat to car and bicycle traffic and the creation of a car-free 'inner ring.' After the opening of the Torontobridge in 1969, Nassaukade, Stadhouderskade, and Mauritskade were designated for car traffic to and from the city center. Marnixstraat, Weteringschans, and Sarphatistraat – the inner ring – were gradually turned into tram and bike streets with one-way car traffic.

However, these measures could only be successful with effective enforcement. In 1983, the wheel clamp was introduced to prevent unpaid parking. Subsequently,

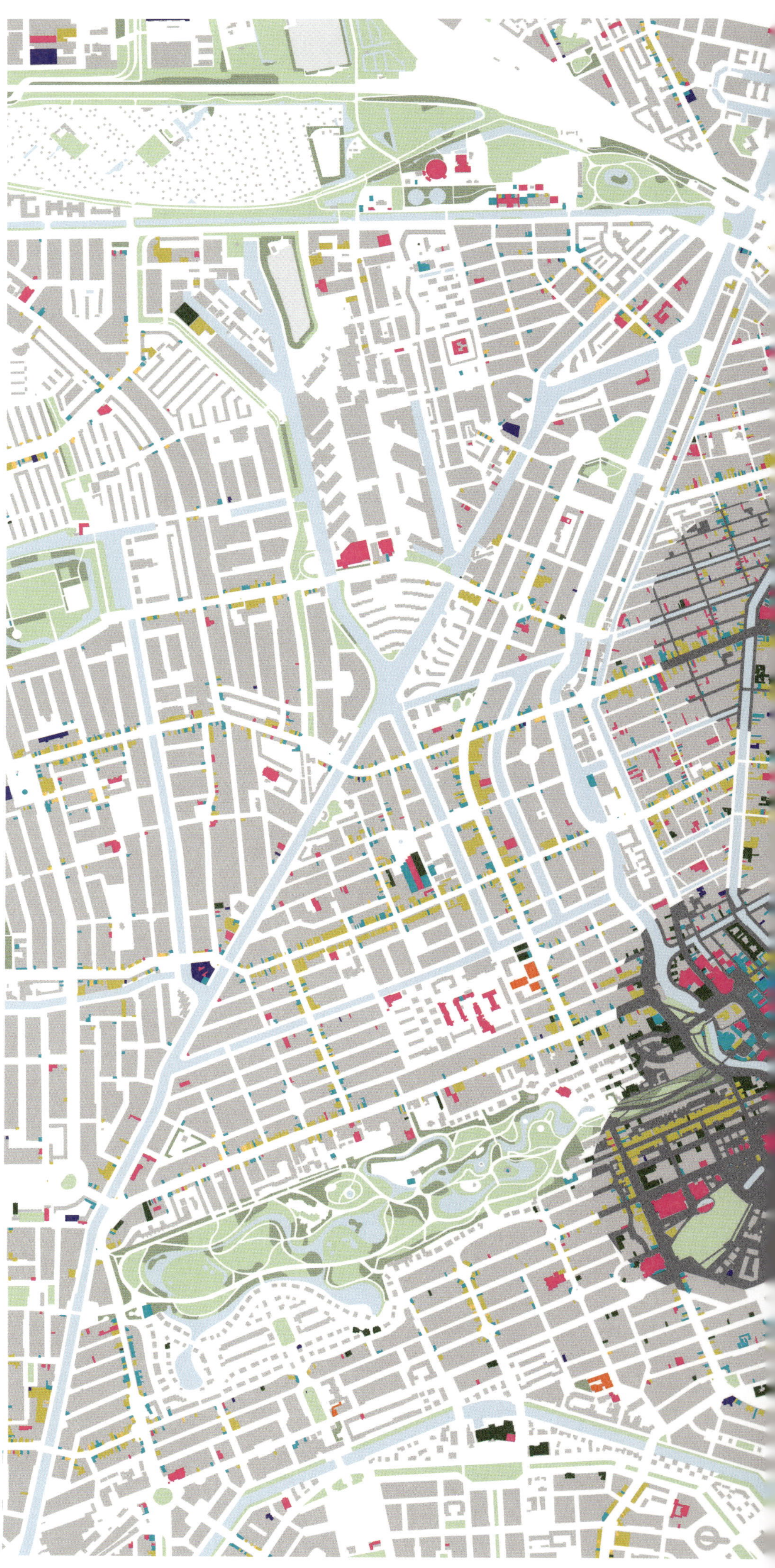

→ Service clusters in the city center

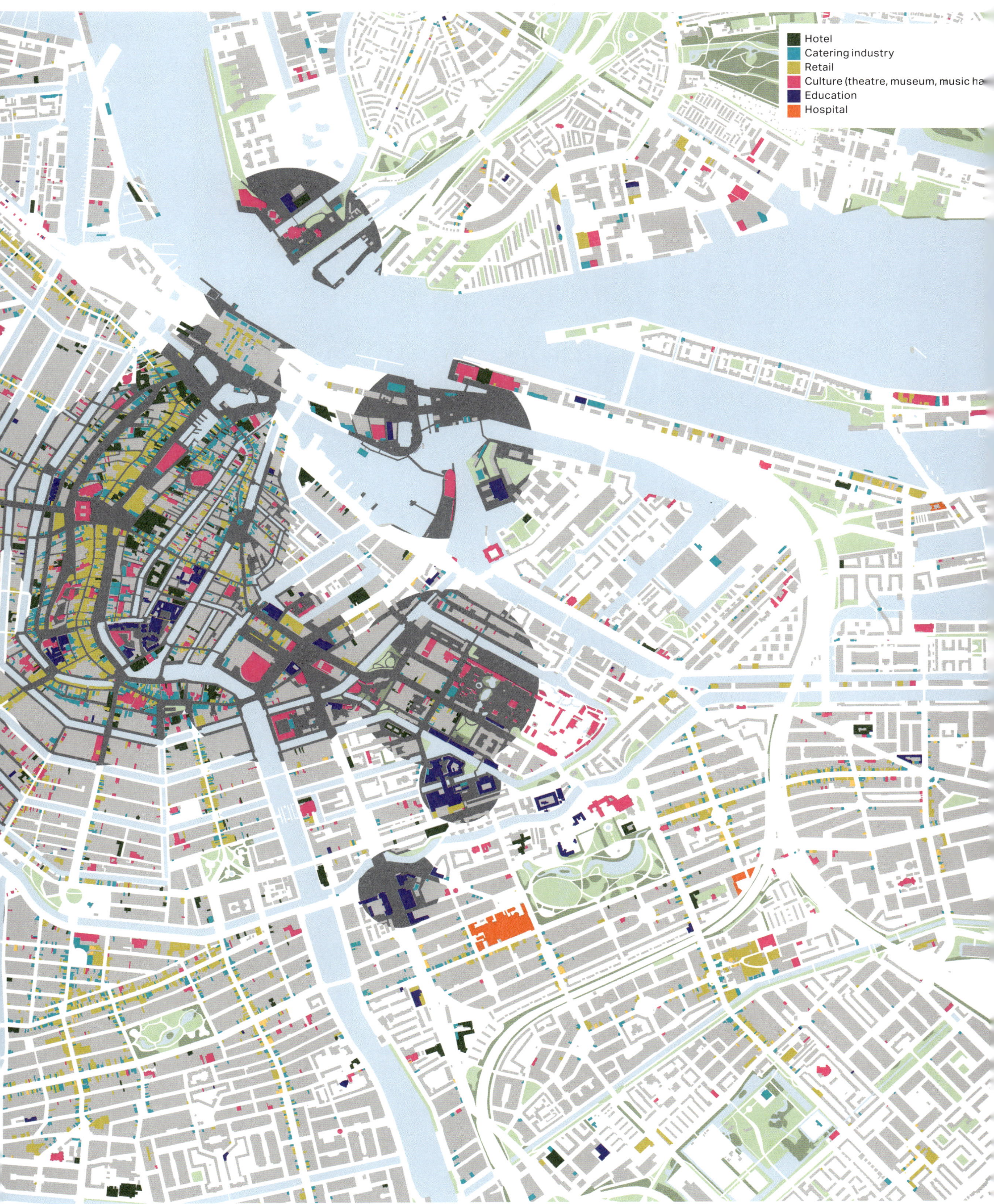

Hotel
Catering industry
Retail
Culture (theatre, museum, music ha
Education
Hospital

1

1 Structural image of Amsterdam city center, city formation with clustering of offices (light blue) and university (black), business activity on the Eastern Islands (dark blue), and 'spreading' of central functions in the 19th-century belt (dashed blue line) (Note City Center, 1968)
2 Redesign of Damrak, 1991

parking fees were gradually increased and implemented in an ever-larger part of the city, just like the spreading of an oil stain.

Zeedijk and The Red Light District

The Zeedijk, with its maze of alleys surrounding it, was traditionally the harbor district of the city, filled with pubs, gambling dens, guesthouses, brothels, and the uniquely Amsterdam phenomenon of window prostitution. In the 1970s, the atmosphere hardened with the introduction of drugs and the associated crime. The heroin trade and street heroin use in particular contributed to a grim atmosphere, which many Amsterdam residents avoided. Estimates suggest that around 1980 there were 10,000 heroin addicts in Amsterdam, along with all the criminal activity, especially around the Zeedijk.[8]

To break the difficult situation, the GGD (Public Health Service) started an experiment in 1979 with regulated distribution of methadone (and clean needles) as part of rehabilitation programs for heroin addicts. The methadone bus became a well-known symbol. The experiment proved to be very successful, leading to a decline in robberies and making the streets feel less grim.

In 1985, a significant step was taken with the establishment of the NV Economisch Herstel Zeedijk. This collaboration between residents, entrepreneurs, and later the municipality focused on purchasing, renovating, and managing as many buildings as possible to prevent further decay of the street. After the repressive and regulatory measures taken in the previous years, this was a new and very effective step in combating drug trade and crime.[9] It marked the beginning of a much broader recovery phase starting in 1985.

During the city's growth spurt, tourism also grew, including sex and gambling tourism in the Red Light District. Could the successful approach of the Zeedijk be applied more broadly? In 2009, Project 1012 was launched, named after the postal code of the central part of the city. The goal was to break the criminal infrastructure and economically upgrade the entrance area of Amsterdam. After acquiring properties and changing zoning regulations, many of the prostitution windows, gambling halls, and coffeeshops in the Red Light District were closed, and the concept of Red Light Fashion was introduced. Vacant retail space was filled with clothing workshops, galleries, and fashion stores. The effectiveness of these measures is evaluated differently.[10] Ultimately, not half, but a quarter of the thousand windows were closed. The vacated retail space in Damstraat was largely filled with a new type of tourist shops: cheese, ice cream, candy, and waffles.

The criminal circuits, human trafficking, and influx of tourists remain difficult to manage, even post-pandemic. A solution is being sought in the construction of an erotic center on Europaboulevard near one of the on- and off-ramps of the A10 South. This fits into the broader tourism distribution policy.

Broader City Center policy

The establishment of the Structure Plan 'The City Central' in 1986 marked a more comprehensive new policy following the reversal of urban decline and the regulation of chaos in the public space of the city center in the preceding years. The approach chosen was a general profile that strengthened both the central functions and residential areas. Some sub-areas received more specific designations. For instance, the area between Nieuwezijds Voorburgwal and Damrak-Rokin was designated as the core retail area. Cultural functions and hospitality were concentrated around Leidseplein, Rembrandtplein, and Nes. As for employment, the expectation was a decrease in the number of jobs, with a goal to retain 80,000 jobs by the year 2000. The redesign of Valkenburgerstraat, Oosterdok, and the repurposing of Binnengasthuis were seen as 'impulses for the city center'.

A concrete measure from the structure plan was the construction of dedicated tram lanes on Damrak, Rokin, and Vijzelstraat, with priority for public transport in traffic light systems. In later versions of the Traffic Circulation Plan, a Main Public Transport Network was introduced, extending the concept of free tram lanes throughout the city.

Prominent developments from this city center policy during these years include the renewal and expansion of the core retail area with Magna Plaza in the old main post office (1991), Kalvertoren at the site of the Heiligewegbad (designed by Pi de Bruijn, 1997), De Kolk (designed by Van Berkel & Bos, 1997), and the redesign of major squares such as Rembrandtplein (1985), Nieuwmarkt (1990), and Damrak (1991). The choice of materials, as well as the design of lighting and street furniture, received much attention. Artists Alexander Schabracq and Tom Postma designed turquoise street lamps, benches, and fences in an expressive postmodern idiom, resembling totem poles and assemblages of disparate, stacked elements. Opinions on the quality were divided. In the redesign of Damrak and Rokin in 2013–2015 as part of the North/South Line project, different materials and furniture were chosen. Only the lighting fixtures at Nieuwmarkt remain as a reminder of this experiment.

At the same time, an intensive debate took place about the necessary redesign of Museumplein. The 'shortest highway in the Netherlands', built in the early 1960s across the square, exemplified the policy focused on promoting car traffic to and from the city center. Following a public competition held by NRC *Handelsblad* in 1988 and a thorough debate, Danish landscape architect Sven-Ingvar Andersson was invited in 1991 to create a design for the square's redesign.[11] His proposal to transform the square into a 'green field' surrounded by major cultural institutions, with understated design elements, raised many questions, especially about the 'ezelsoor' (the dog-ear, referring to the lifted corner of) the sloping grassy area near the Stedelijk Museum. Despite this, the design was implemented in the following years, and the expansion plans for the Van Gogh Museum and Stedelijk Museum followed the design: on the west side of the square, a pleasant, informal walking area was created, with entrances to the renovated museums and, in good weather, sunbathers occupying the *ezelsoor*.

The major issues the city faced at the time prompted Mayor Ed van Thijn to establish a Spatial Strategy Executive Team in 1992. Urban planner Dirk Frieling was appointed as an independent advisor to the municipal executive (1993–1996).[12] An essential part of Frieling's advice was his plea for municipal investments in the public domain of the city center: infrastructure, public spaces, and metropolitan facilities. This led to a long list of investments, building on the decision to renovate Museumplein in 1993. In the years that followed, projects such as the redesign of Spui (1996) and Dam (2001), the cleanup and redevelopment of the Westergasfabriek, the renovation and expansion of the Stedelijk Museum, and the construction of the Muziekgebouw and OBA were largely funded by the municipality of Amsterdam. The city and the national government both contributed to the construction of the North/South metro Line. The national government also financed the large-scale renovation of the Rijksmuseum.

After the new municipal executive took office in 1994, a separate Borough for the City Center was established in 1996. That same year, the municipal memorandum 'Roomfor Quality' and the first *Handboek Openbare Ruimte* (handbook for the design of public paces) were published, along with the New Standard Canal Profile. The focus was on creating more calm in the cityscape and using durable, beautiful materials – out with the bollards, concrete stones, and utility boxes of houseboats, and in with wide natural stone sidewalk curbs, deck slabs, baked bricks, and 19th-century streetlights. In an explanatory sketch, the 'bike-niche' appeared for the first time as a replacement for the traditional bike rack. In 1997, work began on the re-profiling of the first canal, Blauwburgwal. How far have we progressed by now – 30-40%? Not nearly finished! Along with the renewal of 'weak' quay walls, a new wave of re-profiling projects was set in motion, with stricter requirements regarding freight traffic and parking.

In 2001, the Policy Framework for Public Space was published under the title 'Puccinimethod', referencing the taste,

2

1

2

1 Museumplein, 1975–2025
2 Muziekgebouw in 2015

craftsmanship, and quality of products from the Amsterdam chocolatier of the same name. The principles outlined in the Handbook were extended throughout the city.

The new focus on quality also included improvements to accessibility. After the construction of large parking garages at Bijenkorf (1980) and under the Stopera (1986), a series of new public garages were built at the Open Havenfront and as part of the Markenhoven, Kalvertoren, De Kolk, and Oosterdokseiland projects. At the same time, large parking facilities were created on the city's outskirts, near train stations and tram hubs (P+R's), such as under the Arena and the Olympic Stadium, and on Zeeburgereiland. What had seemed like an absurd idea in the 1960s and 1970s – the Provo White Bicycle Plan – became a massive success as the OV-fiets (Public Transport Bike) system from 2000 onward. After taking the train to the city, commuters can easily bridge the 'last mile' with a rental bike.[13]

In 2003, the construction of the North/South metro line finally began.

Metropolitan Development

After the 2006 elections, a red-green coalition took office, led by Lodewijk Asscher of the PvdA and Maarten van Poelgeest of GroenLinks. In the lead-up to the elections, they emphasized the opportunities for metropolitan development and a new role for the city in the region and the country. 'New Amsterdam' could become the place where talent gathers and develops. The coalition agreement expressed the ambition for Amsterdam to be among the five most attractive cities in Europe. However, before the ink had even dried, the office market collapsed, and the financial crisis hit. In 2008, the banking crisis followed. Investors pulled out of the Zuidasdok project, and housing construction in the city almost came to a halt.

However, the development of the city center did not stagnate. On the wave of the significant population increase, the growth in tourism, and the creation of new jobs, investments, led by culture alderman Carolien Gehrels, continued. In 2010, the Canal Ring was designated as a UNESCO World Heritage Site. 2013 became a true 'jubilee year', with, among other events, the reopening of the Rijksmuseum, the 400th anniversary of the Canal Ring, and the King's Day boat trip after the coronation of King Willem-Alexander. The number of overnight stays in Amsterdam more than doubled from 8.8 million in 2007 to 22.1 million in 2023.

The public space policy continued with the redesign of areas like Rembrandtplein, Haarlemmerplein, Overtoom, Wibautstraat and Muiderstraat. However, the most radical intervention in the old city was the 'Red Carpet' project, combined with the construction of the North/South Line stations. Building on the successful experience with 'facade-to-facade' re-profiling, as seen on Wibautstraat, the entire public space was revamped, from the Open Havenfront near Central Station, through Damrak, Rokin, and Vijzelstraat to Ferdinand Bolstraat. The introduction of one-way traffic on Amstel, Rokin, and Damrak created significantly more space for pedestrians and cyclists. A 'cut' between Rokin and Vijzelstraat eased the traditional bottleneck at the Munt. The opening of new underground parking garages above the deep metro stations at Rokin and Vijzelgracht was coupled with the removal of

1

on-street parking in the surrounding area. The Beursplein area was also redesigned in 2019, connected to the opening of the first underground bicycle storage facility in the city center.

During this period, the city center itself expanded. The Oosterdok and the central part of the northern IJ shore were added. In 1997, NEMO opened at the tip of the IJ Tunnel pier, with the museum harbor along the quay, and from 2003, the Arcam Center for Architecture. The real momentum came in 2007 when the new OBA library and other buildings on the Oosterdokseiland were completed, along with the renewed quay and a boardwalk in the water. A significant leap was made after the renovation of the Scheepvaartmuseum and the opening of the Marineterrein from 2013 onward. The temporary occupation of the buildings with various start-up innovative companies and educational institutions transformed the traditionally inaccessible area into a vibrant and diverse urban space. The swimming facilities at the Marineterrein's dock proved to be a stroke of genius.

The Shell site at the Buiksloterweg ferry landing had long been a blind spot. The construction of Eye (2012) and the creation of the walking promenade along the water, with THT, the revamped Shell canteen, brought new energy and public space, much like what had been previously mentioned under the 'Water City' concept. The opening of the renovated

3

2

1 OBA in 2014
2 City Archive De Bazel, 2009
3 Marineterrein, 2023
4 Swimming at the Marineterrein, 2023

A'DAM Tower in 2016 turned the area into a popular tourist attraction, effectively becoming part of the city center.

Through these additions, the Amsterdam city center evolved into a 'supercluster': an exceptional concentration of very specific metropolitan functions within a relatively small area – only 3 kilometers in diameter, easily walkable, and excellent for cycling. This development has progressed much faster and has turned out to be more comprehensive than many had expected.[14]

New Focuses

The COVID-19 pandemic had an unprecedented impact on the functioning of the city center. The number of visitors dropped dramatically, and the streets became eerily quiet. It is remarkable to see how, just a few years later, despite wars and a severe recession, the number of daily visitors in 2023 surpassed the 2019 record, reaching 25.4 million.

The policy aimed at making the city

4

center more attractive and less car-dependent was continued after the pandemic. Leidseplein was redesigned once again, serving as an exemplary model, and this was linked to the creation of an underground bicycle garage and the relocation of the taxi stand. The Open Havenfront and the IJ side of Central Station also received their final, new design, complete with bicycle garages and space for 3,000 OV-bikes (public transport bikes).

In 2024, a speed limit of 30 km/h was introduced throughout the city on non-through roads, resulting in a much more pleasant and peaceful street environment.

Additionally, many redevelopment projects now place greater emphasis on green spaces, trees, and flowering plants. For instance, the Nieuwezijds Voorburgwal gained a park-like character near the former stamp market. When a new Puccini handbook for the design of public spaces was established, it was complemented by the first-ever 'Handbook for Green Spaces'.

A much-delayed but deeply moving addition was the Holocaust Names Monument (2021), designed by Daniel Libeskind. The folded brick walls with names create unexpectedly intimate spaces along the Weesperstraat. At the monument, one lane of the Weesperstraat was narrowed, and this should ideally be done along the entire street.

1 Bicycle garage with 7,000 spaces under Open Havenfront, design wUrck, 2018

2 Holocaust Name Monument Weesperstraat

1

2

PUBLIC SPACE

The marshy ground of the city is not an ideal foundation for public space. The ground sinks and settles quickly, and trees don't grow easily. When streets are opened up, you can clearly see how many layers of sand, gravel, and stones have been used to raise and reinforce the ground. Asphalt is pleasant to drive on but quite inconvenient when it comes to renewing pipelines. Traditionally, small paving materials were used in the city. Concrete stones and tiles measuring 30 × 30 centimeters were the modernist versions, and the city is full of them.

Over the past fifty years, the policy for public space has changed dramatically.

In the 1970s and 1980s, the focus was primarily on making public spaces safer for pedestrians and cyclists. The Traffic Circulation Plan (1978) and the Bicycle Policy Handbook (1981) shaped this vision.

The new Standard Canal Profile (1997) set the tone for an integrated approach, with an important role for design. The Public Space Design Handbook (2009) for the city center built upon this. Ultimately, with the help of the so-called Puccini method, the policy for designing all public spaces in the city was developed in the Red and Green Handbook (2021).

In the thick handbooks, it is outlined which materials should be used in which locations, what street furniture, drains, and lighting fixtures are to be employed, and how transitions, corners, and connections should be detailed.

Sustainability and safety play an important role. This led to the creation of floor maps that document the quality of public space in different areas of the city, including principles for material usage, design, and details for roads, sidewalks, parking, bike paths, and curbs.

A distinction is made between historical cores (including the dike areas and old village centers), the 19th-century belt and garden villages, the '20s-'40s belt, the post-war city, the southern IJ shore, and finally, the Port Area.

The Green Handbook contains the basic principles for planting and greening up the city. This includes assortments of trees, plants, and shrubs, as well as principles for the distance between trees and quay walls or pipelines, for the use of root barriers, tree crowns and mirrors, and for the design of planting beds. As part of the Rainproof policy, so-called wadi's have been implemented in several locations: long, open planting beds where rainwater is slowly drained.

→ **Next page:**
Balcony on the IJ

CANAL STRUCTURE

Key points of the manual

- Use of sustainable materials
- Increase safety and livability
- Minimize application of anti-parking poles

USED MATERIALS

Cobblestone paving
Application
Inner city

Natural stone curb
Application
Inner city

Natural stone deck slabs
Application
Inner city (canals)

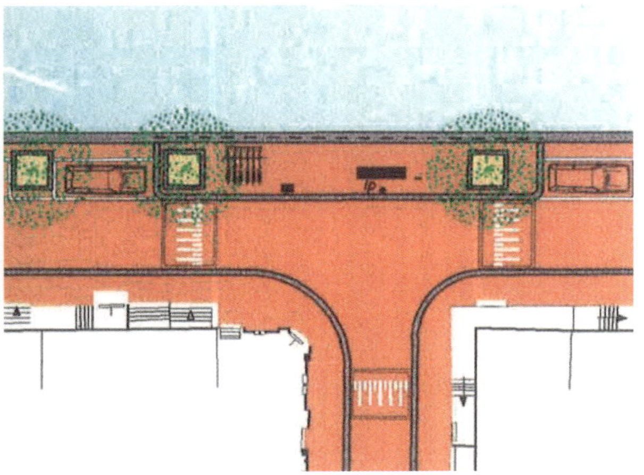

Canal-street connection

Canal profile with parallel parking

Prinsengracht with natural stone curb

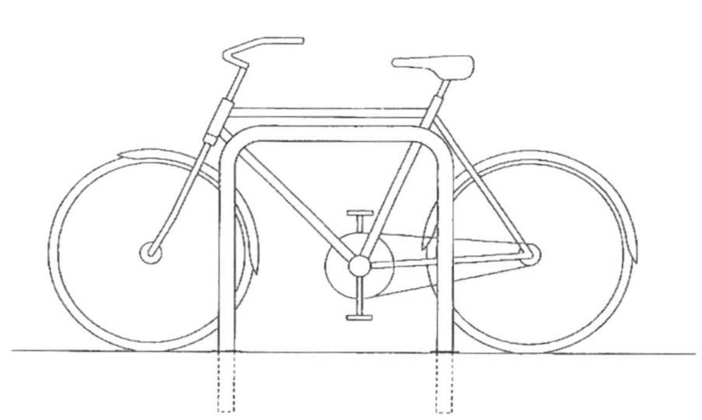

Typical Amsterdam bike rack

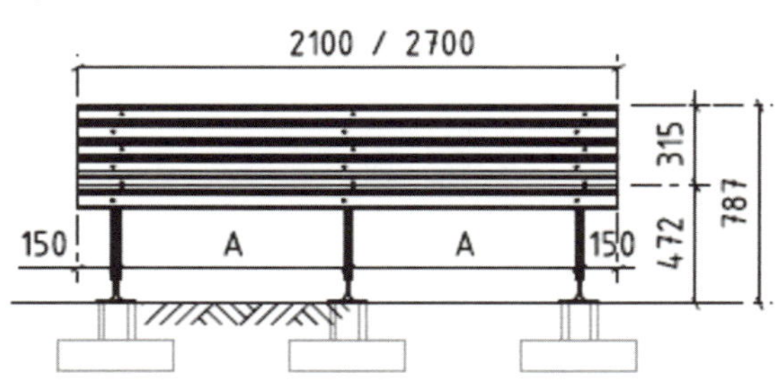

Canapé bench

Pole 1883 with Ritter fixture (left) and with Crown fixture (right)

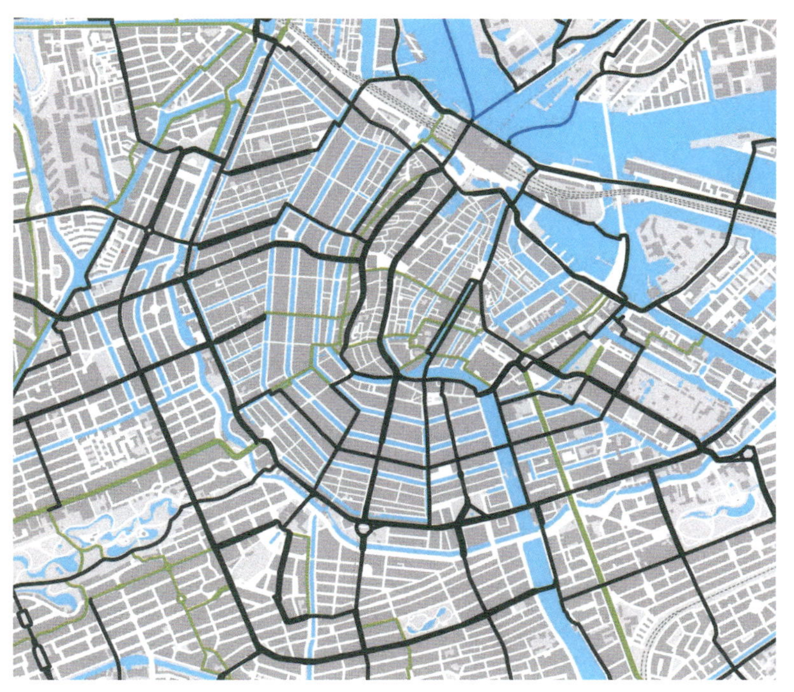

BICYCLE NETWORK

Plus' bicycle network

Main bicycle network

Ferries

USED MATERIALS

30 x 30 cm Concrete tile
Application
city center

Concrete curb
Application
city center

Asphalt
Application
city center

Spui 1980

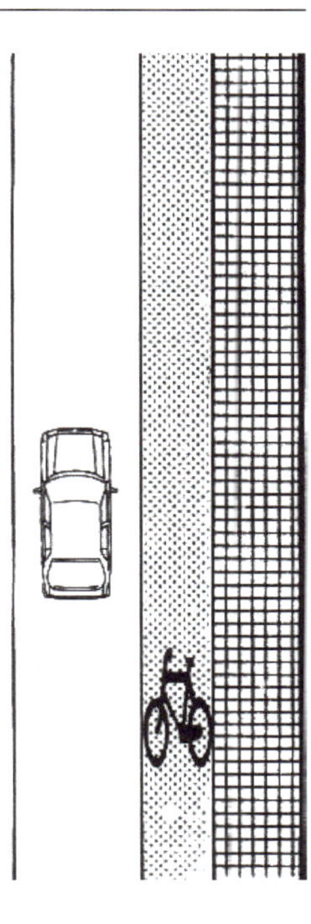

Bicycle lane

Pole 1924 with fixture 1924 (left)
Standard low pole with conical fixture (right)

Nieuwmarkt bench

Prinsengracht with 'Amsterdammertjes' (cast iron anti-parking poles)

PANCAKES

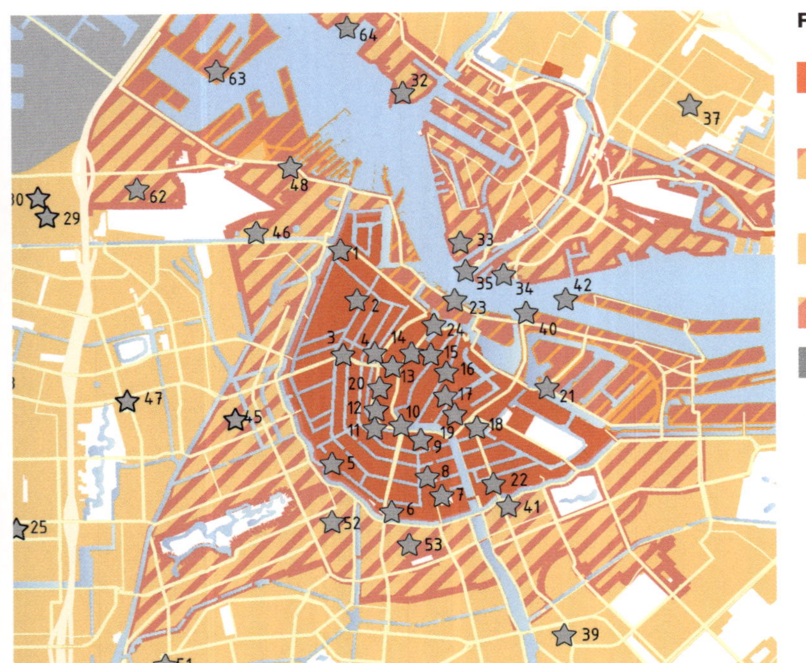

FLOOR PLAN

- City center and historic villages
- 19th-century belt, garden villages, and northern IJ bank
- Belt '20s-'40s and post-war city
- Southern IJ bank
- Port area
- Special spot with number

USED MATERIALS

Cobblestone paving
Size
20 x 7 x 8 cm, running bond
Application
pedestrian areas and sidewalks

Natural stone curb
Application
city center and historic villages

Red asphalt
Application
separated bike lanes and bike streets

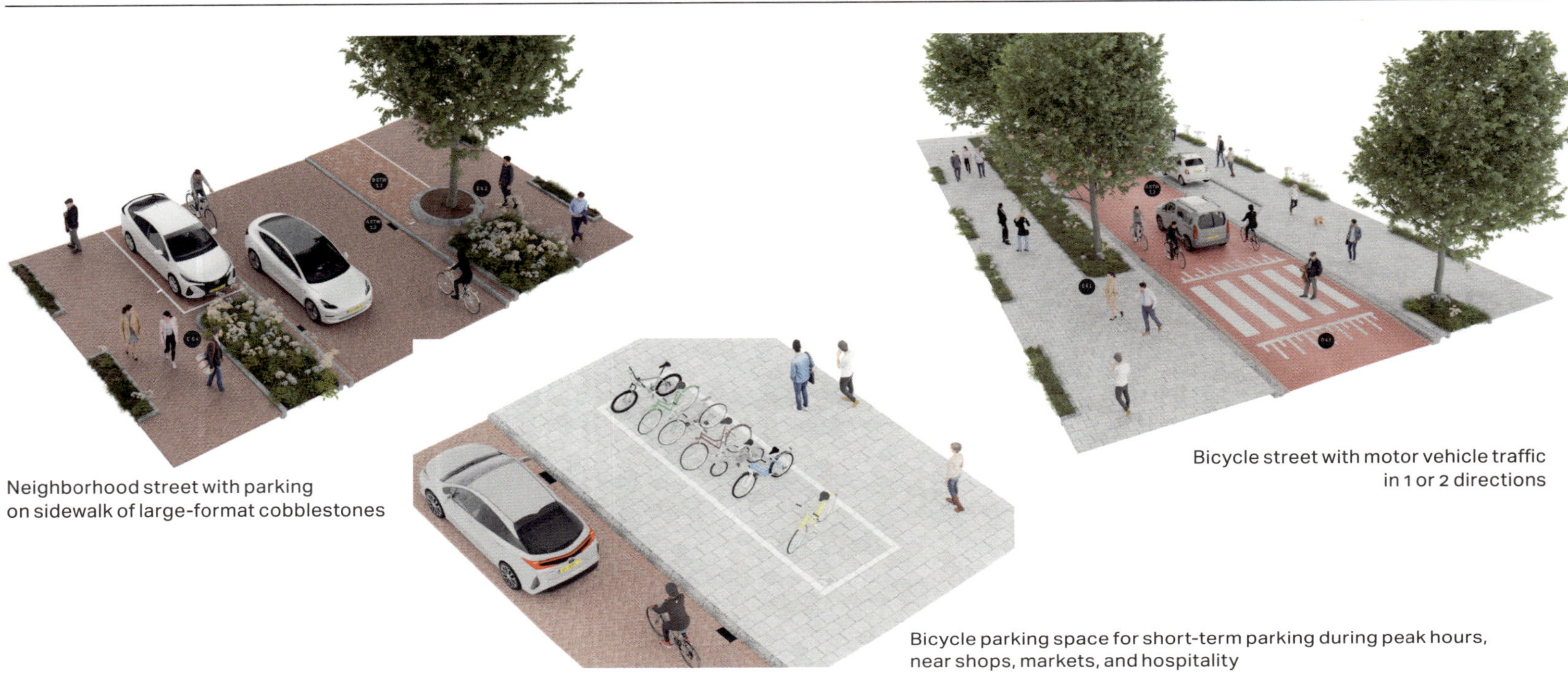

Neighborhood street with parking on sidewalk of large-format cobblestones

Bicycle street with motor vehicle traffic in 1 or 2 directions

Bicycle parking space for short-term parking during peak hours, near shops, markets, and hospitality

Standard trash bin, 1,000 liters with compression mechanism

Wadi, Prinses Irenestraat

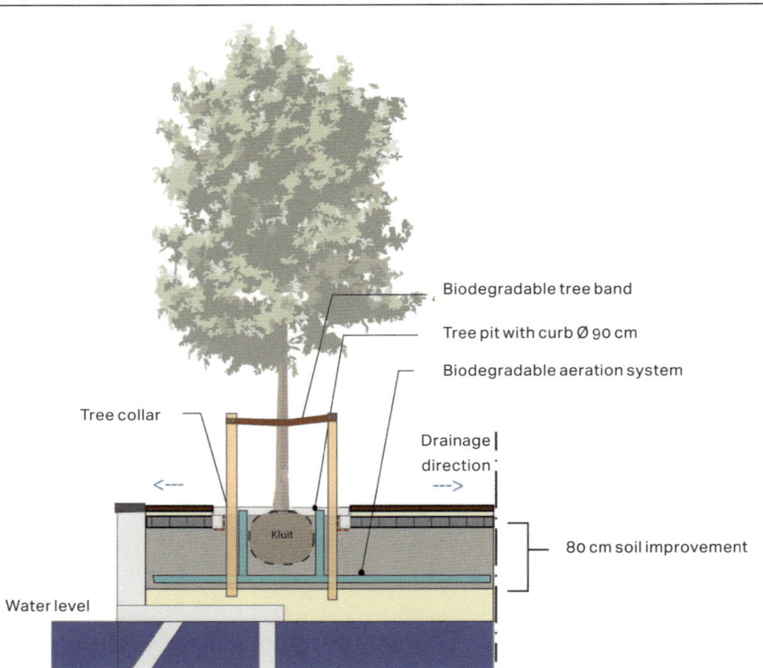

Tree bed, construction details planting bed for trees along canal

MANUAL PUBLIC SPACE DESIGN 2009

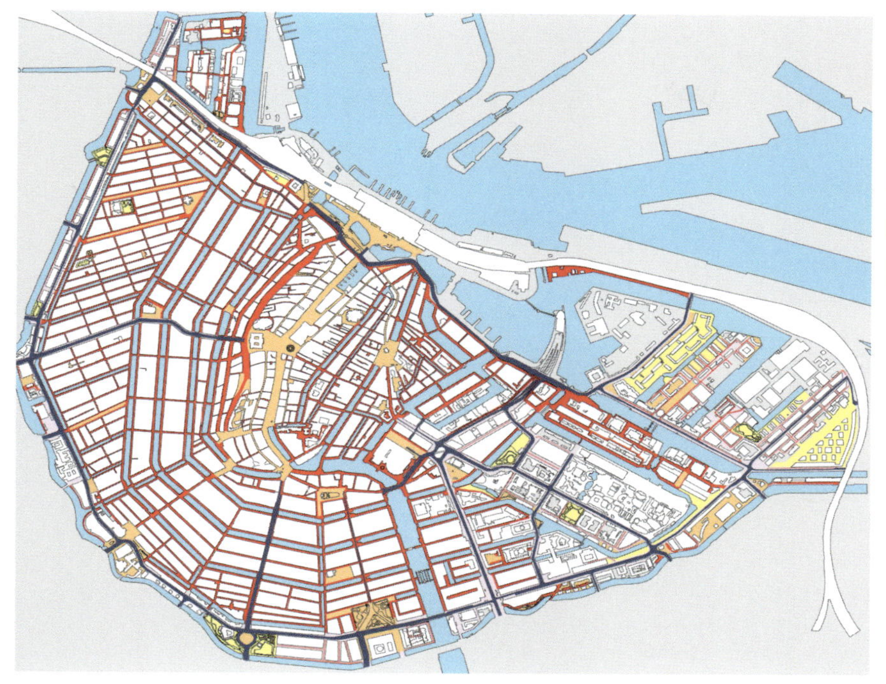

FLOOR PLAN

- Cobblestone paving
- Tile paving (sidewalks)
- Special materials
- Special green space
- Asphalt (roadway and/or tram track)

USED MATERIALS

Cobblestone paving
Size
20 x 7 x 8 cm, running bond
Application
pedestrian areas and sidewalks

Cobblestone paving
Kite size
20 x 10 x 8 cm, herringbone pattern
Application
roads

Granite cobblestones
Used in,
among others, Dam Square, Leidseplein, Nieuwmarkt, Rokin

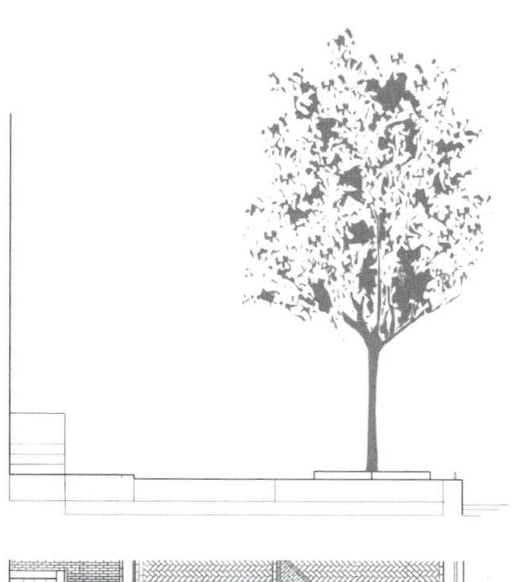

Profile of wide canal

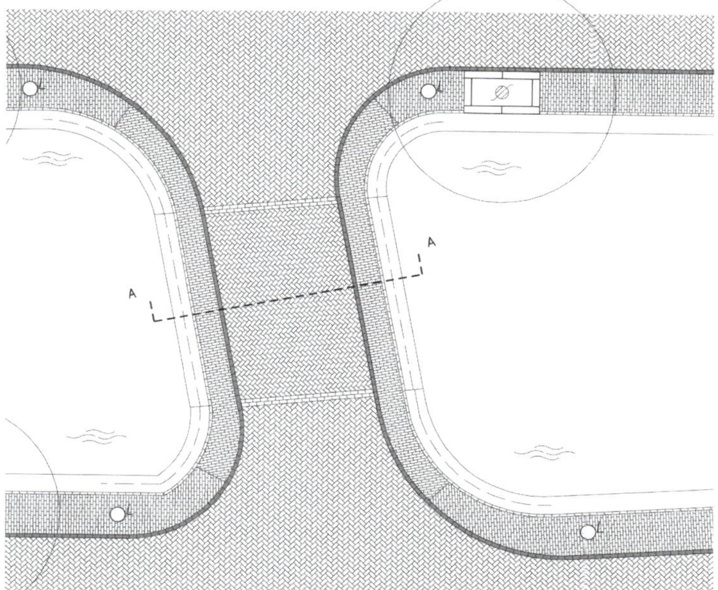

Standard intersection of narrow canal with bridge

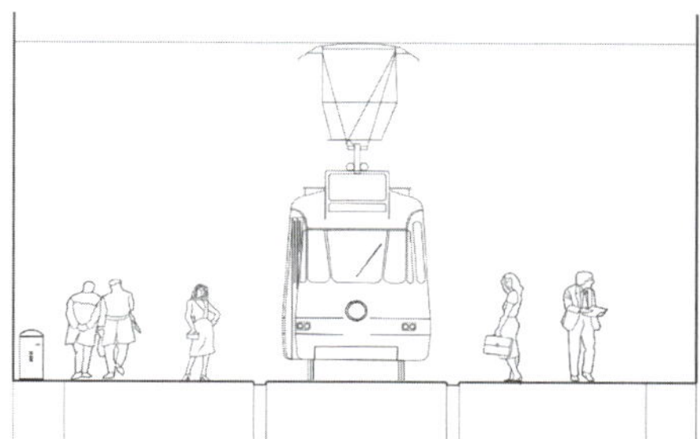

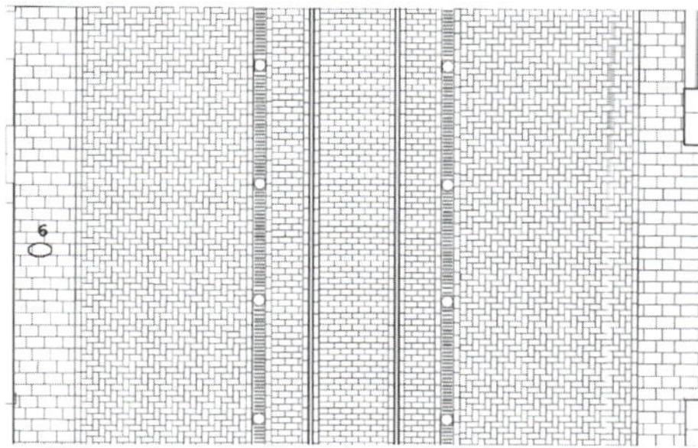

Street profile within city center

Damrak, before redevelopment

Bicycle rack, Amsterdam

'Red Carpet', Damrak

Princess Irene Bridge, Beatrixpark

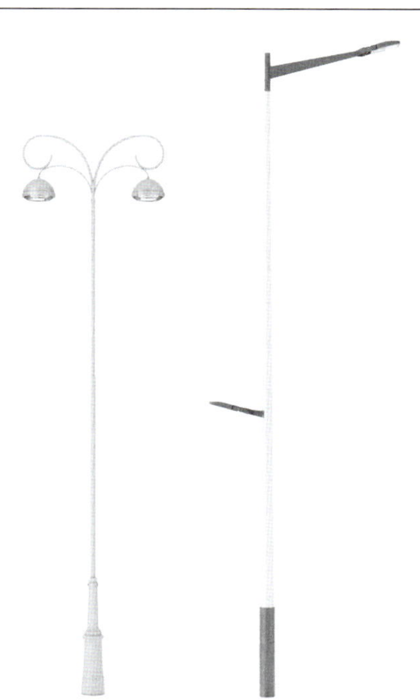

Apollo pole (left) and NPK pole (right)

5A MUSEUMPLEIN

Until 1997, the 'shortest highway in the Netherlands' ran across the Museumplein, as a precursor to a projected city entrance from the A4, Henk Sneevlietweg, and De Lairessestraat into the city center. This fits into the idea of the 'square of plans' or the 'square of missed opportunities.' It was a great relief when, after the redesign, the Museumplein was transformed into a large, green, and car-free field.

The design for the redesign was created by the Danish landscape architect Sven-Ingvar Andersson, commissioned by the Zuid district. Should it be a square or a park? Based on the model of the 'campo' in Pisa and 'greens' in many English cities, a neutral open space was chosen, where the large cultural buildings are subtly situated. Only the pond near the Rijksmuseum refers to the monumental axis of the building. The relativization of monumentality is most explicit in the raised *ezelsoor*, or 'dog ear', at the Stedelijk Museum, which accommodates the entrance to a parking garage and an underground supermarket.

In 2009, major maintenance was carried out; several elements of Andersson's design had worn out. Equally important was that both the Van Gogh Museum and the Stedelijk Museum moved their entrances to the square. The western side of the Museumplein became an informal entrance area.

An additional issue was the bicycle traffic through the passage of the Rijksmuseum. The winners of the competition for the museum's renovation, the Spanish architects Antonio Cruz and Antonio Ortiz, projected the new entrance in the middle of the passage. This met with much opposition. Cycling through the passage is considered by many an authentic Amsterdam experience. After a lot of debate all the way up to the State Secretary for Culture, a compromise was worked out, allowing the passage to remain both an entrance and a bicycle street.

1 Museumplein in 1982
2 Pond near Rijksmuseum, 2023
3 Aerial photo, 1980
4 Aerial photo, 2023
5 Historical development of Museumplein
6 Final design for the redesign of Museumplein, Sven-Ingvar Andersson, 1995
7 Museumplein viewed towards the Concertgebouw, 2013
8 Museumplein viewed towards Rijksmuseum, 2021

1

2

3

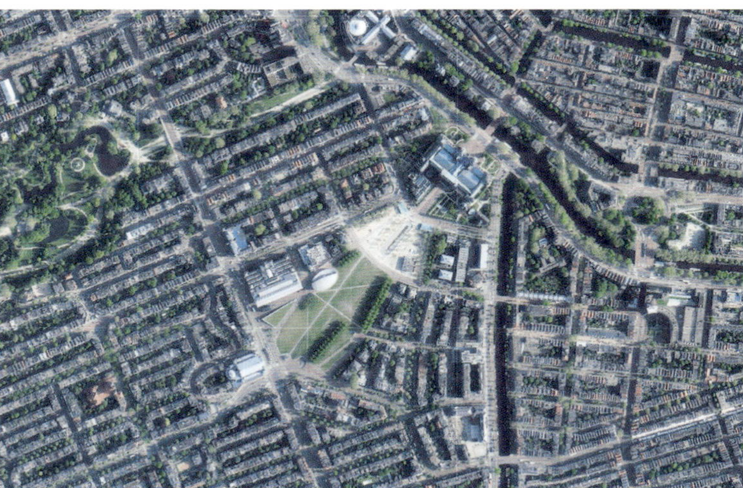

4

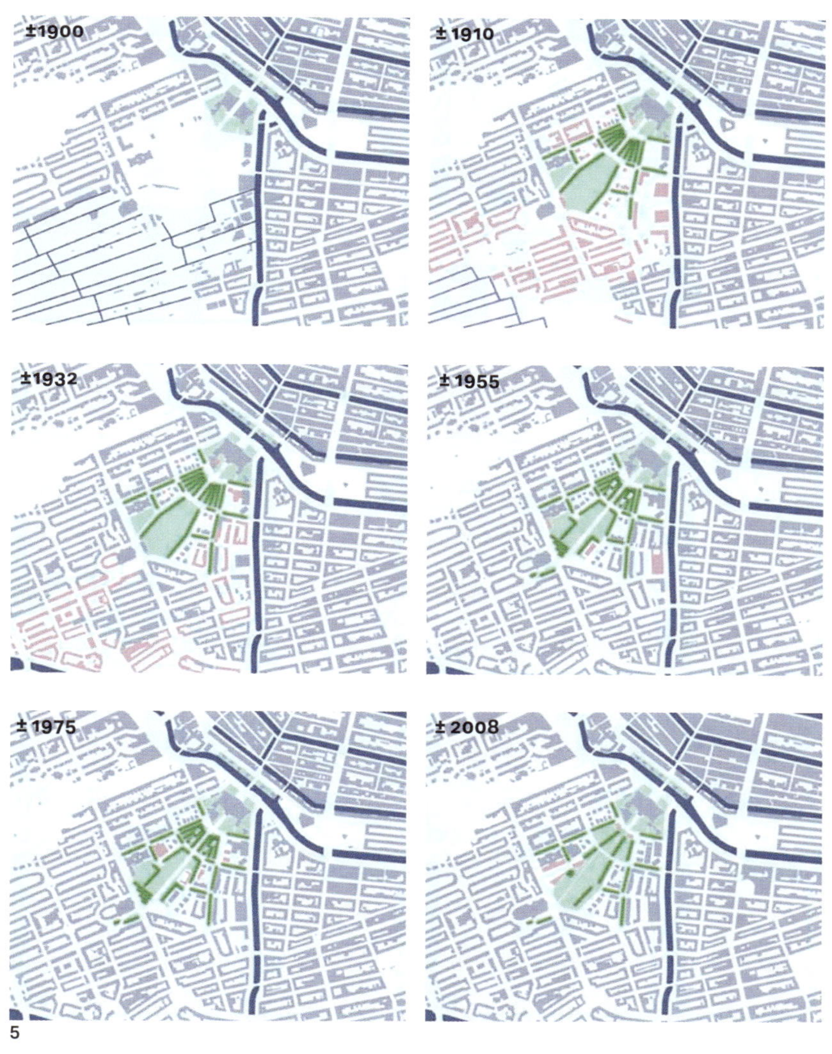

5

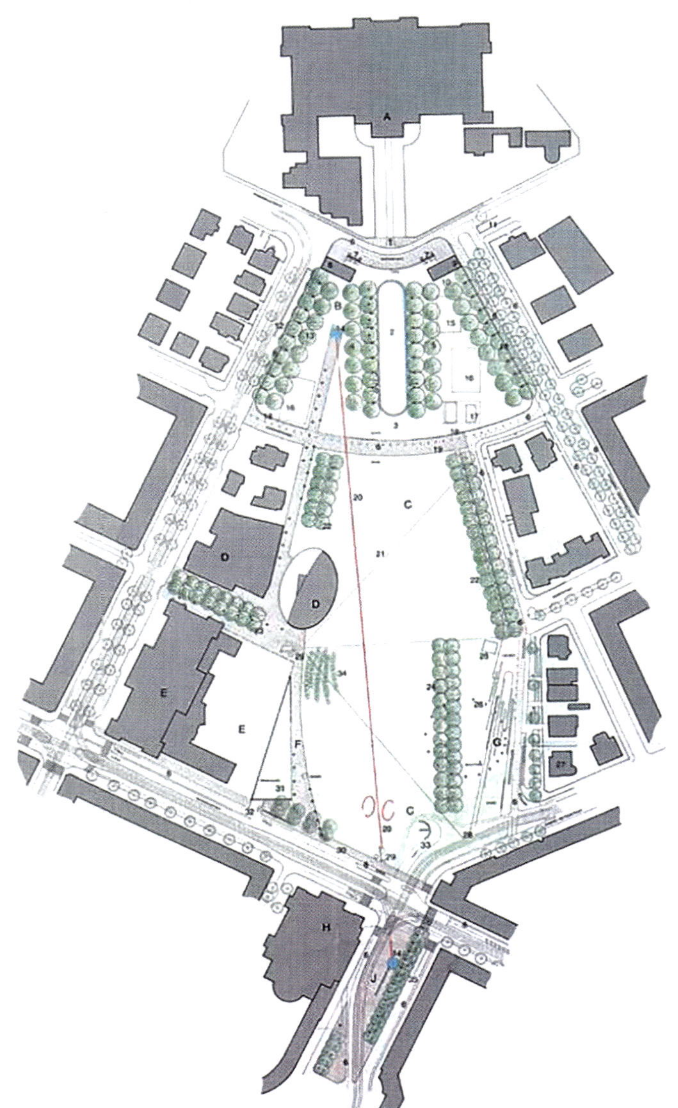

6

7

8

5B THE DAM

For many years, the physical and symbolic center of Amsterdam was a square dominated by cars. Since 1925, there had been a small park on the eastern side. In 1947, this was replaced by the war memorial, designed by J.J.P. Oud. According to Simon Sprietsma, designer at DRO, the Dam appeared fragmented: 'It was a patchwork of cobblestones, hexagonal concrete tiles, bricks, tram tracks, and red and black bits of asphalt. Traffic drove in circles around the palace and the National Monument, creating two huge traffic islands. It was never designed as a cohesive whole.'[15]

In 2001, the Dam underwent a complete makeover, funded by the proceeds from the sale of the Municipal Energy Company. The redesign fit the ambitions of Alderman Guusje ter Horst, who tackled the public space in the city center under the motto 'beautiful, clean, and empty.'

This motto was also reflected in the design for the Dam by Simon Sprietsma. The goal of the redesign was to make the square more organized, attractive, and, most importantly, quieter. Unnecessary elements, such as tram shelters and traffic signs, were removed. This allowed for the creation of a square in the classical sense of the word. The car was given less space. All the asphalt was replaced with a carpet of Portuguese cobblestones from facade to facade. The square was also given a slight convex shape. Overall, the new design made the space feel much more open. The limited street furniture was specially designed, such as the light poles made of polished steel. The reactions to the redesign were generally positive, although there was and still is significant complaint about the bumpy cobblestones.

1 Dam square in 2009
2 New light poles on Dam square, design by Simon Sprietsma (visualizations: Cees van Giessen)
3 Aerial photo before 1956
4 Aerial photo, 2023
5 Repairing the cobblestones on the Dam
6 The Dam in 1996
7-8 Impressions redesign Dam square, design by Simon Sprietsma (visualizations: Cees van Giessen)

1

2

3

4

5

6

7

8

5C NORTH/SOUTH LINE

In 1968, Bureau Stadsspoor released its final report on the future of public transportation in Amsterdam. To keep the increasingly congested city center accessible and to connect new expansions, the tram network was no longer sufficient. The proposal was to build a metro network, a 'city rail,' starting with the East Line. The Ring Line and the North/South Line were also already on the map in the report. The proposal was adopted with a convincing majority. Construction of the East Line began in 1970, but so did protests against the metro project. These culminated in the Nieuwmarkt riots of 1975 and the decision to postpone the construction of other metro lines.

However, in 1992, a decision was made to build a Ring Line, initially referred to as the 'ring fast-tram.' The Ring Line opened in 1997. During its preparation, a feasibility study was conducted for the construction of a North/South Line. In 1996, a positive council decision was made, and in 1997, a referendum followed.

Construction of the North/South Line began in 2003. This was technically challenging. The tunnel would be drilled through the soft Amsterdam peat soil. Furthermore, the tunnel tube needed to

1

2

3

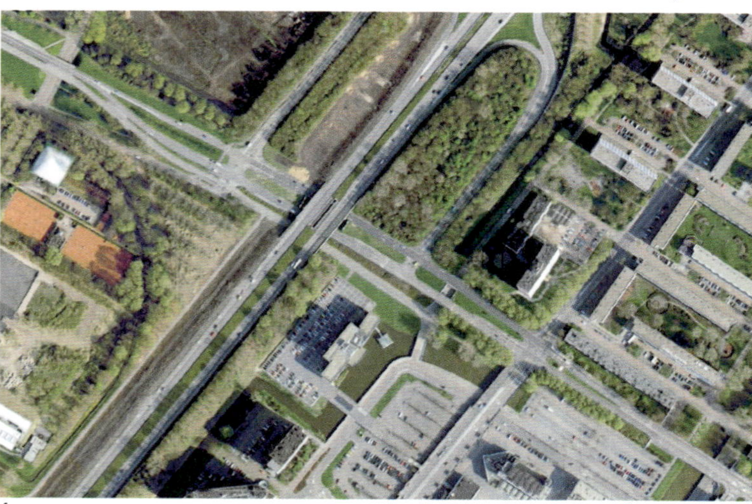

4

5

be lowered beneath the Central Station. Construction was initially expected to be completed by 2008, but due to anticipated budget overruns, emergencies, advice, and discussions in the city council, it ultimately took until 2018 for the first metro to run.

The seven new stations on the line were designed by Benthem Crouwel architects and are as simple as they are spectacular. Each station also features its own artwork. For example, the Rokin Station displays an impressive exhibition of all the finds from the underground Amsterdam mud. Seven years after opening, the line is now indispensable. A report from the Amsterdam Institute for Advanced Metropolitan Solutions (AMS) states that the line's contribution to the city's accessibility is net positive.[16]

1 North/Southline track and stations
2 Construction of Rokin Metro Station, 2006
3 Archaeological finds displayed in Rokin Metro Station
4 Aerial photo, 2005 (surroundings of Noord Station)
5 Aerial photo, 2023 (surroundings of Noord Station)
6 Entrance to De Pijp Metro Station, designed by Benthem Crouwel Architects
7 Canopy of Noord Metro Station, designed by Benthem Crouwel Architects
8 Vijzelgracht Metro Station, designed by Benthem Crouwel Architects
9 Central Station Metro Station, designed by Benthem Crouwel Architects
10 Cross-section of Rokin Metro Station, designed by Benthem Crouwel Architects

6

7

8

9

10

5D CENTRAL STATION

The construction of Central Station in 1889 closed off the city from the IJ. In the following century, the station was expanded several times, and the situation around the station became increasingly confusing. On the city side, parts of the Open Havenfront were reclaimed for bus stops, the entrance to the East Metro Line, and a widening of the Prins Hendrikkade for car traffic. On the IJ side, car traffic also increased, and the notorious 'tippelzone' (a designated area for prostitution) emerged.

Since the 1980s, extensive studies and designs have focused on a new perspective for the station and its surrounding area. After years of work, the new situation is completed early 2025. Meanwhile, ProRail began a new round of renovations on the station itself in 2021 to handle the continuously growing flow of passengers.

The 2005 Masterplan Station Island brought many aspects together: the location of the North/South Line and its connection to the station on both the city and IJ sides, making the station compatible with the OV-chipkaart (the Dutch public transport card), organizing the transport before and after travel by building a bus station on the IJ side, and creating various passages between the city and IJ sides. On the IJ side of the station, a tunnel was built for motorized traffic, and the bus stops were elevated. The ground level in and around the station is now entirely for pedestrians and cyclists. The new canopy gives the station a strong identity on the IJ side.

In the development of the 2012 Masterplan Station Island, further attention was given to the public space on both the city and IJ sides. On the city side, a 'cut' was made for car traffic in the Prins Hendrikkade, allowing the Open Havenfront to regain its original form. Additionally, the largest bicycle parking facility in Amsterdam, with space for 7,000 bikes, was built under the water of the Open Havenfront. The public space has also been completely redesigned, mainly to create a more pleasant environment. A new bicycle passage under the tracks connects the Martelaarsgracht with Pontplein on the IJ side. On the IJ side, after much discussion, a long, gently curved square was created with an underground bicycle parking facility for 4,000 bikes. There, you can relax on the lazy stairs, enjoy the sun, and watch the water and boats.

1

2

3

1 Construction of IJ-side bus platform, 2009
2 Aerial photo, 2008
3 Aerial photo, 2023
4 Stationsplein city side, 1980
5 Entrance to bicycle parking under Open Havenfront
6 Bicycle parking IJ boulevard, designed by Venhoeven CS
7 Visualization of the Open Havenfront city side

4

5

6

7

5E LEIDSEPLEIN

Leidseplein dates back to the mid-17th century and was originally a place where people could park their wagons and carriages before entering the city on foot. It wasn't until more than a century later that it took on its first cultural functions. In the 20th century, the square continued to serve as a parking lot until, in 1971, the northern part of the square and the adjacent Leidsestraat were closed off to cars and bicycles. In 2010, it was decided to make the square car-free. In 2016, the planning process for its redesign began. Ultimately, the revamped square was opened in 2021. In addition to reinforcing the Leidsebrug and renewing the paving, finding a solution for parking bikes and taxis was the main challenge. The square, once a chaotic traffic space, was transformed back into a pleasant public space.

The key interventions in the design by Ruwan Aluvihare, landscape architect at the municipality, address this need. Beneath the Kleine-Gartmanplantsoen, a bicycle parking facility was created, and the taxi stands were relocated, along with the tram stops, to the Leidsebrug. This freed up much more space for cyclists and pedestrians. Additionally, long benches were installed. The complex intersection is now a shared space, a space where one can cycle or walk without curbs or barriers. This results in a calmer streetscape, but also adds flexibility and improves traffic flow.

The underground bicycle parking facility, designed by Eric Smit, can accommodate 2,000 bikes. The entrance to the facility is designed to blend with the brick decoration of the nearby bridge over the Lijnbaansgracht. The bronze lizards, designed by Hans van Houwelingen in 1994, now have a prominent place on the square.

1

2

3

1 Redesign Leidseplein
2 Aerial photo, 2014
3 Aerial photo, 2023
4 Leidseplein in 1988
5 New location for the iguanas
6 Entrance to bicycle parking, designed by ZJA Architects and Engineers
7 Floor plan of underground bicycle parking, designed by ZJA Architects and Engineers

4

5

6

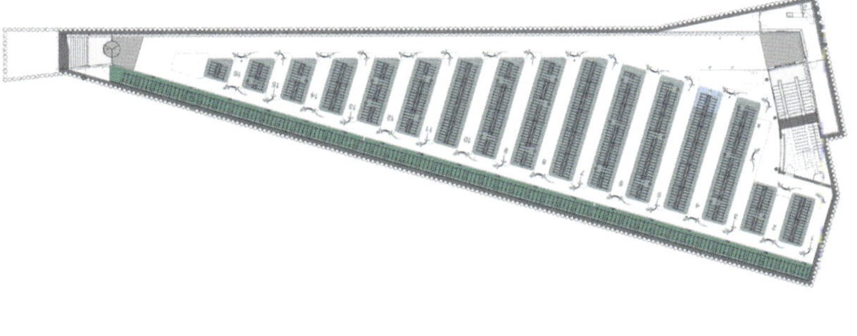
7

5F BINNENGASTHUISTERREIN

The history of the Binnengasthuis dates back to the conversion of a monastery in 1578 into a hospital after the Alteration. In the 19th century, the hospital was modernized. When the Binnengasthuis merged with the AMC in the early 1980s, the University of Amsterdam (UvA) took over most of the buildings.

Since the 1990s, discussions had been ongoing about building a new library on the site. Other possible locations were considered, such as a combination with the new OBA (Openbare Bibliotheek Amsterdam) on the Oosterdokseiland or in the De Bazel Handelsmaatschappij building on the Vijzelstraat. However, it was eventually concluded that a central location in the cluster of Humanities faculties was preferable. In 2000, the Cruz y Ortiz Arquitectos office presented a design for a new building. However, several historic hospital buildings would need to be demolished for this, which sparked significant opposition. As a result, the demolition permit application was withdrawn in 2012. MVSA Architects and André van Stigt created a new design, where a large atrium with a glass roof connects the renovated historic buildings. Construction began in 2019, and the new university library will finally open in 2025.

The new UB is part of a broader area development now called the University Quarter, involving a series of renovations, relocations, and a thorough redesign of the public space. Parts of the area will be made car-free, and wherever possible, trees and plantings will be added.

1 Model of the University Library design, 2000, designed by Cruz y Ortiz
2 Interior courtyard at Oudemanhuispoort
3 Aerial photo, 2008
4 Aerial photo, 2023
5 Design of the courtyard for the new University Library, 2025, designed by MVSA/Buro van Stigt
6 Facade design at the Doelenstraat entrance, designed by MVSA/Buro van Stigt
7 Vision map of the University Quarter, 2021, designed by West 8

1

2

3

4

5

6

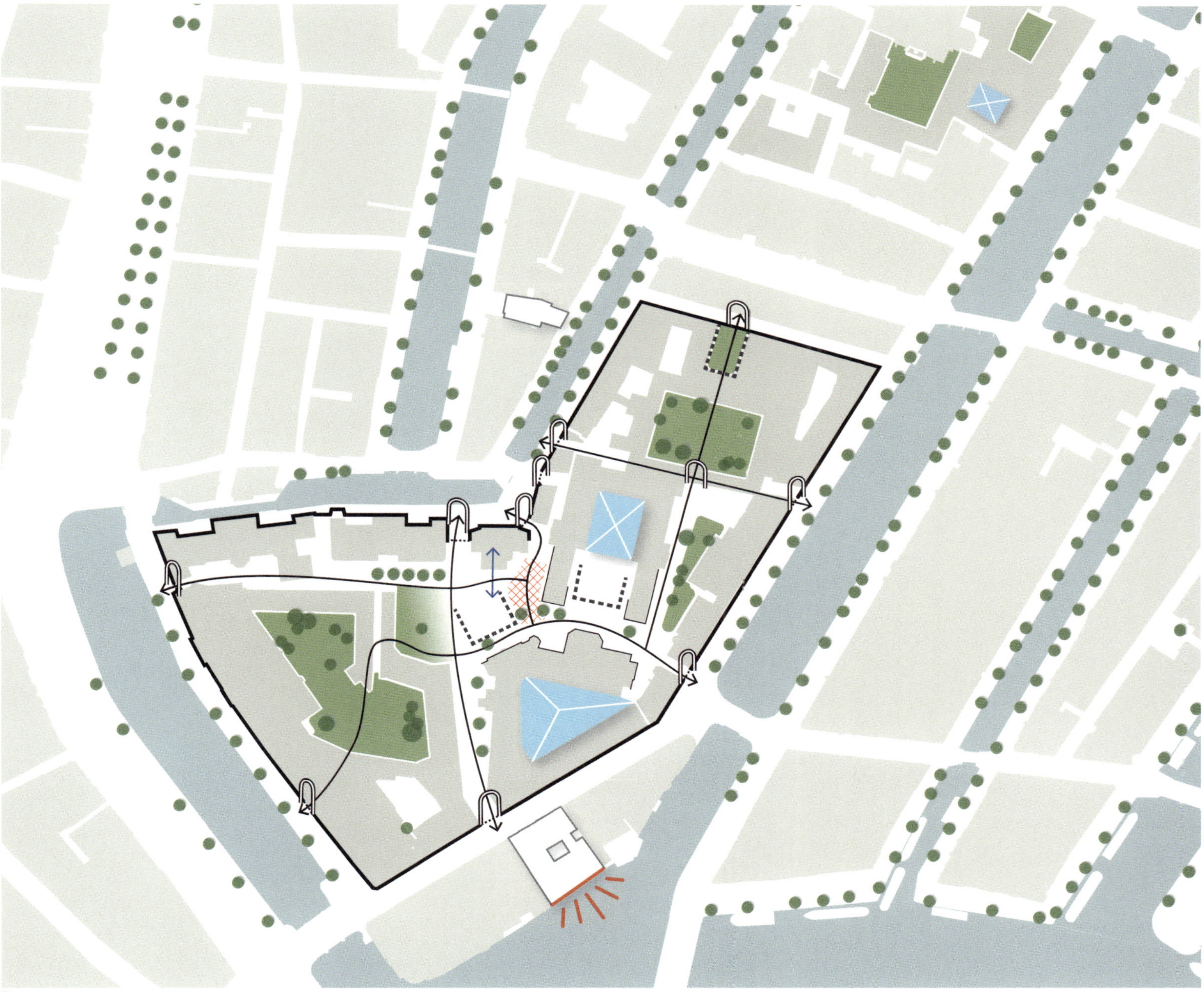

7

PART 3
A BROADER PERSPECTIVE

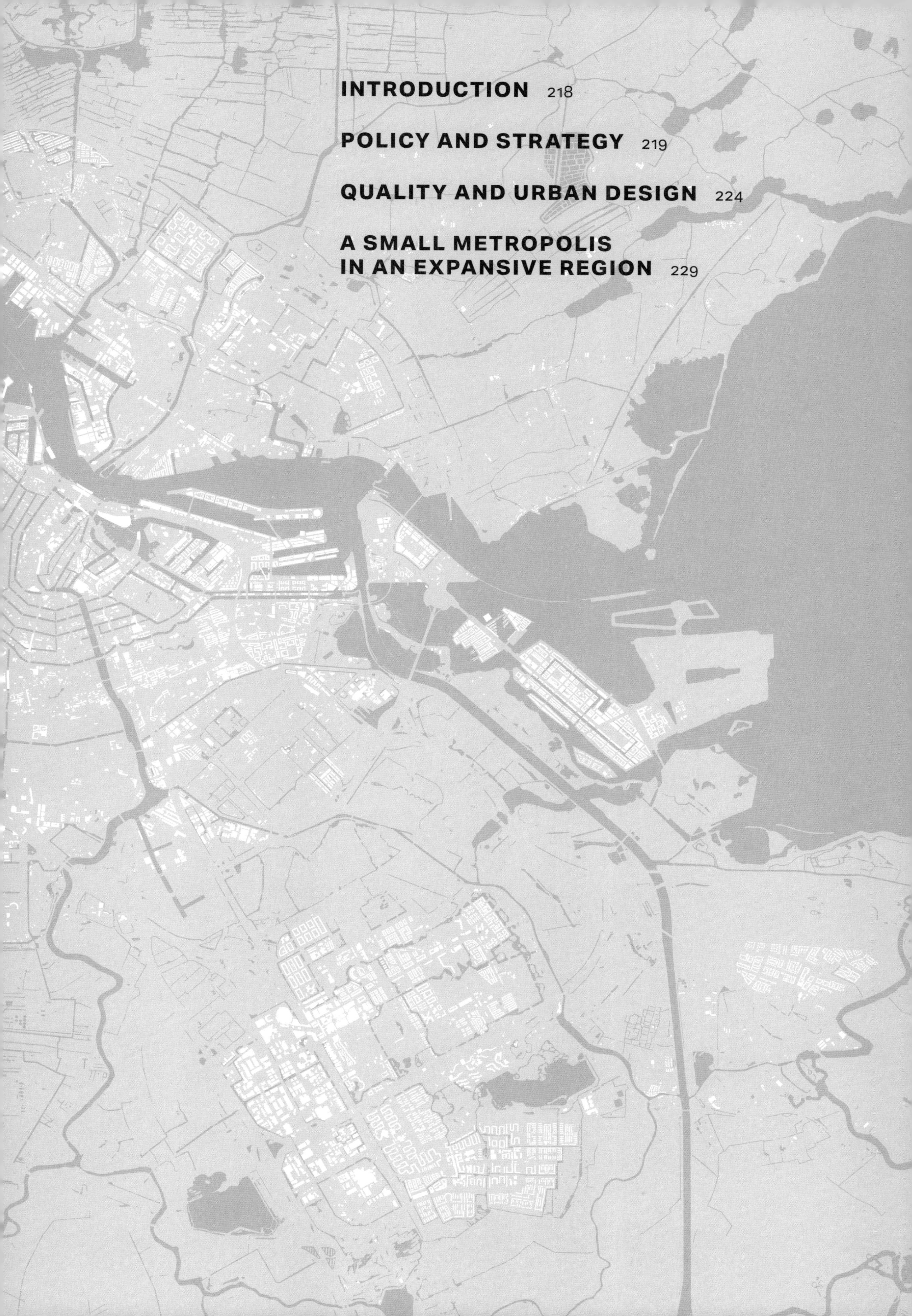

INTRODUCTION

How are the five major movements connected? In this final section, Amsterdam's development over the past fifty years is placed in a broader perspective. First, developments in policy and strategy are examined, drawing on the periodization from Part 1. This is followed by an exploration of urban design developments in relation to experiments in other European cities. For a proper understanding, the regional context is particularly important. Amsterdam has developed into the core city of a rapidly expanding and increasingly interconnected region.

POLICY AND STRATEGY

Amsterdam has built a strong tradition over the past fifty years of using policy instruments to discuss and guide the city's development. Structural plans outlining a vision and the main policy directions – later referred to as the Structural Vision and Environmental Vision – have a planning horizon of twenty to thirty years and have been drafted roughly every ten years. Since 2015, a Development Strategy has also been introduced, focusing on how the vision should be put into practice. This strategy has a ten-year horizon, the time required to complete a project from initiation to realization. In 2024, a new Development Strategy was adopted.

In addition, there are annual work programs, including, for a long time, the Spatial Investment Program. When a new area development project starts somewhere in the city, roads, trams, bridges, and parks must also be constructed – costs that are not covered by land exploitation. These so-called 'off-plan' measures are, of course, crucial in determining the quality of projects.

These policy documents are closely linked to the aldermen who led their development: Michael van der Vlis (*De stad centraal*, 1986), Jeroen Saris (1991), Duco Stadig (*Open Stad*, 1996), Maarten van Poelgeest (*Economically strong and sustainable*, 2011), and Marieke van Doorninck (*A Human Metropolis*, 2021). The names of aldermen Eric van der Burg and Reinier van Dantzig are associated with the Development Strategies of 2016 and 2024.

To reverse the decline of the city, the new municipal executive that took office in 1978 did not require a Structural Plan. Under tight control from City Hall, the movement to revitalize the 19th-century neighborhoods was set in motion, alongside proposals to stop the exodus of the city by developing low-rise areas on the urban fringe. At the same time, the large and powerful Public Works Department was dismantled. In 1980, the Urban Development Section was restructured into the Spatial Planning Department. Its main task was to draft a Structural Plan that could respond to major changes in the port and the financial sector. Eventually, in 1986, the *De stad centraal* Structural Plan was adopted. This plan provided the policy framework for the long recovery phase of the city between 1985 and 2006, which saw the restructuring of the water city and expansion southward. What in 1986 were still relatively vague outlines became more concrete in the Structural Plans of 1991 and 1996, albeit with new points of emphasis.

The *Structural Vision Amsterdam 2040* from 2011 marked a major shift in thinking about the city following the onset of rapid growth in 2007 and the establishment of the Amsterdam Metropolitan Area that same year. The focus turned to the city center and surrounding neighborhoods as a metropolitan interaction hub and to the intensive urbanization of the Ring Zone, the transitional area between the pre-war and post-war city. The economic crisis stalled much of this vision, but from 2014 onward, the housing market picked up again. The *Road Map 2025* from 2016 then prioritized transforming the Ring Zone into a mixed-use urban area with ambitious housing programs. The movement toward low-rise development on the urban fringe was coming to an end; 'renewal' (of Nieuw-West), 'water city,' and 'southward expansion' gained new momentum. Meanwhile, the movement focused on the inner city accelerated rapidly.

The *Environmental Vision Amsterdam 2050, A Human Metropolis*, from 2021 reflects on the city's economic success

➔ Structure Plan Part C – Work, 1978

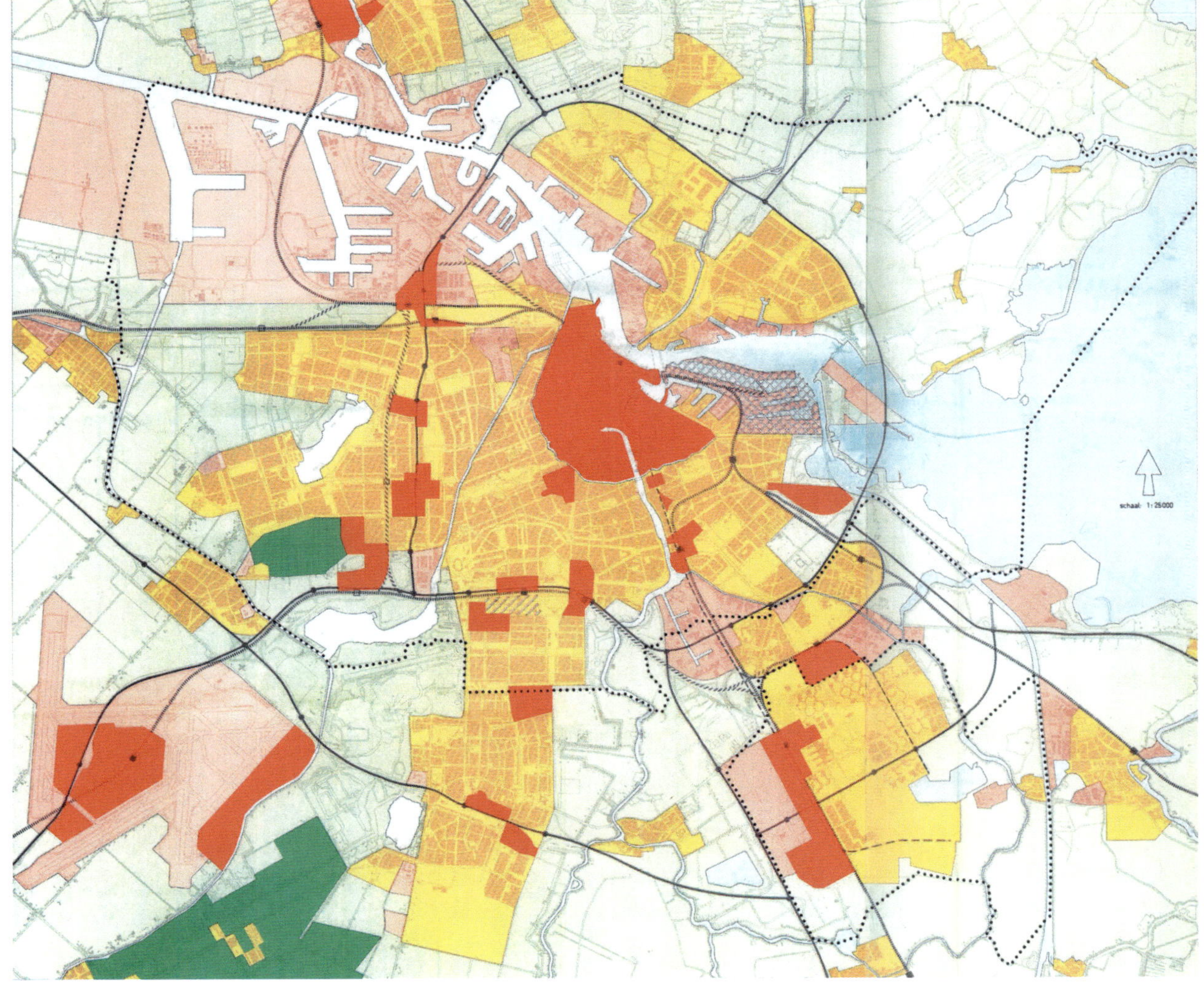

and focuses on decentralization and a polycentric city within a regional perspective. The city center, the Zuidas, and ArenA-Poort had already developed into distinct centers with their own character, while the centers of Noord and Nieuw-West were also emerging. At the same time, there was a stronger emphasis on connections with other hubs in the metropolitan area, such as Zaanstad and Amstelveen, and the broader region. However, recent shocks made the implementation of this new perspective anything but straightforward.

The *Road Map 2035* from 2024, *Building Neighborhoods of the Future*, also emphasized smaller-scale developments to enhance quality and livability.

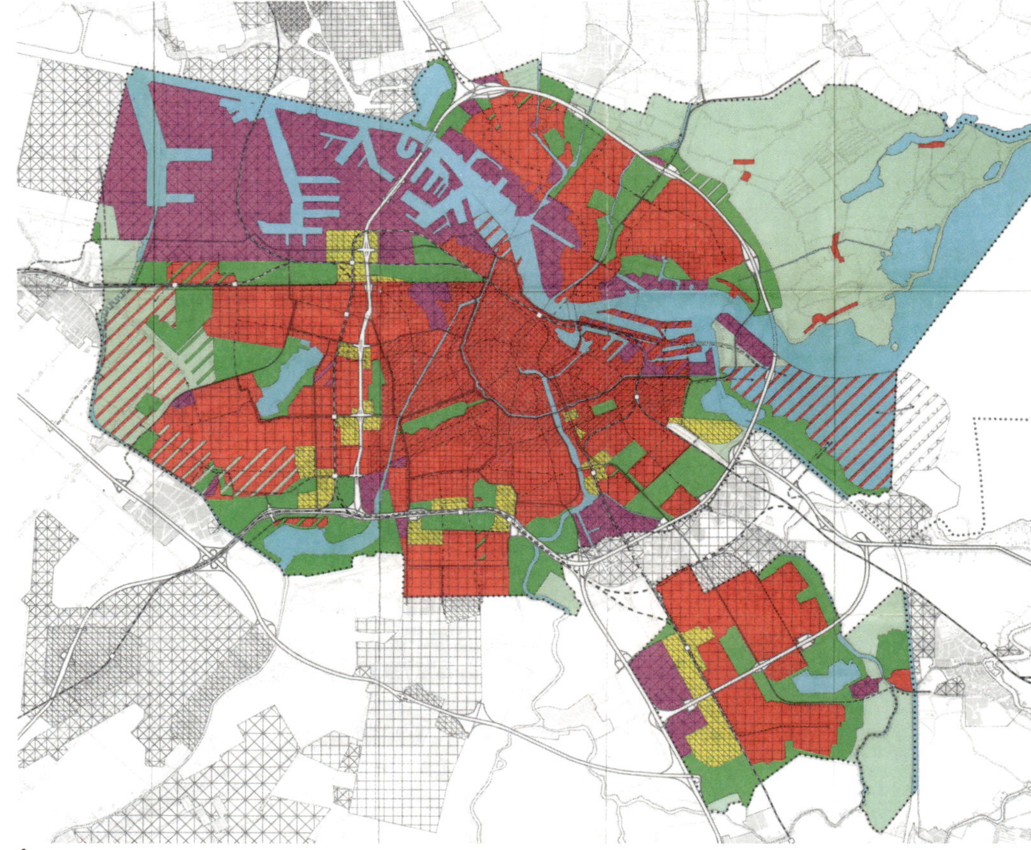

1

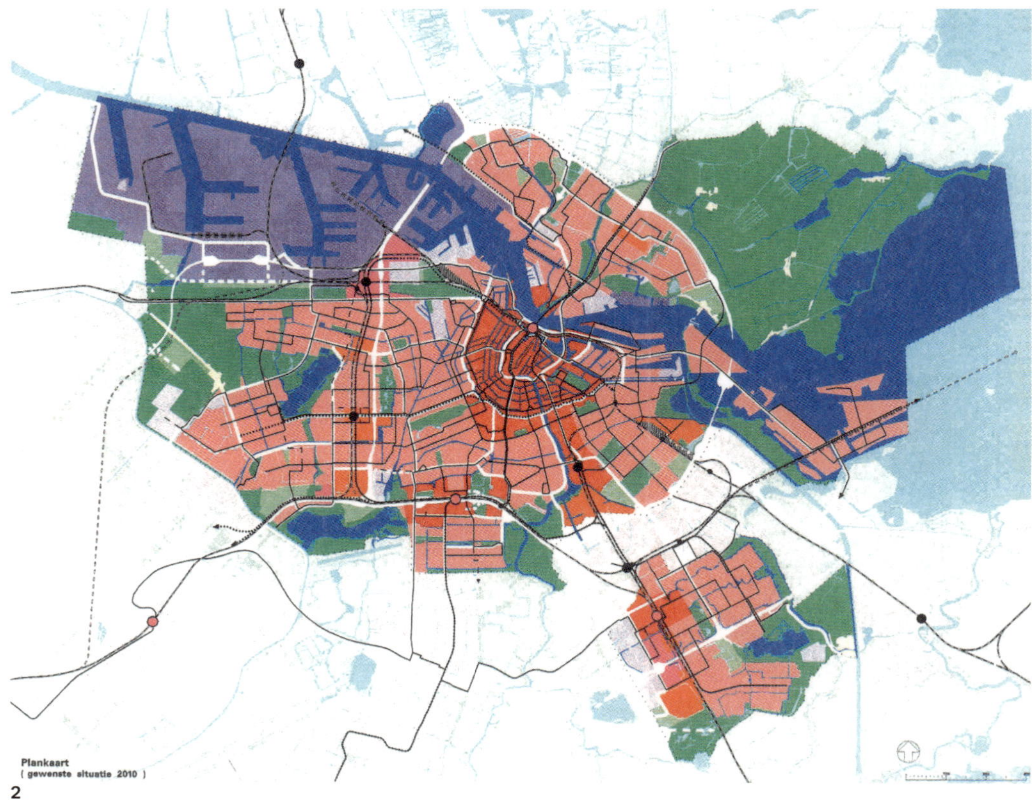

2

Guidance

To guide these movements, a mixed model was initially chosen, assigning different roles to the municipal government, the 'central city', and the newly introduced 'districts'.

After an initial experiment with district administrations in Noord and Osdorp, the district system was officially implemented across all of Amsterdam in 1987, ultimately resulting in no fewer than sixteen districts by 1990. Virtually all municipal powers were autonomized, including the establishment of a District Fund modeled after the Municipal Fund. Elected district councils and administrations were also responsible for spatial development.

By that time, both the 'renewal of the existing city' movement and the 'low-rise on the city's edge' movement were already well underway. Still, there were notable differences in how these strategies were applied – for instance, in the renewal of various garden cities in Nieuw-West, the repurposing of old gas factories, and the parceling strategies of different low-rise neighborhoods. In some cases, the central city and districts formed coalition projects where their interests aligned, such as in the renewal of the Bijlmer, the Bos en Lommerplein, and the Lelylaan.

Responsibility for projects under the 'water city' and 'southward expansion' movements, however, remained entirely with the central city. These areas were undergoing large-scale transformations, which the municipal government accelerated and steered toward its intended goals. In 'water city', this happened gradually, project by project, under strong municipal direction. In 'southward expansion', change came in shocks, with highly diverse collaborations between market players and the UvA emerging around the Omval, Zuidas, Science Park, and AMC.

During the period of rapid growth and following district mergers in 2010, only seven districts remained, now including a dedicated Binnenstad district. From that moment on, the central city and districts worked together in drafting policies and overseeing project organizations in implementation. The 'supercluster city center' movement also became a shared responsibility. While hotel development was facilitated, the municipality and district administrations took the initiative in shaping new urban amenities and public spaces in the city center, making significant investments themselves.

One of the first 'shocks' to follow was the abolition of the districts. Opposed to what it saw as 'excessive administrative layers', the national government forced Amsterdam in 2018 to dissolve the districts as independent governing bodies, reducing them to a limited advisory role. From that point onward, control largely rested with the municipal executive.

Finally, a unique event was the merger of Weesp into Amsterdam in 2022. However, Weesp did not become a district but was designated as an 'urban area'.

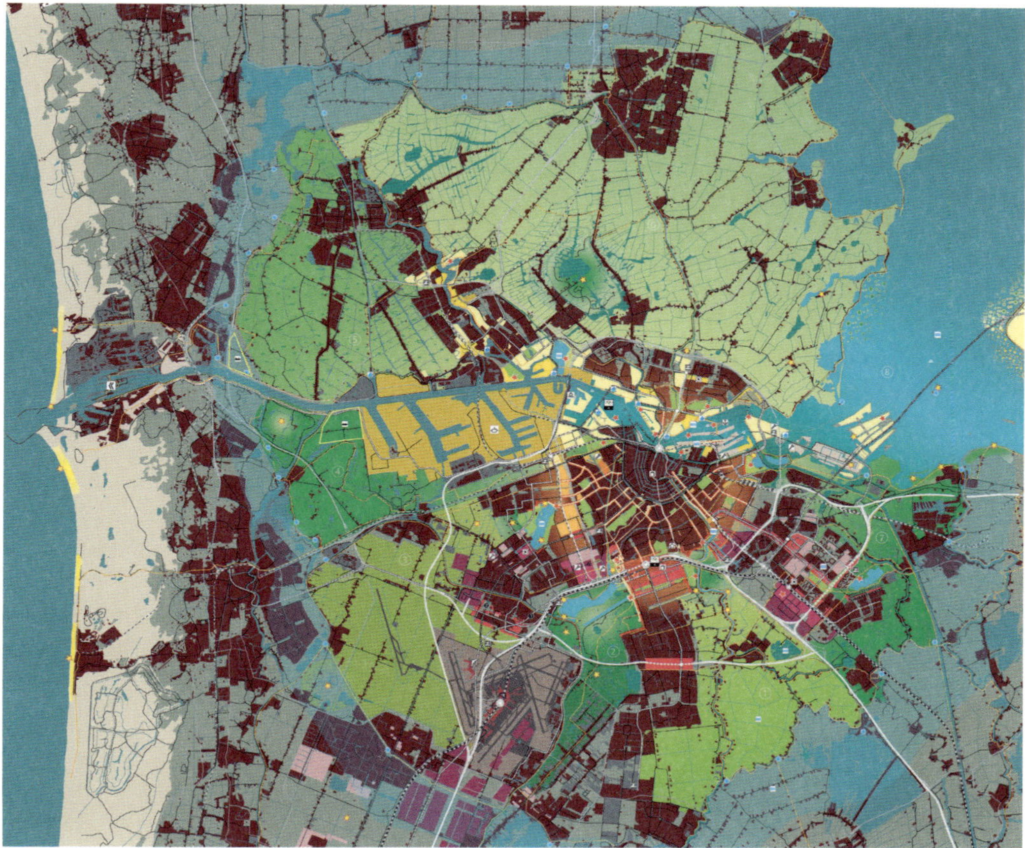

3

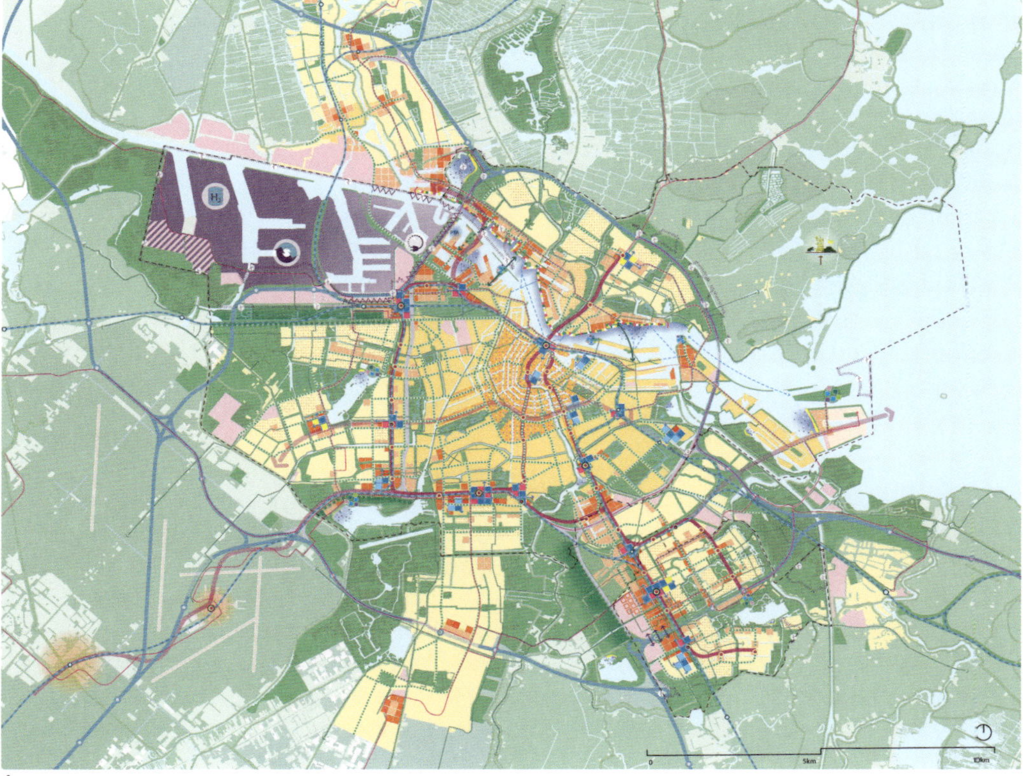

4

1 Structure Plan 'The City Central', 1986
2 Structure Plan 'Open City', 1996
3 Structural Vision 2040 'Economically Strong and Sustainable', 2011
4 Environmental Vision 2050 'A Human Metropolis', 2021

Costs and revenues

It would be interesting to ask financial specialists to estimate the costs of Amsterdam's 'major transformation' over the past fifty years. The total likely amounts to tens of billions – possibly more than a hundred billion euros. Where did this money come from?

Private individuals and businesses invested heavily, but both the national government and the municipality also contributed significantly.

The renewal of the existing city – during both the phase of reversing decline and the phase of recovery – would have been impossible without national government support. This came in the form of subsidies for new construction and the renovation of social housing, as well as subsidies for soil remediation and land acquisition. Land acquisition costs included, for example, the purchase of additional residential development sites, such as the former grounds of the Heineken and Amstel breweries. Heineken used this money to finance the construction of its new brewery in Zoeterwoude. A similar principle later applied to the relocation of businesses from the Eastern to the Western Port Area. National government funding thus served as the financial lubricant for these urban transformations.

This was even more true for the enormous national investments in new rail, road, port, and airport infrastructure in and around the city, which enabled the southward expansion. Schiphol, of course, but also the A10 with its tunnels under the IJ, the A5 and connecting highways, the southern and western branches of the rail network with no fewer than nine new stations, the renovations of Central Station and Amstel Station, the construction of the Hem- and Utrechtboog railway connections, and contributions to the North/South metro line and the Zuidasdok project.

The renovation of national institutions such as the Rijksmuseum and the Maritime Museum, along with funding for the construction or renovation of cultural landmarks like the Stopera, De Nieuwe Kerk, the Theatre School, and the Anne Frank House, further accelerated the transformation of the city center into a supercluster. The national government, in short, made substantial investments in the capital.

And Amsterdam itself? The sale of the municipal cable television network (KTA) and the energy plants of UNA certainly provided a financial boost. But two structural factors have contributed to the city's financial strength over the past fifty years: leasehold conversions and high land revenues.

Like other major cities, Amsterdam operates a leasehold system. Much of the land is municipally owned and leased out in exchange for an annual ground rent (canon), typically set for a fifty-year period. Leasehold conversion involves resetting this rent after fifty years based on the then-current land value. Starting in 1975, all lease agreements originally signed from 1925 onward were gradually renewed. For example, the leaseholds for all homes in Berlage's Plan Zuid were updated. The old ground rent had been based on land values from the 1930s, while the new rate reflected values from the 1980s. These conversions generated substantially higher revenues year after year. The effect was amplified by many leaseholders opting to pay off their ground rent in a lump sum for fifty years.

A second major source of municipal income was high land revenues from new land leases. Over the past fifty years, there were many such leases – covering 200,000 new homes as well as countless new office buildings and hotels. The amount of ground rent varies by land use. For residential properties, a long-standing distinction was made between social housing, which had a standardized, relatively low ground rent, and private-sector housing, where the rent was linked to market value and construction costs. In the early stages of urban renewal, almost exclusively social housing was built – producing little revenue and requiring financial subsidies. However, as the recovery phase began in 1985 and private-sector housing was introduced, municipal revenues increased significantly. Since then, the proportion of housing types has been a key component of coalition agreements formed after municipal elections. These ratios directly impact the city's financial flexibility. For a long time, the balance between social and private-sector housing was set at 60-40, but later years saw shifts to 40-60 or even 30-70, generating considerable revenue.

Amsterdam has a unique method for handling land revenues. First, land income is compared against the costs of acquiring, preparing, and developing the land within each project. Any surplus is deposited into the so-called Equalization Fund, which helps offset deficits in other projects. Early projects in the southward expansion – such as the first new office districts in Sloterdijk and Southeast – were particularly profitable, generating far more revenue than traditional industrial estates. Later, the Zuidas also became a major contributor. The Mayor and Aldermen (B&W) decide how to allocate the fund, based on recommendations from the alderman responsible for Land Affairs. Aldermen who combine this portfolio with Spatial Planning hold significant influence.

Thanks to high land revenues and this unique financial mechanism, many projects were completed that would otherwise have been financially unfeasible – think of the bridge buildings over the A10 at Bos en Lommerplein, the redevelopment of the Westergasfabriek, and more recently, the Houthavens and De Hallen.

In recent years, however, the municipality's financial position has weakened. To ensure housing remains accessible for low- and middle-income groups, a 'middle segment' category was introduced in 2014, and new housing distribution ratios of 30-40-30 or 40-40-20 were adopted. This had a major impact on revenues, making it far more difficult to balance project budgets. Partly for this reason, the city decided in 2017 to reform the leasehold system. Since 2020, it has been possible to buy out the leasehold 'in perpetuity'. While this may provide the city with short-term financial flexibility, it is less favorable for long-term municipal finances, as the recurring conversion benefits will disappear.

The end of gas extraction in Groningen has also weakened the national government's financial position. The new policy approach – 'every region counts' – along with shifting priorities such as defense and the energy transition, makes it less likely that the national government will invest in Amsterdam at the same scale as in the past fifty years. This also explains the difficult negotiations over funding for the Zuidasdok project.

Half a century of urban development

Until shortly before his passing in 2017, Mayor Eberhard van der Laan worked on an exhibition about the challenges Amsterdam faces. The exhibition, *De mooiste stad* (*The Most Beautiful City*), was displayed in 2018 at the Schuttersgalerij of the Amsterdam Museum. The title was based on Van der Laan's statement: 'We have an enormous problem: we live in what is perhaps the most beautiful and pleasant city in the world'. He believed that insights from past solutions could help tackle contemporary challenges in what he called the 'Third Golden Age'.

We might no longer describe previous phases of rapid urban growth as *golden*, given their many downsides. The same may hold true for this era when it is assessed fifty or a hundred years from now. But looking back at the past fifty years, it is undeniable that the city's appearance has radically transformed and improved.

It is also tempting to follow the analogy and compare the city's development steps to those of the 16th and 17th centuries, with the First, Second, Third, and Fourth Expansions, as well as the late 19th and early 20th centuries, with city engineer Jan Kalff's expansion plan and Berlage's three major plans for the Transvaalbuurt in the east, for the south, and for the west.

Will the five outlined movements later achieve a similar status? Or will the defining Structural Plans take precedence instead?

What is certain is that three key turning points can be identified in this half-century of urban development: the 1978 municipal elections, the construction of ABN AMRO's headquarters near Zuid Station between 1996 and 1999, and the 2016 decision to build 50,000 homes in the Ringzone within a decade.

The impact of the 1978 elections has already been widely discussed in this and many other publications. The city's decline was halted by initiating the renewal of the existing urban fabric and offering an alternative to suburban migration: 'low-rise housing on the city's edge'.

The 1986 Structural Plan introduced two new perspectives: the transformation of the waterside city around the IJ and the further expansion of the service economy around the stations of the renewed railway network, particularly to the south. A 1987 diagram captured these new urban development ideas concisely and gave them a name: IJ-as and Zuidas.

But was this enough? In September 1992, during the presentation of his Master Plan for the Southern IJ River bank in a packed Koepelkerk, Rem Koolhaas put it bluntly: without a clear strategy for the spatial development of the city in the new service era, Amsterdam would quickly slip into becoming an 'appendage' of the rapidly growing Schiphol Airport. The airport was booming and preparing for the next round of expansion, with plans for a fifth runway, the construction of new terminals, and the renovation of the underground station with a stop for the planned high-speed trains to Brussels, London, and Paris. Koolhaas' master plan presented an appealing vision for the development of the IJ Axis. The vacant harbor islands on both sides of the Central Station could allow the city center to expand towards the IJ, with a prominent position for the large new banking conglomerates along Westerdokskade and an overbuild of the tracks with a mix of offices and amenities on Oosterdok Island. Koolhaas received an ovation. Not long after, ING, the main financier, pulled the plug on the IJ Axis plans, and it seemed the city was indeed heading for a secondary role.

The decision by the city council in 1996 to agree with ABN AMRO's desire to build its new headquarters at Zuid Station turned everything upside down. The power of this new perspective became visible in the following years. The WTC at Zuidas doubled in size, and a whole series of new towers were built around Zuid Station for increasingly international banks, law firms, and consulting companies. Large companies like AkzoNobel and Arcadis also established their headquarters here.

Amsterdam didn't become an appendage of Schiphol but did turn towards the airport. Meanwhile, the city center developed into an urban, car-free interaction space. Former bank buildings were converted into hotels, new cultural facilities, and co-working spaces. On the islands around Central Station, at Overhoeks, and for now, temporarily at the Marineterrein, a mixed urban program was implemented. The city center thus expanded significantly. The North/South metro line connected everything and also linked Old and New North.

The Structural Vision Amsterdam 2040

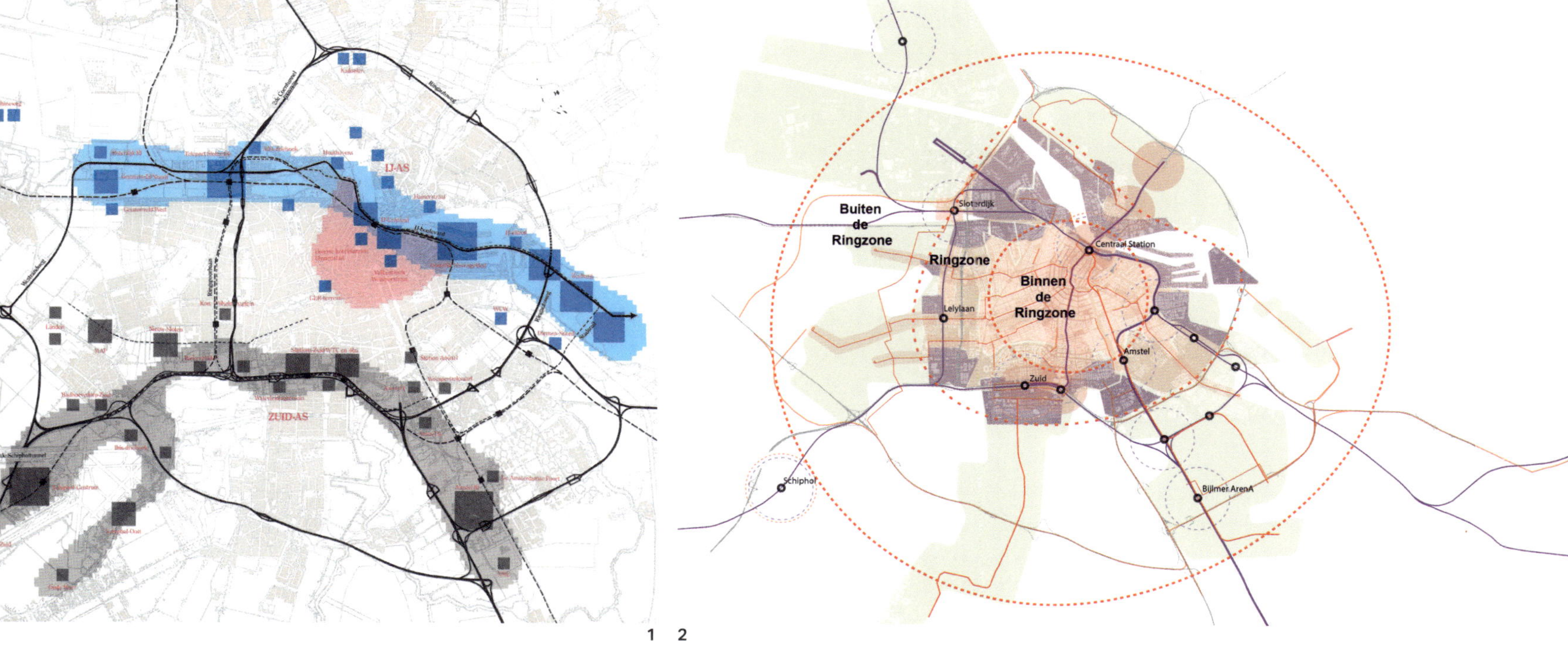

1 2

1 Diagram IJ-as – Zuidas, 1987
2 Diagram Ring Zone, 2013

from 2011 and, following that, the Development Strategy Road Map 2025 mark a new turning point: a much higher construction output. The long-term average hovered around 3,500 homes per year, but that number had significantly dropped during the crisis years of 2007–2014. By aiming for the construction of 5,000 homes per year, 50,000 homes could be added to the stock over a period of ten years. Various new projects were designated in the Ring Zone, but more importantly, densities were significantly increased, even in projects that had been running for longer. The number of homes in the Houthavens doubled to 2,700, and in Oostenburg to 1,900; in NDSM and the Sluisbuurt, it was even raised from 1,500 to 5,000 homes. The average home size decreased to 60 m² in 2022; building heights, on the other hand, were increased. Building blocks took on a more hybrid character: they are composed of multiple building volumes of varying heights. Parking is often located on the inner courtyards, in one or two building layers. On top of that lies a collective but often sparsely landscaped deck.

The new city council raised the housing target in 2022 to 7,500 homes per year. In the period from 2015 to 2024, a total of 54,171 homes were built, averaging 5,400 per year.

A new turning point?

In 2021, the city council adopted the new Environmental Vision Amsterdam 2050, 'A Human Metropolis'. Multicentricity and regionalization became important themes. The further development of the water city in Haven-Stad is seen in connection with the development of Zaanstad, the development of the Zuidas, and the Schinkel Quarter in relation to Schiphol and Haarlemmermeer. An East/West metro line will complete the metro network. Do the concepts of multicentricity and regionalization signal a new movement: the emancipation of the periphery?

Do the shocks of recent years and the limited financial possibilities mean that the growth phase of the past fifty years is now coming to an end? The title of the Development Strategy 2035, 'Building Neighborhoods of the Future', suggests a different focus and a new movement, one where smaller-scale improvements in livability and cohesion take center stage.

In the 1990s, it became common in the Netherlands to view the government as ballast and to move away from the concept of a constructable society. The development of Amsterdam over the past fifty years shows that the city, as a physical structure, is indeed malleable. Not in the form of realizing a future dream, but through clever movement. Sometimes movements were initiated; in other cases, they were supported, facilitated, and prompted. A delightful and instructive game with a fantastic result, leaving one curious about what comes next.

QUALITY AND URBAN DESIGN

How did the new policy concretely manifest in the design of the city over the past fifty years?

From 1956, the Amsterdam artist Constant Nieuwenhuys worked for nearly twenty years on his utopian project *New Babylon*. Through a remarkable series of models, sculptures, drawings, collages, and texts, he evoked a fascinating vision of a new society. In his view, automation would eliminate much physical labor, and creativity and experimentation would play a far more significant role: the *homo faber* gives way to the *homo ludens*. There would be time for unexpected encounters and travel; many would lead a nomadic existence. His views and ideas were widely disseminated through exhibitions, publications, and lectures, and had a substantial influence. The motto for Amsterdam's 700th anniversary in 1975 also referenced this idea: 'live, work, play!'

Fifty years later, it can be observed that Constant's utopia has largely been realized. Heavy industry has almost completely disappeared from the city, and 'play' has become an essential part of life in Amsterdam. The city has been designed for interaction, cultural exchange, and innovation. It has become a city of new friends, coffee drinking, meetings and calls, dining out, performances, and festivals. The public space is dominated by young people, students, and an endless stream of visitors and temporary residents, especially since the city's growth spurt began in 2007. In recent years, the population dynamics have been extreme. In 2023, 90,000 people settled in the city, mostly from abroad, while 80,000 people left. This number decreased somewhat in 2024, but still represents nearly 10% of the city's population! Journalist Marcel van Engelen referred to this new character of the city as 'Hotel Amsterdam'.[2]

However, the current spatial form of the city has a very different character from what Constant envisioned fifty years ago. In his vision, a nomadic existence would include a new type of city with temporary and highly changeable structures that would stretch across the urban landscape. In his maps, he showed how the existing city would make way for new linear megastructures – 'sectors' in various colors, materials, and atmospheres. He drew inspiration for this from the architecture of stations, harbor terminals, and airports. In a speech on the occasion of the opening of the new terminal at Schiphol in 1966, he even suggested that the new airport could be viewed as a 'precursor' to the city of the future.[3] The similarities between his proposals and the current terminal complex are evident.

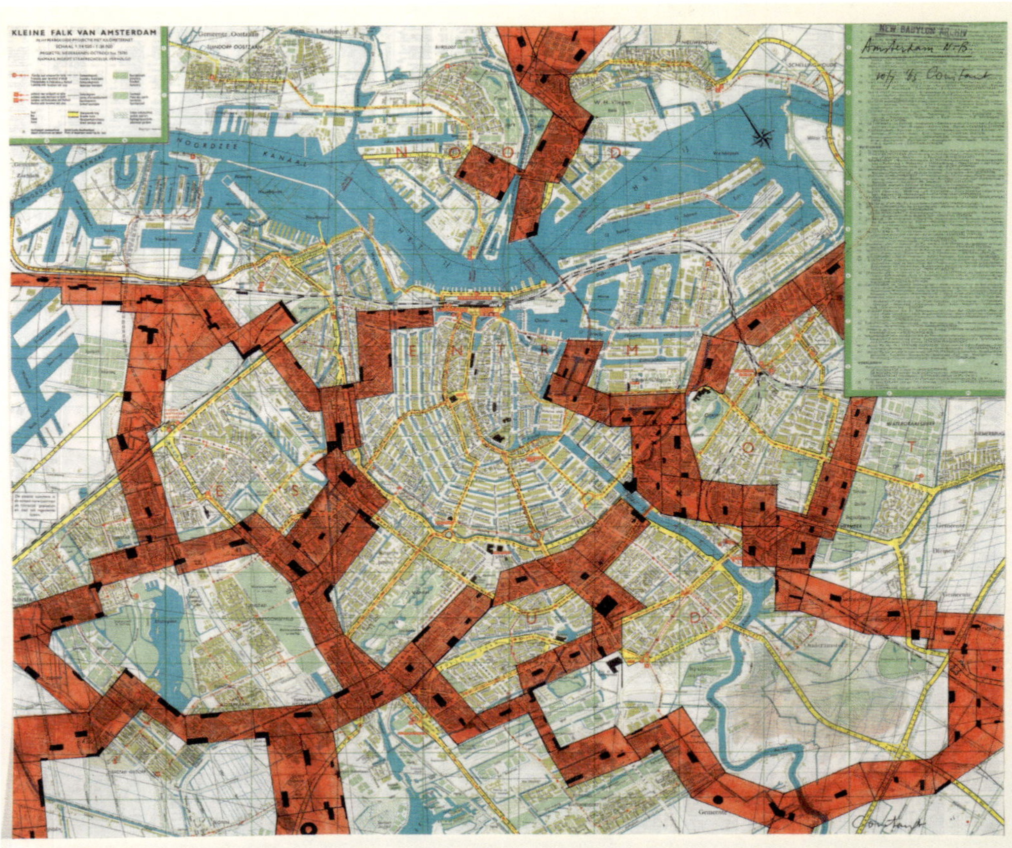

1

He would have followed with interest the experiments of like-minded individuals in England, such as Peter Cook and Ron Herron, the architects of Archigram, with their 'plug-in' and 'walking' buildings, Cedric Price with the open architecture of Fun Palace and Interaction City, or the projects of Richard Rogers. In 1971, Rogers, together with Renzo Piano, won the prestigious international competition for the construction of the new Centre Pompidou for modern art in the heart of Paris.[4] 'Beaubourg' is a prime example of what a city for the playing human could look like, with its construction, escalators, and colorful pipes on the outside, allowing the building's interior to be as flexible as possible and used as a multidisciplinary cultural factory. The dynamism is emphasized by the large square in front, and the joyful fountains by Jean Tinguely and Niki de Saint Phalle next to it.

Willem Sandberg, director of the Stedelijk Museum in Amsterdam and a juror in the competition in Paris, reflected: '...for years I have dreamed of a museum built like a department store, where you can see from the outside what is available inside – goods in all fields – you walk freely in and out – you look for something special and head straight for it, or wander around until your eye or ear is suddenly caught by something. so I thought of a home for all the muses: not only the visual arts but also music, dance, literature, film, and photography: a real mouseion.'[5]

In the past fifty years, Schiphol has expanded with new terminals, shops, offices, and hotels. It has become an extensive and labyrinthine city with endless conveyor belts and lounges, and it is also constantly under construction.

The contrast with what happened in the old city is extreme. A whole series of modernist buildings from the sixties and seventies have been demolished – the Wibauthuis by Norbert Gawronsky, the Jan Swammerdam Institute on Constantijn Huygensstraat, the Station Post Building by Piet Elling on Oosterdok Island, the Andreas Hospital by Marius Duintjer, the Maupoleum by Piet Zanstra on Jodenbreestraat, and of course, a large part of the Bijlmer flats![6] The radical modernization of the city's image and fabric in the sixties and seventies was rejected; instead, the existing was embraced. Even in what has been newly built, there has been a return to tried-and-tested concepts and design tools. Large new complexes such as the WTC, AMC, Roeterseiland, and the ArenA have not spread out à la Constant's structures, but have been integrated into newly designed urban environments with squares and boulevards.

However, this course correction is not unequivocal. That would fail to acknowledge the great strides made in the design of the city. The overarching theme of the past fifty years is, of course, that modernism, with its desire for a different city full

1 Constant Nieuwenhuys, *Map New Babylon-Amsterdam I* (ink, watercolour, 52,5 x 62,2 cm) Collection Kunstmuseum The Hague (photo: Tom Haartsen) © Constant / Fondation Constant c/o Pictoright Amsterdam 2025)
2 Renewal of public space Plaça del Sol Barcelona, design by Bach-Mora Arquitectes, 1981–1985

of 'light, air, and space' and an orientation towards collectivity, efficiency, and repetition, made way for a postmodern view, inspired by the qualities of the existing city, and with a focus on individuality, complexity, and difference. But within this large line, interesting side paths and detours emerge, often building on what has happened in other cities.

Color and small scale

Amsterdam initially had – unlike Paris and London with their design competitions – bad luck with the City Hall competition of 1968. The jury, dominated by architects who had grown up with modernism, chose the monumental plan of the Viennese architect Wilhelm Holzbauer, featuring the sculptural council chambers placed on a colossal pedestal by the Amstel.[7] Ultimately, a happy compromise was reached through the combination of the city hall and the opera building, but the appearance of the complex remains a shadow of Beaubourg.[8]

Color and experimental materials can be found in the architecture of many early urban renewal projects. Aldo van Eyck and Theo Bosch, for example, were outspoken admirers of the complexity in the fabric of the old city and strongly opposed the Stopera, but in their projects like the Pentagon on Sint Antoniesbreestraat, the housing in the Jordaan, the Motherhouse on Plantage Middenlaan, and the P.C. Hoofthuis on the Singel, they experimented extensively with concrete, glass, and aluminum, as well as non-Amsterdam colors like blue, yellow, and purple. In the 'recovery' of the metro breakthrough on Sint Antoniesbreestraat, the building lines were restored, and underpasses, arcades, and small squares were added, but the street view primarily became a cacophony of colors and building masses.

In many other urban renewal projects from the seventies and eighties, yellow or light gray bricks were used, and the woodwork of window frames, doors, and eaves was painted in exuberant colors. The existing street pattern was maintained, but the architecture unmistakably appealed to renewal and improvement. The image of the dull 19th-century belt had to be refreshed. Perhaps you could call this a form of 'late modernism.'

Public space and architecture of the city

A major leap was made with the Piraeus project on the KNSM Island. This project fits into a broader reorientation of the significance of public space and the architecture of the city, in the Netherlands but especially in other cities across Europe.

The rediscovery of the importance of well-designed public spaces is credited to the Barcelonese urban designers, who, after the death of Franco and the democratization of the country in 1979, seized the opportunity to reshape the public space of the city.[9] In just a few years, under the leadership of Oriol Bohigas, an impressive series of squares, parks, and reprofiled streets were created, meant for parading, chatting, playing football, and having coffee. These spaces featured a full arsenal of classic design elements, executed with contemporary materials: benches, pergolas, groups of trees, natural stone, light posts, and sculptures. What stands out in all of these projects is the clear distinction between spaces for cars and spaces for pedestrians. The highlight is the Moll de la Fusta, where traffic moves underground, and the city once again touches the harbor and the Mediterranean Sea. The guiding principle was to give a new shape to the urban landscape.

Similarly, in 1979, the initiative for an IBA (International Building Exhibition) was launched in Berlin.[10] More than thirty years after the war, much of the old city – especially around the Wall – still lay in ruins. Architect Josef Paul Kleihues proposed 'kritische Rekonstruktion' (critical reconstruction) as the theme for the *Neubau* projects: the reinterpretation of the classical 19th and early 20th-century Berlin building block. 'Critical' in this context refers to editing with an eye toward new uses and meanings. Successful examples are projects in Charlottenburg and the southern part of Friedrichstadt, near where the Jewish Museum was later built. International design competitions were held for these locations, and the winning designs were ultimately constructed between 1983 and 1987. The characteristic contrast between the wide, continuous streets with their parcelized facades, and

2

the typical Berlin courtyards, often interconnected, was playfully reworked. Open gaps in the facades were filled with new buildings, often featuring sleek masonry or stucco with a classical facade design: a base, a central part with four or five layers, and a rooftop structure. This restored the continuity of the streets. Within the blocks, you sometimes find new courtyards, as well as successful experiments with new housing typologies, large and smaller inner gardens, play areas, and pedestrian pathways.[11] After the fall of the Wall in 1989, this approach continued to develop in various parts of the city. The fragmented city was thus healed and made suitable for contemporary use.

Through publications in Wonen-TA/BK and Plan, as well as in international journals like Lotus and The Architectural Review, and through education, exchanges, and excursions, many Dutch designers became familiar with the experiments in Barcelona and Berlin.[12] At the universities, research into urban form was conducted, and designing for the city regained a prominent role.[13]

The reassessment of the role of design was already followed in 1982 with the successful AIR event around the Kop van Zuid in Rotterdam.[14] Four foreign designers, including Kleihues from Berlin, were invited to present their vision for the redevelopment of the old harbor area. The results were widely discussed and led to the 1987 Masterplan for the Kop van Zuid by Riek Bakker and Teun Koolhaas, which included a new bridge over the Maas and urban development on the Wilhelminapier.

In 1988, many puzzle pieces fell into place. The plan for the redesign of the public space in downtown The Hague, 'De Kern Gezond',[15] prepared by Alle Hosper, was published, the 5×5 Workgroup was launched,[16] and the Fourth Note on Spatial Planning was released.

From the manifesto of the Working Group 5x5:

> More challenging than the anonymous and bureaucratic, we believe, is a public housing policy that prioritizes quality from all sectors and in various forms. Inspired by societal developments that demand diversity in housing. From the awareness that architecture and urban planning are inherently interconnected. From a sense of beauty. From the joy of living in a city.[17]

In the Fourth Spatial Planning Memorandum of 1988, the pursuit of spatial quality also became a national policy objective. This was manifested, among other things, in the establishment of the Netherlands Architecture Institute in the same year (opened in 1993 at Museumpark in Rotterdam) and the creation of the Architecture Stimulus Fund in 1993. As a result, there was also a growing appreciation in the Netherlands for the classical European city, as well as for an experimental design approach focused on new possibilities for use.

Reserved Amsterdam

Around 1980, experiments in Amsterdam under alderman Jan Schaefer were limited to assignments given to Rem Koolhaas and Carel Weeber to develop urban planning proposals for the IJplein and Venserpolder. These were primarily intended to bring alternative urban planning approaches to the table, in contrast to those of the Urban Planning Department, without a clear 'program' or architectural agenda. This also applied to the Oosterdok competition of 1984, which was only open to Dutch designers.

In urban renewal, priority was given to speed and reaching consensus with resident organizations on the course of action. The 'portieketagewoning' (porch apartments) proved to be a reliable means to create many well-equipped three- and four-room apartments, even on complicated sites. Typological innovations were limited to a few experiments, such as on Bickerseiland and in the Jordaan, and on additional housing locations like the urban villas and towers along the Singelgracht, following the repurposing of several barracks. Herman Zeinstra designed an exciting series of 'filling' open gaps with HAT units. The converted warehouses at Entrepotdok by Joop and André van Stigt, completed in 1987, also attracted a lot of attention, but that was the extent of the innovations.

In these years, however, there was a revival of the architecture of the Amsterdam School and the urban planning of Berlage's Plan Zuid from the 1920s and 1930s. The groundbreaking, expressive projects of architects like De Klerk, Kramer, Van der Meij, and Wijdeveld had been heavily criticized by modernists as 'apron architecture', with traditional floor plans behind them. A major exhibition at the Stedelijk Museum in 1975 reintroduced the quality and importance of their projects. A series of publications followed, emphasizing material use, craftsmanship, detailing, and the plasticity of the facades; implicit calls for a new urban architecture.[18] In the discussions about the approach to the Mercatorplein, there was extensive reflection on the quality of Amsterdam School architecture.[19] When Berlage's Plan Zuid celebrated its 75th anniversary in 1992, a specially established independent foundation took the opportunity not only to showcase the qualities of the plan but also to conduct design research into

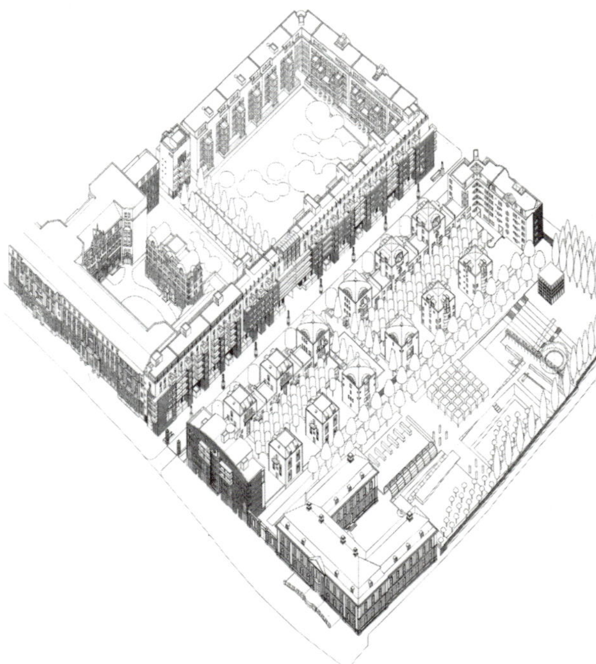

1

1 IBA project Lindenstrasse in Südliche Friedrichstadt, 1983–1987
2 Piraeus KNSM Island, design by Hans Kollhoff in collaboration with Christiaan Rapp
3 Eye Filmmuseum, design by Delugan Meissl Associated Architects, 2012

renewal opportunities for crucial locations.[20] The successful Museum Het Schip in the Spaarndammerbuurt opened in 2001.

Initially, Amsterdam's construction practice took a rather cautious stance toward the new quality discourse. Commissions for the new generation of internationally operating architects were not forthcoming. This changed in the early 1990s. Renzo Piano built NEMO on the IJ Tunnel (1992–1997); American architect Robert Venturi and the Portuguese Álvaro Siza each worked on the expansion of the Stedelijk Museum.[21] But the real acceleration came from Jo Coenen in and around the urban plan for the KNSM Island starting in 1988.

Coenen worked simultaneously on the design for the Céramique site in Maastricht, where he invited a whole range of foreign architects to design various blocks, including Álvaro Siza, Luigi Snozzi, Mario Botta, and Aldo Rossi. For the architect selection for the blocks on KNSM Island, he made a similar list. Hans Kollhoff was ultimately chosen in 1991 as the architect for the later Piraeus block 1. A key factor in this choice – also for the involved residents' organization – was his Berlin IBA projects in Charlottenburg and Friedrichstadt.[22]

Together with his colleague Christian Rapp, who acted as project architect, Kollhoff then created a project that, upon completion in 1994, made a significant impact. It inspired an entire generation of young architects to experiment with classic materials and building forms, often with a nod to the architecture of the Amsterdam School.[23] The majority of Amsterdam's new construction in recent decades owes a debt to Piraeus. A fine, recent example is the Spaarndammerhart project by korthtielens and Marcel Lok.

Other Approaches

The open-minded approach of the 1990s also allowed space for other approaches, such as focusing on innovation and the use of modern materials and constructions. This is reflected in the works of architects like Benthem Crouwel, who designed the RAI, the Stedelijk Museum, the Noord/Zuidlijn, the bus platform, and the new roof for Central Station; Felix Claus, for the block along the A10 in the Laan van Spartaan and the A'DAM Tower; and Hans van Heeswijk, for the Hermitage.[24] The most 'deviant' from the postmodern line is the sculptural design for the Eye Filmmuseum by the Viennese firm Delugan Meissl Associated Architects.[25]

A distinctive trend is also the transformation of existing buildings. Architect André van Stigt was particularly inventive in complex assignments, such as the restoration of the Olympic Stadium, the transformation of De Hallen, and more recently, the conversion of the Chirurgische Kliniek at Binnengasthuis into the University Library (UB). In the renovation of the large shipbuilding hall at NDSM, inspiration from Constant was most explicitly visible.

The combination of rapid growth and crisis led to various innovative solutions. In Buiksloterham, there is a strong focus on circularity, with places like the creative hub De Ceuvel housing workshops and office spaces in old ship hulls, as well as a café, all fully circular and built with second-hand materials on contaminated land. Not far from there is Schoonschip, a development of forty 'autarkic' houseboats, and a series of apartment complexes mainly made of wood, such as Patch22, Top-Up, and Stories.

Could the recent focus on density be considered a new approach? Many recent apartment complexes now feature central hallways, which allow apartments to receive light from only one side. This 'hotel-style' access may work well for temporary housing for young people and students, but it tends to result in lower-quality living conditions for regular residential buildings.

And then, of course, towers! The first towers in the plans for the Sluisbuurt on Zeeburgereiland were still an experiment in unique housing and block forms for each island in the Waterstad. That type of design was new to Amsterdam. But when applied on a large scale, the inevitable question arises: Will Amsterdam eventually join the ranks of other generic metropolises, marked by dreary, high-rise apartment towers with lifeless ground floors?

2

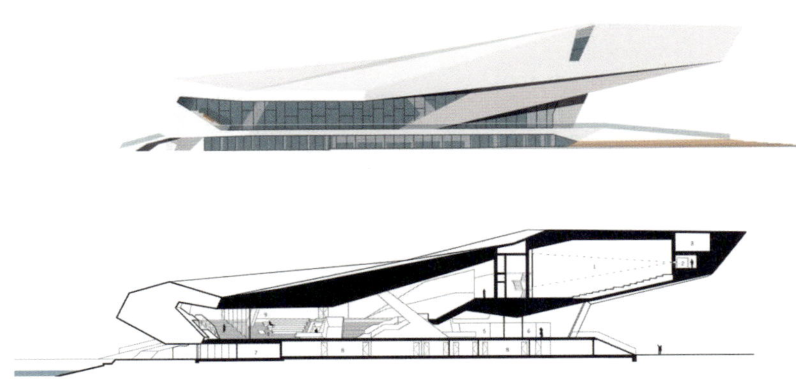

3

Public Space and Landscape

Isn't the quality of Amsterdam also primarily in the public space? We of course have the beautiful canals, but Amsterdam initially wasn't ahead in the design of streets and squares. In the seventies and eighties, the focus was on controlling car chaos and encouraging bicycle use. The introduction of concrete paving stones as a surfacing material and the placement of tens of thousands of 'amsterdammertjes' (small bollards) did not really provide a qualitative boost. Even in terms of public space, the city only started opening up in the early nineties, and it was only then that more attention was paid to sustainable materials and design.

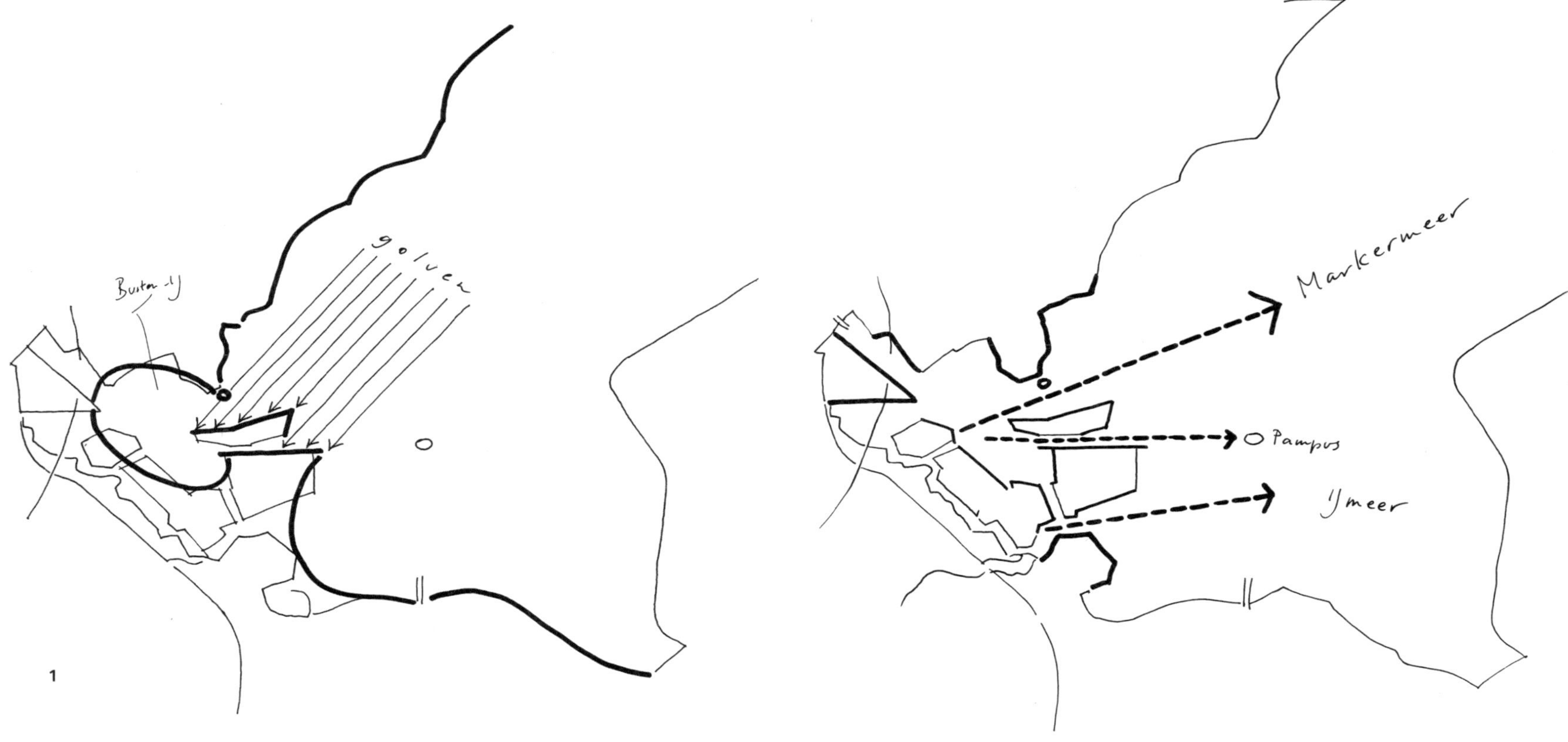

1

The Danish landscape architect Sven-Ingvar Andersson was invited as the designer for the Museumplein. Artists were involved in the redesign of the Nieuwmarkt and Damrak-Rokin. Intense debates about the chosen solutions led to the rediscovery of traditional materials such as baked bricks, Amsterdam hardstone, and the Ritter lanterns, as well as high-profile designs for the redesign of the Spui and the Dam.[26] With a new canal profile and the Puccini method, a new standard was ultimately established.

The power of clear public space and sustainable materials became evident with the creation of the Zuidplein and Arena Boulevard, and especially with the re-profiling of the Wibautstraat, long considered the 'ugliest street' in the city. The new paving and rows of trees even led to a whole series of 'ugly ducklings' like the Bommerhuis, the Volkskrant building, and the Parool complex starting a new urban life.

A similar rediscovery was also seen in urban expansion. The projected polder Nieuw-Oost became the archipelago of IJburg, in the tradition of the 17th-century harbor islands. Moreover, the Buiten-IJ gained a new form due to the thoughtful placement and design of the islands. The IJburg Bay, the bridges, the beach, the harbor, and the views to Pampus added new elements to the urban landscape. Urban planning here became landscape urbanism.

All these developments come together in the transformation of Central Station, with the newly opened waterfront, with cars and parked bicycles underground, with the Balcony on the IJ, and the long vistas to Zaanstad and the Oranjesluizen. The landscape is back in the city.

Conclusion

In the seventies and eighties, Amsterdam was not at the forefront when it came to designing the renewal of the city. Porch houses in closed building blocks and single-family homes in rows, along with concrete paving stones and Amsterdam bollards in public spaces, were the answer to the city's decay. Piraeus and the new canal profile marked a breakthrough in the early nineties. In the long phases of recovery and the subsequent growth spurt, however, there was delightful design in a wide range of new urban housing and block forms in developments that made optimal use of location quality. 'Difficult' XL buildings have found a more natural place in the city. Underground solutions for parking cars and bicycles and a consistent 'car-free' policy brought space – and ultimately the landscape – back into the city. Learning and perseverance occurred not only from designers but also from administrators, developers, housing corporations, and street pavers.

In addition to a new Amsterdam School with lots of brick and attention to detail, there was also room for experimentation, particularly in the design of new infrastructure and public buildings. The inventiveness of designers is proving to be invaluable as circularity, cost-efficiency, greening, and livability are pushing for new solutions to everyday challenges.

In 1995, the residents of Amsterdam overwhelmingly rejected the municipal proposal to create a city province. That same year, the Amsterdam architecture center Arcam published a map showing all the ongoing projects in the region.[27] This convincingly demonstrated the need for regional coordination. As a result, a Regional Consultation Body was established, followed by a Northern Randstad Wing Consultation. Eventually, in 2007, the Metropolitan Region Amsterdam (MRA) was created, a collaboration between the provinces of North Holland and Flevoland and thirty municipalities. Within the MRA, urbanization policies are coordinated. Together, negotiations with the national government are conducted to determine the direction to take. The Amsterdam Transport Region, in turn, coordinates major investments in public transport and regional cycling infrastructure in a smaller area.

The core area of the MRA is the Amsterdam agglomeration, with its characteristic lobed or finger-like city structure. In addition to Nieuw-West, Amsterdam-Zuidoost, and IJburg, Amstelveen and Zaanstad also extend like fingers into the surrounding countryside. The lobes have a strongly distinct identity; take Zaanstad, for example, with its centuries-old industrial history around the Zaan River. Each of them has a major service center: Osdorpplein, Stadshart Amstelveen, ArenAPoort, Inverdan – and IJburg to a lesser extent.

Together with Amsterdam, these lobes effectively function as one urban system with 1.2 million inhabitants. Here, daily relationships are the strongest. The agglomeration is bounded by the remnants of the 19th-century Amsterdam Defense Line: the series of forts, lines, and floodable areas in a circle around 20 kilometers from the city, forming a complete green belt, designated as a UNESCO World Heritage site in 1996.

The MRA also includes Zuid-Kennemerland, the IJmond, and the Gooi. Already in the 17th century, country estates were established here by wealthy Amsterdam merchants along the inland dunes near the sea and extending into the higher grounds inland. In the 19th century and the first decades of the 20th century, these areas then developed into large suburbs of Amsterdam. They are about 30 kilometers from the city and remain popular residential areas. The industry in the IJmond and Haarlem, and the media companies in the Gooi, shaped the identity.

In the urban growth policy of the 1970s, this characteristic was continued. New residential areas were chosen at a distance from Amsterdam. The first generation included Lelystad and Hoorn, 40 kilometers from the city. Later designated new towns like Purmerend, Almere, and Haarlemmermeer are located closer. However,

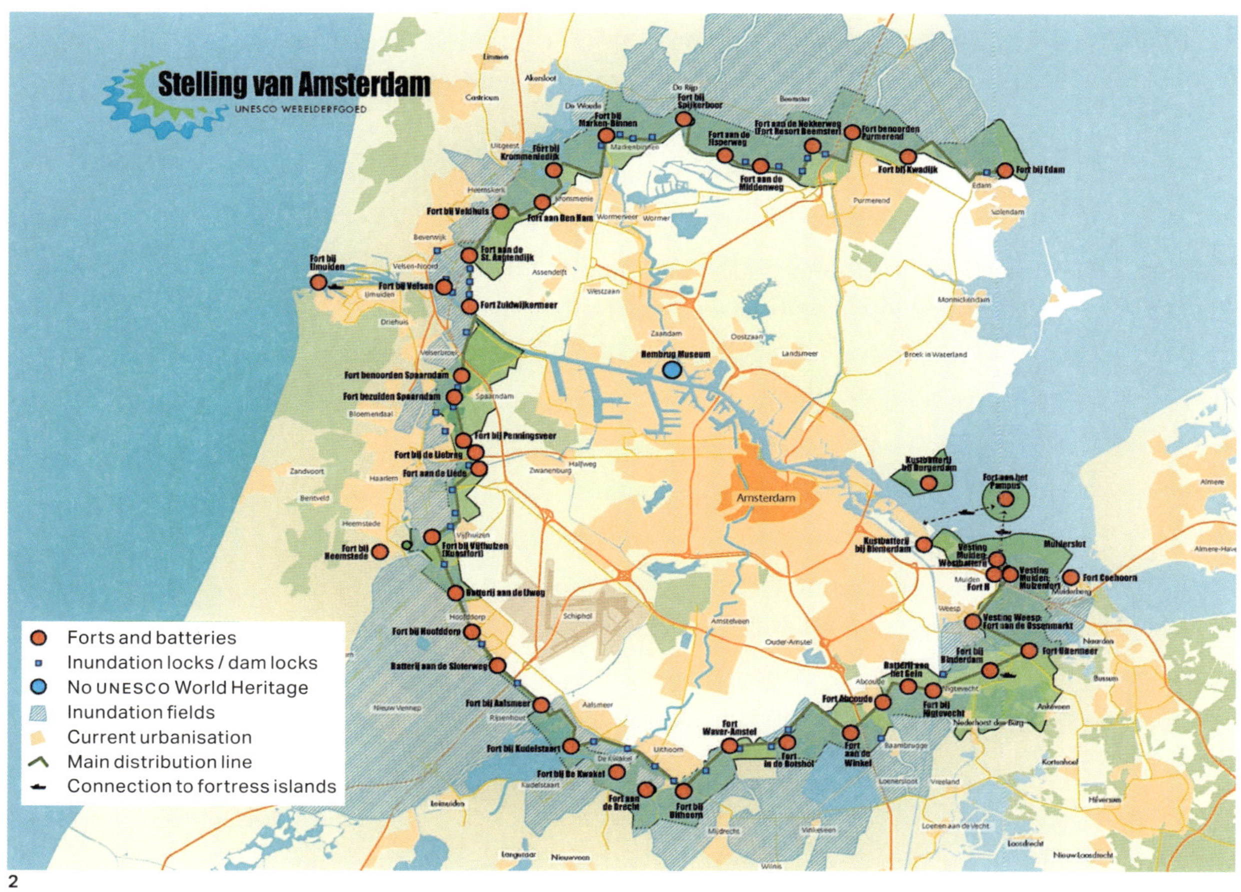

2

1 Diagrams design IJburg: shelter and views, Frits Palmboom, 1998
2 Defense Line of Amsterdam (with the current urbanization outlined)

ORDZEE
IJMEER

the lobed structure of the agglomeration was largely maintained. From the centrally located agglomeration, you are still quickly in the open landscape. Since Schiphol's flight paths run over these sparsely populated landscapes, the openness is also 'guaranteed.' The decision not to reclaim the Markermeer further helped with this.[28] There are no tides in Amsterdam, but the vastness of the lagoon and the horizon can still be experienced daily in the heart of the metropolis.

The total population of the MRA grew from 1.8 million in 1975 to 2.6 million at the beginning of 2025; a growth of 40%.[29] The housing stock doubled, from 600,000 to 1.2 million. A third of the new construction took place in Amsterdam, a third in the new towns of Almere, Hoofddorp, Purmerend, and Lelystad, a sixth in Amstelveen and Zaanstad, and a sixth in the other cores of the metropolitan region (see appendix 1 for statistical data).

Comparing what has actually been built with the ideas about urbanization from the early 1970s, it turns out that the policy of concentration in spatial planning has been very successful. Contributions came from all levels of government. Of course, there are differences with what was originally intended. Amsterdam has become much more compact due to intensification than originally thought; the new towns of Haarlemmermeer and Almere have, in turn, become much larger than initially planned.

The main differences lie in infrastructure and employment. Far fewer highways have been built than were planned in the National Roads Plan – those that were built are extremely wide! Schiphol has also grown much larger. With all the distribution companies surrounding it, the airport is a massive source of employment. The traditional industry around the North Sea Canal pales in comparison. In general, employment in the MRA is highly concentrated in Amsterdam and around Schiphol. There is an extremely skewed balance between housing and employment, with large daily commuting flows! The large buildings seen on the 'Built in the MRA' map in Almere and Lelystad are mostly not intensive job concentrations but extensive distribution companies.

The most spectacular development is undoubtedly the construction of the polder cities of Lelystad and especially Almere. Construction of Lelystad had started earlier, but in 1975, the development of Haven, the first core of Almere, began. Today, nearly 230,000 people live in Almere, in 95,000 homes. These are numbers that seem almost unreal.

← Map Built in the MRA, 1975–2025

The multi-core concept of Almere follows the 20th-century Dutch tradition of dividing large urban expansions into smaller units, such as in Berlage's plans, the garden cities, and the neighborhoods in many other new towns. Here, it also reflects the layout of the Gooi, with a lot of attention given to the spaces between the cores. Early on, forests were planted in the areas between the cores. The iconic feature became the Weerwater, located in the center of the city.

With 2.6 million inhabitants, the MRA is one of the smaller metropolitan regions in Europe. However, a distinctive characteristic of the urban landscape in the Dutch delta, which has grown over centuries, is the strong dispersion in the urbanization pattern. Just to the north of the MRA lie Kennemerland and West-Friesland, with the cities of Alkmaar and Hoorn. The Bollenstreek, Amersfoort, and Utrecht are also not far away. By train, you can also quickly reach The Hague and Rotterdam. The Randstad – the entire urbanized area in the west of the Netherlands – has between 6.5 and 9 million inhabitants, depending on the definition used.[30]

More important than the definition, however, are the agglomeration effects, also known as borrowed size.[31] These provide an explanation for the vast array of specialized services and facilities in Amsterdam. It is not only the size of the region that matters, but also the relative proximity of other large cities and an extensive urbanized hinterland. Due to the relatively short distances, the cities derive part of their appeal from each other. Within the Randstad and the Netherlands, Amsterdam is undeniably the business and cultural center.

A Nordic metropolis

At the development of the Zuidas, some may have dreamed at the beginning of this century of Amsterdam playing a role as a financial center, part of the European top, just below the 'command centers' of the 'global economy' of Saskia Sassen: New York, London, and Tokyo.[32] That did not happen.

Looking at the ranking of cities in various comparative international studies, Amsterdam ranks in the subtop of European cities like Berlin, Brussels, Düsseldorf, Frankfurt, Madrid, Milan, Munich, Warsaw, and Vienna. Amsterdam performs well in the tech industry and on the connectivity of Schiphol. However, when it comes to international organizations and institutions, other cities score much better.[33] This is partly due to the fact that Amsterdam, although the capital of the Netherlands, has many political and administrative institutions located in The Hague.

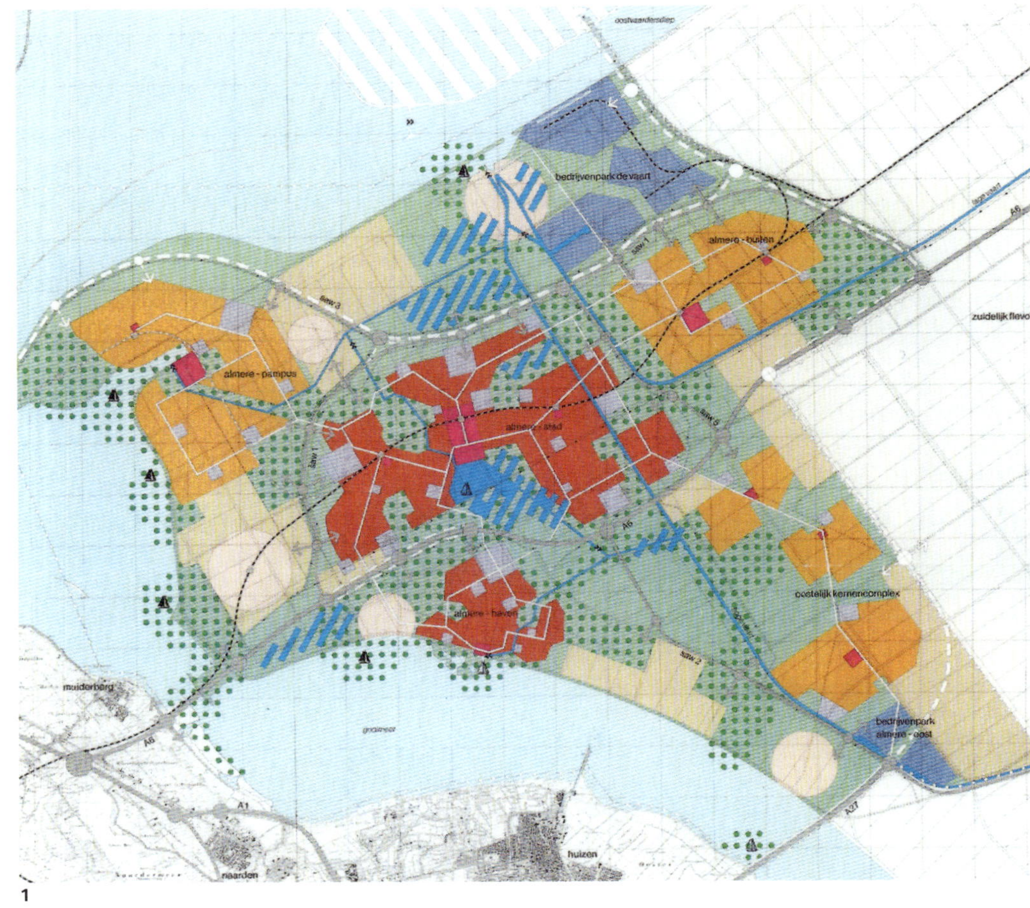

1

To understand the dynamics and specific qualities of Amsterdam, it is interesting to look at other Northern European cities. In particular, the affinity in location, size, and urban form with cities like Hamburg, Copenhagen, Stockholm, Helsinki, Rotterdam, Antwerp, and Oslo is noteworthy. These port cities share a bourgeois, Protestant culture, and in their 20th-century history, social democratic ideas about design and planning have played a prominent role.

Of course, there are differences. The centers of Hamburg and Rotterdam were completely destroyed during World War II. The others were spared, although drastic traffic breakthroughs in the 1950s and 1960s also caused significant damage.

More important are the similarities. First and foremost, the choice not to grow concentrically. Not only Amsterdam, but also Hamburg, Copenhagen, Stockholm, and Helsinki chose the lobed or finger city model in the 1950s to orient their expansions directly onto the surrounding landscape. Amsterdam is the most perfect example of the application of this model.

To accommodate further population growth, a completely new city was built from the 1970s onwards near Helsinki, à la Almere: Espoo. Around Copenhagen, Roskilde and the Køge Bay were developed. Since the 1990s, Malmö has also functioned effectively as a suburb of Copenhagen. A whole series of satellite cities have also been built around Rotterdam: Hoogvliet, Capelle, Spijkenisse. Many of these suburbs and new towns – including Almere – have a suburban character. A notable exception is Espoo near Helsinki. Since the 1960s, a large technical university has been located there, the present-day Aalto University. It is located at the very edge of Espoo, in Otaniemi, and quite close to Helsinki, 11 kilometers from the center, 20 minutes by metro.

Similar processes can also be found within and immediately around the cities. Many harbor functions moved away, and

Tourism and Airports in Northern European Cities

Destination	Overnight stays 2019	Distance airport > city	Passengers 2019
Amsterdam (Schiphol)	18.4 m	15 km > Dam	71.7 m
Hamburg	15.4 m	12 km > Rathaus	17.3 m
Stockholm (Arlanda)	15.3 m	45 km > Kulturhuset	19.6 m
Copenhagen (Kastrup)	9 m	8 km > Kongens Nytorv	30.2 m
Helsinki (Vantaa)	3 m	19 km > City Hall	19 m
Antwerp	2.1 m	5 km > Groenplaats	0.3 m
Rotterdam (Zestienhoven)	2 m	5 km > Coolsingel	2.1 m

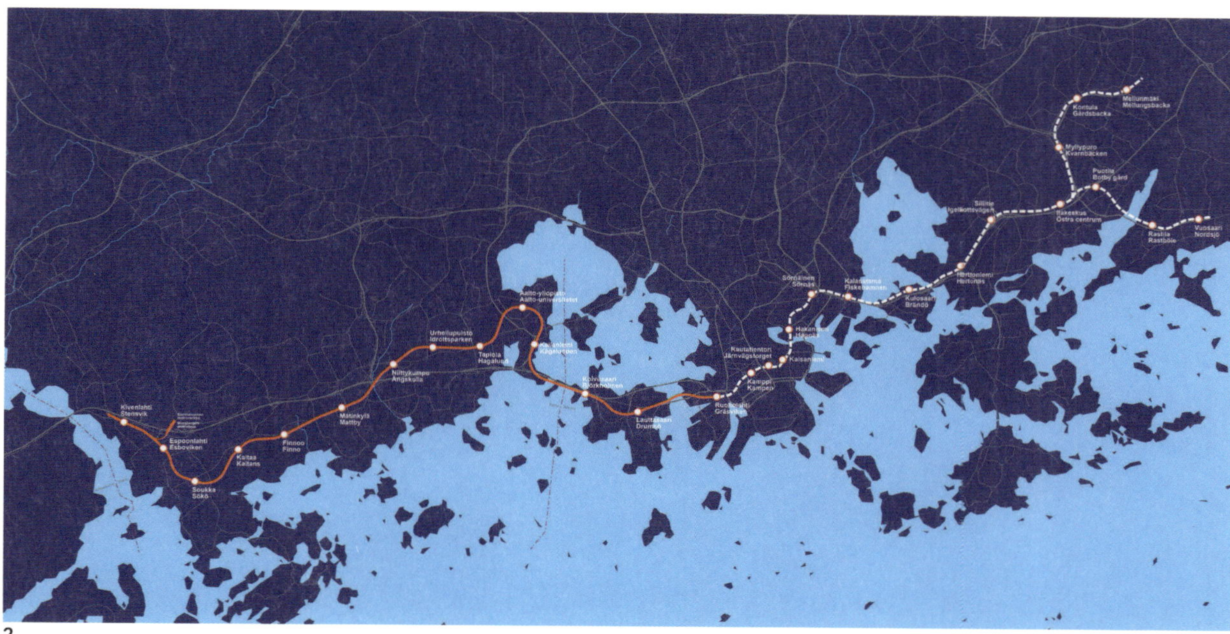

2

1 Structure Plan Almere 1978
2 Satellite city Espoo near Helsinki with Aalto University in Otaniemi, accessible via the East/West metro line
3 Helsinki Pasila 2020, new office area north of the city center on and around a former railway yard, compare to the Zuidas development

all cities developed their waterfronts with a combination of housing, modern employment, and cultural facilities. The list of iconic buildings is enormous, from De Rotterdam, via the Operahuset and the Munch Museum in Oslo, and the MAS in Antwerp, to the Elbphilharmonie in Hamburg. In terms of the scale of waterfront development, Amsterdam stands out with the 50,000 completed homes, unlike the others. In the redevelopment of HafenCity in Hamburg, Kop van Zuid in Rotterdam, the Eilandje in Antwerp, the water city and the new islands in Copenhagen, and the coastal locations in Helsinki, the projects generally consist of 20,000–30,000 homes.

In some of the northern cities, there are also similar shifts in economic activities as in Amsterdam. Most explicitly in Copenhagen and Helsinki. In Copenhagen, for example, the stock exchange complex and the stadium have been moved to Ørestad, near Kastrup Airport and the bridge over the Öresund to Malmö. In Helsinki, the focus of office employment has shifted to Pasila, near the Messukeskus convention center, on a large old railway yard a few kilometers north of the city center. In Hamburg, City Nord has been developed near Hamburg Airport, and in Stockholm, Kista is located on the route to Arlanda Airport, but these are less substantial movements.

All the mentioned cities are fully focusing on tourism. With the exception of Helsinki, all visitor numbers have surpassed the levels of 2019. The table (page 233) includes the number of overnight stays for that year. Comparable data for 2023 or 2024 are not available for all cities. Therefore, the 2019 figures have been included. Amsterdam tops the list. The table also includes data on the distance from the city center to the airport and the number of passengers processed by the airport in 2019. What fundamentally distinguishes Amsterdam from the others is the large airport!

In conclusion, it can be stated that over the past fifty years, Amsterdam has become a small metropolis that ranks among the mid-tier global cities. The agglomeration has around 1.2 million inhabitants, including the lobes of Zaanstad and Amstelveen. The historic city center has developed into a diverse, car-free, and popular interaction environment, and has expanded around the Central Station (CS) towards and reoriented on the IJ. The new urban islands in the waterfront city around the IJ have added a unique urban living environment. On the 'land side', two strong secondary centers developed around the stations Zuid and Bijlmer ArenA, each with its own profile, business-focused and leisure-oriented, respectively.

The city is located in a still relatively intact and protected open landscape and benefits from an extensive urban region, with older suburban areas in the inner dune line near the sea and in the Gooi, large new polder cities, but also with a seaport in transition and an extremely large airport.

The city's growth spurt since 2007 in terms of population and jobs has intensified the skewed work-home balance, particularly between Almere and the central part of the region, and has led to sharper segregation between affluent and less affluent areas, both within and outside the agglomeration.

In 2022, the MRA and the involved provinces and municipalities established the Urbanization Strategy for the region. Just as in the Amsterdam Spatial Vision of 2021 and the Development Strategy of 2024, the concept of polycentricity is now embraced at the regional scale. More balance is needed.

3

EPILOGUE TO 2075!

Ongoing movements

The future is uncertain. But sooner or later, and certainly differently than expected, many projects will be carried out for which the foundation has been laid in recent years.

Some large movements, such as in the 'water city', span centuries. In 1876, the North Sea Canal opened, and the IJpolders to the west of the city were created. In five to ten years, the Oranjewerf, the last waterfront company on the eastern side, will close. All other companies either went bankrupt, merged, or moved to the Western Port Area. The transitions in the port economy will undoubtedly lead to new developments. The southern movement also had a long lead time. After a century of debate, Amsterdam Zuid Station finally opened in 1978. This sparked enormous dynamism in the financial sector and business services. Amsterdam is a water city, but has also become a 'land city.' From Zuid, you're much faster to other cities in the country and Schiphol than from CS. Amsterdam Zuid will certainly become the largest station in Amsterdam, and it is also the most efficient location for international train traffic.

These movements continue. The Amsterdam 2050 Spatial Vision provides the framework for this. Let's systematically review what is still in the works.

The 'renewal of the existing city' will continue steadily with a whole series of projects in neighborhoods from the 1960s and 1970s in Nieuw-West, and in Noord. The centers of Nieuw-West and Noord will be strengthened. Inclusivity and circularity are key priorities. Focus will then shift to neighborhoods from the 1970s and 1980s in Gaasperdam and from the early urban renewal period. The car-free Frans Halsbuurt in Oud-Zuid is a great example for redesigning and greening streets in other neighborhoods. Further sustainability also includes the expansion of district heating networks and experiments with timber construction and building transformation. This is still happening very slowly but will undoubtedly accelerate.

Regarding the intensification of the existing city, the latest 'major' transformation seems to have recently started. The large Food Center on Jan van Galenstraat will become a mixed-use residential and business area. The monumental Central Market Hall has already begun its new life as a business and event center. But what could follow in Weesp or Diemen and Duivendrecht if the choice is made to downgrade and integrate the Gooiseweg?

'Low-rise buildings on the urban edge' are still under construction in Weespersluis, on the northern edge of Weesp. Large new locations are not presenting themselves. For new suburban environments, we can look much better at other centers in the region.

Since the 1990s, 50,000 new homes have been built in the new water city around the IJ. It seems likely that there is room for another similar number: on Zeeburgereiland and Strandeiland, in Buiksloterham, NDSM, Hamerkwartier, and gradually in HavenStad. A few bridges and tunnels, over and under the IJ, will be required.

The southern movement continues, now that the decision has been made to combine living and working in the Schinkelkwartier, Zuidas, Amstelkwartier, ArenAPoort, and Bullewijk. The city is becoming much larger and more compact.

In the city center and around the central part of the IJ, many projects are also in the works. The National Slavery Museum will be built at the tip of Java Island. It would be great if the Marineterrein, Dijksgracht, and Sixhaven could maintain their green and experimental character, slightly apart from the city center, amidst the influx of visitors.

And then there's still an unresolved major issue: the Weesperstraat, combined with the abandoned Mr. Visserplein and the strange grade-separated interchange of Prins Hendrikkade and Valkenburgerstraat. Here, another round of city repairs is needed!

Shocks

But what about the shocks of the past few years? When creating the periodization of 1975–2025, the pattern of reversing the decline, recovery, growth spurt, and shocks was called 'classic'. Does this imply the end of the city's rapid growth and flourishing? Or are the shocks a transitional phase, followed by a new phase of growth?

It is wise to explore potential developments broadly, using what-if scenarios, starting with climate change. What could be possible responses to a rapid sea level rise? And that's just one issue – there are many big challenges that will need fresh ideas and solutions.

Against the backdrop of the wars in Ukraine and the Middle East, and the significant changes in government policies in the US and various European countries, further integration of the global economy is no longer a given. In response, Mario Draghi, the former president of the European Central Bank, outlined a perspective for a stronger and more autonomous strategic position for Europe.[1] Will all member states agree, or will distinct blocks begin to form within Europe? What could the consequences and opportunities for Amsterdam and the region be? A crucial issue for the region is the future of the steel industry. Will there be a strong push for the sustainability of Tata Steel at its current location, or given the high price of energy from wind and solar, would it be wiser to invest collectively, as a European effort, in locations in Norway and Spain, close to clean energy generation sources?

And will international migration continue? This seems difficult to stop or bend. Will English then become definitely the working language in the city? Or are concerns about the strong growth of in- and outflows of the population justified? The social infrastructure of the city seems to benefit from some level of stability. Should we build larger homes for families who want to stay in the city? What would be the effect of a smaller influx of international students?

Can the excesses of tourism be curbed? Strangely enough, hotels are still being opened, and permits are being granted for room rentals to tourists. Supply creates demand. A lesson from the COVID period is that the city could have bought hotels for refugee accommodation and student housing. It is wise to keep such counter-cyclical measures in mind.

Movements

Fifty years of urban development in Amsterdam make it clear that the city's spatial development is not an autonomous process. The five major movements are societal processes in which the municipal government actively took a position, intervened, facilitated, and invested based on the political goals the city set for itself.

The new concept of polycentricity in the 2050 Environmental Vision of Amsterdam from 2021 and in the Metropolitan Area's Urbanization Strategy from 2022 offers points of reference for taking new steps to combat inequality and segregation, improve livability, and restore balance in the city and the region. 'Emancipation of the periphery' seems to be a promising new movement!

How could this take shape? In Amsterdam itself, investments have been made in new construction projects, such as the Meervaart theater near Sloterplas and a large new library at Kraaiennest in Southeast. Such iconic projects help shift the perception of the periphery, but more is needed. For example, stopping the sale of social housing, stimulating employment, combating 'room splitting', and building many elderly homes to get the housing turnover moving. However, the greatest steps can be taken in the relationship between the city and the cores in the agglomeration and the region.

Port

The transition to a circular and post-fossil economy in the port will likely not proceed in a linear fashion. The future energy supply is under pressure. Wind and solar energy are sustainable alternatives, but they also seem to be much more expensive in the long term compared to the cheap gas from Groningen. What does this mean for the production of steel, fertilizer, and catalysts, as well as for storage capacity, electrolyzers, and batteries? Which new industries should space be reserved for?

By actively aligning with developments, the areas around the Petroleumhaven and the Jan van Riebeeckhaven could be freed up. These areas are still used for the storage of various oil products. After the closure of the coal-fired power plant on Hemweg in 2020, the gas-fired plant in this area also has a limited lifespan. By enabling new uses in this area with less environmental impact, room can be made for mixed development and for fast connections to Zaanstad. Could the IJtram continue from Hemweg to Zaandam and later perhaps a metro line? Zaandam may seem far away now, but the distance from CS is just as great as the distance from CS to Centrumeiland in IJburg.

Schiphol

Further growth of the airport and the construction of a second terminal complex are no longer appropriate. It is better to focus on exploring other options. Is reducing Schiphol's size and closing one or more runways an option, possibly in combination with redistributing air traffic to regional airports and scaling down the airport's hub function. In *Onder het luchtruim*, Theo Baart and Tijs van den Boomen advocated for reducing the number of flights to 300,000 and closing the Aalsmeerbaan.[2] In Aalsmeer and Uithoorn, the noise disturbance is extreme. Closing the Aalsmeerbaan offers various development opportunities there, but unexpectedly also in Haarlemmermeer.

Redesigning airspace may help in the short term to reduce negative health effects and free up development sites. How often does it actually storm in the Netherlands, and should the Buitenveldertbaan be used? In 2022, there was one heavy storm, in 2023 there were nine, and in 2024, seven. If you were to argue that the Buitenveldertbaan is indeed a storm runway and only used as such, a very different LIB regime could apply.[3] This could offer a less disturbed and more urban perspective for Amstelveen, as well as the area around Duivendrecht Station and the Bijlmer.

Uneven work-life balance

The urbanization of the IJsselmeer Polders has been the most significant development in the region over the past decades, but this urbanization has so far primarily been housing, resulting in traffic jams and crowded trains during rush hours to and from the more centrally located job areas.

Breaking this imbalance in employment between the polders and the old land cannot happen without major interventions. Analogous to the complex of the Aalto University in Espoo near Helsinki, everything could be done to establish a technical university in Almere, the cradle of AI in the Netherlands. This would strengthen Amsterdam's tech hub.

Or could it be an option to move (part of) the Amsterdam UMC to Almere? Fifty years after its construction, the challenge of sustainability at the AMC will inevitably arise. Will this happen at the current location or at one or more new sites? After the merger, the VU Hospital and the AMC had 19,500 employees. A significant number of them live in Almere!

New public transport

In the Amsterdam Omgevingsvisie 2050, a metro East/West line is tentatively indicated with a dotted line. Imagine this: built beneath the Singelgracht, the 'inner ring' can be freed up from tram traffic above ground, and a cut can be made for through traffic between Overtoom and Boerenwetering. From Vondelpark and the Rijksmuseum, you could walk or bike directly into the city center. Further west, the Lelylaan could become a pleasant city street, and via Osdorpplein and Badhoevedorp, the metro would continue to the center of Hoofddorp.

And to the east? On the map of the 2021 Omgevingsvisie, the dotted line ends at Muiderpoort Station. But wouldn't it be better if the line continued towards Almere, via the Science Park and IJburg? Along the way, you'll pass the NS railway yard at Watergraafsmeer. If this is relocated to the IJsselmeer Polders, significant development space would become available at Science Park and in Diemen.

The two largest regional hubs could then be directly connected to the Amsterdam city center. However, the costs of such a connection would be extremely high. Would 2075 be feasible? Perhaps an unexpected opportunity will arise, but for now, it seems wiser to consider different scenarios and focus on lighter measures first. The IJtram could go to Zaandam. And could tram line 1 not just continue to Haarlemmermeer?

And Almere? At the tip of Zeeburgereiland, at the junction of the A10 and IJtram, lies an excellent opportunity to build a water station. From there, ferries could depart for Vuurtoreneiland, Buiteneiland, Pampus, Volendam, and Marken, as well as a fast boat to Almere and Lelystad.

A small metropolis

The small metropolis of Amsterdam can thus evolve into a more polycentric region, with new hubs in the north, west, and southeast, as well as in Zaandam, Hoofddorp, and Almere. Amsterdam will become many cities.

On the other hand, Amsterdam lies somewhat 'peripherally' in Europe. When developing Schiphol and the internet hub AMS-IX in past years, the city's physical location was less of an issue. However, in the European train network, the city will likely be a final destination rather than a stopover or hub. For strengthening the accessibility of the city and its metropolitan quality, it seems more interesting to focus on expanding the Intercity Direct network to Groningen and Twente, as well as to Brussels, Eindhoven, and Düsseldorf. This would make the metropolis larger and stronger.

One could also argue that the peripheral location is actually an advantage. The landscape around the city, with the sea, dunes, lakes, and large bodies of water, has always been close by. It's not just about the green wedges between the lobes, but also about the green areas of the Stelling van Amsterdam, the Green Heart, Waterland, and the Markermeer. The peat bog areas around the city will acquire an increasingly natural, marshy character in the coming decades due to ongoing soil subsidence, similar to what we see around Nieuwkoop, the Jisperveld and Ankeveen. The redesign of the metropolitan landscape could help unlock these green areas around the city and enhance their attractiveness. In recent years, Lelystad has positioned itself as the 'capital of new nature,' referring to the ecological qualities of the Oostvaardersplassen and the new Marker Wadden near the Houtribdijk. It would be fantastic if, in the next fifty years, the metropolitan landscape could make another leap in quality!

↓ Marker Wadden (photo: © John Gundlach | Flying Holland)

APPENDIX

Development of Population and Housing Stock in Amsterdam and the MRA (Metropolitan Region Amsterdam)

Table 1: Development of Population MRA 1975–2025
Source: CBS StatLine

	1975		2025		increase	
	total	% MRA	total	% MRA	absolute	%
Total MRA	**1,844,349**		**2,624,284**		**779,935**	42
Agglomeration Amsterdam	1,220,518	66	1,661,276	63	440,758	36
Amsterdam	768,193	42	935,793	36	167,600	22
Agglomeration, excluding Amsterdam	452,325	25	725,483	28	273,158	60
New Towns*	141,863	8	575,433	22	433,570	306
MRA excl. Amsterdam	1,076,156	58	1,688,491	64	612,335	57
MRA excl. agglomeration Amsterdam	623,831	34	963,008	37	339,177	54
MRA excl. agglomeration Amsterdam, Almere and Lelystad	598,831	32	648,716	25	49,885	8

* New Towns = Almere, Haarlemmermeer, Lelystad, Purmerend

Table 2: Development of Housing Stock MRA 1975–2025
Source: CBS StatLine

	1975		2025**		increase	
	total	% MRA	total	% MRA	absolute	%
Total MRA	**589,734**		**1,221,776**		**632,042**	107
Agglomeration Amsterdam	397,226	67	793,173	65	395,947	100
Amsterdam	271,398	46	480,852	39	209,454	77
Agglomeration, excluding Amsterdam	125,828	21	312,321	26	186,493	148
New Towns*	34,404	6	238,182	19	203,778	592
MRA excl. Amsterdam	318,336	54	740,924	61	422,588	133
MRA excl. agglomeration Amsterdam	192,508	33	428,603	35	236,095	123
MRA excl. agglomeration Amsterdam, Almere and Lelystad	188,001	32	300,603	25	112,602	60

* New Towns = Almere, Haarlemmermeer, Lelystad, Purmerend
** Q3 2024 figures

Table 3: Population and Housing Stock six biggest cities NL 1975–2025
Source: CBS StatLine, incl. annexations/mergers

	1975		2025		increase %	
	population	housing stock	population	housing stock	population	housing stock
Amsterdam	768,193	295,891	935,793	486,769	22	65
Rotterdam	620,867	239,940	672,330	328,408	8	37
Den Haag	486,280	181,070	568,419	274,172	17	51
Utrecht	256,016	81,591	376,435	168,713	47	107
Eindhoven	192,562	64,245	246,417	119,376	28	86
Almere	0	0	229,570	93,246	–	–

NOTES

Introduction
[pp. 6-7]

1 Marten Middendorp et al., *Atlas 2024. De 50 grootste gemeenten van Nederland op 50 punten vergeleken. Brede welvaart* (Atlas 2024: The 50 Largest Municipalities of the Netherlands Compared on 50 Points. Broad Prosperity), Nijmegen 2024.
2 CBS figures + estimates for Lelystad (not yet an independent municipality in 1975).
3 Geert Mak, *De engel van Amsterdam* (The Angel of Amsterdam), Amsterdam 1992; James Kennedy, *Nieuw Babylon in aanbouw. Nederland in de jaren zestig* (New Babylon Under Construction: The Netherlands in the 1960s), Amsterdam 1995; Herman de Liagre Böhl, *Amsterdam op de helling. De strijd om de stadsvernieuwing* (Amsterdam on the Brink: The Struggle for Urban Renewal), Amsterdam 2010; Fred Feddes, *1000 jaar Amsterdam* (1000 Years of Amsterdam), Bussum 2012; Tim Verlaan, *De ruimtemakers. Projectontwikkelaars en de Nederlandse binnenstad 1950–1980* (The Space Makers: Property Developers and the Dutch Inner City 1950–1980), Amsterdam 2017; Marcel van Engelen, *De Stad. Het verhaal van Amsterdam van 1980 tot vandaag* (The City: The Story of Amsterdam from 1980 to Today), Amsterdam 2024; Bas Kok, *Gogme*, Amsterdam 2024.
4 See www.gebouwdin.amsterdam.nl and www.amsterdam.nl/planamsterdam. The publications mentioned were self-published, with the exception of: Wim Hartman et al. (eds.), *Algemeen Uitbreidingsplan 50 jaar, 1935–1985* (General Expansion Plan 50 Years, 1935–1985), Amsterdam: Amsterdamse Raad voor de Stedebouw, 1985; and Allard Jolles et al. (eds.), *Stadsplan Amsterdam 1928–2003* (City Plan Amsterdam 1928–2003), Rotterdam 2003.
5 The focus on movements over an extended period aligns with the 'longue durée' approach in historical analyses of the French Annales School, with historians such as Fernand Braudel. This perspective emphasizes underlying processes rather than a sequence of events like coronations, weddings, and battles.
6 Hans Aarsman in 2019 on the photographs of Jusopo Arsath Ro'is in the City Archives: www.amsterdam.nl/stadsarchief/stukken/archiefvondsten/brommertje/.
7 At various times, I had the opportunity to reflect on my work for the City of Amsterdam. This sometimes resulted in a study report, such as *Integratie A10* (Integration A10) from 1995, or an online publication, such as the cycling tours of *Tour Groot-Amsterdam*, released upon my departure in 2020. The resulting publications include: *4 x Amsterdam, ontwerpen aan de stad* (4 x Amsterdam: Designing the City), Bussum 2005; *Lange lijnen in Nieuw-West* (Long Lines in Nieuw-West), Amsterdam 2007; *Nieuwe ritmes van de stad* (New Rhythms of the City), Bussum 2009; *De Hollandse Metropool. Ontwerpen aan interactiemilieus* (The Dutch Metropolis: Designing Interaction Environments), Bussum 2013; and (with Anouk de Wit) *SuperWest 2000–2021. Vernieuwing van de Amsterdamse tuinsteden* (SuperWest 2000–2021: Renewal of the Amsterdam Garden Cities), Bussum 2022.

1975 – AMSTERDAM 700 Chronicle of a Turbulent Celebration Year
[p. 8-21]

1 The festivities in 1975 officially took place under the title *Amsterdam 700 jaar* (Amsterdam 700 Years). The organizing bureau also operated under that name. In this publication, the jubilee year is referred to simply as *Amsterdam 700*.
2 City of Amsterdam, *Stedelijk Jaarverslag Amsterdam 1975* (Amsterdam City Annual Report 1975), 1976.
3 Council Proposal *Amsterdam 700*, cited in: *Amsterdam werkt* (Amsterdam Works) no. 10, October 1973, p. 14.
4 Jan van Oostrom (1923–1988) was the head of Bureau Amsterdam 700. Previously, he was involved in organizing major events such as Rotterdam AHOY, E'55, the 1962 Floriade in Rotterdam, and the 1972 Floriade in Amsterdam's Amstelpark. After Amsterdam 700, he organized the 1982 Floriade in Gaasperpark.
5 The sports and play facilities in the neighborhoods were realized at the initiative of various local and district organizations. These included seating areas, fishing piers, mural painting under viaducts, a roller-skating rink, fountains, playground equipment, flower boxes, traffic lights, and a petting zoo. Source: *Overzicht wijkprojecten Amsterdam 700* (Overview of Neighborhood Projects Amsterdam 700), January 1976, archive of Paul Gravemaker, secretary of Bureau Amsterdam 700.
6 In the early 1970s, Amsterdam hosted 25–35 international congresses per year. See: H. ter Balkt, *Amsterdam congresstad in 1975* (Amsterdam Congress City in 1975), *Amsterdam werkt* no. 7–8, July–August 1975, pp. 11–15. In addition to hotels, the RAI and the Royal Tropical Institute were Amsterdam's main conference venues.
7 *Financieel verslag Amsterdam 700 (1975)* (Financial Report Amsterdam 700 [1975]), May 1982, archive of Paul Gravemaker, secretary of Bureau Amsterdam 700.
8 Conference *European Architectural Heritage Year*, October 19–24, 1975.
9 For an extensive analysis of the impact of the European Heritage Year 1975 on Dutch heritage policy, see: Anita Blom and Peter Timmer, *Hersteld verleden van dorpen en steden. Stads- en dorpsgezichten tijdens de stadsvernieuwing (1961–1985)* (Restored Past of Villages and Cities: Urban and Village Views During Urban Renewal [1961–1985]), Amersfoort 2019.
10 Piet de Rooy et al. (eds.), *Geschiedenis van Amsterdam. IV: Tweestrijd om de hoofdstad 1900–2000* (History of Amsterdam IV: Struggle for the Capital 1900–2000), Amsterdam 2007. A sharp summary of the debate can be found in: Tim Verlaan, *De toekomst van de Nederlandse binnenstad 1960–1978* (The Future of the Dutch Inner City 1960–1978), PhD dissertation, UvA, Amsterdam 2016, chapter *Amsterdam. Van herenakkoorden naar politiek primaat* (Amsterdam: From Gentlemen's Agreements to Political Primacy).
11 Den Uyl was Alderman for Public Works in Amsterdam from 1962 to 1965. See: Anet Bleich, *Joop den Uyl (1919–1987). Dromer en doordouwer* (Joop den Uyl [1919–1987]: Dreamer and Doer), Amsterdam 2008. On Nassuth: Daan Dekker, *De betonnen droom. De biografie van De Bijlmer en zijn eigenzinnige bouwmeester* (The Concrete Dream: The Biography of the Bijlmer and Its Maverick Architect), Amsterdam 2016.
12 Municipal Department of Public Works and Municipal Housing Service, *Voorontwerp Tweede Nota Binnenstad Amsterdam* (Preliminary Draft Second Inner City Memorandum Amsterdam), 1968, and *Nota Amsterdam behoeft woningproductie in het gewest* (Memorandum: Amsterdam Needs Housing Production in the Region), Amsterdam 1970. See also: Paul Meurs, *De moderne historische stad. Ontwerpen voor vernieuwing en behoud 1883–1940* (The Modern Historic City: Designs for Renewal and Preservation 1883–1940), Rotterdam 2000; Verlaan 2016 (note 17).
13 Geurt Brinkgreve, *Alarm in Amsterdam. Of, het lot der oude binnensteden* (Alarm in Amsterdam: Or, the Fate of Old Inner Cities), Amsterdam/Brussels 1956.
14 See, for example, Hans Righart, *De eindeloze jaren zestig. Geschiedenis van een generatieconflict* (The Endless Sixties: History of a Generational Conflict), Amsterdam/Antwerp 1995; James C. Kennedy, *Nieuw Babylon in aanbouw. Nederland in de jaren zestig*, Amsterdam 1995.
15 Roel van Duijn e.a., *Provo & Provocaties 1965–1967*, reprint 15 nummers van het tijdschrift *Provo*, Utrecht 2014 (Roel van Duijn et al., *Provo & Provocations 1965–1967*, reprint of 15 issues of the magazine *Provo*, Utrecht 2014). All 'white' plans were proposals for collective and environmentally friendly solutions to the city's problems.
16 The experiment never really took off due to the limited range of the vehicles and technical problems. It ended in 1988. It wasn't until 2011 that the first electric shared cars were introduced in Amsterdam.
17 See also: Herman de Liagre Böhl, *Amsterdam on the Brink. The Struggle for Urban Renewal*, Amsterdam 2010), and *Steden in de steigers (Cities Under Construction). Stadsvernieuwing in Nederland 1970–1990 (Urban Renewal in the Netherlands 1970–1990)*, Amsterdam 2012; Verlaan 2016 (noot 17) (Verlaan 2016, note 17).
18 Eric Duivenvoorden, *Een voet tussen de deur. Geschiedenis van de kraakbeweging 1964–1999*, Amsterdam 2000 (*A Foot in the Door. History of the Squatters Movement 1964–1999*, Amsterdam 2000), chapter '1975', iisg.nl/staatsarchief/publicaties/voettussendedeur/hoofdstuk03.php.
19 Jan Mastenbroek, *'Tussen planning en evaluatie'*, (*'Between Planning and Evaluation'*), a reflection on the public relations aspects of organizing the 700th anniversary of Amsterdam, presented at the RAI, November 1975, archive of Paul Gravemaker, secretary of Bureau Amsterdam 700.

PART 1
SOCIETAL DYNAMICS
[pp. 22-47]

1 See, among others: Paul Schnabel, 'Het zestiende Sociaal en Cultureel Rapport kijkt zestien jaar vooruit', in: idem (ed.), *In het zicht van de toekomst. Sociaal en Cultureel Rapport 2004*, Den Haag 2004, p. 45-90. Schnabel distinguishes, in addition to internationalization, individualization, and informatization, also informalization and intensification – the five I's.
2 For an overview, see: Dietmar Rothermund, *The Routledge Companion to Decolonization*, London 2006. A concise overview is provided by: Dane Kennedy *Decolonization: A Very Short Introduction*, Oxford 2016. From the late 18th century, all countries in North, Central, and South America became independent. The second wave after World War II mainly involved countries in Africa and Asia. After 1975, Zimbabwe (1980) and Namibia (1990), among others, followed.
3 Social geographer Jaap Draaisma, guest researcher at the HvA, closely tracks the development of Amsterdam's population on his website: www.amsterdam-sorteermachine.nl/buitenlandse-studenten.
4 Saskia Sassen, *The Global City. New York, London, Tokyo*, Princeton 1991 (rev. ed. 2001, 2013).
5 Bart Stellinga, *Dertig jaar privatisering, verzelfstandiging en marktwerking*, Amsterdam 2012.
6 Bureau van Statistiek der gemeente Amsterdam, *Jaarboek 1976*, Amsterdam 1976.
7 In 1961, the university's status changed from Gemeente-Universiteit to Universiteit van Amsterdam.
8 Data: Onderzoek & Statistiek gemeente Amsterdam and *Wonen in de Metropoolregio Amsterdam 2023*.
9 Figures: UvA and VU and

Jaap Draaisma (see note 29).

10 Data: Onderzoek & Statistiek gemeente Amsterdam 2023.

11 Veerle Leijnse, *Gebouwen voor vrouwen. De wensen en huisvesting van alleenstaande werkende vrouwen, gebouwd tussen 1940–1965*, master's thesis UU, Utrecht 2022; Salomé Bentinck and Annerieke Vos, *Zedelijkheid en zelfbeheer. De huisvesting van alleenstaande vrouwen 1850–1965*, graduation report Architecture TU Delft, 1981.

12 End of 1980: 712,465.

13 PBL, Hans van Amsterdam et al., *De stad: magneet, roltrap en spons. Bevolkingsontwikkelingen in stad en stadsgewest*, Den Haag 2015.

14 Monique Doppert, *Amsterdam. De roze geschiedenis*, Amsterdam 2023.

15 Peter Olsthoorn, *25 jaar internet in Nederland. De fascinerende herinneringen van de Nederlandse pioniers die Amsterdam tot centrum van het Europese internet maakten*, Amsterdam 2014. www.netkwesties.nl/documenten/25%20jaar%20internet%20in%20Nederland.pdf.

16 Data: CBS 2024.

17 The logistics city hub is now called CTPark Amsterdam City and has a surface area of no less than 120,000 m².

18 At the lowest point of the crisis in late 1983, unemployment in the Netherlands was 10.7%; in Amsterdam, more than 13% of the workforce was unemployed in 1983. While unemployment in the Netherlands as a whole declined from 1984, it continued to rise in Amsterdam, reaching 15% in 1987.

19 Manuel Castells, *The Rise of the Network Society. Volume I: The Information Age: Economy, Society and Culture*, Oxford 1996 (2nd ed. 2009).

20 Compare: Sassen 1991 (note 30). Euronext: the stock exchange merger of the stock exchanges of Amsterdam, Brussels, and Paris (formed in 2000). AMS-IX: the organization that operates the Amsterdam Internet Exchange in the Watergraafsmeer (since 1994/1997).

21 Rob van Engelsdorp Gastelaars and David Hamers, *De nieuwe stad. Stedelijke centra als brandpunten van interactie*, Rotterdam/Den Haag 2006. The concept of the escalator region was coined by A.J. Fielding in: 'Migration and Social Mobility. South-East England as an Escalator Region', *Regional Studies* 26 (1992) 1, p. 1-15.

22 Crimson Architectural Historians, *Een stad van komen en gaan*, Rotterdam 2019.

23 Data from 2005, 2013, 2019: Onderzoek, Informatie en Statistiek (OIS), *Amsterdam in cijfers. Jaarboek* 2006, 2014, 2020. Data from 1975: *Jaarboek 1976* (note 32).

PART 2
Introduction and MOVEMENT 1
[pp. 48-85]

1 Since 2010, many DIY housing projects (*zelfbouwprojecten*) have been realized on leftover plots and residual spaces throughout the city, totaling approximately 3,750 homes. See: *Bouw Zelf Samen. Kijk op (collectief) particulier opdrachtgeverschap, medeopdrachtgeverschap en wooncoöperaties*, Amsterdam 2022.

2 *Onderstukken*: homes that have been demolished down to the first floor. *Nota Open gaten* (1972), cited in: Egbert Ottens, *Ik moet naar een kleinere woning omzien, want mijn gezin wordt te groot*, Gemeentelijke Dienst Volkshuisvesting, Amsterdam 1975.

3 *Bureau van Statistiek der gemeente Amsterdam, Jaarboek 1975*, Amsterdam 1976, p. 150 ('5.3.3. Mutaties in de woningvoorraad, 1970 t/m 1974').

4 The figures come from: *De Amsterdamse stadsvernieuwing in beeld 1993*, part of the report *Op weg naar een duurzaam verbeterde buurt*, gemeente Amsterdam 1994 (table p. 64). From the total new housing production up to 1993, the 1,800 homes built in the *Oostelijk Havengebied* until that point have been deducted.

5 The transformation of the fortifications is described in the standard work by John van Eck, *De Amsterdamse Schans en Buitensingel*, Amsterdam 1948. The series of barracks: *Cavalerie Kazerne* 1864, *Oranje-Nassau Kazerne* 1814, *Militair Hospitaal* 1868, *Rijksmagazijn van Geneesmiddelen* 1889, *Rijkskledingmagazijn* 1877. For an overview, see: www.stelling-amsterdam.nl/kazernes/index.php.

6 Statistically, this concerns the *gebied* Slotervaart and the *wijk* (or neighborhood combination) Kolenkit.

7 Jobs of more than 12 hours per week. Due to the closure of *Slotervaartziekenhuis* (Slotervaart Hospital), this number has undoubtedly declined. However, it is expected that the site will once again host significant employment opportunities.

8 See the forthcoming biography of Dirk Frieling: Fred Feddes, *Samen Nederland maken. De wereld van Dirk Frieling (1937–2011)*, Vereniging Deltametropool, Rotterdam. Also, compare with Frieling's report on the first urban renewal experiment in the *Spaarndammerbuurt*: *Ambtenaren als aktiegroep? Verslag van drie jaar Spaarndammerbuurt*, special issue *Forum* 23 (1972), no. 5/6.

9 Herman de Liagre Böhl, *Amsterdam op de helling. De strijd om stadsvernieuwing*, Amsterdam 2010. Also see: Marcel van Engelen, *De stad. Het verhaal van Amsterdam van 1980 tot vandaag*, Amsterdam 2024.

10 Paul Meurs, *De moderne historische stad. Ontwerpen voor vernieuwing en behoud 1883–1940*, Rotterdam 2000. *Lijst 1895 in Archief PW, Stadsarchief Amsterdam.*

11 The history of the *Gemeentelijke Dienst Volkshuisvesting* (Municipal Housing Department) is described in: Egbert Ottens, *Ik moet naar een kleinere woning omzien, want mijn gezin wordt te groot. 125 jaar sociale woningbouw in Amsterdam*, Amsterdam 1975.

12 *Algemeen Plan voor Sanering*, 1930. The widening and breakthrough allowed for the creation of an *inner ring*: Damrak, Rokin, Amstel, Waterlooplein, Valkenburgerstraat, Prins Hendrikkade.

13 Aimée Albers, 'Ontwerpen met "directe democratie". Buurtbewoners, architecten en de vormgeving van de stadsvernieuwing in Amsterdam 1970–1990,' *Bulletin KNOB* no. 2, 2021, p. 1-19.

14 *HAT – Huisvesting Alleenstaanden en Tweepersoonshuishoudens* (Housing for Singles and Two-Person Households).

15 Martin Mulder et al., *Blijven bouwen. Stadsvernieuwing in de jaren negentig*, Amsterdam: Gemeente Amsterdam, afdeling Coördinatie Stadsvernieuwing, 1987; with insightful interviews with Louis Genet, Enneüs Heerma, and Adri Duivesteijn.

16 Evert van Voskuilen, *Ridders in de Bijlmer. Een wandeling door de geschiedenis van Zuidoost*, Amsterdam: Stadsdeel Zuidoost, 2014.

17 Hilde de Haan and Jolanda Keesom, with a contribution by Rein Geurtsen: *Terug naar de straat. De vernieuwing van de F-buurt, Amsterdam Zuidoost*, Haarlem 2004.

18 *Far West* was a collaboration between housing corporations *De Key, Stadgenoot*, and *Rochdale*; *Prospect* by *Eigen Haard* and *AWV*; *Westwaarts* by *Ymere, De Dageraad*, and *PWV*.

19 See: Maurits de Hoog and Anouk de Wit (eds.), *Super-West. Vernieuwing van de Amsterdamse Tuinsteden 2000–2021*, Bussum 2022.

20 The number of demolished homes is difficult to determine precisely. Due to the merging or splitting of homes in retained complexes and renovation projects, the number of demolished homes cannot be directly derived from the housing stock in 2000 and 2021 and the number of newly built homes.

21 Maurits de Hoog and Ivan Nio, 'Staalmanpleinbuurt. Biografie van een Amsterdamse stadsbuurt', *Super-West 2000–2021* no. 2, September 2022, published by *Van Eesterenmuseum/De Alliantie* as part of the *SuperWest* event.

22 The six office buildings converted into hotels around *Sloterdijk Station* and the new hotel in *Riekerpolder* are not included in this count, as these areas fall outside the *Westelijke Tuinsteden* (Western Garden Cities).

PART 2
MOVEMENT 2
[pp. 86-117]

1 Wil Zonneveld, *Conceptvorming in de ruimtelijke planning. Patronen en processen*, PhD dissertation UvA, Amsterdam 1991.

2 See also: J.J. van der Velde, *Stadsontwikkeling van Amsterdam 1939–1967*, Amsterdam 1968; *Werk in Uitvoering. Orgaan van de Dienst der Publieke Werken Amsterdam* 1964–1972.

3 Victorien Koningsberger, *Schuivende panelen. Hoe architectuur een kind van zijn tijd is. Bouwen en wonen in hoogbouw in Amsterdamse uitbreidingswijken 1945–1970*, master's thesis, Utrecht University, Amsterdam 2011.

4 In 1962, the Municipality of Amsterdam commissioned a study for the new residential neighborhood Het Breed in Amsterdam-Noord to three architects: Jaap Bakema, Aldo van Eyck, and Frans van Gool. See: Endry van Velzen, 'Over vanzelfsprekendheid. De 1138 van Van Gool in Amsterdam-Noord', *Oase* 49/50 (1998), p. 44-65.

5 In the mergers of football clubs, many teams with corporate ties disappeared, such as Shell ('Spirit houdt elk lichaam lenig' merged into Nautilus), NDSM, PTT, AMROBA (AMRO Bank), DENEBA (De Nederlandsche Bank), and AGT (Amsterdamse Gemeentetram). Taba, with roots in the tobacco industry, still plays at Sportpark Drieburg.

6 www.cepezed.nl/nl/nieuws/smart-mobility-hub-een-multifunctionele-schakel/140446/

7 Hartman 1985 (note 4).

8 Anouk de Wit, *Nieuw Sloten. Van tuin tot stad*, Amsterdam: Dienst Ruimtelijke Ordening, 1998; Hilde de Haan and Jolanda Keesom, *Gebouwen in de Aker, Amsterdam-Osdorp*, Haarlem 2002.

9 Municipality of Amsterdam, *Bouw Zelf Samen. Kijk op (Collectief) Particulier Opdrachtgeverschap, Medeopdrachtgeverschap en Wooncoöperaties*, Amsterdam 2022.

PART 2
MOVEMENT 3
[pp. 118-149]

1 Newly built homes 'outside the dikes' 1975–2023, including the large-scale repurposing of warehouses at the Entrepotdok, Kadijken, and Silodam, as well as IJburg. According to figures from the CBS, 46,700 homes have been built by January 1, 2023. With housing production in 2023–2024 in the Houthavens, NDSM, Buiksloterham, Overhoeks, Cruquius, Zeeburgereiland, and Centrumeiland, the total will exceed 50,000.

2 Jerzy Gawronsky, 'Ontstaan uit een storm', in: Jerzy Gawronsky en Raniith Jayasena, *Oeroud Amsterdam. Een zoektocht naar de vroegste geschiedenis van de stad*, Amsterdam 2017, p. 54-91. See also: Ranjith Jayasena, *Graaf- en modderwerk. Een archeologische geschiedenis van Amsterdam*, Utrecht 2020.

3 For a great overview of port development: Roeland Gilijamse en Hans Bonke, *De haven van Amsterdam. Zeven eeuwen ontwikkeling*, Bussum 2009.

4 The Pampus Plan was drawn in 1964–1965 by the Rotterdam architectural firm Van den Broek and Bakema as an alternative to new construction in the Bijlmermeer. The urban expansion on islands in the IJmeer was meant to accommodate housing for no less than 350,000 people.

5 A legendary theatrical performance was *Noordwesterwals* by the Dogtroep in 1994, reprised in 1995.

6 Freely based on Melchior Fokkens, *Beschryvinge der wijdt-vermaarde koop-stadt Amstelredam*, Amsterdam 1662.

7 Famous examples can be found in Florence (from Piazzale Michelangelo), London (Southbank), and New York (Brooklyn Heights Promenade). Closer to home, *De Hoven* in Deventer and Zutphen and *Lent* in Nijmegen offer a similar sensation.

8 'Amsterdam's most beautiful terrace in the 19th century. The Tolhuis at the Buiksloterweg ferry has existed for 350 years,' *Ons Amsterdam* July-August 2012.
9 ENTOS: *Eerste Nederlandse Tentoonstelling op Scheepvaartgebied*, ELTA: *Eerste Luchtvaart Tentoonstelling Amsterdam*.
10 See the report on the design and history of the pavilion by Marcel Westhoff: items. amsterdamse-school.nl/details/objects/1865
11 KSLA: *Koninklijke-Shell Laboratorium Amsterdam*.
12 Bernard Leupen, *IJ-plein Amsterdam. Een speurtocht naar nieuwe compositorische middelen*, Rotterdam 1989.
13 *Structural Sketch IJ-axis*, Dienst Ruimtelijke Ordening Amsterdam, 1987.
14 *Oosterdok Design Competition 1984*, organized by the municipality of Amsterdam, won by Henk de Boer and Alle Hosper, second prize Teun Koolhaas.
15 The planning for the *Eastern Docklands* is documented in: *Oostelijk Havengebied Amsterdam. Stedenbouw en Architectuur*, Rotterdam 2003.
16 See, for example: Lodewijk Brunt et al., *Flaneren langs het IJ. Een opstel over problemen en pretenties van het IJ-oeverproject*, Amsterdam 1991.
17 In the 1970s, NMB built its headquarters near Zuid Station but moved in the 1980s to the spectacular Zandkasteel in the new center of Amsterdam Zuidoost, the Amsterdamse Poort. One of NMB's subsidiaries was MBO, the *Maatschappij voor Bedrijfsobjecten*. In the 1970s and 1980s, it developed, among other projects, the new construction of the Buikslotermeerplein and Amsterdamse Poort shopping centers and, after merging with Postbank and Nationale Nederlanden, expanded into ING Real Estate.
18 The partial designs for the islands were made by various designers, all from the 'OMA stable': Kees Christiaanse (Westerdokseiland), Rients Dijkstra (Oosterdokseiland), Willem-Jan Neutelings (CS).
19 Kees van Ruyven, memo 'Anchors in the IJ', 1995.
20 In addition to designers from the department, external designers also worked on the planning for Nieuw-Oost, such as Ashok Bhalotra. The implemented 'islands' plan was developed by a team of external designers led by Frits Palmboom. The team also included Yttje Feddes and Dirk Sijmons.
21 Vinex: *Vierde Nota Extra*, national spatial planning memorandum from 1992, with a program for the development of large housing areas near cities. The housing density at most locations is 30-35 homes per hectare, compact low-rise; compare with Leidsche Rijn near Utrecht and Ypenburg near The Hague. The density on Haveneiland is 85 homes per hectare. On the other islands of IJburg, the density is lower.
22 By the later mayor Eberhard van der Laan.
23 An important quality of the water city is the countless water artworks in the public space: an extensive collection of locks, dolphins, heads, quays, retaining works, docks, piers, ramps, pumps, buoys, a lighthouse, cranes, docks, ferry slips, steel, wooden, and stone bridges, viaducts, tunnels, ventilation buildings, terminals, warehouses, silos.
24 Compare the slabs on the south side of the Sloterplas in Osdorp, designed by Arthur Staal.

PART 2
MOVEMENT4
[pp. 150-181]

1 Bert van Eekelen, Remko Schnieders, and Sebastiaan de Wilde, *Dokwerkers, Reconstructie van planontwikkeling en bestuurlijke besluitvorming bij Zuidas en Zuidasdok*, Neerlands Diep, Academie voor publieke infra- en bouwprojecten, 2014.
2 It is interesting to make a comparison with Antwerp, where the relationship with the Scheldt remained intact, but the focus of the city's functioning shifted to the station area around the Leien.
3 An important point regarding growth is that Schiphol's 'home market' has expanded significantly. The United Kingdom is Schiphol's largest passenger market after the Netherlands. Schiphol has direct daily connections with 26 destinations in the United Kingdom: London (City, Gatwick, Heathrow, Luton, Southend, and Stansted), Manchester, Birmingham, Edinburgh, Bristol, Glasgow, Newcastle, Aberdeen, Leeds Bradford, Southampton, Liverpool, Norwich, Cardiff, Belfast (City and International Airport), Humberside, Durham Tees Valley, Inverness, Doncaster Sheffield, Exeter, and East Midlands. On average, 256 flights are operated daily between the UK and Schiphol. In 2019, a total of 10.7 million passengers traveled on these routes. Of these travelers, more than 26% transferred to another flight at Schiphol; the others visited the city.
4 L.H. Immers and P.H. Mijer, *Schiphol 2005, prognose van het luchtvervoer, inventarisatie van de ruimtelijke ontwikkelingen*, TU Delft Faculteit der Civiele Techniek, Vakgroep Verkeer, 1988.
5 O&S gemeente Amsterdam. Employed persons working more than 12 hours per week, 2019.
6 Amsterdam Marketing, *Kerncijfers 2017*.
7 Schiphol Group Jaarverslag 2015.
8 Decisio, *Economische impactanalyse Schiphol*, 2015 (in opdracht van het Ministerie van Infrastructuur en Milieu).
9 Barbara Lavell (red.), *Kanjers en knoerten, grote bouwplannen in een historische binnenstad als die van Amsterdam*, Stedelijke Woningdienst, Amsterdam 1995.
10 This is the former GETZ plot, now called UID: Urban Interactive District, a project for 950 homes, events, and theater, designed by MVRDV and DELVA Landscape Architecture.
11 See the informative website: grimshaw.global/projects/rail-and-mass-transit/bijlmer-arena-station/.
12 The Development Strategy *Koers 2025*, presented in 2015 and adopted in 2016, was part of the program *Ruimte voor de Stad*, which ran from 2014 to 2018. The program explored all the major challenges the city faced during its growth spurt.
13 See the Zuidas website: zuidas.nl/theme/zuidas-business-district/.

PART 2
MOVEMENT 5
[p. 182-215]

1 Willem Heinemeijer, Michel van Hulten, Hans Dirk de Vries Reilingh, *Het centrum van Amsterdam. Een sociografische studie*, Amsterdam 1968.
2 Richard Florida, *The Rise of the Creative Class. And How It's Transforming Work, Leisure, Community and Everyday Life*, New York 2002.
3 Business services 30,329, creative services 20,196, ICT sector 17,944 (2023).
4 During the period 2008–2012, a collaborative project between the municipality of Amsterdam and TU Delft conducted research on this phenomenon. The subject of the research were clusters of facilities for interaction in the four major cities as well as in Leiden and Delft. Maurits de Hoog, with contributions from Verena Balz et al., *De Hollandse Metropool. Ontwerpen aan de kwaliteit van interactiemilieus*, Bussum 2012. 'Interaction environments' are spaces for meeting and exchanging people, information, goods, and capital.
5 Data from O&S and Binnenstadsmonitor, DRO Municipality of Amsterdam; see also: Maurits de Hoog and Rick Vermeulen, *Nieuwe ritmes van de stad. Metropoolvorming in Amsterdam*, Bussum 2009. Figures from 2018 are from the *O&S Yearbook 2019*, pages 280 and 290.
6 Data from O&S, dashboard key figures Amsterdam.
7 Municipal Department of Housing, *Sociale woningbouw Amsterdam 1968–1986*, Amsterdam 1986. HAT units and group homes are counted as housing.
8 See the chapter '"Busje komt zo". The Pioneer Years of Methadone Distribution in Amsterdam (1975–1985)', in: Gemma Blok, *Achter de voordeur. Sociale psychiatrie vanuit de GGD Amsterdam in de twintigste eeuw*, Amsterdam 2014.
9 Rebelgroup, 'NV Zeedijk. The Approach, Effects, and Future', Rotterdam 2015.
10 See, for example, the critical analysis by the Rekenkamer Metropool Amsterdam, 'Project 1012. A Study of the Approach to the Amsterdam Old City Centre', Amsterdam 2018.
11 Jouke van der Werf, *'Plein, park of veld? Cultuurhistorische verkenning Museumplein en omgeving'* ('Square, Park, or Field? Cultural Historical Exploration of the Museumplein and Surroundings'), commissioned by the municipality of Amsterdam and the Oud-Zuid district, Bureau Monuments & Archeology, Amsterdam 2008.
12 In semi-annual reports, Frieling reflected on the spatial strategy of the municipality and succinctly summarized his advice. The first year focused on discussions about investment agreements between the Regional Organ Amsterdam (ROA) and the government regarding housing construction, infrastructure, and large city policy/urban renewal. Once these agreements were broadly established with the last Lubbers cabinet and concretized with the first Kok cabinet, attention shifted to organization, planning, and quality of major projects, the renewal and expansion of large urban facilities, and the city's position in the region and in the Randstad. The archive of Dirk Frieling with his semi-annual reports to the Mayor and City Council of Amsterdam is housed in the collection of the HNI in Rotterdam. A second element in Frieling's advice was the introduction of the concept of a metropolis. Against the background of the failed referendum on the city province and the difficult negotiations over the funding of the North/South Line, Frieling advised the Mayor and Aldermen to look more broadly and seek allies to push for national policies aimed at 'metropolitan development': the expansion of the large cities in the western Netherlands, with their economic and cultural activities, and their connections with each other and the world. This was implemented in the Delta Metropolis Association. The Kok cabinet embraced the idea, but the concept of the Fifth National Spatial Planning Memorandum, in which the idea was further developed, was not discussed in the House of Representatives after the resignation of the cabinet in 2002.
13 Fred Feddes in collaboration with Marjolein de Lange, *Fietsstad Amsterdam. Hoe Amsterdam de fietshoofdstad van de wereld werd*, Amsterdam 2019.
14 In *De Hollandse Metropool* (2012), interaction environments in the Amsterdam city center were classified by size and visitor numbers: centers, squares, quarters, districts, and superclusters. In 2012, I expected that some of the quarters would make a quality and scale leap and could develop into a 'mixed city center district' (the old city) and a 'cultural district' (Leidseplein-Museumplein). The city center now functions as a supercluster, a cohesive area with a diameter of 3 kilometers. In addition to the 25 million tourist day visitors (to shops, museums, attractions, and festivals), the city center is also used daily by Amsterdam residents, commuters, and students. This together likely leads to around 50 million users per year.
15 Noël van Bemmel, 'Dam heeft kamerbreed, maar hobbelig tapijt', *de Volkskrant*, May 5, 2001.
16 www.mobiliteit.nl/wp-content/uploads/2021/11/Impactstudie-Noord-Zuidlijn.pdf.

PART 3
A BROADER PERSPECTIVE
[pp. 216-237]

1 The Master Plan for the IJ waterfronts was commissioned by the Amsterdam Waterfront Financieringsmaatschappij (AWF), a partnership – a Public-Private Partnership – between the Municipality of Amsterdam and ING.
2 See: Marcel van Engelen,

De Stad. Het verhaal van Amsterdam van 1980 tot vandaag, Amsterdam 2024.
3 Constant [Nieuwenhuys], 'Over het reizen', speech to the members of the BNA at the completion of the new Schiphol, 1966, in: *Opstand van de homo ludens. Een bundel voordrachten en artikelen*, Bussum 1969.
4 The Centre Pompidou in Paris was designed by Richard Rogers and Renzo Piano, following an international competition in 1971. Jean Prouvé was chairman of the jury. Rogers later built the spectacular Lloyd's building in 1978, also after winning a competition, in the heart of the City of London.
5 Willem Sandberg, as quoted in: Ad Petersen and Pieter Brattinga (eds.), *Sandberg. Een documentaire/A documentary*, Amsterdam 1975, p. 106. Quotation included in: Wouter Davidts, *Museumarchitectuur van Centre Pompidou tot Tate Modern. Verschuivingen in het artistieke begrip van openbaarheid en hun impact op het architectuurprogramma van het museum voor hedendaagse kunst*, doctoral dissertation, University of Ghent, 2003.
6 See for example: Wouter van Elburg and Hanneke Ronnes, *Amsterdam sloopt. Afbraak in de hoofdstad in de 21ste eeuw*, Amsterdam 2021.
7 The jury of the Stadhuis competition consisted of architect Huig Maaskant (chairman), Prof. Jacques Schroder (ETH Zürich), P.J. Pederson (city architect of Copenhagen), Sir Robert Matthew (chief architect of the London City Council), and Amsterdam architects Chris Nielsen (city architect), Frans van Gool, and Piet Zanstra. Urban planner Jakoba Mulder acted as secretary on behalf of the city.
8 A vivid description of the history and construction of the Stadhuis-Muziektheater complex can be found in: Herman de Liagre Böhl, *Rumoer aan de Amstel. Het Amsterdamse stadhuis en het muziektheater 1808–1988*, Amsterdam (special edition of *Jaarboek Amstelodamum* 2015).
9 Oriol Bohigas, Peter Buchanan, and Vittorio Magnago Lampugnani, *Barcelona 1980–1992. City and architecture*, Barcelona 1991.
10 *Projectübersicht, Internationale Bauausstellung Berlin*, 1987.
11 Catalogue, *The Architectural Review*, special *Berlin IBA*, 181, no. 1082, April 1987.
12 Extensive documentation of the Barcelona projects appeared in: *Lotus 23: Catalonia* (1979), *Lotus 39: Beautification of Towns* (1983), *Lotus 56: Space, Time and Architecture* (1987), *Lotus 64: The Other City Planning* (1989), *Lotus 67: Great Transformation Projects* (1990). Cornelis van de Ven, 'Architectuur van Barcelona. Vernieuwing, traditie en nieuwe aanzetten', *Wonen-TA/BK* no. 8, 1979.
13 A widely used series of excursion guides documenting the Barcelona projects was created as part of an educational project by Rein Geurtsen, Max Risselada, and Jasper van Zwol at TU Delft, academic year 1987/88. The study of urban form, including work by Rein Geurtsen at TU Delft, built on Italian and French research. Urban form is understood as the product of successive modifications and in relation to geomorphology and landscape. Atlases became a frequently used means of publishing results. See for example: Rein Geurtsen and Luc Bos, 'Kopenhagen, dubbelstad. Een bewerkte reisindruk', *Wonen-TA/BK* no. 10-12, 1981, pp. 14-51. The approach influenced many studies. See also: Casper van der Hoeven and Jos Louwe, *Amsterdam als stedelijk bouwwerk. Een morfologiese analyse*, Nijmegen 1985; Frits Palmboom, *Rotterdam, verstedelijkt landschap*, Rotterdam 1987; Maurits de Hoog, *4 × Amsterdam. Ontwerpen aan de stad*, Bussum 2004.
14 *AIR – Architecture International Rotterdam* 1982. Besides Josef-Paul Kleihues: Aldo Rossi, Oswald Matthias Ungers, and Derek Walker. The design studies can be seen as an early experiment with what later became known as 'research by design'.
15 Joris Molenaar, 'Opfrissing van een residentiestad: De Kern Gezond. Een inrichtingsplan voor het centrum van Den Haag', *Archis* no. 11, 1988, pp. 16-19. The plan was drawn up by Alle Hosper, then director of bureau B&B.
16 The *Werkgroep 5×5* launched model projects in 1988 in Amsterdam, Groningen, The Hague, Maastricht, Rotterdam, and Zwolle. Results were published in: *Werkgroep 5×5, Initiatief en inspiratie. Thema's voor de kwaliteit van volkshuisvesting en gebiedsontwikkeling*, Amsterdam 1989, and Adri Duivesteijn and Fred Feddes, *Voorbij het gangbare. Een pleidooi voor de kwaliteit van volkshuisvesting en stedebouw*, Amsterdam 1989.
17 *'Manifest 5×5'*, May 1988, www.gideonconsult.nl/voor%20de%20kwaliteit%20van%20stede.pdf.
18 Philippe Panerai, Jean-Charles Depaule, and Jean Castex, *Formes urbaines. De l'îlôt a la barre*, Paris 1978.
19 Hetty Berends, Rein Geurtsen, and Max van Rooy, *Een gat in de ruimte. Berlage's Mercatorplein en de reconstructie van een toren*, Amsterdam 1991.
20 Karin Gaillard and Betsy Dokter (eds.), *Berlage en Amsterdam Zuid*, Amsterdam 1992.
21 1992: Study assignments for Weeber, OMA, Quist, and Venturi. 1994: Study assignment for Siza. Closed competition 2004: Architectuurstudio Herman Hertzberger, Benthem Crouwel Architecten, Henket & Partners Architecten, Diederen Dirrix van Wylick Architecten, and Claus en Kaan Architecten.
22 Images of Charlottenburg Luisenplatz: hiddenarchitecture.net/luisenplatz-developmen/
23 Firms associated with the 'new' Amsterdam School include Winhov, M3H, Arons en Gelauff, korthtielens, Marcel Lok, Geurst en Schulze, Marlies Rohmer, and LEVS.
24 Projects by Benthem Crouwel, Ninedots, Roberto Meyer, Jeroen van Schooten, Claus en Kaan, UN, and Venhoeven CS.
25 www.dmaa.at/work/eye-film-institute with drawings!
26 In this discussion, the *VVAB* played an important role – the *Vereniging Vrienden van de Amsterdamse Binnenstad*.
27 Maarten Kloos and Indira van 't Klooster, *ARCAM KAART*, 1995.
28 In 1986, preparatory work on the Markerwaard was halted. Ultimately, in 2003, it was decided not to develop the polder.
29 CBS figures, and an estimate for Lelystad 25,000 (not yet an independent municipality in 1975) based on Lelystad Online, https://www.lelystad-online.nl/home/historie_lelystad#:~:text=In%201975%20ontving%20Lelystad%20zijn,zijn%20met%20volop%20frisse%20lucht.
30 The population of the three metropolitan regions of Amsterdam, Rotterdam-The Hague, and Utrecht, respectively the four provinces of North and South Holland, Flevoland, and Utrecht (3, 3.8, 1.4, 0.5). The North Wing of the Randstad also includes Ede, Arnhem, and Nijmegen. The South Wing also includes parts of the Brabant Urban Network.
31 E.J. Meijers and M.J. Burger, 'Stretching the concept of "borrowed size"', *Urban Studies. An international journal for research in urban studies* 54 (2017) 1, pp. 269-291.
32 Saskia Sassen, *The Global City. New York, London, Tokyo*, Princeton 1992.
33 See, for example, the biennial ranking by GaWC, the *Globalization and World Cities Research Network*, and the methodology behind it in: Peter Taylor, *World City Network. A Global Urban Analysis*, London 2004 (2010).

Epilogue – To 2075!
[p. 234-238]

1 Mario Draghi, *The Future of European Competitiveness*, European Commission, Brussels 2024.
2 Theo Baart and Tijs van den Boomen, *Leven onder het luchtruim. Hoe Schiphol duizend vierkante kilometer in zijn greep houdt en hoe dat anders kan*, Rotterdam 2024.
3 *LIB = Luchthavenindelingsbesluit*. The LIB now includes a zone around the approach route of the Buitenveldertbaan that excludes housing construction in Amstelveen, as well as in the area around Duivendrecht Station.

IMAGE CREDITS

700 centenboek (700-cent book), Amsterdam municipal Giro p. 13 (7)
Almere Municipality p. 232 (1)
'Amsterdam 1970–1990', *Bulletin KNOB* nr. 2, 2021 p. 1-19, 61 (3)
Amsterdam City Archives p. 12 (2, 3), 13 (8), 14 (1), 15 (3, 4), 19 (2), 20 (1), 53 (1), 56 (3), 57 (4), 62 (1), 63 (2), 71 (bottom right), 72 (top right), 73 (top right), 76 (1, 2), 77 (5, 7, 8), 79 (6), 81 (4, 5), 83 (6), 85 (6), 87 (1), 90 (1), 92 (1), 94 (1), 103 (top right), 111 (5), 112 (2), 113 (6), 115, 119 (1, 2), 122 (1), 123 (2), 126 (2, 3), 135 (top right), 140 (1), 141 (4, 5), 144 (1, 2), 146 (1), 147 (6, 7, 8), 149 (7), 151 (1), 152 (2), 154 (1), 155 (2, 3), 160 (1), 161 (3), 162 (2), 167 (top right), 175 (4), 176 (1), 177 (7), 178 (1), 181 (4), 183 (1), 186 (1), 192 (1, 2), 194 (2), 199 (centre, bottom), 200 (bottom), 201
© Amsterdam Municipality p. 43-46
Amsterdam Municipality, Dienst Ruimtelijke Ordening (Department of Spatial Planning) p. 18 (1), 65 (4, 5), 91 (3), 99 (3), 117 (6), 127 (5), 219 (1), 220 (1, 2), 221 (3), 223 (1)
Amsterdam Municipality, Dienst Ruimtelijke Ordening (Department of Spatial Planning) / Gert Urhahn p. 128 (2)
Amsterdam Municipality, *Handboek fiets (Bicycle Handbook)* p. 199
Amsterdam Municipality, *Handboek inrichting openbare ruimte (Public Space Design Handbook)* p. 201
Amsterdam Municipality, *Handboek rood en groen (Handbook 'Red' and 'Green', part of the 'Puccini Method')* p. 202
Amsterdam Municipality, Monumenten en Archeologie (Monuments and Archaeology) p. 205 (5)
Amsterdam Municipality, *Nieuw Standaard Grachten Profiel (New Standard Canal Profile)* p. 200
Amsterdam Municipality, Publieke Werken (Department of Public Works) p. 91 (2), 190 (1)
Amsterdam Municipality, Ruimte en Duurzaamheid (Space and Sustainability, the Urban Planning Department) p. 85 (4), 96 (1), 112 (1), 131 (3), 148 (1), 162 (1), 163 (3), 211 (7), 212 (1), 215 (7), 221 (4), 223 (2)
Amsterdam.nl p. 146 (2)
Andersson, Sven-Ingvar p. 205 (6)
ANEFO p. 14 (2)
Architecten Cie p. 81 (7)
Bach-Mora Arquitectos p. 225 (2)
belowthesurface.amsterdam p. 208 (2)
Benthem Crouwel Architecten p. 173 (6), 209 (6-10)
Bouman, Daphne p. 143 (8)
Bouwes, Nico p. 56 (1)
Bureau Oslo p. 146 (3)
Burg, Marcel van der p. 73 (bottom right)
BUROBEP p. 143 (6)
Coenen, Jo p. 127 (6)
Costanza, Raiza p. 132 (1)
Coumou, Hein p. 67 (4)
Couprie, Sanne (Amsterdam Photo Bank) p. 157 (2)
Cruz y Ortiz p. 214 (1)
Damme, Sebastian van p. 81 (6, 8)
data.amsterdam.nl p. 76 (3), 78 (2, 3), 80 (2, 3), 82 (2, 3), 84 (2, 3), 108 (3), 110 (1, 2), 112 (3), 114 (2, 3), 116 (2, 3), 140 (2, 3), 142 (3, 4), 144 (3, 4), 146 (4, 5), 148 (2, 3), 172 (3, 4), 174 (2, 3), 176 (3, 4), 178 (2, 3), 180 (2, 3), 204 (4), 206 (4), 208 (4, 5), 210 (2, 3), 212 (2, 3), 214 (3, 4)
Davidson, Hans p. 99 (4)
De jarige stad (the Birthday City), Little Golden Book, De Bezige Bij p. 13 (6)
De Twee Snoeken p. 77 (6)
Delugan Meissl Associated Architects p. 227 (3)
DELVA landscape architecture p. 130 (2)
DigiDaan p. 143 (9)
DKV Architecten p. 96 (2)
Duivenbode, Ossip van p. 169 (top right)
Dynamo Architecten p. 145 (5, 8, 10)
Effting, Katja p. 181 (6)
Eis, Edwin van (Amsterdam Photo Bank) p. 68 (1), 79 (5), 83 (4, 5), 111 (4), 115 (5, 6, 7), 116 (1), 145 (7), 149 (5, 6, 8), 172 (1, 2), 173 (5), 175 (5), 176 (2), 179 (4), 193 (2), 194 (1), 195 (3, 4), 196 (1, 2), 204 (2), 205 (7, 8), 207 (5), 211 (5)
Escher, Gielijn p. 11 (1), 13 (5)
festivalfans.nl p. 117 (5)
fruittuinvanwest.nl p. 117 (4)
Gebouwd in Amsterdam (Built in Amsterdam) (gebouwdin. amsterdam.nl) p. 71 (top right), 72 (bottom right), 73 bottom right), 74 (bottom right, top right), 82 (1), 103 (bottom right), 104 (top right),106 (bottom right), 135 (bottom right), 136 (bottom right, top right), 137 (bottom right), 138 (bottom right), 168 (bottom right, centre-right), 169 (bottom right), 170 (top right)
Geurtsen, Rein p. 65 (3)
Giessen, Cees van der/CIIID p. 207 (7, 8)
Grimshaw Architects p. 175 (7, 8)
Guerra, Fernando p. 179 (6)
© John Gundlach|Flying Holland p. 237 (1)
Gustafson, Porter + Bowman p. 78 (1)
Hanswijk, Frank p. 145 (9)
Hoek, Allard van den p. 137 (top right)
Hogeschool van Amsterdam (Amsterdam University of Applied Sciences) p. 80 (1)
Hoog, Maurits de p. 55, 60 (1, 2), 66 (3), 71 (bottom right), 72 (top right), 88, 100 (1, 2), 103 (bottom right), 104 (top right), 105 (bottom right), 106 (both centre-right), 120, 135 (top right), 136 (top right, bottom right), 152, 168 (top right), 170 (centre-right, bottom right), 184 (sketches), 199 (bottom right), 227 (2)
https://felixmeritis.nl/ p. 12 (4)
https://nieuweinstituut.nl/events/plastic-zipatone-letraset-mecanorma-en-meer p. 17 (3)
https://www.lansimetro.fi/ p. 233 (2)
https://www.pampus.nl/doe/stelling-van-amsterdam/de-stelling-van-amsterdam p. 229 (2)
KAAN Architecten p. 179 (5)
Karres en Brands, KCAP p. 173 (7, 8)
Karres en Brands p. 174 (1), 175 (6)
Kate, Laurens Jan ten p. 142 (2)
Koen van Velsen architecten p. 56 (2)
Kramer, Luuk p. 66 (1)
Kuipers, Marieke, 'Dutch Conversions in Conservation. The European Architectural Heritage Year and its aftermath in the Netherlands' p. 17 (2)
LEVS Architecten p. 167 (bottom right)
LOLA Landscape Architects p. 170 (bottom right)
Maas, George (Amsterdam Photo Bank) p. 113 (4)
Masterplan Helsinki Pasila 2020 p. 233 (3)
Mecanoo p. 79 (4), 114 (1)
ML_A/korthtielens p. 74 (bottom right)
Musch, Jeroen p. 142 (1), 143 (5)
MVSA/Buro van Stigt p. 215 (5, 6)
NFP Photography B.V., Wielerbaan Sloten, ook wel genaamd Velodrome Sloten, aan de Sloterweg, 1972: © c/o Pictoright Amsterdam 2025 p. 113 (5)
Nieuwenhuis, Alphons (Amsterdam Photo Bank) p. 177 (8)
Nieuwenhuys, Constant (1920-2005), *New Babylon-Amsterdam I*, 1963, https://stichtingconstant.nl/catalogue/work/new-babylon-amsterdam-i (foto Tom Haartsen), collectie Kunstmuseum Den Haag, © Constant / Fondation Constant c/o Pictoright Amsterdam 2025 p. 224 (1)
OMA p. 65 (2), 127 (4), 129 (3), 177 (5, 6)
OMA/Willem-Jan Neutelings p. 128 (1)
Palmboom, Frits p. 129 (4), 228 (1)
Parool, Opland p. 16 (1)
Rougoor, Henk (Amsterdam Photo Bank) p. 161 (5)
Sambeek en Van Veen Architecten p. 141 (7)
Sant en Co: 84 (1), 85 (7, 8), 130 (1), 138 (top right)
Schiphol.nl p. 156 (1)
Schot, Jan p. 141 (6)
Sluyterman van Loo, Willem p. 149 (4)
Smalen, Rosa (Amsterdam Photo Bank) p. 211 (6)
Smet, Dennis de p. 68 (2)
Sprietsma, Simon p. 206 (2)
Stelt, Jan van der p. 12 (1)
Tangram Architekten p. 108 (1), 109 (4, 5, 6, 7)
Team V p. 85 (5)
Temp.architecture & studio Nuy van Noort p. 180 (1, 5)
The Architectural Review, april 1987, volume CLXXXI, nr. 1082 p. 226 (1)
topotijdreis.nl p. 108 (2)
Toren, Rindert van den p. 20 (bottom), 42, 53 (bottom), 57 (4), 63 (2), 70, 87 (bottom), 90 (1), 94 (1), 102, 103 (bottom), 105 (top right), 107, 122 (bottom), 123 (bottom), 134, 151 (bottom), 154 (1), 162 (2), 166, 183 (bottom), 186 (1), 192 (1), 198
VDNDP, NL Architects, Chris Collaris Architects, studio Donna van Milligen Bielke, Space Encounters, DS Landschapsarchitecten p. 131 (4)
Verhoef, Arjan p. 34, 36, 38, 40, 58, 93, 96, 124, 158, 188, 230 (maps)
Voedseltuin IJplein p. 95 (2)
Voskuilen, Evert van, *Ridders in de Bijlmer (Knights of the Bijlmer Neighbourhood)* p. 64 (1)
Vries, Isis de p. 71-74, 103-106, 135-138, 167-170 (all drawings)
Vries, Rufus de p. 66 (2)
Waardenborg p. 77 (4)
Waternet p. 143 (7)
Wolk, Wouter van der p. 214 (2)
World Wide Wendel / Nathan Reinds p. 145 (6)
Xerios p. 113 (4)
ZJA Architects and Engineers p. 161 (4), 213 (5, 6, 7), 226 (1)

INDEX

ABOUT THE AUTHOR

Maurits de Hoog (Gouda, 1955) is an urban planner, trained at TU Delft. After internships with the *Aktiegroep Nieuwmarkt* and the *Nederlands Documentatiecentrum voor de Bouwkunst*, he moved to Amsterdam in 1976. He worked with the Villanova partnership in Rotterdam and in 1992 established his own office in Amsterdam: *De Hoog - ontwerp en onderzoek*. In 1996, he joined the city's Department of Spatial Planning, later the Directorate of Planning and Sustainability. From 2008 to 2012, he was professor of urban design at TU Delft, in the chair of *City & Region*, and subsequently quartermaster of the Amsterdam Institute for Advanced Metropolitan Solutions (2013–2014).

His expertise lies in exploring, designing, and guiding urban transformations. In Amsterdam, he was involved in projects such as the development of the IJ riverbanks, the Wibautas, *Panorama-Noord*, the *IJmeeratelier*, *Haven-Stad*, the development strategy *Koers 2025*, and the programmes *Sprong over het IJ* and *Vrije Ruimte*. He participated in the Quality Teams for *Drechtoevers* (1999–2004) and *Ruimte voor de Rivier* (2006–2016), and served as supervisor for the development of *Oostoever Sloterplas* (1994–1996) and the renewal of the 1950s neighbourhood *Jeruzalem* (2006–2010).

He is the author of *Tour Groot-Amsterdam* (Amsterdam, 2020), *The Dutch Metropolis. Designing quality interaction environments* (Bussum, 2012), and *4 × Amsterdam. Ontwerpen aan de stad* (Bussum, 2005).

CREDITS

This book is published on the occasion of the anniversary year of Amsterdam 750 and was supported in part by funding from:

City of Amsterdam, Department of Planning and Sustainability

Concept, text and sketches movements
Maurits de Hoog

Production and project documentation
Laura Smits

Timeline Amsterdam 1975–2025
Tim Ruijs

Maps Amsterdam and MRA
Arjan Verhoef

Isometric drawings house, block and subdivision forms
Isis de Vries

Photography
Rindert van den Toren

Translation
Translation Kings

Design
Maud van Rossum

Lithography
PRDigitaal

Printing
Wilco

Production
Marja Jager,
nai010 publishers

Publisher
Marcel Witvoet,
nai010 publishers

nai010 publishers is an internationally orientated publisher specialized in developing, producing and distributing books in the fields of architecture, urbanism, art and design. www.nai010.com

nai010 books are available internationally at selected bookstores and from the following distribution partners:

North, Central and South America - Artbook | D.A.P., New York, USA, dap@dapinc.com

Rest of the world - Idea Books, Amsterdam, the Netherlands, idea@ideabooks.nl

For general questions, please contact nai010 publishers directly at sales@nai010.com or visit our website www.nai010.com for further information.

Printed and bound in the Netherlands.

ISBN 978 94 6208 906 8
NUR 648, 758
BISAC ARC010000
THEMA RPC

Amsterdam Urban Development 1975–2025 is also availabe in Dutch:
Stadsontwikkeling Amsterdam 1975–2025
ISBN 978 94 6208 905 1
And as e-book:
ISBN 978 94 6208 918 1